Building Adolescent Literacy in Today's English Classrooms

RANDY BOMER

HEINEMANN
Portsmouth, NH

Heinemann
361 Hanover Street
Portsmouth, NH 03801–3912
www.heinemann.com

Offices and agents throughout the world

Library of Congress Cataloging-in-Publication Data
Bomer, Randy.
    Building adolescent literacy in today's English classrooms / Randy Bomer.
        p. cm.
    Includes bibliographical references and index.
    ISBN-13: 978-0-325-01394-7
    ISBN-10: 0-325-01394-2
    1. Language arts (Secondary).   2. English language—Composition and exercises—Study and teaching (Secondary).   I. Title.

LB1631.B72 2011
428.0071'2—dc22   2011000937

Editor: Kate Montgomery
Production: Vicki Kasabian
Interior design: Lisa A. Fowler
Cover design: Jenny Jensen Greenleaf
Typesetter: Cape Cod Compositors, Inc.
Manufacturing: Steve Bernier

Printed in the United States of America on acid-free paper

15   14   13   12   11   EB   1   2   3   4   5

CONTENTS

ACKNOWLEDGMENTS

If you're reading this, you might be checking to see if I've acknowledged you. Who else would take the trouble to read acknowledgments? So most likely, you already know that I should be thanking you, and in that case, I want to start off by saying thanks right here, directly to your face.

If we spoke, then you're in this book. If I worked in your classroom, you and your students are certainly here. If I talked with you about something you were writing or reading, then your thinking shaped mine and fed the streams that became this book. If you were in a class or an audience and asked a question or even just looked interested or confused, then you're here, too. Over the past twenty-five years, I've tried thousands of times to make the ideas in this book clearer to people, more acceptable, more reflective of teachers' real experiences with students, and every one of those conversations helped create this text. This book floats on an ocean of help, and I feel no shortage of gratitude for every bit of it. Though my mind floods with the faces and voices of individuals, I'll organize them here into the communities and conversations that have been especially influential in the ideas in this book.

My colleagues at The University of Texas at Austin have taught, inspired, and challenged me every day for the past decade, and they have shaped many of the educational values and attitudes in this book. My relationships to doctoral students continually push me into new territories of learning, prohibiting the laziness or complacency I would probably fall into without them, and I thank them for that. My work with the Heart of Texas Writing Project, a site of the National Writing Project, provides a container for my ongoing conversations with a community of inquiring and courageous teachers in Austin, while also connecting that community to a network of hundreds of others across the country.

Before coming to Austin, I worked with equally supportive and committed communities of educators in Bloomington, Indiana, and New York City. Colleagues at Indiana University and at Queens College taught me much and gave me space to grow. Before that, at Teachers College Reading and Writing Project, Lucy Calkins and an extended family of literacy educators saw promise in me and let me join in a deep learning conversation for ten years.

NCTE has provided more relationships and communities than I can count. I spent many days with other Executive Committee members and headquarters staff over four and a half years, and we had deep conversations about many dimensions of our profession. The other presidents with whom I served shared even longer, deeper, and more frank conversations that were deeply educational for me—and continue to be so. Hundreds of wise and thoughtful people serving their profession in myriad ways showed me again and again the importance of our shared mission.

Perhaps more important than anyone else have been the hundreds of teachers in whose classrooms I have taught side by side, conferring with individual students, planning curriculum, reflecting on lessons, examining our own thinking and literacy practices. I have worked extensively with communities of teachers across the country, particularly in certain cities—Austin, New York, Indianapolis, San Diego, Los Angeles, and Boston. Those classrooms have been my research sites, design groups, and informants.

Kate Montgomery, Publisher at Heinemann and one of my best friends, was the instigator and chief supporter for this book, believing I should write it long before I did, and right through the times when I lost heart for it. It's here because of her, though as writers always say, the bad parts are not her fault.

This book is about assuming an appreciative gaze, and about the things that become possible in the spaces between people when such a gaze is present. I know about that, at the deepest level, because every day, I become who I am under Katherine Bomer's loving gaze. If everyone were married to someone like her, there would be a lot more books in the world.

Fixing Attention

The Spotlight in the Classroom

" *My experience is what I agree to attend to. Only those items which I notice shape my mind—without selective interest, experience is an utter chaos. Interest alone gives accent and emphasis, light and shade, background and foreground—intelligible perspective, in a word. It varies in every creature, but without it the consciousness of every creature would be a gray chaotic indiscriminateness, impossible for us even to conceive.* "

—WILLIAM JAMES, *Principles of Psychology*

CHAPTER 1

There is time enough for everything in the course of the day, if you do but one thing at once, but there is not time enough in the year, if you will do two things at a time.

—PHILIP STANHOPE (*Lord Chesterfield*) *in a letter to his son, April 14, 1747*

English: What to Teach

Sharon is reading *After Tupac and D Foster* by Jacqueline Woodson instead of doing her algebra homework. The trouble is, she can't stop. She happened upon it last Thursday in her English classroom library and started reading it Sunday. It looked interesting to her mostly because only a few weeks before, her mother had loaded some Tupac songs onto Sharon's MP3 player, and she'd been listening to them since in almost continuous rotation, telling her friends she was getting into old-school hip-hop. Reading Woodson's novel, she thinks it's cool to know that the author has been listening to these same tunes while writing this book, and that Neeka, the main character, and her friends are bonding over those songs. Neeka and Jayjones remind her of her with her friends, so while she's reading, she feels like she's with them. When she sits alone with this book, she just feels comfortable, and as a result, she's read almost the whole thing in the past couple of days—a much more focused and rapid devouring of a book than she has experienced before.

Gerardo and Jay usually go to Jay's apartment after school, where one of the things they do is post on their shared blog. Gerardo does the typing, while Jay lays on Gerardo's bed and bounces a tennis ball against the poster on the opposite wall, now dappled with shallow dents. The computer used to belong to Gerardo's uncle, and it doesn't really have enough memory for a lot of websites, but it works for now to let them compose on the word processor and then paste it into the appropriate field on the blogging site. After the assembly at school in which all the students were cautioned about online bullying, they've stopped writing about their friends on here, though that's hard, since it's about half of what they talk about as they walk to Jay's apartment. At least, on the few occasions when they write about people now, they don't name them. Today, they are in their usual positions, Gerardo at the computer by the window and Jay on the bed, and they talk in short bursts as Gerardo writes about how unfair it is that this one unnamed friend of theirs keeps getting busted for skateboarding. He's not actually arrested but stopped and scolded, either by police or by people with stores near the place he skates. This is today's outrage, and lots of their entries are similar kinds of complaints. Not all, though. It's the entries they write together that tend to get heated up; when they log in separately, Jay from the library, the entries are calmer and often more personal. For either type of entry, they base what they write on ideas they have developed and preserved in the notebooks they keep in their English class.

These two brief portraits, drawn from interviews with adolescents, have several things in common. They represent self-sponsored literate activity situated within students' relationships, spaces, and interests outside their English class—but supported by it. The students are highly engaged in what they are doing; the writing or reading isn't painful, doesn't involve them forcing themselves to get it done out of compliance with authority, so that they won't get in trouble. The kids become focused on their literate activity, and time passes almost without them noticing it. They're developing habits of engaging—ways of becoming involved and invested in literate tasks that are significant to them, not because they were born to love reading and writing but because of the ways the literate activity connects to other things in life that matter to them. Engagement involves motivation, desire, care, and participation, and it is essential to reading proficiency, writing excellence, academic achievement, and college success (Guthrie and Alvermann 1999; Kuh 2009). It is, almost by definition, the central feature of an educated, literate life. The little snippets we have seen in these portraits are not sufficient, of course, to produce either academic success or an intellectual life independent of educational institutions. Those require investment of hours well beyond the brief moments into which we have glanced. But habits of reading, of thoughtful study, of commitment to projects are built upon moments in which a student comes to believe that there is something interesting for them in literate activity. English class should be about making more such moments possible.

Purposeful engagement requires that a person select something out of all the world, then hold her attention there long enough to see more in the object, to develop from one thought to another and to care about it. Attention, as William James said, "implies withdrawal from some things in order to deal effectively with others." It involves selective ignoring in order to make space for deliberate attending.

In today's world, as everyone knows, managing attention is a problem. Our devices bring the whole world to us no matter where we are; nothing is out of reach; every friend is constantly in our face. "Withdrawal from some things in order to deal effectively with others" seems excruciatingly difficult. The email dings, the phone rings, the world beckons, and we respond so as not to be rude, so as not to be out of the loop, so as not to be fully engaged with what was already right in front of us. It's not really a matter of attention deficits resulting from misfires in the brain; it's a matter of an attention economy in which we all live our lives. Everyone wants our attention, but it is in limited supply. A person can really only pay attention to one thing at a time. People like to talk about their powers of multitasking, but in actual fact, they are just describing rapid switching and refocusing of attention, and each switch is costly in the time it takes to complete a task, the degree of engagement possible, and the number of thoughts they can develop as contributions to what they are doing. While we may be able to do background activities, talk to someone while we drive or listen to music and eat something while we read, we're not able to read more than one thing at a particular moment, or to write and read simultaneously, or more generally, to fully attend to multiple meaningful resources at once. What Sharon, Gerardo, and Jay show us in the examples above is that engagement demands that one particular thing occupy their attention while they temporarily hold other agendas at bay. Attention involves selection. This principle guides our ability to construct an intellectual life in this age.

If this difficulty with attention is true of our society generally, it is no less true for an English language arts class. Indeed, our discipline—its history and its position in modern life—presents special problems for our ability to manage our own and our students' attention. For one thing, English language arts has always been pretty ill-defined as a subject. What is it? Throughout its history, people have wrestled with definitions. Partly as a consequence of this vague definition, English has often become a jumble of particles—literature, drama, art, technology, vocabulary, syntax, literate habits, study skills, reading strategies, composition, creative writing, media studies, filmmaking, literary history, linguistics, research strategies, and academic writing for all curriculum areas. Sometimes, it seems this subject is supposed to teach all the skills required for all the other subjects, on top of the already too-complex subject matter often associated with English.

The complexity of English language arts has been intensified in recent years by the changing nature of literacy and the changing population in the U.S. (and all other English-speaking countries). Literacy practices on the Internet are not just speedier, more convenient versions of the old literacy practices—people are doing new kinds of things (see Chapter 14), and young people will need to learn about them to be full participants in digital culture. Today's English classroom should not look like the English classes of the 1940s or even the 1980s, and not just because there are new tools. Literacy in digital environments involves generous participation in communities, construction of innovative texts, selection and pursuit of passions and projects, advocacy and identity work, as well as open-minded civility mixed with critical caution about the advocacy agendas of people whose perspective is different from one's own. If English class engages with the practices of the digital world, then *what to teach* becomes even more complex and multifaceted, and making decisions about what matters requires even more wisdom and foresight (Beers, Probst, and Rief 2007).

Older versions of English language arts also seem to have been built for different people than the students in our classrooms today. Today's English classroom has more diverse students in it than at any time since the early twentieth century, the last huge wave of migration into the U.S.A. Immigrant children are the fastest growing segment of the U.S. population (Suarez-Orozco and Suarez-Orozco 2001), and the adolescent population is significantly more diverse than the adult population (U.S. Census Bureau 2010). Most dramatically, the U.S. is becoming more Latino than it has been in the past, especially with Mexican immigrants and Mexican-Americans but also with Latinos from the Caribbean and Central and South America (Passel and Cohn 2008). More of these students are likely to be multilingual than many of their teachers are, and they are likely to draw upon more varied cultural, literary, traditional, and linguistic resources in their literate thinking. If all our students are to see themselves in the literature they read and to imagine for themselves a meaningful and useful literate life, then the expanding and intensifying diversity in our classrooms will add still more complexity to the planning and design of today's English classroom.

Finally, American politicians seem to have figured out that education is an easy mark. They can declare it heretofore a failure, install some new accountability system, let the grades rise while people get used to the new system, and then claim to be the savior of the nation's future—and then start that cycle all

TECHNOLOGY NOTE

Notes like this one will appear in every chapter in this book and offer connections to new literacy practices that have emerged in digital environments. Sometimes, the notes will be about getting work done using digital devices, but more often, they'll address the ways people are *doing* things on computers and the Internet and will not focus on the tools. We must think of technology not as cool toys or tools as ends in themselves but rather orient students to forms of participating in these new environments.

Multilingual Note

Every chapter will include multilingual notes. That's partly because it's important to be inclusive and multilingual students are everyone's business, not just teachers who are specialists in ESL. It's also important to note the rich resource it is for a literacy class to have multilingual students in it. Our work is about advanced forms of literacy, not the English language as such, and we can teach in a way that supports the developing multilingualism of our students rather than trying to take it away from them by limiting them to English. Obviously, that's a better education.

over again, repeating, it seems, until the end of time. We are in an atmosphere of continuous policy churn—never-ending reform and redefinition of success. At the time of this writing, a new generation has discovered the agenda of college readiness, which was also the main reform effort of the 1890s. Once again, just as occurred over a century ago, stereotypes and simplifications of college curricula are pressed into the high schools and middle schools. Tests, accountability, and prescribed curricula hold teachers in what policy makers proudly call an iron triangle. Despite these powerful forces, the teacher remains the ultimate determiner of the curriculum that actually reaches students, the classroom the only place where the actual experience of education is created. That means each individual English teacher determines students' experience of reading and writing as activities; we should take that responsibility very seriously.

An English teacher has decisions to make about how to apportion attention in his particular classroom. Just as each individual must decide how to control her own mental spotlight in daily life, leaving some things in darkness while lighting up other things, so the English teacher has a necessary obligation to focus. I would suggest that that means deciding the best way to create powerfully literate individuals. Professional English educators owe it to their students to use the knowledge of the profession in order to do the best by their students, and that is sometimes slightly different from just following a prescribed curriculum from one lesson plan to the other. We need a vision of a literate life, and we need to maintain that life as our focus, since it's the goal our students would have if they had the knowledge we do. They don't want only college, because college is a means, not an end; it lasts a few years and then that education, too, is supposed to be activated into the intellectual life of an engaged citizen with personal and social passions, a desire for aesthetic experiences, and chosen relationships that are maintained by participation through many kinds of texts.

A focus on literate lives offers us a way to take as a motto for our class one of the mottos of the U.S.A., *e pluribus unum*, meaning one out of many, a unity built upon diversity. The agenda of supporting each student in developing habits and projects in literacy allows an English class to be designed as a unified and simple curriculum that can contain much diversity and complexity, as we all learn what a literate life is made of, while diverse individuals pursue projects that are meaningful to them. Teaching in such a complex atmosphere means adopting a new understanding of the discipline of English and its traditions, one that also allows the teacher to reorient to students, adopting a position of respect and caring, one that intends to add capacity to those that students already bring to class. The objective is to build habits of engagement and intention, to help students learn to control the spotlight of their own attention.

People in the real world, after all, read and write for a huge variety of purposes. Figure 1–1 maps the Continent of Literate Purposes. Most English classes confine their attention to the very small state of Academia on that map, never voyaging very far into the other territories. In our lives outside of school, however, it's completely common for people to spend much more of their writing lives in Personalia, Civica, Worklandia, and the rest, with only a few of their early years stopping by Academia. Shouldn't a high-quality curriculum include more of this map? People's reading lives, too, span much more terrain than the space given to them in school—over purposes of informing themselves about health, taking pleasure in works of literary art, escaping into other worlds, growing personally, fitting in with a community, participating in spiritual communities and traditions, reinforcing their membership in political

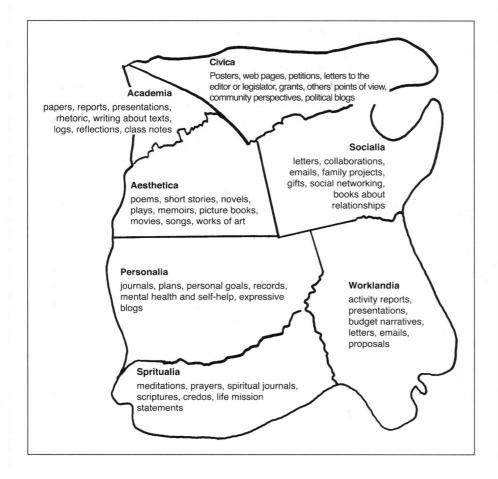

FIGURE 1–1 The Continent of Literacy Purposes

groups, growing professionally, learning about refrigerators, bugs, and other things that keep them company in life, choosing whether to bring their own taste into line with widely shared opinions about fashion and design, deepening their understanding of works of music, art, or architecture, and many other things.

Our students need, in other words, to become independent in their literate lives. Not independent from other people or communities, but independent from their teachers or other authorities that demand literate compliance—the sort of independence that makes it possible to join with others in literate conversations across the many domains of a life history. They need to be able to move flexibly among literate communities in which different reading and writing practices count—those where evidence is the main criterion in an argument as well as those they choose where a particular identity or feeling is what gains respect and audience.

In other words, our students need to be ready for college and/or career, as so many standards movements would have them be, but they also need to be ready to participate in communities well beyond those. It's essential that they be ready to participate in democratic communities, which means not just reading to become informed about those issues that may require a vote but participation well beyond that. Participants in democracy need to be able to let one another know what their lives are like so that a *common good* can be arrived at with consideration for everyone's circumstances. They need to be able to write on the Internet in order to deliberate about possible shared futures as well as debate about the meanings and lessons of a shared past. Large governmental structures like national governments are only legitimate and representative of the people generally when there is a vital democratic culture supporting and informing them. I want students, through their literacy, to have access to that culture and to be able to critique the world as it is, so that they can also imagine new possibilities for themselves and their communities.

Another form of participation readiness is their preparedness to be active members in digital culture. For a significant percentage of the population, the Internet is their chief environment for literacy, and that literacy involves a much more active set of composing practices than made sense in book/print culture. There is an expectation in the emerging environment that people write back more often and more rapidly to what they read, that they will actively connect one small text to another, that they will mix media when they explore or express, and that they will innovate on others' creations. A literacy classroom that doesn't attempt to educate for participation in communities, that doesn't build upon the communities in which students *already* participate is likely to be irrelevant to the literacies that students will really need as they compose their lives.

English language arts, as a discipline and as a class in secondary schools, should be a home to students' curiosity about all these forms of participation as well as some we haven't even thought of yet. It will take some work to get there. Teachers will have to continue to clear out the heaps of novels that crowd the curriculum. To do that, they will have to persuade their departmental colleagues that such a move is possible. (It really is, mostly, department colleagues who have to be persuaded. Neither the U.S. nor any state has a list of books that have to be read in a grade level. For the most part, English teachers do that to the people right next door to them, so the solutions to that curricular crowding are local.) In recent policy discussions about adolescent literacy, it absolutely never comes up that adolescents already have a class in school that is supposed to focus on building their literacy. That's because in everyone's memory, English doesn't do that, because it's about Shakespeare and Salinger. I'm arguing that English should, instead, become about reading and writing lives, about participation in literate communities within the classroom and beyond its door. We, as literacy educators, should be passionately interested in those lives and communities, should take a deep interest in what people do when they read, write, design, attend, and create. We need to create our English classroom as a container for exactly that interest.

A Class Is an Organization of People

Though I know a *classroom* may be a room, an architectural structure, a *class* is really an organization of people. Any plan a teacher makes involves making decisions about social arrangements in which students will talk and work. The possible social arrangements are pretty straightforward: individuals, partners, small groups, or whole class. Each of these arrangements is good for supporting particular kinds of thinking, motivation, and work. In designing a class period, teachers combine these structures for participation in varying, purposeful ways.

Independent Work

A structure in which students work individually allows each person to be in control as a reader or writer, directing the spotlight of her own attention, listening to her own thoughts, making independent judgments, trying out new ways of thinking. In what I will later call *independent reading*, students choose their books and build ideas that connect this book to others they have read in the past or plan to read in the future. This classroom structure is the incubator for an independent reading life. When the class is focused on writing, on the other hand, each writer has to do his own thinking and decision making— what to write about, how it should be structured, what purpose and style would be most appropriate for the audience who will read this. It's in the nature of most writing situations that people do much of the work independently even when they are working in collaboration with coauthors. These kinds of independent work structures provide the most choice to each individual student and so they are especially motivating; people generally get more excited about things they have chosen to do. Just as important, these arrangements put students in the position of tuning into their own preferences, interests, and impulses, so that we as teachers can connect those individual energies to the more advanced work of the discipline.

Independent literacy practices are, in many ways, the bottom line of instruction for future reading and writing lives. We plan that each student will carry away habits, not as dyads or groups of four, certainly not as a whole class, but as individuals who will enter many new communities and partnerships across a life span. Therefore, the other structures of partnerships, small groups, and whole class have to feed into what students can do independently; something we can only know when we ask students to read and write independently.

Of course, independent work is almost always integrated as well into the other structures. If people are discussing a book in a small group, they are reading it as individuals and preparing for those conversations independently in order to have high-quality conversations. In the midst of a whole-class discussion, teachers ask students to stop and write just to take stock of their own thinking at this point. Any one class period may have varied participation structures, even though the overall session may be designed for a specific kind of work.

Partnerships

Partnerships see students combined two-by-two and offer what is usually a fairly easygoing and light way of thinking with someone else. Partnerships can be especially useful in reading, and in them, a pair of students read the same text and discuss frequently as they move through it. This arrangement, more than any other, makes maximum use of the medium of talk, since in a class where partners are talking, at any one moment 50 percent of the students in the room are actually speaking to a listener. In whole-class discussion, by contrast, only one person at a time can speak. Responding to a whole-class text can be facilitated by partnerships, too, as can responding to ideas the teacher has presented to everyone or to a particular student's piece of writing. Sometimes, teachers ask students to take on a writing partnership, a research partnership, or a homework partnership, in which students have someone with whom to check in about their progress and developing habits. Partnerships, therefore, can be quick appointments to talk with one other person, or they can be sustained, deeper engagements, such as Leo and Julio reading *The Burn Journals* together. As such, they can be the focus of class time and a main object of teaching—how to be a good partner and have better conversations—or they can be a few minutes long and in support of independent, whole-group, or small-group work.

Small Groups

Small groups involve three, four, or five students sharing work—either responding to one another's writing, reading a book (or many books) together, or collaborating on an inquiry together. Work in small groups is different from partnerships, in that the work usually involves more development of ideas, sticking with topics longer, and less freewheeling moving from topic to topic. The work is thus a little more rigorous, in a way, though each individual's agenda, choice, and motivation is a little more compromised by having to deal with the interests of more different people. With small groups, talk is well distributed across the room, though obviously less so than with partners; with groups, each person has to wait longer between turns to speak.

Because social interactions in small groups are more complex, more of the teaching has to focus on collaboration and talk strategies. Just putting students into small groups isn't enough to make them successful, and at first, it will become very apparent that they don't yet know how to hold an idea in their conversation long enough to think through it, how to listen and respond to one another, how to differ and get past intense disagreements. Chapters 4 and, especially, 8 will provide much more detail about structuring and teaching into small groups.

Like the other structures, small groups can be sustained or quick. In the midst of a whole-class discussion, a teacher will often ask students to get together into groups of three or four to process what the class has been discussing and how it applies to each individual project. Likewise, during independent work, a teacher sometimes asks students to get together in the last ten minutes of a period and share what they accomplished today, or something new they tried in their writing or reading.

Whole Class

Whole class is of course a very common structure in most secondary schools, perhaps the most common. It's obviously the most efficient way for one teacher to share a strategy, some information, or a new perspective with a whole group of students. And it's obviously also the one in which individual students are afforded with the least choice and asked the least to self-regulate their literate activity. So it's important, but it must always be at the service of the other structures, particularly independent work, in order to make a difference in people's literate lives. Whole-class teaching is the location for demonstrations of and mentoring into things writers and readers do that students have not yet had enough access. It's a structure for introducing these practices and then pointing students toward doing them in their independent work. Likewise, when we read a novel with a whole class, we ought to be making explicit a few select valued ways of reading and thinking about text (see Chapters 5 and 6) and/or media for responding to text (Chapters 7, 8, and 9) so that students can take these habits back to their independent work and from there into their literate lives.

What a Class Period Can Be

With those basic elements—independent work, partners, small groups, and whole class—a teacher designs a class period. The notion of design—of carefully combining elements to achieve a particular purpose—is crucial (Smagorinsky 2007; Wiggins and McTighe 2005). The objective is not to load as many structures as one can into a single class period, adding herky-jerky motion and a number of transitions from one activity to another. In order to accustom students to sustaining attention, rather than just adding to the fragmentation of their day, the class session should be as elegant as possible. That cannot be achieved when people think they have to insert pieces like "warm-ups," "motivations," or gratuitous demands that every class start with a very brief reading or writing time that really goes nowhere. Achieving elegance is slightly complicated, though, by the fact that it is sometimes helpful to be able to plan a class with one or two graceful shifts in participation structures from a short, whole-group lesson to independent work, or from small groups to whole-group reflection. Still, there is important work to be done in English class, and we need to remain focused on that work, constantly resisting the jumble of little pieces.

I'm going to describe four important types of class period, though I'll give substantially more attention to one of them—the workshop structure. Many people, I among them, have found that a workshop structure is especially useful in supporting students' constructions of highly motivated literate lives. But everything is not a workshop, and all the purposes an English teacher pursues cannot be best achieved with only one structure. So I'll also describe, more briefly, three other basic shapes for an English class period.

A Workshop Classroom

A workshop structure (Atwell 1986; Bomer 1995; Rief 1992) takes its name from its similarities to spaces where people work on projects across time. In a workshop, whether in an English classroom or a wood shop, the work is still there waiting when the maker walks in. Every time she comes into the workshop, she knows where the project is, she knows what to do, and she can pick up where she left off yesterday. Sessions of making connect through the maker's intention from one session to the next.

In a writing workshop, then, the main thing one could see by peering through a window would be people writing, there in the classroom. They would have walked into the room, picked up the project they were working on, summoned up the thinking, planning, and intention that could help get the work back underway, and become engaged. In other words, they would have done what any writer outside school would have to do upon returning to the desk. In a reading workshop, likewise, people read—they pick up the text they were reading yesterday, as well as the intentions and ideas that brought them to this text and will carry them into the next one. Or if they are reading with a partner or small group, they might be continuing a discussion of the book they are reading together, in which case, the conversation itself is the object being made, and it will be the focus during work time.

Though there are several structures that support it, the defining feature, the only nonnegotiable element of a workshop classroom, is that time when students actually engage in literate behavior—right here on campus! I have known people to question this: *Why can't they do their work at home? This isn't a study hall!* From that perspective, pretty common in secondary schools, actual literate activity seems unworthy of the time, and the best use of a class is something other than the very behavior that is the target of all the teaching. In order for the teaching of reading and writing to have some place to stick, however, it's important for students to be engaging in those activities where the teaching takes place. If we want them to read or write outside school, we have to value it inside school and also give them a chance to get engaged with the work. Banning literacy from the school day is a bad idea. A workshop classroom in English does the opposite; it centers on students' ongoing literate activity, every day, as the focus of the class.

So the center of the class—the massive guts of the period—is work time. Assuming a forty-five- to fifty-minute class, that's at least half an hour. On the clock, if the period looks like this . . .

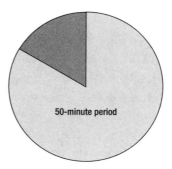

. . . then the class structures look something like this . . .

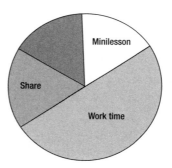

. . . a structure that makes very clear where the spotlight of attention shines—on students working. Work time takes the lion's share of the period, framed by two whole-class meetings, which I will describe shortly. During this work time, students engage with long-term projects they have chosen within the curricular parameters the teacher has established (and those parameters will be described at length in this book). In order to facilitate the completion of those projects, this class structure remains in place, the only thing going on, for a stretch of weeks. It is into the ongoing literate work students have chosen that the teacher instructs, through several teaching structures. That's what makes this very different from a study hall—the teacher's role as an expert and coach on just the things that the students are working on. The teacher is not just reading while they read or writing while they write; there is important and urgent work to be done here.

While students are working, during that selfsame work time I've been discussing, the teacher circulates and confers with individuals, partners, or small groups. These conferences are, in effect, lessons tailor-made for the student, based on where she is in the work right now. It can be a very precise and accurate way of teaching, since it allows the teacher to choose a point to make to this writer or reader, one she may be ready to hear right now. A conference is about one focused idea, something that will not only help with the writing or reading of this text in front of the student, but a lesson that represents a bigger idea or strategy about reading or writing that will help the student in the future as well. A conference is not just a way of making sure students know what they're supposed to do, a clarification of an assignment; it's a moment that is designed to change the student's habits or understandings from now on, if only in a small way.

Though the precise length of conferences vary somewhat, they have to be pretty short, because settling in with one student for twenty minutes is a good way to lose the rest of the class, because there is a need to get around to more than just a couple of students in a day, and because a conference should be about only one idea, not everything the teacher can think of to say to this kid today. In a thirty-minute workshop, I usually make it around to six or seven students. I've gotten pretty good at working quickly over the years, but for someone just beginning to confer, it may take a little while to get up to speed. It may help to remember that if you do have one long conference, you have to pay for it with several brief ones afterward, just to make some progress around the room. By the end of this book, readers will have lots of ideas about the sorts of things conferences will be about.

As I mentioned before, whole-class meetings occur at the beginning and end of the period in a workshop classroom. The first meeting is a minilesson (Calkins 1994), a very focused and brief lesson with a single, laserlike objective, something that most of the students need to hear, most are ready to hear at this point in their work, and, as in a conference, that could benefit them not just now but throughout their literate lives. In a minilesson, good teachers usually begin by giving the students some context, a reason why they've thought to talk about this today. "I've noticed, while you're working on your poems, that. . . ." The teacher then explains clearly what the point of this minilesson is going to be. "So the thing I wanted to talk with you today is. . . ." Then, often, he demonstrates the strategy, actually doing it aloud quickly in front the students. Other times, he might demonstrate it by pointing it out in a published text. If the minilesson up until this point has only taken five minutes or so, he might ask the students to try some quick and dirty version of the objective right now, in the next minute and a half, either aloud with a partner or jotted in their notebook. He then pulls the class back together and explains how this little talk relates to what they are doing now and also when in their future writing lives they might need to use this learning. If the minilesson is too long, it's also possible to introduce the idea and do the demonstration of it one day, then as a part two, to ask the kids to try something the next day.

It's crucial, for the sake of the workshop being about the students' work, that the minilesson not become maxi, that it not start chipping away at the work time as the teacher thinks of more things to say. It's a good idea to banish "oh, by the way . . ." from one's teaching vocabulary. If there's more to say, then that can be tomorrow's minilesson. Because the shortness of a minilesson permits the longness of writing/conferring time, it's a good idea for teachers to time themselves while doing the minilesson until they get used to this particular genre. Again, I would predict that by the time a reader has made it through this book, ideas for minilessons won't be too much of a problem.

The other whole-class meeting, the one at the end of the period, is the share time. If the word *share* seems too touchy-feely, then it might help to think of it as a time for reflecting or self-assessing. It's useful as a moment for students to say, "What just happened? What am I accomplishing? What's next?" They can pull back from the forest of their own content and think about process, direction, and goals. Sometimes, teachers find it useful to ask a student to read aloud a bit of what they have written. Often, they choose a particular student as they confer, someone they talk with today who might be able to spread the word from this conference about a particular strategy. In the conference, the teacher offers the student a new strategy, then asks her to share this new idea at the end of the class. As a consequence, the wealth is spread around and the teaching in conference goes further. Other times, the teacher asks the whole class as individuals to look back at what they did today—in their writing or the pages they read—and name their progress, then set a goal for tomorrow. Still other times, the teacher might ask students to recall the point of the minilesson and then talk with a partner for five minutes about how they applied that idea in their work today, or how they might do so tomorrow. The share time, therefore, used in an instructionally purposeful way, can become a moment for students to name and claim their learning and progress, the problems they're working through, or the strategies they are trying to remember to apply.

As I have already argued, I see the workshop structure as the best collection of teaching practices for times when the focus is on students getting work done, and that should be most of the time. As we examine the details of what there is to teach about the processes of reading and writing, it will be clearer why we want students doing them in the classroom right in front of the teacher, where she can talk with the kids on the spot about what they are doing, complicating and transforming their initial work toward more powerful forms of participation in literate culture.

Some Other Possible Structures

A few times, certain superintendents, excited about workshop's potential to build strength for students, have attempted to mandate workshop as the only structure for teaching. Aside from the political and social difficulties that arise from such mandates, there are some kinds of teaching that just don't fit that well into workshops but that are still worth doing, even if they don't account for most days in a particular classroom's life. I'm not including here things like lectures, because I think the utility of a structure that has students just listening to a teacher talk all period would have to be considered pretty limited. On rare occasions, if the teacher is especially good at talking and can break it up so students have a chance to reflect and process what's being said, maybe lecture is somewhat useful, but it's not a premium way of building a learning life. I do think, however, an English teacher (or perhaps any secondary teacher) would be hobbled without ever being able to use the structures I am calling *mentored inquiry*, *sustained whole-class discussion*, and *shared aesthetic experience*.

Mentored Inquiry

Sometimes, a class is investigating a concept or topic together. Among the concepts that will appear in this book that a class might investigate, for example, are students' existing literate lives outside school (Chapter 2), dialects in the community (Chapter 15), and the differences between oral and literate language (Chapter 15). Sometimes at the beginning of a genre study, like poetry for instance, there might be a few days in which students investigate what can count as a poem, before the class really gets going as a workshop in poetry (Chapter 13). Between units of study in writing, it may at times be useful to inquire for a few days into the structures of sentences (Chapter 15). In such a classroom, there may be a minilesson followed by small-group or individual work time, but the focus is less on picking up on yesterday's work and extending it, and the tasks may be more structured by the teacher in the interest of building the concepts that are the aim of the unit. There is more of a content focus than a focus on habits, agendas, and dispositions that create a literate life. This is content that is designed to make literacy and language more interesting, but it's knowledge *about* language and literacy, not direct use of language and literacy.

Sustained Whole-Class Discussion

Whole-class discussions, when they are actually discussions among the students and not recitations from each individual student to the teacher (see Chapter 8), are common ways of structuring class time in English classes, especially when the class is reading a longer text together. It is possible to think of these discussions as workshops, with the teacher offering a minilesson about a particular strategy for being a high-quality discussant at the beginning, then initiating the conversation among the whole class while he circulates and confers briefly, privately, with individuals about ways of gaining the floor or building on another student's point. But more common is for the teacher to facilitate discussion and participate in it. It's clearly important for students to have the kind of on-fire discussions that might hook them into an intellectual life and to be captured by their teacher's excitement in discussing something interesting. These moments are, for many people, an important source of engagement in literacy and thinking. At the same time, because whole-class structures are inefficient ways of distributing talk, they run a risk of turning a healthy number of students passive, so they should probably be less dominant in student's experience than they now tend to be.

Shared Aesthetic Experience

There are times when the purpose of a class is to share an aesthetic experience—to enjoy a work of art, live with it, inhabit it, and not necessarily, at least at first, to analyze it or do anything with it. This can take the form of looking at and responding to slides of paintings, watching a short film, or participating in an improvised drama that fleshes out the story world of a text that's being shared. These classes don't have the usual kind of "instructional objectives" and they aren't designed to promote productivity. They are, rather, designed as experiences of beauty, perhaps pleasure, for many of the students. Our thinking about shared life should not become so linear, so like a production line, that we can't imagine such an experience as part of an English class. With the arts in education being under continual threat, it's always worth remembering that English is the remaining academic subject that does concern itself with aesthetic knowing, and that kind of knowing is important for people's lives as well as collective life (Greene 1988, 1995).

I don't pretend that the class structures I have described here are the only ones possible; they aren't. I also don't claim that they are equally important; I have found that workshop structures are especially valuable, and they will be the main focus of this book. But teaching well is always a matter of thoughtful, informed adaptation in response to an assessment of what is going on with students (Duffy and Hoffman 1999), not of a monolithic devotion to a single strategy as if it were the perfect method.

In the chapter that follows, I will describe initial assessment that makes thoughtful teaching possible, through leading students into inquiry into their own existing literate lives. In that chapter, the emphasis will be on convincing students that what they bring to school is valuable and deserving of respect in their teacher's eyes and building teaching upon what they discover about their own practices. The chapter after that will discuss the expansion of literate lives and ways of supporting students in developing committed practices of reading and writing that may help them in all sorts of academic work.

CHAPTER 2

When I was in high school, they drug me into the principal's office and told me I had a lot of potential, but that I needed to learn how to study hard and make something of myself. And that's when I quit school. Because I realized that we weren't operating on the same level of reality. Because, you see, I knew that I already was something.

—JOHN TRUDELL, *Native American activist and poet, in the film* Trudell, *by Heather Rae*

Appreciating Existing Literacies

Javier is building a motorcycle "from the ground up," and in order to do that, he frequently consults Internet sites about his project, especially particular mechanical and engineering questions, like how things go together. These sites contain text—advice from people who have built motorcycles, both novices and experts—and also many captioned diagrams that describe the assembly of engine parts. He gets on a particular social networking site most days, quickly replies to the messages that he has already, and gets off right away so he won't be obliged to reply a second time in one day. On his page, he has a recording he used his computer to make of him and his cousin battling in rap to a beat they created on the computer. He has a Mexican flag hung on the wall in his room, and his homeys come over and tag on it. To that group together, it's an important symbol of shared identity. At the beginning of the school year, he asked his teacher if she had Cirque du Freak books, a horror series for young adults, kind of a grown-up Goosebumps. Javier has played the game Halo as a MMPORG (massively multiplayer online role-playing game), and he was the only one in his class with that kind of experience. Javier doesn't do too well in school, and he's not all that easy to get along with as a student, but he has a multifaceted and complex array of literacy practices.

We have begun so far in this book to trouble the questions of what to teach and where to teach it—the classroom structures that create schoolwork in space and time. Let's now turn our attention to the people involved. Who are these kids? What will be our relationship to them? And what is the beginning like for a relationship in which teaching and learning can occur? I am going to suggest that the best possible beginning to a school year just might involve finding out about students as literate people, while also building a relationship with a listening attitude.

If, as teachers, we hold back a few minutes from proclaiming our knowledge, our rules, and our expectations, and instead listen to students talk about their lives, we might be able to meet them in a more respectful way. We might learn ways to take into consideration more of what they are dealing with and more of the competencies and resources they bring into the classroom. When we listen, we clear a space into which students can move, a space for them to grow into. We deliberately create a silence into which they can speak and hear their own voice. I am not suggesting that the teacher will become passive and fail to teach assertively; rather, I'm suggesting that our teaching can be most powerful if it is undertaken with students experiencing the classroom as including space for the details of their existence, rather than blurring their individual faces into a vague generalized identity of "student."

Actually, this listening and inquiring does more than establish a relationship. So much teaching in school meets the learner's mind imprecisely, as a *non sequitur*, answering a question the learner is not asking. A teacher develops a lesson on how to organize an essay, while a student in the class still isn't confident enough about her authority to develop content in her writing. A teacher starts asking comprehension questions while a student is resenting the fact that she is reading yet another novel that has nothing to do with her interests or experience. We need to know what students know and how they think about literacy in order to help make connections to new ideas and practices. We need to know how they have been changing lately in order to transform what they can do tomorrow. We need to know what they think they already are, in Trudell's terms above, instead of beginning by telling them they ought to make something of themselves.

This kind of investigation is real assessment; it is coming to understand the learner. Usually, school assessment ends with a number or grade supposedly corresponding to the student's progress on a linear path of development—like steps on a ladder. But literacy is not well represented as a single line of growth or a single dot on a line. People read and write, even in careers, even in college, with all that they are. Many streams contribute to reading, and many to composing—a student's relationships, values, history, culture, language, and loves. To assess what is going on with a particular kid, the teacher really needs to understand much of that.

The letters and numbers on report card grades and test scores show little to a student, her parents, or the system. These tiny particles of information are part of the school system and are, at least within the imperfect present, inescapable. A teacher's work, however, is starved by so meager a way of thinking about students' literate lives. If a teacher looks at a class full of students and, instead of seeing the faces of particular people she really knows, sees an 82 here or an A– there, superimposed over human faces, I don't see how she can really teach those people. The form of assessment a teacher really needs—a process of coming to understand—is a more qualitative and descriptive kind of appreciation of what a student knows and can do as a reader and writer. It requires a detailed understanding of how literacy works presently in the life of that student and how it has operated in the past, as well as the journey the student is presently making in this class.

So grades and test scores do not form the base of teachers' most important understandings of students—and I want to go further. A teacher's assessment needs mainly to be appreciative. The most useful form of knowledge for teachers is affirming—acknowledging already-existing interests, experiences, knowledge, and skill in order to build upon them—rather than based upon some kind of diagnosis of a problem, impediment, or deficit in the student (Alvermann et al. 2006).

Getting Real About Grades

Grades are part of the job of teaching, though they are so minimalistic as signs that they really carry very little information. When a teacher gives a 91 or an A–, what does that say? It's not really a measurement of anything and even when it is a number, it is not really quantifying anything. The student does not get 91 of anything. It's just a signal that the student did really well, almost as well as the teacher could have wanted, but not quite. Compared to the detailed knowledge of learners we are talking about in this chapter, it's pretty thin business.

Deficit vs. Appreciative Perspectives

Much of my decision making about teaching comes back to a fundamental commitment. I will believe in students' competence and intelligence. I will keep faith, as Don Murray suggested, that they have stories to tell, things to explain, and the language with which to do those things. I will reject any notion that places in my mind a belief in students' deficits—whether those deficits be genetic, cultural, or behavioral. I will treat them as people who can get important things done for important reasons.

Deficit thinking is a perennial hazard in the educational process (Bomer, Dworin, May, and Semingson 2008; Dudley-Marling 2007; Marx 2006; Valencia 1997, 2010). Perhaps wherever the difficult human transactions of teaching and learning are going on, adults in the system might be positioned to worry that there is something wrong with the kids, their families, communities, language, entertainment choices, or brains. Statements like "these kids have no language" or "they have no experiences" are especially pernicious errors in education—harmful in their effects (Collins 1996; Rist 1970; Rosenthal and Jacobson 1968; Varenne and McDermott 1999). Everyone has language—exactly the appropriate languages for the social situations they have inhabited and the roles they've been able to take on in those settings. In some of these situations, such as most families, a little language goes a long way, as words are laden with much shared meaning and so explicitness is neither called for nor appropriate. All human interactions require language—especially if you understand that language includes all kinds of signs. When teachers say that a student lacks language, what they really reveal is that they have not yet found a way to engage this other human being in communication, that the differences between teacher and student have not yet been bridged in the teacher's imagination, and that the teacher is predisposed to thinking all of this distance and misunderstanding is the fault of the kid. That is deficit thinking. (I'll have more to say on language in particular—and supporting students' study of it—in Chapter 14.) Likewise, the claim that people have no experiences seems to ignore the fact that many of the most profoundly shaping experiences people undergo occur before the age of five. People have the experiences they have; those are the things of which literature is made—whatever they are. There is no such thing as the correct amount of experience.

In an era when schools are held accountable for the test performance of every student and where the scores of social subgroups such as Latinos, African Americans, and economically disadvantaged students must be reported separately, maybe it is almost inevitable that deficit thinking will speak through us, even when we don't intend it to. The gaps are always in sight. The students are getting the teachers in trouble. Certain students may, in some states or districts, even be causing the teachers to miss out on bonus pay. That is a situation ripe for blame. But you cannot teach someone in whom you don't believe at a fundamental level. Teaching involves a faith in the competence of the student—an assured hope for her growth.

Recently, appreciative inquiry has arisen in the field of organization management as an alternative to traditional problem or risk analyses and planning (Whitney and Trosten-Bloom 2010). It attempts to build upon the energy, motivation, and inspiration people gain from an organization when things are working well. One of the building blocks of this approach is appreciative interviewing, which many people across an organization conduct with one another, a form of conversation in which participants are asked to recount moments when they—and the organization—were fully alive and at their very best in the work. Analysis of many such moments provides a map of possibilities for the organization's future that allows people to be inspired and confident about their shared life and endeavors.

A comparable perspective also exists in community organizing; the approach is referred to as *asset-based* community organizing (Kretzmann and McKnight 1993). Rather than entering a community and looking for its problems, in this approach, organizers work with community members to identify a community's assets of all kinds and to build shared projects upon that wealth. Contrast this to an organizer who names a community's challenges—say, drugs, unemployment—and then seeks to combat those problems. An asset-based approach is more celebratory and aims to produce more energy, openness, and strength for mutuality and collaboration among the people being served. It finds the resources available in a community—specific forms of knowledge and skill the adults possess, the ways they care for elders, a system of barter and exchange, energy and passion among the youth, a connection to place. Using a discipline of positive eyes and respectful regard, the organizer helps create hope and motivation among the community members.

Both appreciative inquiry and asset-based organizing reject deficit thinking and attempt to replace it with a way of looking, listening, wondering, dreaming, and acting that changes the relationship between someone trying to bring change or help and those who are, supposedly, being helped. In this framework, the person being helped is recognized as a source of information, a base of strength, a network of assistive relationships, a nexus of positive influences—rather than being positioned as a problem to be overcome by the helper. Consequently, the client is more of a partner, an agent in the work, rather than a patient being *done to*.

Many movements in education, too, have taken such a view of student competence, but those advances have often been lost in the noise of an accountability system, of testing and consequences for tests, that seeks to expose problems wherever they may try to hide. In the midst of that system, however, good teachers have realized that it is more important than ever to regard students with appreciation and to speak to them about their assets. In bilingual education, for example, educators hold to a principle of additive education (Lambert 1975)—accepting and building upon the linguistic strength that is already present in students who are becoming multilingual. A subtractive education, by contrast, removes language, relationship, knowledge, and skill from students, asking them to replace much of what they care about with someone else's agenda, supposedly in order to get ahead in the world (Valenzuela 1999). In such a system, school takes away capacities the students had when they walked in the door; it makes them poorer.

Recently, researchers and teachers working in the field of adolescent literacy have developed a similar agenda of seeking to understand the resources students bring to school. Noting that decades of research have demonstrated that school is not always a site of highly motivated, rich, and joyful learning for adolescents, these educators have sought out the physical locations, time frames, and forms of activity when adolescents *do* have such learning and literacy experiences. Educators, like managers and community organizers, are attempting to build their relationships to students upon appreciation of success that might otherwise go unseen and upon recognition of the assets available for this particular person in this specific situation. Conversations with students about the times when texts do count for them is a better place to meet them than with a page assignment for a particular novel, a grammar lesson, or a reading strategy.

Appreciative Inquiry into Existing Literacy Practices

To teach an adolescent or adult, one best begins by finding ways of showing him respect, by bringing him into the relationship as a whole, strong, worthy person. In a literacy classroom like an English class, one way to do that is by receiving students' existing literacies—beginning the conversation with extended and explicit acknowledgment that most of the things we're going to learn in this class are just expansions on things they already do all the time because they want to. The existence of high-level literate behavior in their lives is, for most students, not something they will already be aware of, or even willing to agree about. So the teacher's job is to convince them of what they are already doing.

Before I start describing my conversations with students, let me clarify what brings me into contact with them. I'm a former middle and high school English teacher now making a living as a university professor, researcher, and teacher of teachers. I still spend a good deal of time in secondary classrooms, working alongside other English teachers and their students—researching, trying out ideas, coaching teachers, and demonstrating strategies. Recently, I talked to a ninth-grade class about their reading lives. All of the students were from working-class or poor families, most of them African American and

Latino. If many middle-class Americans were going to think that youth do not have literate lives, some of these would be the kids who would spring to mind first. But that would be wrong.

I said: "This is English class, so you know this class is about reading and writing—let's call it *literacy*. English class, you know from your experience in school, is all about literacy. But you use literacy in other places besides English class, too. For one thing, you know you use literacy in other classes. You read and write stuff in social studies. In biology, you might read a diagram that shows how a plant uses sunlight, how energy and nutrients flow through the plant. In algebra, even if all you're doing is getting ready to solve an equation, you read it—you see what patterns you recognize in it, how it's similar or different to other problems you have seen. That's literacy, too, looking at something and making meaning of it.

"You also have literacy all through your lives outside school. Maybe you go to a church, temple, or mosque, and in those places, there is all kinds of literacy, especially interpretations of a particular book—the Bible, the Koran, the Torah. . . . You may have literate stuff you do in your religious or spiritual life. Or in your social or family life—there may be people you write to, just to keep in touch. You might like sports or music, and there might be literacy you do connected to those. And in a way, it's even bigger than that—much bigger than reading and writing. You read situations all the time. If you go into a new restaurant, you read that room—not just the menu, the whole room—to figure out what they have here, what's good, how I order, how I figure out where to sit. That's a sort of reading, just like when you read a book and you have to bring your knowledge to it and figure out what's going on. If you are on a subway platform, you read it, try to see who's crazy, who to stay away from, where the door of the train might end up, which side goes in which direction. You read the street you're on—you constantly read people and situations."

One girl offered, "We're reading you right now."

"Like what do you mean?" I asked.

"We're trying to figure out what we have to do and what you're talking about."

"Well, you know what I'm talking about, because that's it exactly. Reading a teacher is a special kind of literacy. Let's see if we can come up with a few more examples of special kinds of literacy like that—or else just reading and writing—how different kinds of literacy happen in your life away from school."

Students volunteered several varied forms of print literacy. A boy said that his mother leaves him notes about the day because she has to leave for work before he gets up. A girl offered her letter writing with her family back in her country, and several other students agreed. Many of their ideas were pretty conservative in their definitions of literacy—they weren't yet convinced that literacy could be broader than reading and writing, despite the insight that they were reading me right now. One young man said that he frequently checks fashions on the Internet—especially sneakers. He also mentioned that my shoes were pretty fine, so that was an especially valuable contribution. The mention of the Internet brought a flood of new ideas, and several students mentioned their pages on a social networking site. I asked how many had such pages, and almost everyone in class raised their hands. I asked where they accessed the Internet to manage those pages, and they said the public library and also school, though the school blocked the site. They said that they knew ways of getting around the school's security software, and I said there's another literacy right there.

I asked them to take about five minutes to make a list, thinking through their day, of all the forms of literacy they could come up with in their lives outside school. And after that, I asked them to get together with one or two people sitting around them and see how many different kinds of literacy they had come up with. During the writing and the talking, I circulated and conferred, with individuals during the writing and with small groups during the talking.

I knelt down next to Ruwan, who at first said he didn't have a reading life and then glowered at me, I guess to try and make me go away. He said he didn't like to read and never did it. I asked what he did like to do, and he told me that he was a rapper and liked making music, listening to music, and keeping up with his favorite artists. I asked who he liked and how he kept up with them. Realizing that there was reading there, he gestured to concede the point and said that he buys several different music magazines, especially *Guitar* magazine, when he could afford it, at the candy store. How, I wondered, did he read these magazines? From cover to cover? I asked this because it was clear that he did not even see that he had a reading life, so he certainly hadn't thought about or valued the details of his own reading processes, the kinds of purposeful and intelligent choices he habitually made as he navigated text. He said no, he didn't really read from start to finish; he read the parts that were interesting. Of course, I asked how he could know which parts were going to be interesting if he hadn't yet read them. What was he using to decide? He said that the beginnings and endings of those articles were usually not that interesting to him, but that usually somewhere in the middle, the artist talked about how they got to be who they are. I asked if he meant how they became rich, successful, famous, and he replied that no, that wasn't the point. He wanted to know how they became so good at what they do, what they had learned about playing their instrument and how they worked at it. I asked him why that's the interesting part, and he said, "Because that's where I'm at. I'm trying to learn how to get better so I can become successful at my music. Not like famous and rich, but good at what I do." I asked if there were other things that helped him learn about those ideas, and he talked about websites he had read from school and in the public library (because "there's not a computer working in my house right now").

I came to understand that Ruwan was using his most focused life project, his developing sense of craft as a musician, to create an avenue of purpose in his reading, and he moved along that avenue through complex texts that weren't necessarily built to accommodate the question he brought to them. He had to read selectively and purposefully in order to get what he wanted from them. In this conversation, I came to admire his sense of purpose and his power as a reader, in making text work for him, and I told him so. I also told him that, as our talk in class about reading continued, we wouldn't just be interested in book reading or English class reading; we were interested in the reading that really happens in life, the easy and useful stuff he probably didn't even notice himself doing.

Devorah was reading *A Boy Called It* and said she was on page 81, but she didn't have the book with her at the moment. At the moment, this period, her twin sister had the book, in her science class, and she was on page 63. Of the same book. Devorah said this is the way they often read, sharing the same physical book, passing it back and forth, both intimately aware of the other's progress through the book. They talked about the book, but they had a rule that the conversation today had to stop at page 63 so that the one who was ahead wouldn't spoil any surprises for the other.

Devorah showed me that students are already thinking in intricate ways about the social relationships and the sharing practices that surround a successful reading experience. She and her sister had braided their lives around the reading of this book, which meant they had developed strategies for selecting books, for determining the sequence in which they would read them, for using a text of which they had a single copy, and for talking (and not talking) about the text. They each knew which one needed help with particular aspects of reading, thinking, or understanding, and she could talk with substantial detail about how they were different as readers, as well as about their similarities. This kind of social awareness of other readers is exactly what this curriculum attempts to build into the classroom community.

By the end of that class, students had a position from which to revalue their own literacy achievement—not solely within the context of school but more broadly in the practicalities and pleasures of life. And a conversation was underway, one that could be sustained not only for the next few weeks, but throughout the school year.

What to Expect: What We Know from Research

An individual teacher, embarking upon an exploration of students' existing literate lives, will undoubtedly be surprised again and again by the inventiveness and variation students will reveal. Who knew that Mario had an extensive annotated stamp collection in several albums and a shelf full of reference materials, that Shari—who seems never to read for class—spends her summer vacations indoors reading horror novels, that Bhabani can write in Bengali and maintains a correspondence with her cousin in Bangladesh? Although the variety of individual differences may keep teachers on the edge of their seats as they learn about their students, there are some predictable patterns, well established in research about adolescent out-of-school literacy. For meticulous reviews of much of this research, some readers may want to read sections of *The Handbook of Research on Adolescent Literacy* (Christenbury, Bomer, and Smagorinsky 2008). Some contemporary teen literacy practices might be more exotic to many of us than the literacy practices of certain nineteenth-century novelists!

Many common practices among youth are fairly similar to academic literacy practices. Some young people keep journals, diaries, or sketchbooks; they read novels and participate in organized theatre companies. Though these practices are motivated in different ways when kids undertake them away from teachers' authority, they are right next door to school literacy practices. *Zines*—small-circulation print publications consisting of both original and copied text and images—are, by their nature, unofficial and are often intended to be subversive (Guzzetti and Gamboa 2004; Gustavson 2007). Still, they have existed for centuries and some of their genres are similar to those taught in English classes—poems, book reviews, parodies.

For at least the past sixty years or so, songs have been an especially important kind of text in the lives of adolescents. Kids' ways of thinking about song lyrics—including (maybe especially) rap—are really not substantially different from those of serious readers of poetry. Their interpretive practices are very like those of poetry readers—sometimes, when a song speaks to them, they think more deeply about it, actively making meaning of symbols or oblique and compressed statements; other times, they stay outside the words' meanings and just accept their sound. They sometimes listen to the song first and then read the lyrics on the Internet or CD material, and other times, they study the lyrics before listening to the songs. Most can explain why they do it the way they do (Alvermann and Hagood 2000; Christenson and Roberts 1998). Many youth also make music (a much higher percentage than among adults), either performing or actually writing it (Jennings 1999; Lipsitz 1997; Straw 1997). And that activity sponsors many literacy practices as well, from reading advice on playing an instrument to writing lyrics. Music creates fan cultures and communities around particular artists, styles, and genres, and increasingly, fans find one another through literacy on the Internet.

Some youth engage in the literacy practice known as "tagging," in which they write their nickname, initials, or other form of "tag" in stylized letters on walls and other unofficial writing surfaces. Though some adults condemn this as a criminal behavior, it is also a literacy practice, and several scholars have looked closely at it (Cintron 1997; Cowan 2004; Moje 2000; Smith and Whitmore 2005). We know that tagging represents a strong connection of literacy to identity—that kids feel that these tags represent them. We know that many people who tag have developed a strong sense of craft about it and take pride in their skill. Many tags are signals of affiliation with particular groups, and some are tributes to people who are important to the author. In other words, many of the motives and purposes in tagging are precisely those that fuel every literate life—identity, craft, affiliation with groups, affirmation of relationships—and students would be well served if their teachers tried to tap into those motives and help the students accomplish the same things with additional forms of literacy. These same motives have driven the use of all kinds of signs through much of human history.

Of course, the Internet has offered young people a huge number of spaces that did not previously exist, and all of these spaces are mediated by some form of literacy. The Pew Center for the Study of the Internet and American Life claimed that 93 percent of teens are online, and 64 percent of those are content creators on the Internet (Lenhart, Madden, Smith, and Macgill 2007). That means they have worked on a blog or personal Web page, either on their own behalf or for an organization or school; they've shared original content such as art, photos, stories, or video; or they have remixed content they found on the Internet to make something new. Numbers such as this are difficult to credit fully, but many, many students in middle and high school classrooms have some kind of presence online. Very often these days, that presence is focused around a social networking site like Facebook (though perhaps its prominence fades as soon as I type the name and by the time this book is published, it will seem nearly as ancient as the Etruscans). These sites involve a wide variety of literacy practices.

Another intricately networked form of literacy is texting—the use of cell phones or PDAs for sending quick keeping-in-touch messages to people. I dislike seeing this practice in an organized class time as much as the next teacher, but part of the reason it is often a problem is precisely because the practice is so engaging and important to its users. If the practice becomes part of what we study when we study our literacy, then it has powerful potential to help students identify as people who read and write all the time. One student recently figured out with his teacher that he sends over one thousand messages per day. That's pretty constant writing, even if lots of the messages are just "lol" or " 'sup" or whatever.

Most youth watch television and movies, and teachers should recognize the potential contributions this viewing can make to a literate life, instead of thinking—as educators too often do—of mass culture as the enemy of literacy learning. From students' preferences for particular kinds of worlds in TV and movies, we can begin conversations about the sorts of books that might appeal to them. If we find out they like particular kinds of character types, relationships among characters, settings, tones, feelings, or language, we can help them find books with similar features. Furthermore, the energy that takes students from one movie to the next, a sense of agenda, is a valuable feature of a reading life. Since the development (in the 1980s) of home viewing of self-selected videos and the increasing ease of seeing what one wants when one wants, a viewing life has become much more like a reading life. People decide to see the movies by a certain director or writer, or all of a particular actor's movies, or they become experts in a genre. Students have grown up with this capability, though they may need some help becoming more purposeful and strategic viewers. And these capabilities can make them more deliberate and passionate as readers, too.

Organizing Appreciative Inquiry into Literate Lives

Whole-Class Conversations

In order to plan a class period in which students and teacher collaboratively investigate, two areas demand advance attention—the thematic questions that will be the focus for that particular day and the social structures in which students will do their inquiring and talking. Thematic questions can be broad or narrow, depending upon how the conversation has been developing with that particular group of students. Usually, it's best to begin with broad investigations like "What is my life history as a reader?" and then move to "What are some similar experiences that people in this class have had as readers?" As the conversation develops, it makes sense to narrow and focus inquiries toward topics like "What has been the most productive place for me to read in order to enjoy and escape, and is that a different place from where I read in order to learn something new?" It won't be possible to investigate every conceivable subtopic as a

> ### TECHNOLOGY NOTE
>
> Though I believe we do need to acknowledge the many rich things that students are doing in digital environments, I do not subscribe to the view that young people are digital "natives" and older ones are digital "immigrants" (Prensky 2001). Besides slandering immigrants in inaccurate ways, that framework seems to suggest that younger people are naturally good at the literacies necessary to participate in digital culture, which is simply not the case. They may know how to operate devices and navigate certain kinds of software, but they still need plenty of support to become thoughtful, critical, and powerful readers and writers in cyberspace. We need to receive their expertise, yes, but we also have a responsibility to extend it.

whole group, but it will add detail to students' self-assessments if they have an opportunity to develop some close attention to aspects of their literate lives with the teacher's guidance and the stimulation of the whole class full of stories.

Our experiences of internal processes also make us different from one another. In Chapter 5 about reading and Chapter 10 about writing, we will discuss this further. For these early investigations, it is worthwhile to ask students what reading is like for them inside their minds. What do their minds do when they read? See? Hear? Question? Resist? Escape? And it's also interesting to find out whether writing and reading feel similar or very different, on the inside, when a particular student engages with them. This conversation leads conveniently toward kinds of thinking that are sometimes called *reading strategies*, but it should be undertaken not as a list of prescriptions about good readers, but as a description of difference—how reading and writing as thinking happen for a particular person who is different from the kid in the next chair or any other student in the room.

Overall, these inquiries work best when students do some of the work independently with maximum amounts of choice and control, some of the work with partners, some with small groups, and some with the whole class working together. As I've discussed in the previous chapter (and will do often throughout this book), varied social structures like these help to maintain a balance among a variety of factors in thinking and learning. As I have described, I begin this work with students in whole-class conversations, because it allows me to get everyone sharing the inquiry and understanding what I'm asking them to think about, even though sustaining the investigation is going to involve lots of independent and small-group work. These whole-group conversations also add to the crucial agenda, early in the school year, of the class becoming an accepting community for one another's risk taking across the year.

Uncovering common literacy practices—finding out, for instance that we both play a massively multiplayer online role-playing game—can be opportunities for affiliation and connection. We may not be friends in other areas, but we have the connection of that practice. And differences, too, are important to community. Knowing that Sonya keeps a notebook about her relationship to her boyfriend, and that they write back and forth to each other in that notebook, makes her a specific someone in this room, an inventive, intelligent, and loving person whom others care very much about. We need ways of beginning the year that allow people to emerge from the anonymous crowd, in order to develop a sense of us.

As students offer their contributions to the whole group in a whole-class discussion about literate lives, wise teachers take care to write down what individuals say. This whole-class conversation might be the only time that Mike brings up the importance of Spiderman in his learning to read, because he was, from very early on, taken by the superhero's inventiveness with technological gadgetry. And that fact could provide a useful seed for further reflection later on, or it could provide a foundation for building curriculum and teaching on students' existing literacies, as I will discuss below. Mike's probably not going to write it down in the middle of taking the risk to share it with the class, so the teacher needs to document it in her notes. Likewise, when conferring with individuals and small groups, part of this initial assessment—as with ongoing assessment through the rest of the school year—involves the teacher making notes as she teaches. It's an important habit to develop, because it is the only thing that makes organized reflection possible so that moments in class add up. Figure 2–1 provides a list of activities that may prove appropriate for whole-class work, for partners or small groups, and for individual inquiry.

FIGURE 2–1 Activities for Investigating Existing Literacies

Activities for Investigating Existing Literacies

- Student/student interviews
- Public interviews in which everyone questions a particular reader
- Writing about the differences among readers
- Writing answers to questions about ourselves as readers
- Keeping a journal in which we "spy on ourselves" as readers
- Focused ethnographic investigations of one another's homes, rooms, habits, and reading conditions
- Drawings of ourselves at a representative moment in our reading lives
- Metaphorical drawings of what reading is like for us
- Drawings representing ourselves as readers now and at some time in our lives when we were different
- Acting out critical incidents in our reading lives
- Acting out private moments in our reading lives, with props, to show the conditions we set up for reading or times when reading is hard to accomplish
- A letter-writing cycle about life as a reader initiated by the teacher writing about his own life as a reader, with students writing back in dialogue
- An invitation to bring in landmark books in your life history as a reader and share them with a small group
- Bringing to class books that are easy and books that are hard and share them with a small group, talking about what makes them easy or hard
- Sociograms—or any kind of diagram or chart—representing the social networks of our reading lives, or the social groups that make a difference in the ways we think
- Using sticky notes on every other page to keep track of what we see ourselves doing, mentally, as we read

Individual Inquiries

Central to these investigations is the principle that individuals are different from one another and the social practices of literacy fit into each individual's life in a unique constellation of ways, though the commonalities are still interesting to investigate. Consequently, many of the activities to investigate existing literacies have to be carried out as individual inquiries, with each student pursuing the questions, "How do reading and writing work in my life? What makes me different from other people in this class?" As each student discovers things about herself as a reader, the others in the class also become more interesting, as studies of difference. Even the individual inquiries, then, support the class becoming a community.

The first individualized tasks, as I have mentioned, occur within the context of whole-class conversations. Upon introducing the question of where reading or writing happens in your life, students think about their own lives, jotting some notes, and later, after some discussion and opportunity to hear what others are thinking, writing more extended reflections. This rhythm between shared conversation and individual application gives all students the chance to test the group's conversation against their own experience, to consider how widely shared social practices play out in their own lives—or do not.

As the conversation moves across days, several homework projects as individual self-studies extend the work of examining individual practices. An example of a homework assignment has been to have students make a list of all the different kinds of text that exist in their homes overnight— including songs, TV shows, newscasts, print texts, stories. Other examples have included surveying the things people use literacy to do in their neighborhoods. Examining the ways their mind works, the kinds of thinking they do (see Chapter 6) when they play a video game, watch a television show, read the sports page, or engage in any other easy and pleasurable form of transacting with text.

Across time, each student's consciousness of himself as a user of literacy builds up like any other edifice of knowledge. The teacher's notes, reviewed periodically, allow the teacher and the student both to develop a three-dimensional view of the varied settings and practices of literacy in this life. In addition there need to be opportunities, every week or so for a while, for the stu-

A Homework Example

Tonight, look around your home for possible reading spots and make some notes about what you find. What kinds of places can you find? Make notes about whether certain places might be better for different kinds of reading. For example, the kitchen table might be good for some things; your bed might be good for other things; the steps outside might be good for still other kinds of reading. If your home isn't the place where you would do your best reading, then write about a place you could get to easily that might work better for you.

dent to pull it all together in response to questions like "What have you been learning about yourself as a reader? What do you know now about your writing life? What do you now know about how literacy fits into the universe of things that you enjoy?" Some teachers have used these summative kinds of reflection as questions for course exams their schools require them to give, so that they keep focused on what matters to them—and their kids, even through the official evaluation process. Others have asked students, by the end of the first marking period, to write a "paper" describing the most important things about their literate lives. In such cases, the official genres of school become support for the unofficial genres that populate students' real lives—and vice versa.

Partners and Small Groups

We come to know ourselves in part by thinking about how we are similar to and different from others. There is no such thing as a generic reader or writer, no such thing as a standard literacy in a particular life. And so one of the ways we become aware of what we do and how literacy and thinking work for us is by listening to what others do and realizing that, hey, that's like me, or hey, no way, I'm totally different from that. Partners and small groups are especially useful structures, then, for allowing that kind of exploration to occur.

It may take time to see adolescents feeling productive and successful in partnerships and small groups. At times, they may seem to be having inordinate difficulty in these structures, but that does not make the structures useless. Students may resist engaging in conversation or resist the social risk of trying something new. They may be awkward revealing parts of themselves that have not been part of the disinfected environment of school, especially in a direct way to other students. Even the stiff beginnings of such a conversation are worthwhile, however, and the only way around the difficulty is through it. Just abandoning opportunities to share thinking with other students will not result in growth. The teacher can help by circulating, listening in for a while from outside the circle, and then contributing one thing to the conversation that students can continue working on as the teacher leaves. And of course, the teacher is also, always, taking notes about what she and the students are discovering.

As with independent structures, partnerships usually begin situated in whole-class discussions. During the first conversations about our literate lives, the teacher asks students to turn to people sitting around them and share, for example, the things they like to do and the ways reading fits into those. When they come back to the whole group, the teacher asks about the differences they found and the commonalities. The differences are where the really good discussion and discovery come, because when two classmates are describing a difference between them, all the other students have to ask themselves, "Am I like one or the other of them, or am I different from them both?"

Students often look first for points of commonality, but difference is really more crucial for forging a specific identity and for thinking together about what makes a literate life. Often, the teacher's role is to help them see the differences in what they are saying. Still, frequently, students only realize what they do in their life outside school when they hear someone else name it. It can be inspiring and exciting for a teacher to hear how they build on one another's noticings and insights.

Partners have also served as coinvestigators into the details of each partner's practices. They follow one another home, to the comics store, and to church; they observe their partner's activity on a computer. Having someone else point to their activities and label them as *literate behavior* contributes to the revaluing of ordinary life and connection of that life to academic work. The observation and note taking that the partner does, moreover, is clearly an academic behavior, and

FIGURE 2–2 Exploring Habits with Reading and Writing

Questions for Interviews or Written Reflections

How would you describe the best reading experience you could possibly have?

How would you describe your very best writing experiences?

How do you set up these things for the best reading or writing time you could possibly have?

- Light
- Music
- Body position
- Food and/or drink
- Wiggling or being still
- Nearness of other people

How long does a writing or reading session need to be for you to get really involved and get a lot of work done?

What is the best place for you to get lost in reading?

What is the best place for you to get lots of concentrated writing done?

How have you set yourself up in this classroom to have the best possible reading and/or writing time?

---

so students, even as they value the literacies that are not usually a part of school, engage in many of the practices that are valued in academic settings.

Temporary small groups allow the teacher to make inquiry questions about outside literacy more concrete and embodied in the room, as well as allowing for more extended talk among individuals than is possible in a whole-class discussion. Austin teacher Deb Kelt established small-group conversations by setting up groups of student desks around the room as centers for a ninth-grade class. Once, for instance, she set up areas corresponding to different ages—early childhood, primary grades (K–2), intermediate (3–5), middle school (6–8), and the present. In each center, she set up materials—books, photos, pieces of writing—that might provoke memories of students in that area. Students rotated among these stations in order to reminisce and revisit sites of literacy through their lives. Similar centers have drawn student attention to different kinds of texts—instructions for games and other things; CD liner notes, lyrics, and other music-related texts; photos of graffiti; cereal boxes; advertisements; and newspapers. Rather than thinking of a list of questions through which the whole class moves in concert, the teacher disassembles the questions and builds them around the room as engagements through which students move during the period, while the teacher circulates and confers with individuals and groups.

Context: Getting Inquiry Started as Other Literate Activities Are in Motion

In order to really have something to reflect about, and in order to get the other work of the year launched, this study of selves-as-readers-and-writers needs to be undertaken alongside other work in reading or writing. Some people begin with writer's notebooks, which I will describe more in Chapter 9. Others begin with independent reading, which I'll introduce in Chapter 4. The line of inquiry that allows both the teacher and the student to learn about ongoing literacy in life is not something that should be contained within a single little unit anyway—it's an ongoing agenda across the year. The focus on it that I am describing here usually lasts one to three weeks, and then the consciousness here developed allows the student increased access and meaning in subsequent work.

Domains of Investigation

I ask students to think about themselves as readers by opening up inquiries into their histories, their physical reading habits, the social networks surrounding their reading, and the way their thinking goes while reading. These inquiries make use of familiar strategies of investigation in many disciplines: direct observation, note taking, reflective writing, examining artifacts, graphic representations, dramatic reconstructions, interviewing. What makes them especially valuable is their application to reading as an area of ordinary but unexamined experience: students are asked to become conscious that they have particular identities, preferences, experiences, and styles as readers and that they are constantly making choices and doing something other than "just reading." Figures 2–2, 2–3, and 2–4 list some questions that have been helpful in probing areas that don't necessarily come naturally to students when asked. Here, I will also briefly discuss some of the major domains that have rewarded investigation.

To a large extent, we are the readers and writers we are because of a specific life history with these activities. Some people have intensely pleasurable and satisfying experiences with them, and some people—maybe even some of the same people—also have painful, emotionally fraught, identity-threatening experiences. In order to make literacy visible, it helps to have each person investigate some memories of literacy, in and out of school, from very early childhood to the present.

In the spirit of appreciative inquiry, it is especially useful to investigate the pleasures that are available from textual encounters of any kind. Here, as often, it is crucial that popular culture texts be enfranchised into this conversation, since they are most often the kinds of texts with which students (or most adults, for that matter) engage when they are seeking pleasure. The conversation involves naming the pleasures one takes—a type of character, a feeling, a kind of world in a movie—and then trying to analyze what makes that pleasure so great for this individual (not that the question can ever really be settled, but the habit of analysis is worth opening up).

Like most things in our lives, we engage with particular texts—or kinds of texts—because others with whom we identify also engage with them. A particular video game is important because some of my people say it is. The Bible is important for the same reasons, as is a work of Shakespeare or a newspaper. So the social networks that exist around texts for us are keys to what those texts are doing for us.

Similarly, the social groupings in which we construct our lives cause us to read from particular perspectives. We read as a member of a particular gender, and many people are especially aware of their identity as male or female and so may draw on that aspect of themselves more intensely. We read as a member of a particular racial and ethnic group, because that's part of what makes us who we are, even if, because we are a member of the white dominant group, we aren't usually called upon to recognize it. Our social class, sexual orientation,

FIGURE 2–3
Exploring Life Histories
with Literacy

Questions for Investigating Life Histories with Literacy

Reading

What do you remember about your earliest experiences of reading?

Did someone read to you?

What was that like?

Did you have books? Where were they?

When do you remember first noticing reading?

What were your earlier experiences with reading in school like?

What have been times when you have done things outside school that have involved reading?

Are there religious or spiritual texts that are important in your family or faith community? How do people read those? How do you read them?

Writing

When do you remember first noticing someone writing? When have you seen someone older—someone you admire—writing?

What do you remember about drawing when you were little?

What do you remember about making up stories or playing stories with friends?

When you were younger, if you could have written a children's book to teach other kids about something you knew about, what would the topic have been?

What memories do you have of letter writing? Keeping a journal? Email? Texting? Making websites? Making videos? Writing plays, shows, or songs?

Other Media

What do you remember about characters or stories from movies or television that have been important to you in the past?

What kinds of stories in movies, games, and television tend to appeal to you the most?

What kinds of feelings would you describe mostly having in response to the movies, games, and television shows that you're most interested in?

Can you think of a time when you thought about how people wrote or made a movie, game, or TV show when you were interested in the craft?

What do you remember about times you have enjoyed something on TV or a movie or game with other people? How did you talk about it?

FIGURE 2-4 Exploring
an Individual's
Experience of Literacy

Exploring an Individual's Experience of Literacy

Pleasure

What sorts of things give you the most pleasure in reading? What do you like to see in a text?

How do you like the text to relate to the real world? Do you like seeing yourself in it? Do you like it to tell the truth about things you didn't know about?

What kind of language most pleases you in texts? What are the words like when you really like what you're reading?

When have you been reading and felt the impulse to try writing in a similar way?

Reading as Thinking

How do you see what you read, in your mind's eye?

What kinds of things are easier to see and make richer pictures in your mind? Is it like a movie or like a painting?

How do you hear it?

How do you picture characters, and what kinds of things do you think about them?

How do you respond to confusion or difficulty?

What kinds of feelings are often generated as you read?

What other texts come to mind?

and political commitments also influence our reading. It's not that we only read things that are like us, but even the ways we encounter difference when reading (or imagining the audiences for which we write) make our location in the big social world visible.

This chapter is about engaging the whole class in an investigation of reading and writing experiences, practices, and identities. There are two groups—often very different from one another—that need special attention in this regard: students who speak languages other than English as their first language, and students with a history of struggling in school. I offer here separate discussions of these students, because it is especially important for a teacher to build an understanding of details about them, of their resources, strengths, and gifts, as well as the sometimes more evident areas of work ahead.

Students Acquiring English as an Additional Language

I interviewed a young Somali woman in a Boston tenth-grade class one day. I had asked the class to write a notebook entry about their life histories as readers. As soon as she started talking to me about her reading history, she got sort of confused about what I wanted. The trouble was that she first began reading in Arabic, as part of her religious education, but soon after that, in school, she learned French and Af Maxaa, the official Somali language her school taught. She was writing about this literate history in English, of course, like the native speakers of English sitting next to her. In the course of our conversation, I eventually discovered that none of these languages was her mother tongue, the language in which she first established loving relationships with her family—that was an ancestral tribal language unrelated to all the others that, as far as she knew, had no writing system. Here is a student who could be called an English language learner (ELL), or might be called limited English proficient, or might be called a second language learner. But English wasn't her second language; it was her fifth. Though the school typically positions such students as deficient, she probably knew more about language than anyone else in the room, including me.

It is very important for an English teacher to know the varied linguistic resources available in the room. Increasingly, schools are becoming wealthy with multilingual students, and their knowledge, even when it does not match that of the teachers or the students from dominant groups, is too significant to be squandered. Unfortunately, educators too often tend to see students who speak languages other than English as their first language as deprived rather than rich, as problems to fix rather than resources to draw upon.

That is because, if a student is learning English as an adolescent, one of several things may be going on. They may be newcomers to the U.S., though this is not the most common explanation. If they are recent arrivals, they may have had some English language instruction in their home country, or they may not have. If they did, they may have had limited opportunities to interact with native speakers, so even though they may have learned vocabulary, perhaps even some reading, they may still have difficulties understanding what native speakers are saying—especially when they are speaking to other native speakers.

Perhaps a more common reason adolescents may be in a U.S. school but not yet fluent in English is because, though they have been in the U.S. for years (potentially even most or all of their lives), they have moved mostly in communities that speak a language (or multiple languages) other than English. They

Multilingual Note

It's important to explore the role of each language in multilingual students' lives. When do they speak Spanish (or Cantonese or Urdu or Russian) and when do they speak English? How does each language live in relationships they have with particular other people or with groups? When do they notice themselves thinking in their first language and when in their second? If they dream in both languages, what is the dream about when it is in the first language versus the second? What stories in their lives take shape in either language, and what domains of expertise are easier to explain in which lexicon and grammar? In other words, both students and teacher need a detailed account of how language use is shaped in the students' experience, how it is working for them now, and what new possibilities they can imagine working on together.

may identify strongly with the ethnic group that speaks that other language, and viewing themselves as dominant in English might create identity conflicts for them. Understanding these conflicts reveals much about the human story of learning that must be engaged in order to teach such a student.

There are some students who may be identified as ELLs (English language learners) or, as in federal law, the deficit thinking term *LEP* (limited English proficiency) who may actually speak English but whose test performances and academic languages still do not match their informal knowledge of the language. Even when students are orally fluent in English as well as their first language, they may be classified as long-term ELLs when their academic literacy still lags behind school expectations. School is not set up to recognize and reward the many ways their multilingualism may be growing, and so they may have been disadvantaged by the fact that they have not been learning academic language in the language they knew first, while the demands of school have been established for the benefit of native speakers of English.

These are just a few of the complex ways multilingual development might interact with school history. What is important to realize is that whatever a multilingual student is going to learn, it must be built upon the existing resources she brings to the classroom. The identity she takes on as she develops in academic areas—especially English language arts—needs to be that of a strong, capable, admirable person with prodigious strengths at her disposal as a product of her multilingualism. The best place for a teacher to begin is to get such students to reconstruct and reflect upon the road that brought them to where they are now, making it a point to name the patterns of experience and expertise that are already present in their life history and their habitual practices as a user of language and literacy.

Caring for the Vulnerable

In early assessment, one of the teacher's important tasks is to attempt to understand what is going on for those students who have been made vulnerable by the school system—those who have experienced school as confusing, boring, and harmful to their sense of self. In an English class, this is likely to mean people who have so far found reading and writing difficult or less than completely engaging and pleasurable.

Even as it is important to notice and reach out to students who are likely to be vulnerable in this way, doing so can introduce the hazard of deficit thinking. If a teacher goes on lemon patrol, scanning the room for kids who can't, won't, or aren't, then he may start to regard students as deficient, start thinking of them in terms of their weaknesses rather than their resources, tools, and strengths. There is a balance to strike between noticing struggles and redirecting attention toward strengths. On the one hand, we want to receive all students as equals and respect them as competent people. But to launch into a shared novel without knowing that the book is going to be impossibly difficult for four students in the class is a mistake. To start independent reading without actively learning about the sort of book with which a particular student will be successful is also a mistake. To launch writers' notebooks without calibrating our expectations to the performances we're likely to see on the page could make us design lessons that go right past our learners. The trick is to help all students feel recognized, known, and cared for, even as they are also safe from harsh judgment or embarrassment.

It requires a little more attention on the teacher's part to act ethically toward those students who struggle the most and tend in school to experience the work as punishing. They need a bit more attention than other students do, and attention of perhaps a different kind. Sometimes, especially when a teacher is not used to the population of students she is working with, it may seem at first as if all the students are struggling, and that may in some sense be true. I am talking here about realizing that some students need disproportionate attention because of their vulnerability in the context of their peers. It's not that they need to be coddled or that they will be unable to do the kinds of work described in this book, but teaching them requires careful assessment, more than anything else.

As part of this project, it's important early on to gain a perspective on students' reading. While it is not usually helpful to listen to every student read, it can provide very important information for students who struggle. The difficult question is how to arrange to listen to a few students read without making them more vulnerable to embarrassment as the class catches on that the "bad" readers are being identified by the teacher. Some combination of listening to a wider sample of

Adolescents and Reading Aloud

When a teacher wonders what's going on with a particular student's reading, it's a good idea to create an opportunity to listen to that student read. We need a clearer picture of what he is doing with difficulty, whether his miscues are making sense or poking holes in the text's meaning, and whether his reading sounds like meaningful language in its fluency and intonation. But listening to adolescents read aloud in a secondary classroom is tricky. I am certainly not talking about going down the rows and having everyone read a paragraph from a book, or any other whole-class structure. Rather, while students are reading independently the books they have chosen to read (see Chapter 4), the teacher circulates and confers, sometimes asking a student to read aloud.

After a student reads, I usually say, "I haven't read this book; can you tell me how that part fits in with what's been going on before?" I may ask a few follow-up questions, in a natural, conversational tone, that try to get at whether the reader was handling detail adequately. This can provide a window, however hazy and partial, into the reader's processes with text.

students during class time (while the class is doing independent reading) and asking students to come in after school usually provides a reasonably sensitive solution.

But what are you listening for when you listen to students read? One important lens to have in mind is to analyze the differences between what they say and what is on the page. Everyone makes these miscues, and the question is what quality they are. Making two columns and jotting the differences down can facilitate a quick analysis. The main question is whether a student is making miscues that leave the text meaningful. If she is, then things are going well. If the miscues are poking holes in the text's meaning, then either the text is too difficult, or the student has developed a way of reading that attends so much to the details of letters that she isn't really reading for meaning. In that case, she needs help reconceptualizing the act of reading and developing new habits.

It's also important to listen for whether the student's oral reading sounds like language. Does it flow? Does the melody of his voice correspond to the meaning of the sentences? Does the phrasing make sense? If the reading is very choppy, word by word, if it is completely robotic, or if his reading doesn't sound like meaningful language, then it lets us know that the student will need some work on fluency—something that I discuss as "listening" in Chapter 5.

Looking closely and respectfully at students' writing is also helpful. First of all, does writing seem to flow easily for them? Are there signs of reticence, starts and stops? Do cross-outs seem to signal anxiety about getting their thoughts out there? Second, it is, of course, most important that we listen carefully to the meanings in students' writing. What are they saying, and what in it is important to them? How is it arranged? Even if it appears "disorganized" to us, we need to recognize the system that the writer was using, even if it's only the order in which thoughts occurred to her.

Then, of course, it's easy for teachers' attention to be drawn to the conventions of writing, and when we do attend there, we need to ask questions that can really help us teach, rather than just judging it as good or bad, based on how many mistakes are on the page. Are language patterns in the sentences drawing upon the student's knowledge of multiple languages, or speech patterns common in his family and community? Might those affections and connections be especially important to this person? What understandings about the sounds that letters make are evident in his unconventional spellings? What gifts of pattern noticing are evident in those spellings, even when they are not the ones in the dictionary? The forms of teaching I will describe in this book offer opportunities to work with individual students on the aspects of literacy that need attention for that individual—so this kind of assessment helps to set the course for a sort of personalized curriculum for these particular students.

One thing to keep in mind as we orient ourselves toward students for whom school success requires more effort is that, like other adolescents, the real answer always hinges upon identity and engagement. The approach we take to them cannot offer them the identity of "poor student," or else that identity will prevent them from taking on the kinds of purposeful projects we require. We also can't make reading and writing more boring, pointless, and meaningless to them by radically reducing the complexity of their work—it needs to be achievable yet challenging in order for them to find it engaging.

Building Teaching upon Students' Existing Lives

Envisioning Projects and Their Appropriate Social Structures

One of the ways knowing about students' existing literacies can help teachers plan instruction is in using that knowledge to envision projects and the appropriate social structures to get them done. If a teacher has discovered that several aspects of Jirio's literate life involve music—reading about it, writing it, and attending to lyrics—then it's a short step from there to think that music might be a topic for his reading and might be a topic, a set of genres, and a domain that includes audiences for his writing. Beyond that kind of one-to-one topic match, it may be that Jirio's orientation to sound provides a hint about a kind of thinking that might be important in his reading and composing—perhaps he has something to teach the class about listening. Furthermore, if we know that he mainly engages in his musical literacy with his cousin, it allows us to develop a hunch that working with a partner might be a supportive social context for his work. Knowing about his existing interests and dispositions provides a context for building work for English language arts that he is more likely to be motivated to carry out with passion.

Remembering to Return at the Right Moment

A shared conversation about existing literate lives in the classroom community also allows the teacher to build a storehouse of analogies to which he can return at the right moment later in the year. When teaching something that can be difficult for students to understand—say, interpreting symbols in literature—a teacher can remember a previous conversation about tagging, when students talked about how most teachers cannot decipher tags or other signs and symbols in graffiti, though many of the students can. They know the social world out of which the signs are made, recognize the signs as meaningful, and restore to the sign all that is not said explicitly. Talking about interpretation, the teacher supports students' use of one practice in another context by pointing out that when they come upon an object that seems important in a story, adding back to that object all the cultural knowledge about meaning and feeling that they already know can help them develop some hunches about an interpretation. Remembering the earlier conversation about what students already know they can do allows the development of new practices to build upon what is already there.

Getting Books into a Classroom Library

A clear outcome of knowing students' interests and practices outside school is that it makes it easier to choose, for a classroom library, books that will have immediate appeal and connection to the students' most motivated literacy practices. Finding out that many students are rap fans helps the teacher to identify books about rappers like *Tupac Shakur: Legacy* by Jamal Joseph and *After Tupac & D Foster* by Jacqueline Woodson, and other biographies, criticisms, and lyrics as potentially popular selections. Discovering that students keep up with the drama of one another's lives through texting and social network sites has led some teachers to put together collections of books around the idea of "gossipy books about people like me"—which in this case meant authors like Rita Williams Garcia and Paula Chase Hyman—that can appeal to the same feeling of connection to characters that people are pursuing in their keeping-in-touch literacy. Learning that a particular group of kids reads online or in newspapers about sports—at least the scores—every day has clued teachers into the need for more sports books—by authors such as Chris Lynch, Mike Lupica, and Chris Crutcher—in their classroom libraries. Because finding out about literacy practices embedded in people's lives is a way of finding out about the activities and topics that matter to them, it's a source for connections to more traditional academic literacy—the reading of books and pursuing topics across those books.

Connecting Academic to Everyday Practices

Another way teachers use the information they get from students about their outside literacy practices is by connecting those practices to the ones that are necessary for the new practices the class is attempting to help students grow.

That is, they figure out what a user of literacy is doing in the outside practice, and draw parallels to the kinds of literacy called for in the curriculum. When a girl is collecting statements and signatures from friends in a "friendship book" as a voluntary, unofficial practice, it provides an interesting way to think about a writer's notebook (see Chapter 10)—as perhaps also memorializing social relationships, as being a book of friends, at least for that user, at least until other notebook purposes capture her. Notebooks will feel different to a student who loves gathering collections of different sorts (shells, comics) or a student who keeps a prayer journal. For a student who loves to draw, inquiring into writing as a process of designing documents provides a useful way in, and talking about reading as envisionment also draws upon the practice of seeing what is not yet present. For a student who follows a specific sports team, focusing on just that one bit of news from the daily flood of information, the outside practice provides a context for talking about following specific questions and interests across novels or across sources of information. A student who likes hunting, tracking, and trapping is already participating in some of the human behaviors that millennia ago gave rise to literate capacities, and those interests, energies, and skills should be connected to the looking for and noticing of little signs, like footprints or symbols, and the perseverance to follow a trail to discovery.

Even the rather minimalist composing forms on the Internet, like uploading photos for sharing, reveal motives and processes that could benefit academic literacy—by understanding that uploading as the impulse to share, which can also fuel the publication of writing (perhaps more frequently for such students, with more deliberate audiences) and the sharing, with a select group, of thinking in response to a text. These are more than metaphorical or facile connections; the outside literacies do draw upon intelligences and habits that are useful in academically significant literacies. While academic literacies require different skills and forms of knowledge for their growth, they do share underlying motives, processes, and forms of thinking with the unofficial forms of literacy.

The degree to which it is possible to build a curriculum on students' existing literacies will vary, but each teacher can ask: "How permeable is possible? To what extent can I poke holes in the curriculum to receive students' lives and values from outside school?" Because it's to the degree we make the curriculum connect to life outside that students will actually use the curriculum in life outside. We only make reading and writing lives by receiving them, transforming them, and pointing them back to the world. The next chapter addresses ways of building new, valued forms of literacy into students' lives, inside and outside the classroom—literacy that actually gets somewhere.

CHAPTER 3

Teaching Reading and Writing Lives

I'm pretty sure almost no one thinks that leaving a student texting, tagging, and watching TV is the final goal of school literacy instruction. While it's important that students are recognized for the diverse literacy practices with which they engage in ordinary life, that doesn't mean that the teacher should just leave students where they found them. The precise nature of the end goals may not be easy to agree upon, and they are often not adequately named in official standards documents, but school does seem to be about striving, about reaching beyond what is already there, even when it does include respect for students' assets.

There are ways with text that adults in schools want to add, and those textual practices are going to be discussed in the rest of this book. I don't mean that I will adhere to the zombie literacy practices that are common in school—the walking dead "reports" and "papers" that none but the coerced have ever attempted to make, the ghostly reading experiences that glide through the lives of students who never read anything but the "classics" they are told to read. Teachers may be pursuing important literacy ends with such assignments, and I think some of what I offer in this book may be alternative means to those ends. But much of what passes for curriculum in English is nothing but old habits dying hard, and we can do better. We can build an approach to English that allows happiness, satisfaction, for the actual young people we teach, that helps them become disposed to using multiple forms of literacy for practical, spiritual, social, personal, and political purposes their whole lives long. School should be about becoming an educated person.

Allow me to state a few educational values. Educated people should know how to pursue their own intellectual projects. Educated people should have agendas that take them to texts. Educated people should have habits that allow them to have reading and writing lives. Educated people should live with writing integrated into many parts of their lives. These should be goals of school, because school should be about becoming educated people.

To work on academic literacy is not just a matter of teaching the genres that will be valued in future years of schooling. Academic literacy includes those practices, habits, and knowledges that mark one as an educated person. It's an academic literacy to have favorite living novelists, to be able to name a few contemporary poets who really speak to you, to know some nonfiction writers whose work you like to read no matter the subject they're writing about. If that's not academic literacy, what is it? Wouldn't such knowledge, the vestiges of hours of meaningful reading, be a mark of an educated person? What kind of academic literacy has a shelf life of only a few years? Shouldn't the forms of education we offer students last beyond their twenty-second birthday? I'm always struck when my college seniors cannot begin to provide an answer in response to any of those questions—favorite novelists, poets, or nonfiction writers—even if I give them a week to think about it and look through all their books. It seems to me that they should be asking for their money back for their college education. What did it give them instead? Denying the significance of their existing literacies, their teachers didn't even provide enough literate education to help them sound impressive at a cocktail party.

It's an academic literacy to know your friends as readers and writers, to be comfortable talking with them about what they are writing about and their responses to the texts they are reading together. Recommending books to people you care about is an academic literacy—not a universal, and also not informal, not part of an ordinary life.

The ability to tune into your own thoughts—to listen inside and find out what you're really thinking about—that is an academic literacy. Without that ability, one cannot respond to the texts one reads in any thoughtful or original way. And it's another important skill to be able to compose new thoughts in words—not just to find out what you're already thinking, but to make yourself think something new.

Multilingual Note

It would seem to go without saying that multilingualism is an asset in academic knowledge and intellectual life. Unfortunately, we in schools get used to thinking of these *pobrecitos* as in some way to be pitied because their English speaking and writing may be accented or because English idioms may still give them trouble. Instead, we should get behind the development of their multilingual literacy, providing opportunities to read and write in any language in which they may have even the beginnings of competence. Just because we can't control their language does not mean that we should hold them back.

This ability, to say not just what's on your mind but to come up with something that until this minute wasn't even on your mind, is foundational to academic literacy—thinking mediated by language.

Consciousness of your areas of interest is another academic literacy. Too often, we seem to expect students to evenly balance their interest in every conceivable kind of text or story. But no scholar can afford to be interested in everything equally. English professors say, "I work on eighteenth-century British novels" or "I do literary nonfiction" or "mostly Eliot." Really, they need broader expertise than that, but at any moment in development, and very often for a whole career, a scholar (of any age or education) pays attention to a limited number of topics. Growing specific areas of interest should be one of the things we help students do in order to become more scholarly. Academic curiosity is precisely the sort that selects something from the range of possibilities and then pursues based on that selection.

For the purposes of this book, we are concentrating on specific sites for building literate lives. Writing workshop, especially with writers' notebooks, is a useful structure for building composing into people's lives, and Section 3 of the book will detail that structure. Reading workshops in which students are working on independent reading is an ideal location for examining and developing reading lives, as Section 2 will show. These structures are ideal for the development of highly supported, academically rigorous individual literate lives. In addition, students must learn to be part of a literate community, and so throughout this book, we investigate ways of creating mutuality, awareness, respect for others, and a disposition toward collaboration.

Getting Real About Literacy in People's Lives

Much attention has been paid in recent years to making sure everyone graduates from high school "college and career ready." While I agree that all secondary teachers should have high expectations for their students' literacy, the reality is that most of the things people have identified as college- and career-ready standards are excessively narrow and not really very high at all. (See, for instance, National Council of Teachers of English 2009.)

Viewing curriculum solely as preparation for later years of schooling, even college, is shortsighted. People spend a short stretch of time in school, and that time is supposed to prepare them for the rest of life—school is not supposed to be about school. School is short, and life is long, and a quality curriculum ought to help students become people who can live literate lives beyond school.

It would help us serve students better if we kept in mind the realities of people's lives. Everyone is not an English major. Everyone is not even a college student. Though estimates vary, only something like 75 percent of students complete high school (Heckman and LaFontaine 2008). That means, out of a statistically random ninth-grade class of twenty-four, six of those will not earn a high school diploma. Those students are not failures, or write-offs. They're human beings, American citizens who will earn a living, vote, have a family, and live meaningful lives. They are entitled to an education that is useful and significant in those lives, that improves not just their work performance but the wide range of purposes for which people use literacy.

Of their classmates who do complete high school, one-third will end their schooling career when they earn a high school diploma (U.S. Department of Education National Center for Education Statistics). That's another six of the kids in that class of twenty-four. Half of that ninth-grade class isn't going to college. Mind you, the ones who do go to college are not necessarily more intelligent or worthy or anything else. Mostly, they just have more funds, leisure, and social connections to people who went to college. And the ones who don't go to college will still have literate lives and deserve an education that helps them to construct those lives, honors them, and makes them as powerful as possible.

Only about half of those who attend college will complete degrees. The Census Bureau in 2007 estimated that 28 percent of U.S. adults aged 25–29 have college degrees. And it's that quarter of our ninth graders for whom the curriculum is built, if school is designed narrowly to create better college students. Even thinking about that minority of students, they're only going to be college students for four years. That's what all this is about? Getting them good at school for four more years of it?

What Are You Working On?

To bring these ideas home, the reader may want to pause right here and ask herself: What are you working on right now in your literate life? What are the things you're trying to get better at?

Once you have thought about that for a minute, reflect on the nature of these hopes for your own literate life. Did most of them involve topic sentences, comma placement, essay structures? Did they mainly concern plowing through a book someone else is making you read? What wisdom of insight is available for your teaching from your hopes and plans for your own literate life?

I would argue that our teaching has to go beyond the forms of literacy demanded by any schooling, toward the entire continent of purposes for which people use language and other sign systems for meaning, communication, expression, and participation. In order to meet that challenge, some of our teaching needs to be aimed directly at literate lives—the details of the preferences, choices, habits of mind and body that make a life literate. In the rest of this chapter, I will detail some of this teaching for habits, even though I'm aware that this teaching is not exactly the same thing as teaching reading and writing as such. Most of this book *will* focus on the details of actual reading and writing, but in order for all that important and delicate teaching to have some-place to grow in students' lives, we need to take care with building the nest.

Habits and Conditions in a Reading Life

People with productive, deliberate reading and writing lives can talk about their habits—the ways they set up the physical conditions for a session of reading, the things they do to get ready for a decently productive writing time. Students benefit from invitations to describe their current reading and writing habits, and to try out experiments with possible new conditions (Figure 3–1). Often, people have habits with writing that are quite distinct from the ways they set up their reading, so it's best to invite students into

FIGURE 3–1
Questions to Explore
Reading Lives

Some Questions to Explore Reading Lives

With slight modifications, these same questions could be useful for writing instead.

- How does your current book travel around with you? What exact part of your backpack, pocket, purse, or whatever is involved?

- What are the regular sections of your day? What little reading appointments might be possible in there?

- What are some possible places for reading? How might different places go with different types of reading? Like what could you read on the bus, in bed, at the kitchen table, in school? What are the challenges about each of those places, and how do you deal with those challenges?

- Who knows what you're reading right now? Who do you sometimes think about telling about your book? Who gives you recommendations? Whose reading do you wonder about?

- How does the book you are reading now connect to the last one you read? And to the one before that? How long have you been exploring this kind of text or these ideas? What do you think you will read next? What ideas are coming up in this book that you could think about in that next one?

- What could you choose to read if you wanted to pick something that would go superfast, something that would give you no problem at all?

- What could you read if you wanted a real challenge, something you could understand, but that would make you work?

---

these investigations with either reading or writing specified as the activity under consideration.

As homework at various times throughout the school year, students should carry out investigations and experiments to establish what chairs, rooms, and conditions offer them quality reading time. These can just be assignments printed on small slips of paper, which students can tuck into their writers' notebooks or reading logs to carry home:

> Investigate three different reading sessions this week—away from school, at home, or someplace else—and write half a page about each in your notebook before our discussion on Thursday about how we're similar to and different from one another. Consider some of these things: how you arrange your body to read, where you are, the time of day and how long it lasts, the kind of light you have, whether you are doing anything else (like eating), whether you have music playing, and anything else you can think of.

If students do this in September, February, and April, there might be interesting changes in how they are setting up their reading time—evidence that they are developing as readers.

Body Position

Reading may seem to some people like a disembodied act, because readers mostly need to be still in order to keep their eyes on the page or screen. But being still is not always easy. Get a roomful of teachers sitting still for ninety minutes or so, and you will hear a lot of complaining. "We're not used to sitting for so long," they'll say. "Now we know how the kids feel!" Yes, well. Sitting still is hard for almost everyone. And with reading, it's not just a matter of sitting still—there is a need to get the page or screen near enough to the eyes, which usually involves a flexion of the spine and/or arms. Sometimes, it helps people to assume a studious persona if they lean over a book set on a table or desk. For more transported reading experiences, lots of people lounge or lie down and hold the book up in front of their face. People who read while sun tanning (if there are any such people left) are aware of the intricate sets of arrangements one has to make in different baking positions. There is never, of course, a single method for any of this, but the physical act of reading is far from transparent, and students

---

Designing These Investigations Alongside a Reading or Writing Curriculum

As important as these investigations are, they are not, in and of themselves, the entire curriculum. They are more like threads to pull through the year. It's hard to do much studying of your reading life if you aren't also reading. And you won't learn much about how your own peculiar ways of thinking integrate with writing unless you have at least a writer's notebook underway (see Chapter 10). Therefore, the best design is probably a week or so getting the conversations described in this chapter underway, and then revisiting some aspect of reading/writing lives, as appropriate, once or twice a week in either minilessons or share sessions. Some teachers begin the year with writers' notebooks (Chapter 10) and others begin with independent reading (Chapter 4), and either of those is a perfect opportunity for supporting students' study of their own and one another's reading or writing lives.

can benefit from being made conscious of it, so they can try to give themselves more effective reading experiences.

Then, there is school. Some teachers attempt to vary the available body positions available to students in their rooms by having chairs, rugs, tables, and sofas available. Others just make students aware of their options for body postures with the desks or tables available, and they help individuals think about it: "If *x* is a good body posture for your reading outside this classroom, how can you get a little closer to that here?"

Light

Reading is visual (at least for sighted people), and people's eyes and minds respond differently to varied lighting conditions. I like to read outside for other reasons, but sunlight is usually too bright for my best reading experiences, and I'm usually a little head-achy and relieved to get back inside afterward. My ideal light would be a pretty dark room with warm (yellowish) indirect light. Of course, as a student in a classroom, that wouldn't usually be available, but a teacher could help me situate myself with the best conditions possible for a reading time in this particular room.

TECHNOLOGY NOTE

If you are like most readers I know, you're trying to figure out the role of e-readers in your life. Will you use a dedicated e-reader, a laptop, a handheld device, an iPad, stick with paper? The material and embodied nature of text has seemed unimportant and natural for most of my life, and maybe yours, too. Now, I'm conscious of the physical presence of a book on different devices I own and having to make all new decisions about how my body interacts with text.

Movement, Food, and Drink

Some people like (or need) to keep moving, releasing physical energy while they are sitting still. This is the reason some students get up and wander around while they are supposed to be reading. Figuring out something small to focus on and fiddle with sometimes give them a way to move while remaining still. Knowing that I need to wiggle my leg, squeeze a tennis ball, or roll a coin over my fingers while I read might make the difference in me being able to get through enough text to begin to engage with its story or argument. Snacking, too, can be as much of a kinesthetic release as a sating of hunger. The small movement of picking up a drink and setting it back down allows little vacations from my body position that can release tension and ultimately help keep the reader more engaged with what is happening in the text. For in-class reading, the teacher can help students who need a wiggling strategy to find a rubber band or pencil to wiggle in a way that won't bother other students.

Proximity to Other People

There are some people who really settle down only in the presence of people they are comfortable with. Proximity allows them to concentrate. Such people may read better when someone is reading near them; the presence of the other body at the margins of consciousness is what allows them to get lost in their text. Other people, perhaps more familiar to many English teachers, prefer solitude for reading. They want only their book for company, and they find others a distraction at best. For young readers to be continually at work figuring out how the presence of other people interacts with their optimal reading conditions is important for their construction of a literate life, and also for the possibility of talking sensibly about classroom management issues in a reading classroom.

In a classroom, there are other people around, so for students who prefer solitude, that may seem to intrude on their serenity. At the same time, young people spend most of their day in school, around other people; if they can't read with other people around, that means they will spend most of their time not reading. Some more refined thinking may be in order. It's not simply the physical presence of other people that is at issue. Many people might be able to read on a plane full of strangers but not around the people in their family. The issue, then, is the degree to which it is OK to separate from the people around for an extended time, to disengage and dissociate into a book or screen. In other words, the issue is about personal boundaries, about being able to mind one's own business and not stay continually tuned in to others. Some people's families have taught them that it is rude to disengage from others in the room, to do something independent with company around. Wherever we are, outside school, the people around us right now don't want us to just start reading, and basically, they won't tolerate it if we do. Yet to have academic success and a literate life, one has to read a lot: that involves some kind of negotiation with one's social world, a negotiation that is not easy for anyone to figure out. Therefore, it's important to talk with students, either as a class or independently, about what happens when one is trying to read with all these friends around, and to strategize, mutually, about how to keep working through the difficulties that can arise.

Places

Because people are bodies, they are always located somewhere in space—even when they are reading about a place far away. And locations can be extremely important in the construction of a reading life. Everyone's reading life has a geography—the places where reading is unlikely, where it is possible, and where it is ideal. Though most reading isn't done in the ideal spot, it's very helpful to know what a special spot might be, so that when trouble arises, at least you know a place where reading usually works for you. That Callie knows that she reads books with stories down by the creek and books that help her learn at a table at the library near her apartment is not simply a matter of comfort and convenience—she's using places to distinguish purposes for reading and mental stances that she takes toward text. That Alvaro has figured out that he can read on the fire escape outside his apartment makes the difference in him being able to read at home, since his five sisters tend to be distracting inside. When Ford figured out that he didn't have to go any further than the stairs in front of his house to have some time alone, it made all the difference in his reading habits—the difference between reading almost every day and never reading.

If a student says to me, "I don't have a place where I like to read," the conversation is not over. I say, "Yeah? Well, we've got to figure out someplace you'll like, compared to other places. Where do you think you'll try out tonight? Will it be in your room, somewhere else in your house, in a library, or what?" As with all the other categories here, this isn't meant to be a light survey of likes and dislikes. Each of these areas is an inquiry, something about which every single person will develop things to say, across the time he is in this class. We just don't have to accept, "Oh, I have nothing to say about that." The whole purpose is to develop something to say about all these aspects of a reading life, even though there may be nothing in an individual's mind about it upon first being asked the question.

Schedule, Frequency, Duration, and Impulse

How do you know when to read? It may seem like a silly question, but it's actually kind of a hard one, too. Students will often say, "When I don't have anything else to do." But what does that mean? No one is around? The TV won't work? Often, when people get some reading done, they have planned ahead that they are going to do so. They know that after dinner, they're going to find some space with their book. Or they know that they will read the news on the Internet for another thirty minutes before they get back to their family. Maybe they catch moments during the day, but only if they are looking for them. The commitment to reading occurred in advance of the impulse. It's helpful with students, then, to help them think through their usual day. Are there times in school when you might do some reading? What happens when you first get out of school? Then what? Then what? What about when you get up in the morning? What about right before bed? This discussion—conducted perhaps with the whole class, but more importantly with individuals—scaffolds students' survey of their typical days, so that they can begin to live with the question, "When can I get back to my book?"

Developing a Writing Life

As with reading, our students need more time writing than we can ever provide in school. They need a writing life, if they are going to grow. Don't get me wrong—they need to be writing in school, too, during the school day, which means during class time. But if they are to develop a literate life, writing needs also to grow into a part of life outside school. That's the whole idea, the ultimate goal of writing instruction. But the idea of writing itself—just loving writing—isn't going to be an easy sell for most students. It needs to fit into the things they already do and care about—music, friends, TV, nature, spirituality, politics, family, sports, games. It needs to borrow love and energy to get going, because writing itself is often confusing and laborious—not characteristics of people's favorite activities. But as writers develop a sense of ease, an ability to relax and get comfortable amidst all the gray uncertainty of composing, they may find it possible to bring that medium to other domains of life—like academic learning, the creation of art, and the crafting of arguments about important topics. Some of the categories for constructing writing lives are like those for reading, and some are different. (See Figure 3–2.)

FIGURE 3–2
Questions to Explore Writing Lives

Some Questions to Explore Writing Lives

With slight modifications, these same questions could be useful for reading instead.

- What have you found about the best possible writing session you could have? Are you at a desk, outside, on your belly? What do you need nearby? What tools help you most?

- When conditions aren't right for your very best writing time, what have you found to compensate for this? For instance, how do you compensate in class when things aren't perfect at writing time?

- When you get distracted, what do you usually do in order to re-engage with your writing?

- Has there ever been a time when you just suddenly had lots of writing done and it was so easy that you hardly even felt like you'd done it? Where were you and what was it like? What can you learn from that?

- What topics are you considering your own important writing territories these days? Which are at the center of your map, and which are on the outer borders?

- What are the clubs or groups you belong to, and how could you develop writing projects that might help or support those? Maybe making them more famous, or trying to get some contributions, or educating the public about things that group cares about?

- When was the last time you were writing and you realized you were changing? Maybe you were changing your mind, or maybe you realized you'd grown as a writer? When was the last time you surprised yourself as a writer or observed yourself learning as you wrote?

Conditions: Setting Up

Another thing young people will work on long past the day when they are no longer young people is the relationship of their body to the activity of writing. In corporate lingo—ergonomics. The setup of the physical environment for composing. Like reading, writing is an embodied act as much as a mental one, and many writers attempt to solve problems of energy, attention, and motivation through changing the way they have set themselves up to write.

Places

In his wonderful book *Tuned In and Fired Up*, Sam Intrator (2005) describes the surprising degree of student engagement that arose from a teacher's simple decision to ask students to write outside on the baseball field instead of in their usual classroom:

> Now that the students have settled in, a palpable change is evident in the outfield. Things are quieter, more serene. They have surrendered to the experience. Vincent, earrings gleaming in the sun, reclines against the tree. He stands up and traces his fingers down its coarse bark. He's a four-sport star who once told me that he thinks he has an attention disorder. He later told me that on this day he became "lost in the texture of the bark." Linda, her white elevator pumps off, is rubbing her bare feet against the grass. She stops, writes, glides her toes over the grass, and writes again. Later she told me that she was "reading the grass with her feet," which was something that she had done when she was younger. Trey, who had originally mocked the assignment, twirls a blade of grass, scrutinizes it from every angle, and laces it into a ring. He later said he was trying to envision what the grass looked like from the perspective of the ant that had clambered over his sneaker. (31)

It's interesting that just a change of place seems to have made a difference in students' opportunities to perceive and take the world in, and sadly strange that such an event was novel to the students. But powerful as it was, it was one day, and the choice of place was the teacher's. What if students also engaged in ongoing inquiry into the inspiration and energy available from different places on their writing selves? Undoubtedly, place is a component of the above discussion of setting up optimal conditions, and it is, for some writers, such an important variable that it is worth special consideration. Whether a desk, a picnic table, a corner of a coffee shop, or a big rock by a creek, a special place to write can be an aspect of a writing life. Of course, for many people, including most teenagers, it is necessary to be somewhat adaptive, to avoid saying, "I can't write except in my special chair in another state," or even "my bedroom." Still, part of the inquiry into a writing life should include awareness of the variability in how different spaces affect the writer and analysis of what it is about those places that contributes to the productive state of mind. Bobby says he has, a couple of times, found that he can write in this one chair in his house that sits right up next to a window. Thinking harder about it, he guesses that he likes the light from the window, the possibility of looking out at nothing in particular when his mind rests from a sprint of composing, the twisting way he sits in the chair that isn't quite upright but also isn't reclining, and the fact that he can rest his notebook on the window ledge. That analysis of the features of the place provides some things he can try in other specific places, including the classroom.

The assignment to investigate writing places can produce those insights. To complete the investigation, it needs to be possible for students to experiment, consciously and deliberately, with places in the classroom and perhaps the school building, where they can be most inspired and productive. One good minilesson is to invite them to think through a plan about a spot in the room, then to try it for today's writing time, and then to reflect, during the last few minutes of class, how that went.

Times

Writing demands a particular kind of energy and sense of time, and that energy and space do not feel equally available at all times in an individual's daily life. Every writer struggles across a life span to discover the time of day, length of time, and frequency that are both possible and supportive of writing. Naturally, the class' hour can't be negotiated on the basis of students' individual feelings of readiness, nor can the need for productive writing during that time. But it is also important for each student to search in the spaces of her day to explore when writing can occur. When I first get up? On the bus to school? In study hall? When I first get home? At the end of homework? Moreover, if students learn to break the large task of, say, writing an article into small, achievable subtasks, then even some of the seams and margins of a day can become writing times. An inquiry into such moments is part of developing academic work habits generally, but especially for writing, that development needs support and attention in school.

It's also useful for students to learn to reach for their writers' notebooks in *caught moments*—sudden, unplanned, opportunistic writing sessions. Keeping your book and notebook handy for minutes when you would otherwise be bored or instances when a set of thoughts begins to form is an important early lesson in either independent reading or writers' notebooks.

Tools

If a person has ever taken much pleasure in writing, they can probably talk to you about the tools they prefer. Being able to integrate writing into the steps of their lives requires attention to the physical fit. Where could they keep a pen so they can be sure to find it? When does a pencil fit the job for them? Kids may not talk about the rag content of paper or the nibs on their fountain pens, but they can still be pursuing the question of what pen or pencil might please them more because of the way it looks on paper or feels in their hand. They can examine notebooks—the one that fits in their hand, the one that is easy to find at the store, the one with the wide lines, the one that slides easily into the pocket of their backpack. Moreover, the tools for composing aren't at all limited to those that produce print. Composing in new literacy environments may require (or at least invite) the use of cameras, paints, people's bodies and voices, images cut from paper or copied from websites. The thingness of writing intensifies as it becomes easier to combine words with sound, images, enactments, and movement. This makes composing more complex, but it's good, because it offers a wider diversity of pathways into literacy.

And like all writers, they need to figure out how they are going to move between computer and paper, computer and computer—all the permutations of tool relationships that are common now—and will continue so for the imaginable future. There are enough free software programs available for writing that everyone—consciously or unconsciously—chooses from among a wide range of available options every time they open a new document. I have five that I use regularly: Word, as you might expect, but also Pages, DevonThink, Tinderbox, and WriteRoom (two of those changed between the first draft of this and the time I submitted it to the publisher). I fire up the software I want, depending on lots of different conditions of my mind and my circumstances when I get ready to write. But I'm writing (the first draft of) these words with a blue Pilot G-2 pen on a pad of thick, off-white paper that I special order. Most students aren't going to be as obsessive as I may be about these things. Nevertheless, the tools they use will become important to them, employed strategically to make writing easier—or at least possible for the time being—and they need to get on board the inquiry into writing tools and technologies, where they will spend their whole writing lives.

Getting Started

Writing, for many people, goes pretty well once they have started. They focus on their topic, their thoughts, and text unfolds as they turn it over in their attention. Engagement with the material in mind drives the process. But for lots of people, it's getting started that is the hard part. So helping students explore potential routines, then settle on one and use it, is another lesson or set of lessons in developing writing lives. For Joshua to discover that it helps him to read over what he's written the past few days is a big boost to his writing life, because it's an action he can control and repeat each day. Yesenia's practice of opening her notebook and writing anything that's on her mind for five minutes, even if it makes no sense, makes her feel like she "gets out" her first thoughts and can then focus on the topic she really wants to write about, whether it's in a notebook or a draft. She also keeps her notebook out the whole time she is writing so that when a stray thought distracts her, she can just write it down and get refocused on her work. Jamie has found that he has to say what he's going to write to someone before he gets started. It's easy to talk, and so just getting some words into the air helps to pull his attention toward his topic. At home, Daniella lights a candle before starting to write; at school, she just draws one at the top of the page. Again, it's easy to do, it calms her down, and it lets her do something other than stall or feel empty. Beginning to write is a move from silence into speaking, and it's difficult for many people. Establishing a ritual or routine as a beginning can be supportive of a writing life, one that is very like those of people who write for their professional work.

Getting Started Is the Hard Part . . .

- It helps Joshua to read over what he's written the past few days.

- Yesenia opens her notebook and writes anything that's on her mind for five minutes, even if it makes no sense.

- Jamie has to say what he's going to write to someone before he gets started.

- At home, Daniella lights a candle before starting to write; at school, she just draws one at the top of the page.

Writing Habits

What do you do, in your mind, when you write? What's it like for you? Some people hear the language they are about to produce, but since writing is slower than mental listening, they keep repeating words they are planning until they get to them. Their attention is focused on listening to an inner voice. That can be true for people who are able to slow down the language they hear, too. Their inner monologue is moving at the speed of text production, relatively slowly producing phrases and sentences. But they're still listening—it's just a listening that is transformed. Do the sentences come one at a time, so that each one is a world for a few minutes, while the horizon of your thinking slowly reveals itself across the sentences? How often do you notice yourself moving from your overall plan to the details of what you're writing now? How important is that plan to you? Ask a fourteen-year-old any of these questions, and you will usually get a blank stare for a while. But once students have begun observing themselves from the inside as they write, some brave person will attempt to describe what it's like for them, and as soon as they do, others will begin either agreeing or contrasting themselves. As with all these personal characteristics and practices, people often come to know themselves when they hear someone describing the process in a way that's different from their own. They develop awareness through difference—even more than through similarity.

Modalities, Genres, and Languages

People have their own mixes of modalities, genres, and languages that they use for the disparate purposes and forms of thinking they do through writing. Whether they realize it or not, every time someone sits down to write, they make a set of decisions about modality, genre, and language. By modality, I mean the combination of sign resources that include print, spoken words, images, sound, movement, and visual features of writing (like handwriting, font, color, size). By genre, I mean the conventionalized form of the whole text, such as poem, short story, joke, essay, comic strip, or video documentary, to name a few. By language, I mean both lexical language, like English or Spanish, as well as the language variety, such as so-called Standard Written English or African American English (see Chapter 14 for more on language variety). Within language, we might also include the degree of formality, or register, and the particular discourse, or language style of a community, such as those of education, medicine, or entertainment media.

Sitting down to make a notebook entry or to compose a message to a particular audience, a writer makes decisions about all those things. Some of it may seem natural—like writing a notebook entry with words. But as we'll see, a notebook entry could begin with a sketch, could be written as a cartoon or comic strip, could be made three-dimensional with flaps, cards in pockets, and paper sculptural elements. On a digital device, even with free software, a notebook entry could be a voice recording over a musical background. So the selection of written words is a choice, just as those other things would be. For multilingual students, English is a choice; there's nothing natural about its use. Some entries should be in another language, if they have it, because memories, thoughts, and ideas might more fittingly germinate in the soil of that language. Native speakers of English learning another language, say Japanese or French, ought on occasion to try it out in their notebook writing or certain kinds of projects, because that language is becoming a part of them. The repertoire each of us continually builds of these resources is part of what makes us the writer we are.

Larger Literate Life

Managing Attention

It seems obvious, but we teachers have rarely paid much attention to it. Both reading and writing are activities that demand self-management of attention. In many ways, attention management is the essence of both activities. When writing, we invest our attention in subject matter, and that engagement in what we are writing about is one of the most important moves a writer makes. Attention must be paid. We also shift our attention from the details of the phrase or sentence we are writing right now to the larger view of the chunks of meaning and the overall purpose and design of the whole text. We move between engagement with the subject and planning of structure. While reading, we are reminded of our own relationships or of other activities by incidental memories that arise as we engage with the meanings of the text—and we have to organize our attention either to stay with the new thought or to stick with what the book is telling us. Literacy is largely control of attention, control that necessarily has to come from the reader/writer.

Each of these moves is a shift, an interruption, a change of mind, and every time we successfully make one of these moves, our attention has to migrate without picking up something else along the way. However, we are often unsuccessful at these minute transitions—very, very often. We hear a bit of music from the other room or a noise in the hall; we think of something we forgot to do earlier; our email program dings. We are often distracted. This is true of everyone, though it is less often true of people who are very productive, who've found strategies for managing their attention and remaining involved in the task before them.

Attention, then, requires attention, and it is an important topic for discussion in a classroom that supports people's reading and writing lives. Teachers accomplish this by asking students to think aloud, with partners, the conditions under which they are most successful at remaining concentrated, what they have to do to set up a focused reading or writing time. They also talk with students about making conscious decisions about what is most important to attend to for a stretch of time, so that students learn to have a clear object of attention rather than continually distracting themselves. I've asked students to pay attention to their concentration for a whole reading or writing time and to have out a piece of paper on which they jot down a word or two that can remind them of anytime they find themselves distracted. It may be either by something social like a friend trying to catch their eye, or a thought unrelated to the work, or by some other aspect of the work taking them away from what they are doing right now. At the end of writing time, we talk honestly and realistically about the vicissitudes of attention, and strategize together about how to deal with them. Of course, then the conversation has to be repeated frequently; it's not something you tell them once and then they "know" it.

Attention management has become increasingly important in a world in which we are bombarded by information and by what seems like our continual availability to everyone in the world. For that reason, we will think more about attention management in Chapter 13, which is about new literacy practices in digital environments. (I would be ashamed to say how many times I checked email while writing just this section, so I won't.) For now, it just seems important to understand that attention management is an important dimension of a literate life.

Using Literacy to Manage Literacy: To-Do Lists, Records, Goals, and Plans

One use of literacy that is extremely common, important, and also often overlooked by educators is the use of literacy for self-management—in particular, the use of literacy to manage one's work on literate projects. I'm talking here about to-do lists, written goals, schedules, and the like—the texts that tell us what to do with our hands (Figure 3–3). In fact, this form of writing is not a matter of creating a single text, but of building a system that keeps projects in focus and eliminates the clutter of extraneous materials to which one is not presently attending. Used this way, literacy is a visual support for remembering, focusing, committing attention to specific tasks, and becoming more fully engaged in them.

Writers need ways of capturing thoughts, information, and plans, and the writer's notebook (discussed in Chapter 10) is a useful tool for those purposes. It can also be a good location for jotting reading plans—the books one plans to get around to reading, the metaphorical stack on the nightstand. The notebook is a capture device—a net to keep things from slipping by. And it's a place one returns in order to be told what to do by one's more planful, in-control self. It can be a place to dream up goals—"I want to finish four books by Thanksgiving"—or to record what has happened—"I wanted to read four books by Thanksgiving, but I only did two—even though they were really long books!" And they can be places where students reflect and assess how their literate lives are adding up: "I think I've been slowing down in my reading lately, but one thing I notice is that I'm thinking so much more about characters and why they do things. I wonder if that's why I'm slowing down. Maybe I'm pausing sometimes to think about characters' reasons for things and so not getting through as fast."

Topics in the Study of Literacy as Self-Management

1. You need a capture system—a way of writing things down when you think them—right away, so that they don't get lost. Some things you need to capture are ideas. Other things are just tasks. Are those going to go in the same place?

2. You need to make sure that the things you see all the time are the things you need and want to pay attention to. That means you need to put clutter away where you can find it but not see it and attend to it.

3. You need a system of storage for all those things you need to put away but find later. Students, meet file folders and binders—the ones you choose for your own work, not the ones you are required to buy for school.

4. You need a list of all your ongoing projects. A project is anything that takes more than two steps or actions to accomplish.

5. You need to go down the list in #4 frequently and figure out the next step on each project.

6. Next steps need to be easy and achievable steps—clear directions to yourself that you can obey.

7. A list of next steps needs to be handy at all times, so that you can see it whenever you might have a few minutes to accomplish one of them.

FIGURE 3–3 Topics in the Study of Literacy as Self-Management (see Allen 2002)

They also need to learn how to plan very small and achievable "Next Actions" (Allen 2002), especially for writing and investigating, breaking unwieldy tasks into unintimidating pieces. When I sit down to work on this book, what appears on my to-do list is not "work on book," but something more like "draft three paragraphs on using literacy to manage literacy." The bigger and vaguer the task, the more likely it is that I'm going to avoid it completely; and when I find my self avoiding work, one solution is to make the task easier—something I could do when I feel like a lunkhead. Working with students on becoming detailed task analyzers helps them to develop a lifelong habit of clarity of action and of kind self-management.

Particular People's Projects Across Time

It will probably come as no big surprise that a significant part of my own identity as a writer is that I am spending several years working on this book, and that I have in the past been an author of similar sorts of books. Projects carry us across time. When we set upon a long-term project, we place an anchor in our future and haul ourselves through all the days between now and then by pulling toward that anchor. And even though a particular piece of writing may be a project and may indeed take a long time, any one piece is a subset of a larger project, a longer journey. This book is just one instance of longer life themes for me—connecting to school life, appreciation of students' strengths, literacy as identity, expanding the meanings of literacy that students experience in school. These passions—just a few of many—have become permanent projects in my life as a writer and reader. But I have others that are not professional—I really love books (and blogs and articles . . .) that make me laugh out loud, and I have been pursuing these texts actively since I was a child. I notice styles of writing across these books, and I have developed certain ideas about what is likely to make me laugh. So the project of reading isn't just a matter of liking a certain stack of texts; it's a construction of a set of thoughts across those texts—the relationships among them.

A challenge that is important for any reader or writer of any age is to find the intellectual projects that will carry her across books, across notebook entries, and across pieces of writing made for audiences. They don't all have to be books about the same topic or in the same genre or by the same author; the connections are made by the reader, not by the material. And it's an important role for a teacher to help each student find and develop those projects. It's got to be part of what English class is for.

Knowing One Another in the Community

One benefit of this work, of course, is that each writer/reader comes to know himself. Another kind of profit comes from students' knowledge of one another as diverse members of a community. Hernan and Rashid are sitting side by side; they're reading partners, each with his own copy of their shared book. I see Hernan nudge Rashid, who's lost in the story; Rashid barely looks up, and Hernan points to the page. When, later in the period, it's time for the partners to talk, I ask Hernan why he was signaling to Rashid earlier. "Oh, there was a part on that page," he answers. "I knew when he got to it, he'd say, 'That's racist.'"

"Oh, yeah? Did he say that?" I ask.

"He sure did," he says.

"Did you think it was racist, Hernan?"

"Kind of. But I knew he was going to say it, because he always does. Always with these books, he's talking about 'racist.'"

The three of us go on to discuss their thinking about race, the book, and the author, but what's important about this story for now is Hernan's knowledge of Rashid. He knows his friend as a reader. He recognizes him, is familiar with him, not as good or bad, not as liking or not liking, but as a particular reader with habits of thinking and doing. Among many other peculiarities, Rashid notices and thinks about racism in stories—books, movies, and everyday life. He knows this about himself, and Hernan knows it, too. And Rashid knows that Hernan knows it, which reinforces Rashid's sense of his own identity as that kind of reader.

One of the most important aspects of making specific identities explicitly available to students is the provision of a public forum for being known as that identity. This curriculum is not just about "getting to know myself," but also getting to know others in this class and how they are different from me, and sometimes, though probably less often, also similar to me. The class needs lots of opportunities to talk about peculiar aspects of our literate practices and identities, and the concept at the center of these conversations has to include an assumption of difference. It's a difference that makes people give a specific and detailed account—indeed, it's the encounter with difference that even wakes them up to what exactly they're doing. Just as a conversation about how one dreams in sleep or what one's family's holiday traditions have been can produce a sense of exoticism about other people's lives, so can talking in detail about reading and writing lives and habits. Of course, these differences are not simply as individual as the proverbial snowflakes; they are also cultural. We read as a member of a racial and ethnic group, as a particular gender, as a set of language traditions, as a member of a social class, and other kinds of heritage. But these social influences are assembled and innovated upon by a very specific person in a very particular social context. Rather than being Everyreader, the reader becomes her own name, one very specific reader, inheriting many particular traditions from many different groups in which I participate and also riffing on those traditions in an individual way. And having others recognize and accept us, in all our weirdness, creates a sense of belonging, an acceptance of who I am now, and also the possibility of growing into some new, strange creature.

Now What Are You Working On?

Now, having considered all of those dimensions of both reading and writing, think again about what you are working on in your literate life. What are you working on now?

Reading Outside the Skin

Making Thinking Visible

> " *A person's* consciousness *is the way in which he or she thrusts into the world. It is not some interiority, some realm of awareness inside the brain. Rather, it must be understood as a reaching out, an intending, a grasping of the appearances of things. Acts of various kinds are involved: perceptual, cognitive, intuitive, emotional, and yes again, imaginative.... By attending, listening, gazing, a perceiver structures what presents itself.* "
>
> MAXINE GREENE, *Releasing the Imagination*

CHAPTER 4

Environments for Building Readers

I often see college students who have done everything they were supposed to do for their teachers, put in time with books, taken tests, written essays, but they have no particular agenda with regard to literature, no favorites, no list of books they plan to read next, and no self-sponsored habits of literary reading. I'm not suggesting they don't have resources, knowledge, or literate lives. But they don't have very developed identities as readers independent of school work. That fact becomes understandable when you ask about their life histories as readers.

The most common narrative I hear is that, during their childhood, up until middle school, these students liked to read, and they can name the children's novels they enjoyed. Sometimes they chose these as part of their schooling, and sometimes it was just for self-sponsored pleasure. Then they came to middle school, and the story changed drastically. Beginning in middle school and continuing through college, they have had someone constantly telling them what to read. No pattern is clearer in these life histories: people stop liking to read or having conscious preferences at middle school. In extreme cases, they stopped reading entirely, figuring out ways of faking it rather than reading what the teacher assigned. Their resistance to reading can almost be like an eating disorder—a way of asserting their control of their own mind and activity.

If they are in college now, and you ask them what their reading lives will be like when they get out of college, you will usually get a blank stare. They haven't thought about it. Why would they? The purpose in secondary and tertiary education was to make sure they read good things; the result is that they don't really read anything. And I always have to remind myself: these college juniors and seniors are the most successful students. At my university, they were almost all in the top 10 percent of their high school graduating class. They have made it through a rigorous and often not very supportive college career. They so strongly identify with school that they want to become teachers. What about the vast majority of people who were in middle and high school English language arts but don't show up in my classes, because they didn't go to college or get this far in that particular, narrow journey? Is it really likely they fared better in their construction of reading lives than these students?

In this section of the book, I am going to assume that we want to do better than that, that we would like to set up a relationship between readers and their texts that is constantly engaging and motivating. I think we want to support all readers in habitually having a reading agenda, a text they mean to read next, and then a list of several more after that one. They need to be conscious of the kinds of texts that excite them, the authors with whom they identify, and the ways reading teaches them about the world. For any of that to make sense, of course, each reader needs to be able to make sense of text—to understand what she reads in a way that other readers would recognize. And for many, many people of all ages, coming to such an understanding is not as unproblematic as many English teachers like to think. I would argue that we want to teach in such a way as to be certain that our students understand what they read independently, and that when text is difficult for them, they know some things to do to work on it. We want to graduate readers who can give themselves intense experiences of beauty in literary art, who can participate in communities of readers, who can try to improve their own lives and those of others by engaging with texts. We want them to be able to interpret what they think a text is really getting at, what its point is and why that point might be significant for this and other texts, and we want them to make these interpretations themselves, not only under our close guidance and based on our own readings. We want them to be able both to submit to a text's power while reading it and also to step away from it and critique its assumptions, to slip free of its control of their mind. We want them to be able to recognize the patterns of ideology in the popular texts around them and to assert alternative values. These are ambitious goals, and they require a rigorous curriculum of a very specific kind, a curriculum that actually aims directly for these goals rather than hoping for them as a magical outcome of doing something completely different. Students tend to learn what we teach them, sometimes all too well. The goals are achievable, and not for just a few advanced students—for all students—but it will require a refocusing of our efforts in reading.

I am sorry to say that I don't think it will happen with English language arts curricula that are like those most common in the U.S. "Doing English" in the usual way just is not designed to produce those outcomes. Reading a string of novels and plays as a whole class, followed by formulaic, controlled pieces of writing, peppered with some vocabulary and grammar instruction—that is the typical English class. What's so unusual, in a time of awful education policy, is that this form of teaching English is in no way supported by a single state's standards or assessments. No one is holding an English teacher to a list of books except the other members of her department, the people teaching right down the hall. Clearing the way for better curriculum design involves social and political work, but frankly, this social and political work isn't that hard; it begins with just talking to friends.

Talking to Colleagues: Proposals to Bring to Department Meetings

- Use some of the money that would go toward anthologies or textbooks to buy classroom libraries.

- Expect only a single particular book-length work among all classes on a grade, instead of seven.

- Focus more intently on the state standards, only requiring the particular texts required there (none).

- Install at least one four-week independent reading unit into the shared expectations at every grade level. This should be expanded for students who might sometimes struggle with reading.

- Make more of the literature curriculum support the genres in which students write–to teach contemporary poetry when students write poetry, short story when they write short stories, and so forth.

- Arrive at a shared set of contemporary short works appropriate for readers at each grade level (the purpose being to deflect attention from the list of novels).

In order to provide students with an opportunity to assume a more productive identity of a reader, we need to design a classroom that positions them as such a reader now. Education should involve students in the ways of living that we have in mind for their futures, not doing some other thing in preparation for those futures. If we want them to become active, intentional, interested decision makers as readers, we have to treat them like such people—now. We have to create a classroom that asks them to find what they are interested in reading, that expects them to find an answer to that question, that asks them to develop some intentions about reading. That means handing over more control to the students, more responsibility for making decisions, not toward the production of either chaos or lazy inactivity, but with a full expectation that they will find meaning in literate activity if we provide the right kind of assistance.

The rest of this chapter will discuss details about how to do that, including the use of the social structures I first described in Chapter 1—independent reading, reading partners, small groups, and whole-class texts. I will describe a workshop structure for the teaching of reading and the use of minilessons and conferences as sites for instruction. I'll also discuss the logic of a school year in reading, how a reading year might begin and progress in time. For the most part, this particular chapter will not talk about what to teach about reading or other aspects of the content of teaching—that will come in the five chapters following this one. This chapter is about structures—the containers for all those important lessons. But before I get into all those architectural elements of a reading classroom, I need to say a bit about texts themselves—issues of value and status for different kinds of reading material.

Reading Material: What Is There to Read?

An initial difficulty in teaching reading for many English teachers often involves thinking through the meaning and importance of what some people call "the canon." It's a little tricky, though, to get a grip on what that means. High school English has never really been concerned with the English canon as it would have been defined by, say, a college English department in 1950. With very few exceptions, no one is talking about Spencer's *The Faerie Queene* or Milton's *Paradise Lost*, though those are undoubtedly part of the canon for those who value such a thing. Rather, we're more often talking about texts like Steinbeck's *Of Mice and Men* and Lee's *To Kill a Mockingbird*, alongside a few Shakespeare plays and perhaps *The Odyssey*. Possibly, in those schools or districts that have given some thought to race and gender in their selections, the list would also include something like Cisneros' *House on Mango Street* and Morrison's *The Bluest Eye*. The fact is, few scholars who staunchly defend a strong sense of canon would make the case that *To Kill a Mockingbird* or *House on Mango Street* would really be included. The titles in the high school "canon" are mostly the books that are in the book room, those of which there are enough copies available. To be sure, they tend to be books that teachers have found valuable and successful, which is why *Silas Marner* isn't usually one we fight about anymore. But these books aren't really a canon—more of a convenience—and consequently we don't really need to worry ourselves about the conflict over a canon, because it's simply not the issue in most schools.

What might be of more concern is the notion of literary merit. While *To Kill a Mockingbird* may not be one of the greatest monuments of Western civilization, it's well written, engaging to read, and usually great to talk about. Of course, many other books have those qualities, and more come out every day. Just because many of us find reading Harper Lee's novel to be a good experience doesn't mean it's a one-of-a-kind experience or one that has to be imposed on everyone.

Furthermore, good, meaty discussions can be built upon lots of different kinds of texts—from poems to TV commercials to novels to movies. The quality of the thinking a reader does or the conversations in which she can engage is not contained between the covers of a particular book. The chapters following this one will discuss more about teaching for high-quality thinking and talking in response to a very wide array of texts. For now, I'll just say that we aren't choosing between thoughtfulness and mindlessness. We want, rather, to teach mindful, intelligent, meaningful reading and response in such a way that it is more likely in more different parts of life. In order to accomplish that, we'll need to open our classrooms to more varied kinds of text.

Tools of the Literacy Trade: Well-Equipped Classroom Libraries

Even though many secondary schools have school libraries and some of those are pretty well stocked, it is important that a teacher be able to respond to students' interests and needs by placing books directly into their hands. That means the books have to be nearby, and the teacher has to know the collection well. And that means that classroom libraries are important for English language arts classrooms. The more variety in the classroom library, the more possible it will be to meet the purposes, interests, and levels of difficulty appropriate for particular individual students. A classroom library, especially in a secondary school, needs a lot of books, though when a particular teacher gets started, of course, that's not going to be the case. But access to appropriate and diverse print materials is a huge determiner of reading achievement, and these libraries, each serving over a hundred students, need to get big fast, and they need to contain appropriately varied materials to serve very diverse student interests, preferences, and needs.

One type of text with which English language arts teachers need to acquaint themselves and pack their classroom libraries is young adult (YA) novels and story collections. Though there are precursors earlier, this market and therefore this genre began expanding geometrically beginning in the late 1960s. Since I started teaching in the mid 1980s, there are not only thousands more YA novels available, but almost all of the collections of short stories have appeared. That means there is a generation of authors who have grown up in the midst of these books and became writers with this as a career path, who chose young people as their audience. As with adult novels, there is of course a range of quality, but there are literally dozens of YA novels appearing every year that are well written, engaging to read, and great to talk about, just like *To Kill a Mockingbird*. Most adult readers can get through most of them very rapidly, so it is possible within a few months to have surveyed a substantial library of these texts, and I consider it part of an English teacher's responsibility to do just that.

One of the new roles we take on in helping students compose reading lives is to be one of their resources for finding books that might hook them, so for that reason, it's very helpful for us to know about a lot of books. As time goes on, our knowledge grows exponentially from just talking with kids about their reading, even if we haven't read all their books. Because students are going to be making more decisions, it's inevitable that they're going to be reading things we haven't, and so it doesn't take much effort for us to learn about them from the kids. But it's also important for each of us to have a substantial collection of YA books under our belt. Of course, since the trappings of youth culture change so frequently, only the newest books are likely to seem relevant to the moment (and even they are probably always at least somewhat out of date in a youth culture that changes as rapidly as ours does). Many English language arts teachers, along with some of their students, enjoy the extra excitement of keeping up with new releases and award winners.

Another kind of text that appeals to many students and has grown at a rapid rate in recent decades is graphic novels. I am positive that I learned to read from reading comics in the backseat, and so any literate form with drawings and speech bubbles is very dear to my heart. Advances in technology have made productions of these texts increasingly possible and affordable, and to many of us, they enjoy as much legitimacy as novels and stories with only words in them. As I will discuss in Chapter 13, the new forms of literacy that are emerging in digital environments are built around more deliberate use of visual design elements and texts that communicate through different modalities, including visual images (Albers 2010; Burke 2008; Kist 2005; NCTE 2005). In such a world where what counts in texts is shifting so rapidly, it seems almost irresponsible not to include graphic novels and comics as part of a classroom's literate environment. Once students are reading them, there are plenty of interesting things to inquire about, the ways the text and pictures work together, the passage of time and motion represented in frames, the communication of emotion through multiple modalities. The ability to read these signs, these forms of literacy, in a society that bulges with visual information everywhere you look, are important and interesting to discuss in a literacy classroom.

A Few YA Authors to Launch a Reading Journey

Jacqueline Woodson	Julia Alvarez
Sharon Flake	Francesca Lia Block
Chris Crutcher	G. Neri
Walter Dean Myers	Linda Sue Park
Angela Johnson	Rick Riordan
Short story collections by Don Gallo and Michael Cart	Suzanne Collins

A Few Graphic Novels to Launch a Reading Journey

Jimmy Corrigan: The Smartest Kid on Earth by Chris Ware

Maus by Art Spiegelman

Ghost World by Daniel Clowes

Epileptic by David B.

Hey, Wait . . . by Jason

Bone by Jeff Smith

Blankets by Craig Thompson

American Born Chinese by Gene Luen Yang

Persepolis by Marjane Satrapi

Watchmen by Alan Moore

Understanding Comics by Scott McCloud

Graphic novels and YA novels have met with opposition from parent and community groups and have been challenged as inappropriate in schools. For a teacher to open up the availability of a wider range of texts in a classroom necessitates engagement with questions about appropriateness and censorship. Then again, even those who don't try new things may meet challenges. Older novels that are typically taught, such as *Huckleberry Finn*, *Nineteen Eighty-Four*, *To Kill a Mockingbird*, and *Of Mice and Men* have been challenged and censored. And so have recent titles that are hugely popular, such as the Harry Potter series and the *Hunger Games* books. The challenges can come because of sexual content, of course, but also because of language, violence, magic and witchcraft, political content, and less specific complaints of general inappropriateness. English language arts teachers and librarians are perhaps uniquely positioned in society to protect young people's access to the kinds of ideas and topics that the adults around them may want to silence, and their professional organizations are especially well equipped to lend a hand when such things come up (National Council of Teachers of English 2010a; American Library Association 2010). In addition to being prepared to defend students' right to read, it's also a concept that it behooves students to consider—what makes a book appropriate, why people would want to limit access, and how the history of censorship interacts with technology and political ideas.

To add YA novels and graphic texts to the mix of what's available to students multiplies the kinds of stories that are available to the diverse readers constructing reading lives in our classrooms. Then again, everything is not a story. Indeed, as much as I love narratives—memoirs, novels, short stories—I, like most people, spend more time reading nonnarrative, expository texts of various kinds than I do narratives. I do seek out well-written expository texts, and I have favorite nonfiction writers, such as John McPhee, Susan Orleans, and Bob Herbert, whose work I enjoy regardless of the topic. We need, in a classroom library, to make nonnarrative books, magazines, and collections of feature articles available to students, and these will undoubtedly be favorites for a substantial number of readers who, without these texts available, might appear to their teacher to be unmotivated and struggling. For some students, magazines are indeed the place to meet them, though I do think there are goods to be gained by moving them into a book–length work as soon as they can find one that isn't repellant to them. Meaning builds up across a longer text, and the knowledge a reader has to summon to keep momentum becomes less hard to access because one remembers the section just previous to the present one. These gains in experience

Multilingual Note

Reading in Multiple Languages

Multilingual students are sometimes marked as readers who struggle. However, it's important to remember that they actually have more than one language, and part of a literacy educator's responsibility would be to provide space for their literate development in the languages they know. Might there be books in the classroom library for the languages most common among the students in this community? Some teachers have found it useful for books in international languages to be easier than the English books, partly because multilingual students may have experienced some interruptions in their schooling as they migrated, and partly because easy books in other languages might encourage the native English speakers to explore them with the multilingual students' help.

with text are valuable. But without expository text, these students might never even get on the bus, and magazines often provide ready access to friendly expository text.

In building a classroom library, it's also important to look especially hard for books by and about Latinos, African Americans, Asians and Asian Americans, immigrants, and gay and lesbian youth. People like to see themselves in the books they read, and always to be seeing someone who is not like oneself in the texts in the classroom argues strongly that one's group is not as good as the one all the books are about. Sometimes we teachers think, "Well, they should also be able to learn about people different from themselves through reading." And maybe that's true. We can have that conversation productively and honestly, as soon as all the straight, white males are reading about people different from themselves as often as the black lesbians are. It's a particular kind of privilege to see your experience legitimated over and over in the books on your teachers' shelves (McIntosh 1988). Because the world doesn't just automatically become fair and just, teachers have to work extra hard to mitigate that privilege. The classroom library is one location for that work, as well as in our selection of whole-class shared texts.

Overall, the classroom library must reflect—and make the case for—the usefulness of books and other texts in an ordinary life. How do our students think about the roles of literacy in their lives? How are they able to carry ways of reading across these domains, when appropriate, or at times, to distinguish peculiar reading practices among them? Aesthetic reading practices are not generalizable across all these domains, and neither are academic ones. Neither are the efferent ways of extracting the news from websites about diseases appropriate ways of having the richest aesthetic experience of a poem. What we read and how we read it should be in constant dialogue with the wide range of reading practices in which students presently engage and with which they can easily imagine a future.

TECHNOLOGY NOTE

For young people and adults, more and more of our reading lives these days occurs on screens, handheld devices, e-readers, and other means of accessing the Internet and local digital text. It will be increasingly common and increasingly desirable for the reading workshop to include digital text. We will need to mentor students in reading strategies that are more important in those environments than in print culture. It's not something to avoid; the Internet is a huge sponsor of literacy, and we need to be in there with our students helping them to navigate and be thoughtful, critical readers of digital text in all its forms. Just as English language arts teachers have embraced magazines, comics, and popular culture, we need to reach out to students in the new literacy environments in which they are composing their reading lives.

Readers and Levels of Difficulty

We do not learn to read once and for all at age six and then continue to apply those same skills to every text from then on. In fact, we learn to read again and again across our lives, as we encounter new forms of text and new practices in reading that count in different communities. We can therefore be strong as a reader in one domain but struggle in another. Anyone can be a struggling reader in a particular context—including you and me. One thing is sure: more adolescents have trouble with the texts they are asked to read in English class than most English teachers realize. And if they cannot understand what they are reading, then they will not grow from putting in time with their eyes on the print. Want to find time for more of the high-quality experiences described in this book? Let's cut out the experiences we know cannot help—and may well be hurting—the readers in our care.

It's an important reality for literacy educators to face: readers will not get better at reading from holding books in their hands that are too hard for them to read. It doesn't matter how great the book is if the reader can't make sense of it. To grow, readers need to spend most of their time reading texts at an appropriate level of difficulty. And in many secondary English classrooms, they aren't spending any time in such texts. Talking of standards or of college won't change the reality of the texts being too hard for the readers to learn from. There is only one choice: to lower the level of difficulty until the reading experience is meaningful for the reader and then to gradually raise it again.

As important as it is for readers to be working with text at an appropriate level of difficulty, it is also hard to know how to gauge that appropriateness. Static definitions of text levels—like "level 31" or "fourth grade"—are just convenient shorthand for certain features of texts such as the length of words and the length of sentences. But *difficulty* is not really something contained inside the text; rather, it names something in the relationship between the text and the reader. For example, if Jared picks up a book about fish written for a popular adult audience by a marine biologist, it may have some language that is difficult for him and some unfamiliar vocabulary. But if Jared is a guy who really likes fish and marine life, has been learning about it for some time, if he is interested and motivated, if he has relationships with other people around fish, then he may very well be able to make meaning even with more scientific text features than he is used to. On the other hand, many texts are written with quite ordinary words and simple sentences but are about worlds that are far away or long past, depending, through their simple vocabulary and syntactic structures, on domains of shared knowledge in which a particular reader does not participate. Another text could appear simple but leave huge gaps unexplained, or could express literary strangeness, or could be structured, as a whole text, in a way with which a particular reader is unfamiliar. Consequently, trying to slot kids and books into neat "levels" is usually not nearly as accurate and scientific as people like to think.

Difficulty in reading, then, is not really a single continuum. It is not a ladder from low to high, on which we can place students on a particular rung. There are many more than one continuum. Picture first a Cartesian coordinate system with an x- and y-axis. Now picture a depth axis, so that the x and y are also in 3-D. Now picture that moving through time. That's more what we are dealing with—a continent of possible locations, not a single rung, with others arrayed neatly above and below.

If that metaphor is apt, it means that students are different in more varied ways, and there are even more possible ways in which a single, whole-class text may prove less than helpful for a particular reader. What we need to teach them for independent reading, though, is not to go only for books at a certain predefined level. Instead, we need to teach them that reading is understanding, and that the experience of reading should feel like other experiences in which they know they understand, rather than experiences that are confusing. This difference in the experience of understanding versus the experience of confusion is an essential part of a reading life—both in determining what texts to read and in a disposition toward insistence on meaning. The next chapter will have more to say about that.

Since students need to be reading texts at levels of difficulty they can understand, in order to be able to grow toward more complex and challenging ones, it's important that a variety of texts be available in the classroom. There need to be easier books, but ones that, to the extent possible, aren't too embarrassing for adolescents to be holding. There need to be books with picture support along with text. There need to be, especially for areas of popular interest among students in this particular community, books at varied levels of difficulty from easy to hard. There also have to be many conversations, connected to the discussions described in Chapters 2 and 3, about the fact that readers are different and that one of those differences is in the type of book that feels like understanding to them. It does no good to have the texts available if there is no legitimate way, socially, for a student to choose them. Some teachers have called them "quick reads" or "lighter books" in order to position them toward students as something anyone might want to pick up once in a while. Beers' (2003) Chapter 14 has a bunch of tips about the features of texts that are especially supportive and manageable for what she calls "dependent" readers. Teachers in reading classrooms have to legitimate the reading of texts at appropriate levels of difficulty, even as we hold onto sincere ambition for growth for every student.

Organizing Social Structures for Readers

Independent Reading

The first social structure for teaching reading I will describe, one that has already come up in our exploration of building literate lives (Chapter 3) is independent reading. In this structure, individual students choose their own texts for reading, and read them silently to themselves in class, in a workshop classroom structure (Chapter 1). The work time is reading time, and it is framed by a minilesson (about the topics detailed in Chapters 3 and 5–7) at the beginning and a share session at the end in which students reflect and self-assess about how their reading is going and what they are trying in order to stretch themselves. During reading time, the teacher circulates and confers with individual students on the same kinds of topics that might also be minilessons (i.e., the topics in Chapters 3 and 5–7). Homework is to keep reading the same book; sponsoring that reading outside class is part of the point of the reading inside class—to allow them to get hooked on something so that there is less resistance to picking it up in a different context. The structure repeats, predictably, every day during the unit of study in which the class is attending to independent reading.

Independent reading is the baseline and foundation of the reading curriculum. There isn't much reason to do any of the other things to grow reading if they don't become part of a person's independent reading life. If we read in whole-class structures, I would assume we do this because we think it will affect the ways students engage with texts in the future. But if we only read in whole-class structures, how will we know whether that worked or not, and when will students have an opportunity to try out whatever we are teaching? If we have students working in small groups, presumably we think that is good for each of them as a reader, but they also need opportunities to integrate what they have learned into their own relationship to a book, the one they will have when they aren't in this class anymore.

Students are most motivated when they have the most choice. Raise the degree of individual choice, and up goes motivation, efficacy, and energy for the task. Independent reading, among all the possible structures for reading, offers students the most choice. A student can read what she chooses (I suppose I should say, within the limits of appropriateness for school). The teacher may at times try to push students toward something new or something that would be more of a challenge.

Exploring More of the Continent of Reading

The continent of reading has within it many countries and territories. People do read works of art to be transported and transformed, for pleasure, reflection, and entertainment. They also read a variety of texts because they are trying to figure out how to live and how to think about their lives. Some of this reading might be described as personal, therapeutic, and some of it is spiritual—either religious or just oriented toward the highest values we credit in a community or culture. People read for civic purposes—to participate in political culture and democratic decision making. Civic reading also involves enhancing their understanding of shared principles and values, such as equality, liberty, and fraternity. They read for social purposes, to stay in touch—to find out what a writer (whom they may or may not know) has been thinking, suffering, and celebrating. More reading than we may think is situated within figuring out how to do something physical—how to make a dinner, fix a machine, program a device, exercise to best effect, fertilize a garden, play a game more skillfully. We read in order to make decisions; finding out that we have a physical condition, we will often read for days on end to consider what course of treatment we prefer. People with chronic conditions can have an entire thread of their reading and writing lives devoted to inquiry and community around that purpose. Shouldn't a curriculum in reading be oriented to the ways reading fits into people's whole lives, not just to preparation for the next year of school or the first year of college?

When he does so, he always has to weigh that pushing against the potential risk of losing some engagement and motivation. Sometimes, I think it's worth it, but one has to count the cost and remain humble, because we really just don't know what the outcome of our insistence will be. Without interference from the teacher's agenda, a student in independent reading has the opportunity to think in the way she will when she's not in school—planning the next thing she will read, and what she might read after that. She starts to construct thoughts between books, allowing her reading life to become an intellectual journey.

One thing that is especially clear from research on readers is that those who achieve on tests at a high level are also those who read a lot, and those who don't spend much time reading do not do well. It's not surprising, but those who have access to books they would like to read are the ones who read a lot, and they are the ones who do well on tests and other measures of reading success. Moreover, when teachers devote class time to reading, students are more likely to read outside class as well, because they get interested in their book. The need for reading volume argues against placing independent reading as a once-a-week activity and hoping it will suffice, because that clearly isn't enough to make much of a difference. An approachable review of the research on the relationship between reading volume and reading achievement is in Allington (2005).

There are, however, things that independent reading doesn't accomplish as well as other structures. If this is the only structure for reading, a teacher may not see students growing much in their habits of interpreting and reflecting about meanings, or even their responses to texts beyond just liking or not liking. Even if the text is supporting nuanced and complex thinking, those ideas are not necessarily going to come out in talk, because to understand, the other person would need to have read the book, too. Because it's usually impossible to assume shared knowledge of the plot, readers reading on their own tend to spend all their energy in retelling the plot, whether in talk or writing, an act that both reduces the subtlety of the text itself and also takes air space away from deeper considerations of meaning and motive. In this way, it becomes clear that independent reading does support the psycholinguistic work of reading—the connection of thoughts as a text proceeds—but it does not support all of the participatory dimensions of reading—being competently a member of a particular type of conversation. A reading life does need both of those things. It's also possible for some adolescents who've gotten used to reading being relatively meaningless for them just to keep putting their eyes on print and getting nothing or very little out of it. This perseverant text fixation without accompanying thought needs to be interrupted, and all by itself, independent reading doesn't necessarily support that. This is not to argue against independent reading, not by any means, but it's worth noting that these social structures are like tools, good for some jobs, not as good for others. Students need to move through different social arrangements in a reading year, in order to provide them with the range of practices they need to develop.

To accomplish what it does best, reading time itself must be the focus of independent reading—not any activities designed in support of it. It's reading time that most has to be preserved and protected. It's not good to read a short story aloud for thirty minutes, discuss it for ten, and then have ten minutes of silent reading. That's not independent reading. It's not good to have a lesson on a reading strategy that lasts twenty-five minutes and then have twenty minutes for reading, or to have five students share their books for most of the period. That's not independent reading; it's about the reading time itself.

During this reading time, the teacher confers. Some people have advocated the teacher reading during this time, but there is much to do, and reading conferences are powerful opportunities to expand the thinking that students are able to do—all of them, including the students who don't see themselves as having difficulties with reading. Sitting there reading, while it sounds pleasant, isn't necessarily the best use of the teacher's time and talent. It is true that it's important to demonstrate the value of reading and adult engagement with a text, and that can be done with a few minutes at the beginning of reading time and by sharing one's reading as a part of minilessons. Another motive for the teacher limiting her activity to reading has been to keep the room quiet rather than having conversation that can distract. This seems to be an argument against any conferring ever, including in writing workshop, and I just can't agree with it. Sure, it's a compromise to have thirty readers in a room and the teacher talking quietly with one of them. It's not the same as each person being alone in a silent room. But people get used to reading under all sorts of conditions. I've seen noisy Internet cafes where half of the people are talking and half are completely absorbed in what they're doing. And conferring is too important to sacrifice this easily.

The likely content of reading conferences is what the next few chapters will be about. Here, however, I will describe the structure of conferences. They're not usually times when the student reads her book aloud to the teacher (only if doing so might shed some light on some mystery about this reader), and they're not just summaries of the text to check whether or not they are getting it. At first, it's necessary to get on the same page with the reader—to find out how she is thinking about her book today. So the first conversational move is just an invitation to give an account of her thinking. If she starts telling me the whole story, I interrupt and ask again how she's thinking about it (mainly so that I won't be there all day). In what she says, I listen for some kind of thinking I can support beyond what she is doing now, and an objective or teaching point for this conference emerges. Sometimes, that objective might be the same point as that day's minilesson, though much of the time, it's based uniquely on what this student is thinking today. The purpose is not to correct her understanding of this particular book; it's to teach something about reading that will support her both now and in the future. Usually, I engage her in a dialogue for a minute or two about the kind of thinking I have in mind, trying to get her to use talk to think in a new or intensified way. Then, I leave her doing something concrete (such as one of the externalization strategies in Chapter 7) in support of the thinking I introduced during the conference. That way, she keeps thinking about the conference beyond the point when I have moved on.

Minilessons during independent reading might be about several things. Often, they are about the kinds of thinking described in Chapters 5 and 6. They can also be introductions to particular books in the classroom library, or types of books that are available. They may be about management of the workshop and how to be productive within it. As part of some of these minilessons, I may share aspects of my own reading; students are usually well aware of the book I have going, because I use it so much in minilessons. For the most part, the agenda of minilessons is set by what the teacher observes students doing, what it seems as if they might need to work on. Often, it's that there was something they learned to do in small groups or whole-class work that now they need to take up into their independent reading.

Reading in Partnerships and Small Groups

At first, when kids started asking me if they could read with their friends, I said, "Oh, right. Just sit down and get back to reading." Gradually, I started to realize that they were not little criminals after all; this was exactly what should be happening. Here they were, engaged with texts, often having the impulse to talk with someone about them. Sure, they also wanted to visit and talk about other things, just like people do, but they, like most readers, also enjoyed company in entertaining new events and ideas, someone with whom to share the satisfactions and outrages in stories. Reading is social, and we all have voices in our minds, whether we're anticipating what someone we know would say, remembering what they have said, or just answering back ourselves to the authors whose words we are reading. These voices want to be heard, and they want other voices to talk back so that they can feel themselves defined in difference with others or agreement with them. In many classes, then, the impulse to read with partners begins in independent reading, and the impulse for small groups, likewise, begins when two partnerships would like to get together. There is often, among readers, a social magnetism that pulls individuals together toward one another. As readers get to know other students in the class *as readers*, the idea emerges that they might be able to work together. And if it doesn't, the teacher can sponsor it.

The social impulse is good, because talking about reading can help with both comprehension and also further thinking about a book's characters, relationships, and themes. In conversation, readers hold onto ideas longer than they do when they read alone; talk makes thinking visible, negotiated, and generative. It works differently when there are two conversants than when there are four or so. For two people, it's very easy to get started talking, easy to change the subject, and often easy, too, to just drop the conversation. That means partnerships are good opportunities for students to make sure they're actively processing what's happening in the text and to have some light discussions, holding an idea slightly longer than they individually would be likely to do. Groups of four or so will hold an idea still longer, sustaining their thinking while different people weigh in on it. They are slower moving, less likely to change direction suddenly, but each participant gets fewer chances to talk. They support different sorts of thinking, and do different jobs.

Conversational Frequency

Neither partnerships nor small groups need to meet every day. Twice a week is plenty, with the other days devoted to getting the reading done and any response activities that the group has mutually assigned. More frequent meetings tend not to have enough business, and the meetings are more likely to disintegrate into playing or bickering.

Compared to independent reading, choice in both partnerships and small groups is compromised. If two people have to agree on a book to read together, then each individual's initial impulse is likely not to be in sync. That becomes even more true with four. So these forms still preserve choice for students, as opposed to the teacher, though each individual's freedom is limited by the needs of constructing a shared decision. It *is* important, for these groups to be as effective as they can be, that the teacher allow them to self-govern, serving only as a consultant (even if sometimes an insistent one) to their work. Groups should be required to come up with legitimate, rigorous work, and hold one another to high expectations. In my experience, they not only rise to this requirement of self-governing; they end up having substantially higher standards than a teacher is able to enforce. When peer pressure begins to fuel academic work, whole new worlds become possible.

There are different ways of getting groups together. Some people ask students just to put themselves into groups. Some people ask students to list the people with whom they would like to partner or be in a group, and then the teacher assigns the groups on the basis of that information. Put together in this way, a group can stay together across the reading of multiple texts, having a long-running discussion that bridges more than one book. I call those kinds of groups reading clubs. Other people prefer what they tend to call "book clubs," meaning that the group comes together for the reading of a particular book. They don't choose one another; they choose a book.

Both minilessons and conferences in partnerships and clubs are as often about ways of talking (Chapter 8) as they are about reading and books. This is appropriate, since skills of teaming and collaborative work are essential for students to learn. In addition, the forms of talk with which students engage become the forms of thinking they can entertain. Conferences when work time is talk time (as opposed to reading time) usually involve the teacher circulating around the room, sitting just a short distance away from a group, and after listening for a bit, interrupting to try to teach something that they can use not just today but other days as well. In other words, the teacher has to resist the temptation to fix everything and take decision making away from them. Instead, she has to reason morally with them, attempt to persuade them of a different way of operating together in order to teach the important skills of collaboration.

Struggling Readers in a Group

The text a group chooses might be too hard for one of the members. There may be other ways for that member to access this book, by listening to a recording, for instance, or by reading with one of the other members. In the case of a group, it's most important to be a full member and to participate in the discussions. It is worth keeping in mind that if a particular reader is not benefitting from a book in a reading club, he should have an independent book selected at the same time that *is* more appropriate for him.

Whole-Class Texts

Independent reading and the aforementioned smaller, more student-governed collaborative structures of partners and clubs best embody the goals of the reading classroom—supporting students in their development of the habits, processes, and practices that characterize an ambitious intellectual life outside school, independent of teachers' authority. What, then, is the purpose of whole-class texts? It isn't to teach the text itself. How would that support an independent reading life? In fact, because no particular text is going to be at an appropriate level of difficulty for all students, a whole-class text might be seen as a risky proposition—risky that we may be wasting time, risky that we may be further tangling up the confused reading processes of some students, risky of bruising developing reading identities, risky of forever souring students on a valued text. On the other hand, reading in a particular community carries with it particular values and practices that support these values. Reading is not a transparent psychological process—but one rooted in cultures and communities. Part of what we are legitimately charged with, as teachers of English language arts, is inducting students into valued ways of reading, and that means the teacher has an affirmative and important role to play.

For the teacher to have the opportunity to mentor students into valued ways of reading and responding to texts, it helps to have at least a few times when the teacher takes a more active role in leading students in their thinking about a text. My ideas about the content of that teaching will be clear in the rest of the chapters in this section. The objectives for the teaching are not themes in a novel, certainly not plot details in texts. Rather, the teacher is pursuing purposes about reading—ways of thinking while reading (Chapter 5), valued habits of response and reflection (Chapter 6), strategies for mediating and extending ideas (Chapter 7), ways of talking with other readers (Chapter 8), and forms of writing that support a reading experience (Chapter 9). There is, in other words, much to teach, things readers need to consider in constructing a literate life, and a whole-class reading experience provides a crucial site for getting a few practices introduced to the whole class, practices that, to be truly valuable, have to be taken up into independent reading lives. We should therefore only teach practices to the whole class that we want to become habits, that make sense in a real reading life outside school.

Why Whole-Class Texts?

Whole-class texts, when everything works well, can help create community, a sense of shared experience, work, and purpose, and can provide an important shared reference point for future conversations. They can be moments when everyone in the room cares about something and keeps track of characters together. With a little luck and a lot of work, that can help to bond a class together.

It's not necessary for a whole-class text to be a novel or other book-length work. It is likely possible to teach the same practices with one or two short stories that one would engage in a whole text. And upon finishing the short text, the students can then more expeditiously get using it in their independent reading. Some kinds of thinking, such as *calling other texts to mind* (see Chapter 6) especially benefit from being discussed across multiple short texts. But if there is some whole-class text that a particular teacher is being required by colleagues to teach, and the political work of changing that fact is not yet complete, then using the shared reading of that work as an opportunity to teach several kinds of thinking and strategies for response will provide a useful way of making sure the teaching does have some potential impact on independent reading.

So what does it mean to read a text with a whole class, really? We have discussed the fact that it does no good to ask students to put in time with their eyes on text they can't understand; in fact, it can do damage. Teachers have often worked out a collection of ways students can be able to access a text: it isn't essential that each student read it to herself, because the eyes-on-print work of reading is not the purpose here. One possibility, if it's workable in the situation, is just for the teacher to read it aloud; everyone doesn't need a copy, since the purpose is ways of thinking about the text and responding to it. Another way of accomplishing oral distribution of the text, one that is easier today than imaginable a few years ago, is for the teacher to get the best actor she knows (maybe herself, maybe some other easy mark) to read the text aloud into a digital voice recorder and then put the MP3 file on the class website. Students can listen over the Internet or download the file to their MP3 players. My point is that the focus for a whole-class text isn't just on the getting of the text in the first place; it's on the discussion—entertaining ideas, considering multiple perspectives, and experimenting with new modes of response.

Orchestrating the Elements of an Environment for Readers

Reading is organized by one or the other of these four structures—independent, partners, small groups, or whole class—because the book choice and sharing falls to one of those units. But that doesn't mean there is no role for varied forms of grouping within any one of those structures (Santman 2005). For instance, during independent reading, obviously there are whole-class moments, such as the minilesson. In a minilesson, good teachers often ask students to turn to a partner and think through some idea or practice. In a whole-class reading experience, likewise, there are things teachers ask individuals to do (say, make some notes about their relationship to a particular character in the story) or that small groups do (talk for fifteen minutes about a big question that came up in the whole-class discussion). Small groups might get together and talk about new things they are trying to do in their independent reading, or ways of talking they are trying with their reading partner.

The materials that we gather into the room and the arrangements into which we organize our students for their reading represent our invitations to them to participate in the community of readers. They don't have to become bookish or literary, but if we have been successful in recognizing them for who they are, they might be less resistant to naming reading as a part of their lives.

CHAPTER 5

Building and Inhabiting the World of the Text

English teachers show students how to read. So we need to think carefully about our responsibilities to the readers in our classrooms. We need clear and active knowledge about what we are teaching when we are teaching reading. When Yelena can read aloud anything we put in her hands, but has barely any thoughts in response, she needs to learn how to formulate her own answers to what she reads. What she does not need is for her teacher to hand her yet another novel to plow through, passively and obediently. When Jim, twenty-five pages into an assigned novel, is completely confused about what is going on, he does not need someone to explain to him all the things he didn't get so that he can struggle through the next part until someone helps him with that bit. He needs to be reading a book in which he can be and become a strong reader, making meaning confidently, building habits that will last a lifetime. When Brittany avoids reading altogether, saying she hates it, as if that's just part of her identity, and never completes assignments or knows what is going on in discussions, she does not need to be tested and held accountable, punished, and failed. She needs support in locating texts that are most motivating to her and experiences of reading when it pays off meaningfully. To support all our students in becoming people who love reading as much as we English teachers often do, who can use literacy powerfully and flexibly in varied life contexts, we, their teachers, need deep and explicit knowledge about what happens when someone reads successfully. This chapter and the next are about some of the mental actions that readers engage in. We explored, in Chapter 3, the ways reading occurs in bodies and habits. In the last chapter, I discussed reading in terms of texts and readers' relationships to them and the arrangements of readers that support their thinking. In this chapter, we are concerned with reading on the inside—in the mind.

As long ago as 1908, in some of the first research ever done on reading, Edmund Burke Huey wrote that reading is thinking. Since that time, reading research has taken many turns and detours, but there still exists substantial agreement among scholars that reading is indeed thinking. When someone is not thinking, they're not reading, even if they are accurately saying the text's words aloud or to themselves. When someone is reading, they are making thoughts in dialogue with an author's thoughts. Their thoughts are not replicas of the author's originals, or direct reflections, or smooth transmissions of meaning, but they are experienced as an understanding of someone else's thoughts. Really, the reader's thoughts are of the reader's own making, through specific mental actions she undertakes in dialogue with the text (Goodman 2003; Schoenbach et al. 1999; Probst 1988; Rosenblatt 1978). Each individual reader learns those actions and develops habits of how to employ and coordinate them from her participation in a particular, local community of readers (Bomer 1996). That's why English language arts teachers are so important for developing reading lives: we create those local communities that create people's reading practices.

If students are going to get better at reading, their teachers need to understand what readers do with their minds. What are the kinds of thinking that add up to successful reading? What can a reader do, on purpose, to intensify her thinking? What can make students comprehend? You can't grab a kid by the shoulders, shake hard, and command them to "comprehend!" Comprehension is not a blunt thing that you just do. It's an outcome of an array of different intellectual actions, and literacy educators need to know what those actions might be.

The purpose of this chapter and the next is to describe a range of mental actions readers undertake. Some people have called these "reading strategies," but that phrase makes it sound as if one could read without doing these things, and I would suggest that that is not the case. These kinds of thinking are things people must do when they read in the ways we value in school. I wouldn't call them "natural," because reading itself is not natural—it's cultural. And they may not be exactly universal, because the world is full of all kinds of people, cultures, and situations. But they are common enough among those of us who know how to do school that they are worth teaching to students—as kinds of action, things to do in intricately individualized ways, not just as words to pronounce in order to get through a lesson.

Growing as a Reader for a Lifetime

Attending to one's mental actions is not necessarily a correction to some deficiency: it's a way of playing with control, a method of entertaining ideas, a way of taking delight. And anyone can grow at it. Sometimes people assume that fluent and comprehending readers don't need to engage with these metacognitive strategies, but anyone can envision, listen, or attend to expectations more than usual and, with flexibility of attention, gain more from a reading experience.

All readers, regardless of how many successful experiences with text they've had, can grow at thinking. This chapter is not just an agenda for those who find reading difficult. I, for instance, can read lots of kinds of text, even some hard ones, without paying much attention to my thinking, allowing myself to get lost in the content of what I'm reading. Still, if I read even a pretty "easy" text and really pay attention to the images I make in my mind, or the voice of the text, I can amplify and intensify my experience of that text. I'm especially weak at seeing images of what I read, but I'm pretty good at listening to text. Everyone's built differently but we often need to do things at which we are less natively strong.

Furthermore, despite my confidence about being a pretty good reader, I certainly come into contact, from time to time, with texts that can knock my confidence down a notch or two. And when I do read about, say, physics or postmodern theory, I always become more aware of thinking deliberately. I deliberately try to picture what I'm reading, whisper the sentences so I can hear them, look forward to see how much longer this section will be and what the next will be about, try to apply things I already know to what I'm reading. When we experience difficulty—and everybody does—is when we are most conscious of using mental actions strategically. But those moments are just intensifications of things we do all the time, when we read or when we think. In a sense, mental actions are mental actions. Someone tells you a story and you picture it; sometimes you can't help but have some feeling about what is coming up next. You look at hermit crabs in a terrarium, and you think about it as a character, developing your attitude toward that character, beginning to interpret its shell as "home," which it carries around wherever it goes. These are everyday kinds of thinking, they apply across disciplines and domains of life, and we are reminded of them when we make thoughts as we read.

There is a lot to know about the kinds of thinking that make high-quality reading experiences, so much that we might be tempted to make students stop reading while we explain it all to them. But, of course, that would be like trying to teach someone to drive by yanking them out of the car. Instead, we need to teach short lessons well distributed into students' work as readers. Teachers need a full and deep understanding of readerly mental actions so that they can teach them in response to what kids do. And teachers can bring a particular cognitive move into focus for the whole class by teaching a string of mini-lessons about it. I will have more to say about such minilessons at the end of the next chapter.

I'm going to discuss these readerly kinds of thinking in two categories. First, I will describe kinds of thinking that allow the reader to create and live within the world of the text. By that, I mean those mental actions that allow the reader to know what is going on, creating a solid ground of meaning. One might reasonably think of these kinds of thinking as the elements of com-prehension—the things one can do on purpose in order to understand. For my discussion in this chapter, I am grouping the following kinds of thinking in this first cate-gory of building and inhabiting the text world: envisioning, listening, expecting, monitoring, activating knowledge, and creating relationships to characters. The second cate-gory, discussed in the next chapter, will be called "reflect-ing about the world of the text." The separation is false, really, and you probably can't do any of these kinds of thinking well without doing some of the others simultaneously. But at this stage in my constantly revised theory of reading, I find it useful to divide things this way.

> **Mental Actions That Help Readers Build and Inhabit the World of the Text**
> - Envisioning
> - Listening
> - Expecting
> - Monitoring
> - Activating knowledge
> - Creating relationships to characters

All of these kinds of thinking should probably be understood as overgen-eralizations, not precise prescriptions that combine into a perfect reading event. Any two readers will do them differently (as I discuss more fully in the next chapter, under the heading Teaching These Kinds of Thinking as Inquiry). And a particular reader will assemble them in response to a particular text, according to the demands of the reading situation, the text, and the reader's history, dispo-sitions, hopes, agendas, and uniquely personal qualities. Even with all these caveats, however, there seems to be good reason to believe that helping students attend to and energize these cognitive practices might pay off in making read-ing more full of meaning and life.

Envisioning

Most readers see things in their mind's eye when they read, and all of those readers can also get better at it. Often, envisioning what the text is referring to is the essence of understanding. If you're not seeing it, you're not getting it. This is obviously true of descriptive passages, like this one:

> Marguerite's leading me through the parquet foyer into a living
> room "done" like no living room I've seen (and I've seen a few) and

that the staid Quaker exterior gives no hint of. The two big front windows have been sheathed with shiny white lacquered paneling. The walls are also lacquered white. The green-vaulted ceiling firmament has tiny recessed pin lights shining every which way, making the room bright as an operating theater. The floors are bare wood and waxed to a fierce sheen. There are no plants. The only furnishings are two immense, hard-as-granite rectilinear love seats, covered in some sort of dyed-red animal skin, situated on a square of blue carpet, facing each other across a thick slab-of-glass coffee table that actually has fish swimming inside it (a dozen lurid, fat, motionless white goldfish), the whole objet supported by an enormous hunk of curved, polished chrome, which I recognize as the bumper off a '54 Buick. (Ford 2006, 99–100)

Envisioning is also an important action in understanding descriptions of processes. Take, for instance, this description of the flow of sap through the xylem of plants, which most readers must try to envision, even though the vocabulary may be new to us:

Transpirational pull: the most important cause of xylem sap flow, is caused by the evaporation of water from the surface mesophyll cells to the atmosphere. This transpiration causes millions of minute menisci to form in the cell wall of the mesophyll. The resulting surface tension causes a negative pressure in the xylem that pulls the water from the roots and soil. (Wikipedia 2010)

We usually have to envision instructions or directions, if we hope actually to arrive at our destination. Our envisionment from the text interacts with the road we actually see before us:

As you stay on 180 East, you will be led out of the city. You will pass many stores and fruit stands, and be heading toward the foothills passing fields, scattered houses, and a couple of gas stations. You will want to fill up your gas at one of these stations.

Continue on 180/E. Kings Canyon Road. Pass through the small towns of Centerville and Minkler. Turn left at the intersection after the towns. You will see a fruit stand at this intersection and a sign pointing left that reads: Kings Canyon and Sequoia National Parks.

Narratives involving physical action also demand us to engage in visual work:

One of the men on horseback managed to pull his rifle free of the scabbard before a shell burst in his stomach, sending him back over the cantle of his saddle. His horse lunged forward and he did a somersault, landing on his feet, but his knees were already dead. The other horseman stood in the saddle of his whirling horse, firing his short-gun in all directions. When it was empty he threw it toward the thicket and spurred his horse up the shallow gulch. (Welch 1986, 294)

Even some abstract texts may be imagined diagrammatically. However difficult their concepts may be, we often work on understanding them through envisionment.

> I do not explicitly learn the propositions that stand fast for me. I can discover them subsequently like the axis around which a body rotates. This axis is not fixed in the sense that anything holds it fast, but the movement around it determines its immobility. (Wittgenstein 1969, 22e)

A kind of thinking is, in many cases, cued by the text. We turn up one kind of thinking or another in response to the reading demands of the moment, and at any particular moment in our reading, several kinds of thinking may be at once most active. I picture a reader's coordination of thinking as being sort of like an equalizer at the back of a concert—some levels up high and some almost off completely.

As always, there are exceptions to my generalizations. People who were born blind experience the world through means other than sight, and they use those other senses to compensate for the dimensions of real-life experience that are materially absent when one reads text. We live in bodies and senses, but the whole body is not present in a word; in order to bring meaning to a word, we have to bring the body back to it. In addition to the blind, a few other adult good readers have explained to me that they and people like them in fact do not think visually at all, under any circumstances. I have a hard time understanding what this must be like, even though I'm not an especially visual person, but if they say so, I have to believe them. Despite these interesting and important exceptions, it remains that most people do visualize when they think, and therefore, that it helps to do so when we read.

Listening

Texts have a sound, or voice. Effective readers cue in to the sound of the particular text they are reading, and they let its rhythm and melody carry them through sentences. Readers make their own internal monologue, the inner speech of their own thinking, conform, to some extent, to that of a text.

Naturally, people who were born deaf can and do read, and so this kind of thinking needs to be alert to the same level of human diversity we entertained discussing envisionment. It's likely that there is a range of sensitivity to sound that has nothing to do with reading as such, but for most people who have oriented their thinking and learning to hearing, listening will be a very important part of their thinking with text.

Listening, as a reader, means attending to the voice of a text—tuning in, with one's mental ear, to the way the sentences sound. I am not thinking of voice here as a quality of "good" writing, but as a quality of all texts. A news article, a poem, an entry in the encyclopedia, even the driest administrative memo—any text can be understood as having a voice. To listen is to make oneself conscious of that voice. Listening also means noticing shifts in the voice. In stories, the voice changes every time a character talks, and then again when a different character talks. It is probably pretty rare for readers to have precise ideas about what every character sounds like, but they do sense a shift in sound without exactly hearing a new vocal timbre. The voice in some texts shifts for reasons other than dialogue, too. There may be a shift from an anecdote to an explanation. Texts that are made in a pastiche form—like, say, Eliot's "The Waste Land" ([1922] 1971) or Avi's *Nothing but the Truth* (1991)—require shifts in listening to accommodate the multivoicedness of the text. The same is true of multigenre texts, such as those Tom Romano has written about (Romano 2000). To read those kinds of texts without hearing a shift in voice is to lose much of the pleasure of the text, and is also probably a good sign that the reader is not making meaning. If you don't perceive that something has happened when a scientific voice breaks into a folksy narrative, you're not getting it.

Then too, listening involves attending to the sound in narrative scenes. When readers do this, listening is related to envisionment. It's part of making the movie of the text in our minds, or more actively placing ourselves virtually into the place where the story occurs. We hear the sound of a storm and crashing waves while characters yell to each other in *The Perfect Storm*. We hear a gunshot, or the sound of someone breathing. Of course, a film director will add sound to a scene that is not given in the words, and any reader might do so as well, as an extension of listening to a text. But for some sounds actually given in a text, if a reader doesn't hear them, that reader is not experiencing the text as fully as she could.

So far, I have described listening mostly as part of the reader's experience of the text, a source of understanding and pleasure. Listening, however, is even more fundamental than that, since it creates the reader's relationship to sentences and parts thereof. One of the resources successful readers draw on as they read is the way language is supposed to sound. Take, for example, this sentence, from Adam Schwarz's story "Where Is It Written?"

> I told her I knew she might be disappointed, but I wasn't rejecting her; I only wanted to spend more time with my father, to know and love him as well as I knew her. (1994, 82)

If instead of "I told her I knew she might be disappointed," a reader read, "I told her I knew she might be disappoint," she would notice, if all was going well, that that did not sound right and correct it. The resource she would be drawing upon is what Goodman called the syntactic cueing system, the knowledge a reader always carries, if he is paying attention, about the way one's community's language goes and what it should sound like (Goodman 1967). That this cueing system operates as part of silent reading shows us a reader's habit of listening to written language.

But there is more to a reader's monitoring of sound than just checking syntax. In order to read the above sentence and understand it, readers must, on the fly, decide on the phrasing—they must hear what goes together and where there might be pauses or lifts in the flow of imagined sound. Anyone who doubts it can just try doing it wrong. For instance:

> I told her. I knew she might. Be disappointed, but I wasn't rejecting. Her I only wanted to spend. More time with my father to know? And love him as well as I knew her.

Multilingual Note
Differences in language and culture naturally shape cognition in very different ways. Though I think it would be undesirable to say that a particular ethnolinguistic group does not envision or interpret, we should imagine that it won't be for them exactly as it is for those of a different group. Listening is one kind of thinking we know will be very different, since most people are very attached to the melodies of language they have been hearing since before they were even born.

If you read it that way, it doesn't make sense. It almost seems to mean something different from the original sentence, but mostly, it just doesn't mean anything. You can fix it, but only by regrouping it mentally as you go. You have to hear it right, or else it does not sound like language. We also are most secure as meaning makers when we hear the melody of the sentence—the intonation—such that it underscores what the sentence is saying. It isn't enough to get the phrases and pauses right, if we still hear the above sentence all on the same pitch.

Intonation, stress, and phrasing in language are called *prosody*. Before babies even learn to say words, they babble in the prosody in which they have been immersed. Usually, their parents and other caregivers have been speaking to them in exaggerated prosody (so-called *motherese*), wherein the upward inflections go way up and the melodies of language have larger musical intervals than adult speech usually has. This dimension of the sound of language seems to be foundational to our experience of talk and meaning (Schreiber 1991). Prosody is not just actors' decoration on sentences; it is the way we organize thought structures in relation to one another within and among sentences. It is structure and meaning.

Prosody is also considered an aspect of reading fluency. Too often, especially with older readers, fluency is thought of as speedy mechanical competence. As seems ever to be the case with reading, the aspects that are easier to measure are the ones that end up counting the most in "accountability systems." For more on listening, see Bomer (2006).

Expecting

From the moment they pick up a text, readers begin predicting, making informed guesses about what will be in this and how it will go. As they read along, they have some scheme of probability in mind—the way an overture in a musical or opera lets you know what the rest of the music will sound like. If the text were an explanation about eighteenth-century weddings, and in the third section, a passage narrating a spaceship's landing appeared, a competent reader would notice and think something was amiss. That is because we mostly understand texts as being unitary and coherent. We think that a reading of a text is an experience of one totality, and so we shape our minds to the totality. We have to predict, then, in order to know our current place on the map of the way through this text.

Readers build expectations partly upon their constantly shifting understanding of how the text has been going up until now. Because we understand things that have happened so far in a narrative, we have some ideas about the range of things that are likely to come. At least we have questions we think we'll probably have answered by the end. Even if our expectations like this are sometimes thwarted, we do have the expectations nonetheless.

Also, expectations arise from our experience of reading texts like this one. If we are reading an encyclopedia article about rats, we might expect that a section of the article will be about how rats reproduce, because we've read other texts all about a particular species and that is one of the predictable parts of that kind of text. (See Calling Other Texts to Mind, in Chapter 6.) Sometimes, moreover, a text cues us to predict something is going to happen in a narrative, through foreshadowing, or through some clue dropped in a mystery. Or a gun gets loaded in the first act that we expect will go off by the third. It is always the transaction between reader and text that prompts a particular kind of thinking, and these text-invoked instances of expecting are good examples of that fact.

Time and Reading

To say that readers have expectations draws attention to the fact that every present moment contains a future. This page suggests future pages, this part of the world reaches toward potentialities. Everything is in the process of becoming. If I understand the past of this world, I can't help but have expectations about its possible futures, except if I'm just sitting passively, letting it all float by.

Readers do not necessarily predict the way a gambler bets on a horse, with specificity and certainty; rather, they entertain a range of possibilities about how the text might go. I have seen some classroom practices that seem to ask students to predict in this narrow kind of way, and you probably have seen this, too. After a chapter is over, the teacher asks, "What do you think is going to happen next?" It's clear that the teacher is using knowledge of the reading process to pose this question. But the kids answer with very specific predictions about what will happen next, and then they're right or wrong as they read along. It really is like a wager on a boxing match. When they're right, they sometimes slap each other five. Perhaps it's better than complete passivity. But this behavior does not feel like the level of predicting or expecting I do when I read or that I think anyone should really do when reading aesthetically. Have you ever been to the movies and sat in front of someone who could not stop predicting? "Ooh, he's going to be in the closet! This is not going to be good." You want to turn around and say, "Just. Watch. The. Movie." Mature readers, I think, want people, especially with narratives, to be open enough to uncertainty and to the unfolding nature of experience just to let the story happen.

Often, effective readers try to build a broad outline of what's likely to be in this text, before they start attending to details. They might read very quickly the first time through, or just skim across the big points of what they are going to read, like looking at a whole map before striking out on a journey. This deliberate futuring is reflective of the use of expectation in a text. We need to understand the text as a totality, to have the whole thing together, and prediction is really an effort to get our arms around it all at once—to totalize this text. Working with students who aren't making all they could of the whole text, it's sometimes helpful to talk very specifically about expectations. With most readers, it's more instructive to keep this talk open and tentative, with a "let's see . . ." kind of attitude.

Monitoring

Effective readers check in on themselves as they read, making sure that the text is adding up to meaning for them. When they have stopped making sense, they notice and either attempt to correct their understanding, stop reading, or decide temporarily to ignore the confusion and see if the whole makes sense as they read further. This is something that many adolescents who struggle with reading do not do. For many such readers, a state of confusion when reading in school is so normal, so much the usual state of things, that they don't really see it as anything to address. The text rolls off them like water off a duck's back, because reading (at least in school) never makes sense. The expectation of meaninglessness is confirmed every time they read and so does not feel like a problem.

I notice myself monitoring for sense almost every night. I read when I go to bed, and often, I don't get far into the book before I realize that I have no idea what has been going on in the last few chapters. Sometimes, I'm even hearing voices and words that aren't on the page, and I say to myself, through the haze of fatigue, "Hey, that doesn't make sense. It doesn't go with the rest of the book." And then I stop reading and go to sleep. I've come to realize that many people who struggle with text have that kind of experience all the time—of the text not really making sense, of pages going by that don't mean anything. But for them, it seems normal, not like a realization that the system has broken down.

Continuous Self-Assessment

Monitoring, as a kind of thinking, is a form of self-assessment. We monitor our reading life, as well as our understanding of a particular text. We make sure that the things we are reading generally fit with who we are as a reader. We know the kinds of books and reading experiences that work for us, the kind that do not.

Part of the reason students come to feel so settled, perhaps hopeless, in that state of being is that school demands it of them. Given homework or a reading assignment during class time, they often are asked to approach the text completely passive—read to the end of Chapter 3. So they start reading, with no thoughts active, just doing what they were told, beginning at the top of the page and putting their eyes on the print to the bottom. Let's say they put in their time, dutifully, "reading" word after word, sentence after sentence. All they are asked to do is get to the end, to put their eyes on all the words, and presumably, to say the words to themselves. Never mind that the words don't answer any question they have, that they really aren't asked to care about what they're reading, that they have no purpose, nothing to head toward out of this eye-on-print conscripted service. This happens all the time with many college students, as well. They're given a reading assignment, and they dutifully carry it out. But they really don't know much about what they have read, because all they really did was put in time saying the words to themselves.

When a reader successfully monitors for sense, she continually recommits to the experience of understanding, of meaning. She continually self-assesses the quality of this experience and weighs the importance of the outcome of her assessment. If she's momentarily confused but she decides it doesn't matter to the total reading experience, she may keep reading. If she's confused but it's not worth the time to repair the confusion, she may keep reading. But when the reading situation is motivated and purposeful and the reader is engaged, the reader will make the overall experience make sense, even if there are some confusing spots along the way.

Activating Knowledge

Words on a page can only summon a world we know—they cannot install it in us. So readers must activate whatever knowledge they can, in order to fit what they read with their preexisting understanding. This kind of thinking is sometimes referred to as "using prior knowledge," but that expression seems redundant to me. If you have the knowledge, then you don't need to say it's "prior," do you? It's just knowledge. And it's sometimes called "background knowledge," but that seems inaccurate to what we want to emphasize. We don't want to tell kids to keep this knowledge in the background; we want to teach them to make it active and usable. Literacy educators, especially English language arts teachers, should care about the words they use to communicate with students, and the fact that terminology is already fossilized in the profession may be a reason to examine whether those words are doing the job they should. Here, the action we want readers to learn seems to be *activating knowledge*.

In addition to examining our own language, we need to listen carefully to the ways students speak when they talk about their interior reading processes. Too often, their language too becomes fossilized and uninhabited: "Ooh, Miss, I made a text-to-world connection!" The trouble is, this can easily become cant, just procedural display, the demonstration that they know what their teachers want and they're willing to supply. To keep all our thinking supple and accountable, we need to keep opening up the language, asking for more detailed description, asking students what they mean by the words they use, especially when they're the very words we taught them and expect from them.

Readers who have difficulty making sense of text often may successfully read the words of a text but fail to connect it to the knowledge they already have (Santman 2005). They read about a party and have little or no expectation about what might appear in the text about partying, not believing in their own experience and knowledge as relevant to something that would appear in a book. The text, then, is beyond an arm's length for them—distant and irrelevant and meager in meaning. What they need to do is think—on purpose, for a while—about their own experience of parties, the parties they know of but have not been to, what they know about parties and the language that surrounds them. Then, they can return to the party in the text and more nearly experience it.

To be efficient at using their knowledge, readers may consciously tap into the pockets of knowledge they think will be relevant to this text. They will use

Knowledge and Difference

To arrive at a truly shared understanding of a text, a community of readers would need to be drawing upon shared knowledge. That is why so often our understandings don't match those of other readers—and it's why discussion and negotiation can be so enlightening, as we come nearer to shared knowledge and assumptions—or at least more insightful about differences—looking again at the same words. Reading independently, by contrast, we simply have to rely on the knowledge we have as an individual.

whatever knowledge they have that seems analogous, even if it's not exactly accurate for this text. So if they are reading about killer whales but really don't know anything about killer whales *per se*, they may draw upon something they saw about dolphins or sharks. They bring what they have to the table, regardless of whether it's exactly what was on the menu. This willingness to compare the known to the new is what allows us to bootstrap ourselves into new knowledge—using what we have as an analogy until we get an accurate enough picture of the new material. But if we always had to bring accurate information with us to the reading event, we would never be able to learn anything new from text.

The knowledge readers bring to text is not precise and fully assembled beforehand. It's there just in case it's useful, tentative, potential. Readers employ their knowledge responsively, in an ongoing dialogue with the text's content and meaning. They habitually check what they read against what they know about that kind of thing.

Creating Relationships to Characters

When there are people in a text, the reader develops a relationship to those people. We do this in very much the way we would with a person in the face-to-face world (Hynds 1989, 1997). We may like or dislike a character, or wonder things about them. Sometimes, reading a biography or narrative, what keeps a reader hanging on is waiting for particular characters to come back. Sometimes, the world of a text can be almost unbearable because we just cannot stand these people. People in texts frustrate us with their bad choices, and raise our hopes with their desires and ambitions. We are social beings, and so of course we bring those habits of thinking to our reading. These relationships are an important source of the energy that propels many readers through a text.

Character and Identity

Exploring the boundaries of our own identities, we may think characters are like us or not like us, that a particular character either is or is not our kind of person. We identify, or we push away. This negotiation of who we are, and who we are like, is an important purpose for reading for many people.

Sometimes, the narrator's voice or the author is a personal presence to the reader. Our relationship to the text's speaker, the person doing the talking, is the center of our engagement with the text—almost as if we are reading a letter from someone we know. And sometimes, the reader does this kind of work even if the text does not prompt it. I am not explicitly writing about particular characters right now, for example, but you are still populating these words with relationships, imagining yourself, other readers you know, your students, and the social worlds you inhabit.

William Zinsser, in his classic book, *On Writing Well* (1976), advises nonfiction writers to find the characters in what they are writing about, even if it

100

seems like an impersonal topic. And if you think about it, many nonfiction writers do this. If they are writing about a technology, a business, or an institution, they find characters who bring it to life, making what is unfamiliar more approachable by creating people the reader can relate to. When that's the way writers work, it will be the way readers think, as well.

It may be the case that some readers are more prone to this social kind of thinking than others. In early work on reader response, some scholars (Flynn 1986) suggested that this relational kind of reading was more common among female readers. They were building upon Gilligan's (1982) finding that women reasoned in more relational ways, as opposed to a more objectifying kind of abstraction that males had for centuries promoted as logical and ethical. I suspect that it is common for most men also to form relationships to characters, even if there are more specific gendered differences, and I'm equally sure that there are some women who would say this is not really part of their reading process. Still, questions about gender differences are always interesting to carry into one's classroom.

We are used to living in a world populated by others, keeping up with what they are doing, forming judgments about them, feeling in response to them. Far from being a solitary endeavor, reading involves importing our knowledge from that social world into our transaction with the text. What we bring to a text will always be populated, by those we have known and those we expect to meet.

This chapter has described some of the kinds of thinking that readers do as they build and inhabit the world of a text. In the next chapter, we'll take a step back away from that world, and examine how readers think in response to the text, or about the text as an object.

> ## TECHNOLOGY NOTE
>
> Digital environments, especially the Internet, provide new and complex purposes, contexts, and social landscapes for reading that do not negate the kinds of thinking discussed here, but they do condition and shape thinking differently than a book or print environment. These contextual, environmental differences far outweigh the superficial ones of page versus screen that get so much attention when people talk about reading in new environments, even though the materials and tools are also changing in important ways.

CHAPTER 6

Teaching Toward Interpretive Reading

Here, we turn to the second major category for considering kinds of thinking readers do. This category takes a step back from the world of the text, as we consider intellectual moves a reader makes in thinking *about* the text—making judgments and interpretations, organizing this text in relation to other ones, and formulating answers back to the ways the text represents the world. I will include in this discussion the following kinds of thinking: remembering; connecting to other texts; interpreting; developing and pursuing questions or topics of inquiry; and critiquing social worlds. Now, it is not the case that a reader *envisions* (a kind of thinking discussed in the previous chapter) and then moves on to *interpret* (a kind of thinking in the second). In fact, envisionment always involves some interpreting; you couldn't picture things if you didn't fill in many of the ideas that the writer has left unsaid. And it's certainly not the case that *envisionment* is a seventh-grade skill and *interpreting* a tenth-grade one. People begin to interpret in early childhood and continue to do so all their lives. The first category is not lower or prior to the second. The convenience in arranging the categories in this order concerns the degree to which, in the first category, the reader is inside the text world and subject to its influence. In the second, the reader has assumed a slightly different stance, stepping back out of that world to get a perspective on it. As Scholes (1986) made clear, these moves are useful for readers at any stage of development, and at any point in the reading of a particular text.

Calling Other Texts to Mind

One of the ways we develop our expectations of what might be in a text, and one of the sources of our active knowledge, is our memory of other texts we have read. Those texts may be much like the one we are presently reading, or they may be oral stories, movies, or TV shows. I'm going to give an extended example of this kind of reading in the paragraphs to come. I don't expect any particular individual reader to make the same connections to other texts that I make or even to understand most of my references. That is the point. Each one of us will draw actively upon different intertextual resources when we read. What is important is that we draw upon *some* web of connections to varied texts—whether those be books, other written material, movies, art, or stories from our grandparents.

I pick up *Red Glass* by Laura Resau (2007). It's a young adult novel, and I've read lots of that kind of book before, so I know it will have young characters, most likely thrust into situations where they have to act independently in ways that make them take risks, learn, and grow. The title is pretty spare, so I have to do a little work to make it bring anything to mind. It actually makes me think of *Raise the Red Lantern*, which is Chinese, and *Red Glass* seems like it could be the title of something Asian, though this book is about Mexico. It also makes me think of "red light districts," which is a concept I really only know from other texts, but that's not likely here. I try to think whether I have ever seen a painting with red glass or an image from a film, but I come up pretty dry for direct associations to that, so I let it go. Sometimes titles can bring up memories of other texts, but this one isn't doing so for me. I might be able to draw upon personal memory or on general knowledge about red glass, but here I'm focusing my thinking on how I can use other texts as a resource in thinking about this book—the intertextual thinking I can do.

I know that Resau writes about Mexico but that she's a white U.S. citizen and that brings up a few (surprisingly few) other writers I know like that, such as Harriet Doerr and a book I recently read by Charles Portis called *The Dog of the South*. Once I start thinking about those writers, I think of the tensions in Caucasian U.S. Americans writing about Mexico—that the necessity of writing about the differences and the otherness in the encounter raises the possibility of

---

Mental Actions That Help Readers Think Further About the World of the Text

- Calling other texts to mind
- Remembering autobiographical experience
- Developing and pursuing questions or topics of inquiry
- Interpreting: developing hunches and following them
- Critiquing social worlds and assumptions

---

seeming racist or of exoticizing and romanticizing Mexicans. I think of characters from Mexico who are represented mostly with great respect, though there is always a mystery, because their motives and real thoughts are unknown to the white narrator. As is the case with summoning any kind of knowledge to the fore as one begins a book, I'm not really sure whether any of this will apply. It's just a consciousness of other books that helps this text to fit into a network of other, possibly related, ones. I'm already curious about how some issues are going to be handled in this book, just thinking about others I know. I don't want to impose them too strongly, because the work of art has to speak for itself, but I do have these tentative questions as I begin.

So I open the book to begin reading, and I see that before the page on which the first chapter begins, there is a part 1 page, with its own title, "The Desert," and an epigraph. I have read other novels that are divided into parts like this. No particular one comes to mind right away, though I could remember if I thought about it; what's important is the structure—I get it how this is going to go. These parts are superordinate units of meaning and time. I am asked to stop and consider in between, to ask how this larger chunk works with the smaller and larger parts. And this epigraph is from *The Little Prince* by Saint-Exupery, which I've read, though it's been a long time. I do remember that there is a substantial part in the desert (the title of Part 1), mostly because I remember those illustrations. I look ahead to the first page of Resau's Part 2 and see that its epigraph is from *The Little Prince*, too. So that makes me think I should see what I can remember about that book. I'm not going to go get it, just to start this other book, but I seem to remember that he's precious, emotional, otherworldly (coming from an asteroid and all), lonely, doesn't belong anywhere, and he's riding around on a spaceship. He speaks in very poetic language, as he's doing in this epigraph, which he addresses the narrator (or reader) for some of the book, and that he dies or goes away at the end. It's interesting to me, too, that this French story is working explicitly as an intertext in this novel about the U.S. and Mexico.

I begin Chapter 1, which is entitled "Sleeping with the Chickens." That makes me think of movies I have seen with rural people, usually from countries other than the U.S., living with their chickens in the house. Asian and Latin American countries come to mind as the contexts for these received images. And reports about avian flu also come to mind, since that kind of contact with birds is likely to be a source. Though it wouldn't ordinarily be this conscious in

Reading in a Web of Texts

This intertextual thinking is important because we live in a world that is, increasingly, populated by texts—we speak to one another and make meaning via an intricate system of reference, analogy, quotation, and citation of other texts. The more connection we have to one another—via the Internet, popular culture, and so many other texts—the more we must draw on that web to make meaning. So calling other texts explicitly to mind—which has been important since medieval times—is increasingly crucial for our students.

my mind, I suppose I associate sleeping with chickens with third-world poverty (though I also know that in much of the developing world, having chickens means it is not poverty). The chapter's narrative begins:

> Even before the boy appeared, I thought about the people crossing the desert. I imagined how scrub brush scratched their legs as they walked at night, how the sun dried out their eyes during the day, how their hearts pounded when they threw their bodies to the ground, hiding from la migra. I imagined them pressing their cheeks against the dust, thinking about the happy lives they would have if only they reached the end of this desert. (Resau 2007, 3)

This is immediately recognizable to me as drawing upon narratives of people crossing the border on foot, across the Chihuahuan desert into the U.S. southwestern states. I know it from textual experience, not direct experience. Because I live in one of those states, I have heard people describe such experiences, and that's mostly where I know the phrase *la migra*—border patrol. So some of the texts that come to mind are oral. I've also seen movies that represent the physical conditions and the feeling of being far from other people who could help: *El Norte*; *Mojados: Through the Night*; *Sangre de mi Sangre*; *Babel*; *Lone Star*; *The Three Burials of Melquiades Estrada*; *No Country for Old Men*. These images immediately come to mind when I read the paragraph above, because its language activates memories from those other texts—movies. Thinking about them, I can picture the scrub brush and cacti, the dust and rock, the sun, the dusty skin and chapped lips, the jugs of water. So there is much in my mind that is not explicitly in the text. And that is how reading happens. The reader is constantly restoring much that is missing from the written word.

Also, readers, as soon as they begin reading, have an idea of how this text is going to be structured and what it is going to sound like. Those structural predictions, including genre, help them to create a space of thinking in their minds that has the shape of this text. One way that readers can make these structural expectations clearer and more explicit in their minds is by thinking more deliberately about how other texts are built, even getting those texts out and skimming across them to be reminded of the similarities and differences between the structure of the old text and the new one. For thinking about the architecture of *Red Glass*, I could look at the ways chapters are divided and then at that superordinate structure of Part I, Part II. And the language of that first chapter does plenty to set up expectations for plot structure, since the introductory clause lets me know that a boy is going to "appear."

It's sometimes tempting to think that we adults have all this stuff in our minds and that kids don't have anything because they haven't been alive as long, or because they haven't read the right books or seen the right films, or because they play too many video games, or have too few experiences. To be sure, kids will have different things in their minds. But they will have something, and whether or not their existing knowledge is an exact match for that of the author of the text they are reading, it's what this reader has to work with, and it will do. The job of the teacher is to teach them to use what is in their minds, to formulate questions, guesses, hypotheses, and approximations on the basis, partly, of the other texts that this one brings to mind, whether they are books or stories, song lyrics or fairy tales, movies or television commercials. Their initial attempts will be sketchy and uncertain; and they will get better at it as they read more texts thinking this way.

Remembering Autobiographical Experience

A reader's knowledge about a topic, feeling, or domain of experience includes memories related to it from her own life. Reading a story reminds us of experiences that are analogous—kind of the same in some way. We read about grief and remember our own moments of grief, about love, and recall our own. This is often one of the great pleasures of reading fiction or memoir: the ability to revisit our own past within the structure of a fixed, organized story.

Knowledge and Memory

Autobiographical remembering is closely related as the activation of knowledge I discussed in the previous section—and it's also related to calling other texts to mind. After all, memories of experiences and memories of texts are kinds of knowledge. But we usually think of knowledge as a bit more organized and memory as a more embodied sense, something that might rise to consciousness incidentally, more charged with emotion and relationship, imbued with awareness of how time passed as we experienced something.

Even if we are reading nonfiction, we draw upon personal memories. If I read about sharks, though I have, thankfully, no personal encounters to remember, I do think of what it's like to be under salt water; I remember seeing dolphins swimming in water. Reading that sharks are propelled by a constant need to feed, I remember what it's like to feel hunger. It may be the case that, as you read this, you are remembering reading experiences of your own, and conversations with others about those reading experiences. Those may not be memories full of feeling and important identity themes, but they are autobiographical experiences upon which you draw to make sense of what you are reading. Far from being distractions, these memories are necessary to the understanding of read text, especially when the memories are congruent to important ideas in the text.

The management of the move between personal connections and the otherness of the text world is complex and difficult for most people. If we focus so intently on the text and do not attend to our memories, then we may fail to make even literal sense of the text—fail to interpret—and certainly miss much of the only-alluded-to world it means to invoke. We will have difficulty knowing what is important in the text and what the significance is of the important parts. Then again, if we indulge too much of our memory, we lose the sense of what is new for us in this experience, overwhelming the text with our own preconceptions. We become lost in what was already familiar to us at the expense of really listening, attending to someone else's words, as if when listening to a friend, we wandered off in our own thoughts. (A close friend would complain.) Either of those extremes represents a failure to grow. But even apart from the extremes, most readers are usually teetering in one direction or the other, now tending more to see themselves, now fixating on the text and not attending to relevant experience. The perfectly balanced transaction is probably a myth, because attention is always selective—we choose what to think about.

Developing and Pursuing Questions or Topics of Inquiry

As we read, we start to wonder about things, and these wonderings help fuel our journey through a text. We read in hope of getting an answer to our questions. In the beginning of *The Hunger Games*, for instance, we hear about an event called "The Reaping," which seems to have everyone pretty bothered. If we are reading actively when we first hear about it, a question opens up in our minds: what is this reaping, and how does it connect to the bigger things going on, like the games in the novel's title? For a short while, we read with this question open, collecting small clues, until the scene comes that settles that question—and opens lots of others. Our reading proceeds like this, fueled by wondering and trying to find out, perhaps never completely satisfied, even after the final word of a text. Our engagement is driven by desire.

At least, that's the case when all is going well. Some young readers have trouble catching onto this habit of opening up and pursuing questions as they read. They get started reading a magazine article, and no questions begin taking shape; they don't wonder about anything. Pressed to answer a question about their questions, they may say they're wondering about a simple thing—how old he is, what they eat—that really is not going to pull them far in the text. They need to develop more substantial questions that will fuel their quest for discovery over a longer time. As we will see with the kind of thinking I call interpreting, growth at questioning involves moving to a somewhat more abstract level of thinking. This skill at opening high-quality questions is important not just in literary thinking, but in science, social studies, math, and other areas of inquiry. And it's not enough to receive good questions from the teacher; to become an independent reader with a rich reading life outside school, each student needs to become a questioner, a wonderer, a fully engaged inquirer.

In practical terms, students at any moment in a journey through a text should be able to brainstorm possible questions. Then, they should be able to evaluate those questions and select one, two, or three of them that are actually investigable, to which they can't find a simple answer because they're the kind of question that needs thought over time, with consideration of evidence. They should then be able to sustain their interest in those questions, coming back to them frequently to see if they are still the right ones to be asking. Can those questions be addressed with this text? Are the questions still open and interesting; are they still fuel for reading? Maybe some seemed important at first but now have become irrelevant or just trivial. Readers interested in thinking more about the quality of teachers' questions—and therefore students' learning to ask questions—should read Leila Christenbury's chapter about this in her book *Making the Journey: Being and Becoming a Teacher of English Language Arts* (2006).

Whose Questions Count?

For students to have sufficient opportunities to engage in shaping questions, teachers need, first, to resist being the questioner. Whenever there need to be questions, teachers can ask students to come up with them—and then lead them in a serious evaluation of their level of thoughtfulness. Teaching students the difference between low-level, fact-based questions and interpretive, investigative questions would also teach them something very important about reading.

There are also times when the question or agenda is what brought the reader to this text in the first place. This questioning, then, is not cued by the text so much as by the reader's intentions. When a student has chosen a text—or even collaborated on that choice with a partner or small group—she had the wondering going even before putting her eyes on the print. There may be a very focused question, like how do I know if I have this disease, or there may be a more general curiosity, like I'd like to know more about moths. The question may be what else Katherine Paterson does with religion in her novels, or what does it feel like to be in the other worlds Rick Riordan creates, or whether Mark Twain is as funny as my grandfather says he is. When students are reading out of their own intentions, it's often not a struggle to get them to bring questions to the book. (It is, admittedly, sometimes hard to get them to admit out loud that they are curious about anything in a book.) Often, though, even with independent reading, teachers do find that they need to help students more often *use* the questions they brought to the text, to think with them as they read. Asking investigable questions can connect us to the asking of interpretive questions, and interpreting is the next form of thinking we will explore.

Interpreting: Developing Hunches and Following Them

English teachers are acculturated to value interpreting highly, to think that a text's interpretation is the reason it exists in the first place. But an interpretation, of course, doesn't really belong to the text. It's a product of something a reader has done. Consequently, we serve our students better by teaching them the process of interpreting rather than our own (or some other expert's) interpretations of texts.

Interpreting is not only something people do when they read literature. There could not be a legal system without interpretive thinking about legislation, the Constitution, and other documents that serve as law. And interpreting is a part of everyday life and language (Hanks 1996). If your partner says to you, "It's cold in here. Is the window open?" and you see that the window is indeed open, then you close it. How did you know that was what you were supposed to do? The words "close the window" were not part of the utterance. No text, even the most explicit-seeming one, completely states all its assumptions, connections, or implications. Every language act contains fewer words than are possible about that topic and context. Listeners and readers always have to put meaning together from the wider world and restore the wholeness that is lost when booming and buzzing life becomes language—or when speech loses its melodies, facial expressions, and gestures, and becomes text. Any receptive language act, then, involves mentally putting back what has been left out. That is interpreting. Interpreting means restoring what has gone missing, putting back from our common knowledge the unspoken or unwritten dimensions of a communicative act.

Lists of reading strategies often leave off interpretation and include inference (see for instance Keene and Zimmermann 2007; Keene 2008; Olson and Land 2007; Pearson and Gallagher 1983; Pearson, Roehler, Dole, and Duffy 1992; Pressley and Afflerbach 1995). The two notions are similar in that they are both moments when a reader puts back meanings that have been left out of the words. *Inference*, ordinarily, is a term that describes filling in much closer to the literal meaning of a particular sentence or string of sentences, and *interpretation* is more often used to describe an attempt to construct an understanding of the overall point—or some set of large, encompassing concerns—in a whole text or collection of texts. They're nearly the same act, however, the filling in of the blank spaces of meaning in language.

From very early on in a reading event, a reader starts to get a feeling about *what this text is really all about*, or *what the author is trying to say*, or *what I'm supposed to be understanding on a level that transcends just the events of this text.* This feeling is the beginning of interpreting, and following those little, tentative hunches until evidence begins to confirm or disconfirm them is the process of building a reading. A reader's interpretation changes as the text moves along, as long as it is not frozen by someone else having so-called right answers. Just as the significant questions to ask shift across a reading event, so does the thinking produced through interpreting, as the reader attends to new information and discards guesses that seem out of place now.

How Parallel Texts Aid Interpretation

Thinking through autobiographical stories or the other texts that connect to this one can aid in interpretation. Asking *what do those two stories have in common?* forces the reader to make a more abstract statement about the story being read, a statement that is large enough to hold two stories underneath it. Such a statement sometimes makes a step toward interpretation.

Interpretations vary from reader to reader, because our appraisal of what gaps in a text need to be filled in varies from reader to reader. Still, how persuasive an interpretation is to a community of readers (who demand substantiation from what is shared, i.e., the words of the text) is a test of their validity or usefulness (Fish 1980; Rabinowitz and Smith 1998). An initial interpretive comment may be nothing more than a Rorschach test, providing information only about the commenter. But when she can point to parts of the inkblot that made her say what she said, others may begin to see it, too, even if it is not what came to their minds in the first place. This expanding sense of possibility in a text is the stuff of rich discussions, about literature, about ideas, about beliefs and values. Sometimes, a number of people in one discussion may come to share one big idea or group of ideas, but that is not the only purpose of the discussion, and that big idea is not valued because it is the only correct one or the only one with the power of the teacher behind it.

Critiquing Social Worlds and Assumptions

Every text and every reading event exists in a set of social relations and political relationships. A reader has more or less power than the author or other readers, is situated in a huge web of relationships that position him as strong or needy, experiences a text world as making a statement on her own life experience. Texts also portray social and political relationships that exist in the world. Someone is central, others marginal; some groups are represented as normal, others as deviant; the social world is fixed and final or in transition, subject to revision. Readers need to be able to detect social and political themes and relations in texts and ask whether they are fair, ask who benefits from this representation of reality, and ask whether the ideology of the text is one that represents their own interests or the interests of a common good. Texts may also cause us to ask new questions about fairness and justice in the world.

Many see this kind of critical reasoning as the ultimate goal of reading instruction in a democracy (Bomer and Bomer 2001).

Every text is partial, in both senses of the word—that it favors some people and that it's never the whole story. A novel can only let us know about a slice of the social world, no matter how sprawling its canvas. What is included is what the author privileges, but there are other possible thoughts, ones the author excludes, that a reader might add back in. The fact that we can name its partiality doesn't mean we shouldn't like it. But we should try to identify the shape of a text's incompleteness and tell what is being omitted. A website is always written, posted, and maintained by someone with an agenda—something they'd like to see happen in the world, which motivated them to post the text in the first place. Texts are always motivated, located, and structured by interested parties—even songs, poems, love stories, chatty letters, and other kinds of writing that may seem innocent and non-political. They ask the reader to buy into a version of reality, to accept certain givens and attitudes toward those givens. There is nothing evil or malicious about this (usually): it's just the nature of language.

> **TECHNOLOGY NOTE**
>
> Since everyone writes with agendas, readers need to approach texts with a determination to sniff out the purposes and commitments encoded in the text. Critical reading on the Internet is even more important perhaps than with books, because there are often none of the traditional, institutional publishing filters between anyone with a computer and the readers in our classrooms.

Because texts often do not come right out and announce their agendas, it is important to teach students critical habits of reading. And even when texts *do* frankly state their perspectives and purposes, powerful readers must have ways of assessing a text's role in creating the world this reader hopes to inhabit. Being able to think about oneself as entitled, indeed obliged, to make such judgments does not come naturally to most people. And a habit of thinking actively about *what kind of world we should share* is also not something people are born with. These are democratic dispositions, and as democratic theorist Benjamin Barber puts it:

> We are inescapably embedded in families, tribes, and communities. As a consequence, we must *learn* to be free. That is to say, we must be taught liberty. We are born small, defenseless, unthinking children. We must be taught to be thinking, competent, legal persons and citizens. We are born belonging to others; we have to learn how to sculpt our individuality from common clay. . . . The literacy to live in civil society, the competence to participate in democratic communities, the ability to think critically and act deliberately in a pluralistic world, the empathy that permits us to hear and thus accommodate others, all involve skills that must be acquired. (1992, 4)

When students read literature, perhaps even more than most times in their schooling, they hold in their minds other people's visions of the world. Their habits of entertaining these visions, negotiating their perspectives with the reader's own, and then further negotiating with other readers about what is available to think in response, can contribute to the competencies Barber describes.

But how does one *teach* people to think in the interest of democracy? I've found it helpful, as Katherine Bomer and I discussed in *For a Better World: Reading and Writing for Social Action* (2001), to teach critical reading by teaching students to hold certain ideas in mind. And more recently, I've been thinking that there are three foundational concepts in a critical perspective that are especially useful to make explicit to students: groups, power, and fairness. Without these ideas, students' attempts to read critically can be disorganized and driven only by feelings of being bothered by people's meanness rather than a habit of analyzing critically the systems of privilege and oppression that may be naturalized in texts. With these concepts in mind, no matter what they read, students can use that trio of ideas as a parallel text to lay alongside the text under investigation. The ideas do not tell them what to think about a particular text; they just provide some commonly understood values that might not otherwise come to mind when reading. I'm suggesting here that teachers explain these concepts to groups of readers, discuss them apart from books, and then see how they inform the readers' thinking and conversations in response to texts.

1. Groups

In order to have a vision of *social* justice—or social anything else—it is essential to first develop the concept that people always, necessarily, live their lives as members of groups. Any person can be viewed as the person they are—an individual—and at the same time as a member of many overlapping groups. Part of the way an individual gets to be *herself* is by picking up the attitudes, beliefs, and feelings of the group or groups she belongs to, by being like others around her. Some groups are pretty clearly defined in most people's thinking: males, females, Latinos, blacks, whites, Asians, poor, rich, gay, straight. We are pretty much born into those categories. Even though these categories seem rigid in our culture, they are often more fluid in particular people's experiences, since for a particular period of a person's life, it's possible to feel closely allied with groups other than the ones we are born into. We are members of a gender group, a racial group, and a class group, but many of us have complex, overlapping memberships even in those categories. In addition to those groups we inhabit from birth, we also choose some groups, and people should be able to form purposeful, emotionally significant connections with others—in other groups beyond their own group. We may form alliances with members of the group "joggers" along with people from other gender, race, and class groups. We can then act to make our lives better as joggers, without being divided by our differences.

Being able to see people as members of groups, not just as solitary individuals, can, by itself, change the way we read. Though nothing can keep us from enjoying characters as individuals, we can also see them as representations of a female, or as Latino, as deaf, or as poor. A social lens can give us an additional way of looking at stories and represented worlds, whether fiction or nonfiction. Though no single member of a group can be taken as an emblem of the whole group—that's stereotyping—it is worthwhile to investigate the ways authors represent groups—what they are like and how they are situated with respect to other groups.

2. Power

For a social perspective to become *critical*, it has to be able to give an account of power and its distribution among different groups. When one group gets more money, more political offices, more control of media, more control of institutions (like schools and churches), more chances to make decisions that affect other people's lives, they have more power. And a group that has more power gets its perspective accepted as if it's the only way things could (or should) ever be. Those folks' perspective just comes to seem natural—as if nature made things the way they are. Because of money, control of the military, control of police, and control of information, groups in power can force others to accept their point of view, or at least force them to pretend to. This is true not just in dystopian worlds like that of *The Giver*, though it's especially obvious in such works; it's also just as valid a perspective for reading works that do not attempt to force us to see such dynamics. But I would suggest that those works that keep power and its dynamics hidden are participating in the naturalization of the perspective of the group in power—making everything seem fine and dandy, obscuring the workings of power.

Changes in power relationships—and emancipation for groups who are disadvantaged—can only occur through the work of groups. And because only groups can change things, talking about people only as individuals helps to keep power relations just as they are. That means that most narratives, since they tend to focus us on the misfortunes and heroic acts of individuals, are necessarily incomplete in that they posit that problems can be solved by solitary heroes. We need to be able to add, in our thinking, an imagining of big groups working together to create new social worlds. We can love stories of individual striving, but we need also to imagine collective action in response to oppressive circumstances, because individualistic stories might prevent us from engaging in the only sort of work that can produce real social transformation—and more justice.

3. Fairness

We might think of social justice as fairness among groups. That's slightly different from the justice among individuals that criminal and civil law are concerned with. Here, we're thinking of fairness that can mitigate the power imbalances among different groups. Justice, or fairness, is a different kind of concept from those of *groups* or *power*, because where the previous concepts are ways of thinking about how things *are*, fairness asks us to think about how things *should be*. Justice concerns itself with *oughts*. People in groups, for example, should have similar chances to have a happy life. No people should have to struggle too much just to keep their bodies healthy. No particular group should be more physically vulnerable to harm or deprivation than any other group. Being smaller, in size or number, should not reduce someone's chances of pursuing happiness, and more powerful groups should not get in the way of less powerful groups' going after their purposes (assuming the less powerful groups' purposes do not include the oppression of some other groups). People who hurt others or keep them from living fully should make it up to them. Members of stronger groups should care about and work for the interests of more vulnerable groups, and other people's pain should always be significant to people, even if the other people are from a different race, gender, class, nationality, or set of beliefs. Working to make those *oughts* become realized in the actual world would be work in the interests of justice.

Likewise, attention to the groups represented in texts and their power relations is not just a cold exercise in counting up the benefits to a particular group or the disadvantages accruing to another. There is a moral pressure in critical reading toward wishing for a just outcome—imagining a fairer world and thinking through the shortcomings of the worlds represented in a text. Furthermore, when reading critically, we allow texts to point our attention toward aspects of the real world that need redress, that need action toward more fairness and restoration from harm. Critique, then, is not just a habit of finding fault; it's a habit of hoping for something better—seeing when social worlds fall short, sure, but also imagining how things should be.

As with all the other kinds of thinking we have been considering, one doesn't learn to critique by having other people do the thinking. Students need chances to learn these concepts, most likely through reading shared texts with their teacher's guidance, and then to apply them, self-sponsored, to texts they read in small groups, with partners, and independently. Nothing could be more pathetically ironic than students being taught to become dependent on someone else for their critical perspectives (Bomer 2007). And without a doubt, students will not imagine fairness, or analyze the groups to which characters belong in identical, cookie-cutter ways. Just as they envision textual worlds differently, they will also critique their social worlds in widely divergent ways.

Teaching These Kinds of Thinking as Inquiry

As I have said, there's no one way of doing any of these kinds of thinking, no standard practice that all readers must achieve. The text itself does not create the way a reader thinks it; the reader does, and a text's realization is made of memory, perception, expectation, feeling, attribution—all things that come from that reader as an individual. For a teacher to try and impose a particular envisionment or even a manner of envisioning would be counterproductive, because in fact it would *stop* a reader's thinking, while he attends to what he is supposed to do rather than to his experience of the text. What gets readers to tune into their own thinking is the expectation that they'll have to show how their way of envisioning is distinct from others'—a focus on difference.

> ## Multilingual Note
>
> Students learning English as an additional language possess ample resources for the kinds of thinking we have been examining in this chapter and the last. They do not need to wait through several years of vocabulary or grammar instruction before being asked to draw on those resources and participate in meaningful conversations. It's important to use these larger acts of self-aware thinking to build an infrastructure of deep understanding, meaning, and knowledge that will support them in learning the details of their new language.

For example, when Jeannette said she envisions like a movie, Raul said his picture really wasn't something he sees on a screen but more like he was living it: he envisions in 360 degrees. Russell says he never sees in color, that the books he reads are all in black and white. He asks the others if they visualize their stories in color. Both Jeannette and Raul do see color, and they think it's weird and amazing, and maybe a little sad, that Russell's visualizations are all like old movies, which they think are more boring than color ones. He says no, it's not depressing and not like an old movie—it's not that vivid. It's more like a pencil drawing that moves. It's like his dreams. Now the others are amazed to find out that some people dream without color. For Russell, Jeannette, and Raul, envisionment isn't a switch that's on or off—something "good readers do." And, despite what I said earlier, it isn't even a sliding control that is simply pushed up or down. It's something that each reader has to describe in detail—the ways they are peculiar—like the ways they dream, or kiss, or play.

A conversation like that one produces much more accountability in a classroom of readers. Rather than asking students to parrot the teachers' words, falling into the expected cant that is part of every classroom's life, it requires that they really pay attention to the details of their own thinking—and therefore that they really think something. Of course, the first such conversation that occurs with a particular group may include a certain amount of *acting as if*—kids pretending a level of self-awareness that wasn't really there when they were reading. That's OK. In fact, it's great—because having acted as if he's envision-ing the last time he read, the student might actually attend to what he really sees the next time he reads. As long as we come back to this same conversation over and over so that students can revise their thinking and their accounts of what's normal for them, it's productive even to sponsor students' *imagining* their active reading into being.

So for any of the forms of thinking I have described in this or the previ-ous chapter, it's far more interesting to teach them as inquiry than to teach them as static content—something everyone should accept, remember, and know. These forms of thinking should be questioned, renamed, interrogated, as things we are all continuing to wonder about and entertain as living, trans-forming ideas. The language we use in these kinds of conversations will sound substantially different from prescriptive statements about *what good readers do*. It will add to the theme I discussed in Chapters 2 and 3 of this book, that a liter-acy classroom is a Center for the Study of Us as Readers.

Minilessons

I have tried to give a decent overview of some possible reader thinking actions, though this is not an exhaustive list. I'm sure every reader of this book could add, with a few hours of self-observation, several different lines of growth to what I have provided. But even with this poor little beginning, readers may be thinking that there is an awful lot to teach. How do we begin to bring a particular kind of thinking to a class full of readers?

First of all, when we do ask students to read a novel as a whole class, we can choose two or three of these kinds of thinking to sustain as teaching objectives across the book. It's not that the readers won't also be doing other things, just that whole-class conversations will attend to a few selected kinds of thinking. It's also possible that, in response to reading club conversations about a book, a teacher might name the kind of thinking they are negotiating, and ask them to keep attending to how that particular kind of thinking goes as they proceed with their journey across the book.

But I want to suggest that students' independent reading provides an espe-cially fertile context for this teaching. When they are engaged in books they really want to read and understand, then our lessons about reading as thinking have some preexisting motives to stick to. In a reading workshop, people teach minilessons about these kinds of thinking, and they are likely to be the central topic of conferences. A particular kind of thinking, that is, becomes an objec-tive for instruction. The teacher is trying to teach the students *to envision*, rather than teaching about the possible meanings of Curly's glove in *Of Mice and Men*, or what happened in Chapter 4, or how Steinbeck's life might have informed what he wrote. The teaching objectives come from a precise analysis of what a reader does rather than things in a particular text. It's not that one doesn't sometimes discuss a text, but the focus of discussion is on action, with the text just being the thing that is acted upon.

Here is an example I've chosen from among my recent classroom collaborations, one that encapsulates a bit of teaching born of thinking about the actions readers undertake in their minds. Recently, another teacher, Maya, and I worked on minilessons with students who were each reading a self-selected book. From our conferences with them, we noticed that they were drawing on some of the kinds of thinking they had done in a recent whole-class experience with a short story, but they weren't presently drawing upon the kind of *interpretive* thinking Maya had worked on with them. On the one hand, we knew that their deepest interpretive thinking would most occur with small groups or whole-class experiences, because conversations allow students to hold ideas steady and grow them together. Even most mature readers are better at interpreting in more collaborative arrangements. On the other hand, we were trying to focus on handing thinking over to every student, and we thought we would only really be successful at teaching each student to interpret if we could get them doing it in self-sponsored, independent reading. We thought perhaps they needed to learn how to follow those hunches and build theories about the texts they chose to read on their own, not just in shared reading events. With complex kinds of thinking (as they all are), we knew one, single minilesson about interpretation on a particular Tuesday morning was not going to do the trick. We would need to teach a little, let them read with that idea, and repeat.

We thought we should reintroduce the idea of *interpretation*, so we started with a minilesson about asking "What's the point?" (Vipond and Hunt 1984). Say you walk up to someone and ask them about that building right there, and that person says, "Let me tell you a story. . . ." If you can't see the connection between her story and the question you wanted answered, you're bound to ask, "What's your point?" You want to understand what's not being said—the connection, relationship, or meaning that relates that story to this building or some relevant aspect of the context. If someone's telling you a story in just about any context, you do expect to be able to see the point. It's the same with books. It's good to ask of any text what its overall point is—how it connects to the rest of life and the world. What big idea is behind this text? Maya asked her students to start thinking about that with their book, even if they were just getting started, adding that it was something she or I might be talking with them about as we conferred with them.

The next day, I brought in a short poem, "The Cities Inside Us," by Alberto Rios, and asked the kids to read it, aware the whole time of when they had a hunch about the point and when that hunch changed or was confirmed. (You can find the poem on the Internet.) We looked at the title and generated a few hunches, and then read the first couple of lines to see what changes happened in our theory building. We talked after the next two lines, too. Then I asked them to read to the end and notice the points at which their thinking changed. We did not try to exhaust the meanings in the poem, or to discuss every idea we had. It was just an opportunity for students to notice their acts of interpreting with a little bit of assistance and attention directing from me. We weren't concerned about them "getting it right," just with the actions of following hunches and building theories.

The next day, Maya asked them to think about times when they have done this kind of interpretive thinking before. She reminded them that some of their families, we knew from the explorations of their lives as readers, often taught them by telling them stories that had a special, pointed meaning. Some of them had experienced religious instruction that did lots of its work through stories with a point. All their lives, Maya reminded them, people had been using narratives about things that happen in order to teach them lessons. Maya asked them to jot down three or four times in their lives when there had been a story from which they were supposed to learn a lesson and then to talk with a partner about how and when they started to catch onto what they were supposed to be learning from this story.

In the fourth of this string of minilessons, I gave every student four sticky notes, reminded them of the thinking we had been doing over the past few days, and asked them each to open their own book where they noticed themselves thinking something like "I bet I get what the point of this book is" or "My previous hunch doesn't seem valid anymore, and now I think this other thing," or "That confirms my theory about what this book is all about," or any other thought they could call "interpreting." The fourth sticky note was for them to keep out at the ready, while they read today, and at least once, when they made an interpretive move in their reading and thinking, they should jot a very little note

Breaking Down Minilesson Topics– Another Example

Each kind of thinking has multiple possible teaching points discussed in this or the previous chapter. Any one teaching point is best taught across a series of minilessons.

Teaching a Kind of Thinking: Listening

Teaching Point of Minilesson: Hearing How Sentences Sound

Day 1: All sentences have a melody to them. Notice today times when you have to reread because the intonation was not right in your mind the first time.

Day 2: Here's a sentence from my book that I had to work hard to hear. . . . At the end of class, I'll ask you to read to a partner one you had to work to hear in your book today.

Day 3: Part of listening to how sentences sound is hearing the words that get extra stress, usually because you hear the pitch on that word going higher. See where you notice that in your book today–what words in particular sentences get stress.

about the idea and stick it to the place where they got that notion. In the seven-minute share time at the end of the period, students talked with a partner about their decision making in placing the fourth note, and how it fit with the first three. This use of sticky notes to mark a spot involves *mediation*—using a tool to support or extend thinking. The next several chapters will expand this idea.

CHAPTER 7

Teaching Thinking Devices

English class needs to help students become more powerful readers. That means it should make reading easier and at the same time, more thoughtful, critical, and satisfying. Because it's important for kids to become stronger and more fluent readers, I sometimes worry about all the extra activity that accompanies it, making reading more of a big production than it needs to be. Reading, for secondary students, is often laden with *projects*. Students answer essay questions after reading. They do research about an author and write about that. In classrooms that value some "creative" projects, they may do something with art, or make something like a book cover, a game board, or a poster. In the name of digital literacies, these same clever projects now may take the form of social network pages for characters, or websites about a business or organization in a novel. The precise motive for these projects is often unclear, except that the teacher feels compelled to have students "do something with the novel." This need to "do something with it" is a symptom of schools' commodification of knowledge—the way knowing always has to be displayable, assessable, gradable, as if it doesn't count if you can't see it.

This tendency to make learning into a thing may be destructive to people's ability to develop reading habits they can carry into their lives outside school. The continual imperative to commodify makes reading seem like a huge bother with a lot of nonsense attached to it—especially for students who don't find reading particularly easy in the first place. You don't go from hating an activity to loving it by making it take longer and require more labor.

For several years, in my teaching, I wanted to avoid all these forms of extra work in order to clear the way for young readers, to make reading easier and lighter, to allow students to focus solely on their relationship to the text they were reading. I wanted ease, and I asked students to put down books that were too difficult for them to read successfully, to pick up books that made them strong, to build the habit of reading faster and of finishing books with ease. Adding external activities, especially writing, would just add burden to their processes. And to a great extent, I still think that same thing.

Despite the fact that this whole chapter is going to be about ways of externalizing thinking in response to texts, I believe students are most strengthened as readers when their teachers use these strategies only in limited ways. Some students just shouldn't be weighed down with all this work. We need to exercise judgment about how much activity can get stuck onto reading without making it more difficult, and one option should be that we prioritize and focus on the act of reading itself and minimize other activities around it. There is substantial research support for the notion that students get better at reading when they read more and have easy access to books they want to read (Elley 1991; Fader and McNeil 1979; Krashen 2004; Pilgreen 2000; McQuillan 1998; Worthy, Moorman, and Turner 1999; Worthy 2000). That research suggests that all the stuff we make kids do *around* reading can get in the way of the one thing that will actually help—reading.

At the same time, one of the difficulties of learning to read is that one never sees others' processes, and one's own reading process is never seen and responded to by others. It's hard to observe yourself envisioning or relating to characters, so it's hard to work on it. One of the difficulties of teaching people to read in new ways—like the ways I discussed in the previous chapter—is that a teacher cannot just reach into readers' minds and mold a new set of mental actions (Bomer 1996; Todorov 1981). Reading is invisible, mental, and so cannot be affected directly. In order to affect how people think when they read—in order to create inquiring conversations about thinking among students—there has to be some means of externalizing it—of bringing reading outside the skin (Wertsch 1991).

I have come to think, moreover, that the externalizing activities we ask students to take up need to be not only limited and supportive of actual reading but also plain and ordinary—not at all clever or creative in themselves. They should be, for the most part, the sorts of things at least some people outside school actually do in order to think more about their reading. They ought, usually, not to take a long time to complete so that most of the reader's time is devoted to reading. A literacy education involves learning to use tools for thinking, and to use those tools in concert with one another in such a way as to produce thoughtfulness and to negotiate meanings. So every reader has to learn continually to take advantage of her actual present environment to find the just-right combination of reading, talking, and using other thinking devices.

Tools for Thinking

Lev Vygotsky (1978, 1987) theorized that people always think with tools. Sometimes those tools are inside us, as when we think in words, images, or sounds. Vygotsky called these "psychological tools," because they're tools we use inside our minds, to make thoughts. But these psychological tools are the products of our engagement with external tools—concrete things we use to help us think (Vygotsky 1978; Wertsch 1991, 1998). In school, the most common external tool is talk (Cazden 1988) and it's so important that we are going to deal with it both in this chapter and on its own in the next chapter.

Reading involves the use of an external tool—the text. We think with the text, and so the text is a tool. The text itself is not really doing anything; the person using the text is changing what they think by engaging with this tool. The text is an external medium, and we are doing our thinking with that medium—mediating our thinking. This concept of mediation is central to a Vygotskian, or sociocultural, approach to thinking, learning, and literacy (Cole 1996; Vygotsky 1978; Wertsch 1991, 1998).

We humans also mediate our thinking with other tools—ones that don't try to tell us what to think about, the way a text does. We mediate our thinking with a pen and paper when we think on paper, or write in order to think (Bomer 1995; Elbow 1981; Fulwiler 1987; Langer and Applebee 1987; and see Chapter 10 of this book for much more on writing to think). We mediate our thinking with crayons or charcoal or watercolors when we draw or paint. We mediate our thinking with the software we use on our computer, whether it's a program for graphics, sound, word processing, or for determining the length of each page and location of links in a hypertext. Each of the arts represents a set of external tools for thinking (Harste, Woodward, and Burke 1984). It is very common, in any of these media, for artists, thinkers, or makers to begin engaging with the material without knowing in advance what they are going to make or how an object will come out. They create, build, and extend new thoughts through their engagement with the tool; they put their thinking into the medium. They mediate.

What if we brought together readers' thinking with these externalizing, extending media for thinking? Might it be possible for a reader to think more about the text, her life, and her world if she uses writing, sketching, and other mediational tools to develop ideas? Isn't that really the reason teachers want students to write about their reading? Isn't that why we, as readers, want to talk about what we've read? So that we can hold onto our thoughts, build them up, and allow them to take us somewhere we can only begin to imagine with these first inklings we carry away from the reading experience?

As one way of describing these tools for mediation, I like the term *thinking devices*, from Wertsch (1991). This chapter is about how teachers introduce and support the use of particular tools for thinking in response to reading—thinking devices. That means I began this chapter by arguing against much of its content.

It wasn't just an accident. We do need to be conservative about adding to the difficulty or complexity of reading, just as we need to be thoughtful more generally about eliminating all the distractions in the curriculum (as I discussed in Chapter 1) and planning for sustained, concentrated attention. I also wanted to clear away the assignment mania that dominates the teaching of literature in school. Though the thinking devices I will describe below involve the arts and support creative thinking, most of the assignments traditional teachers think of as "creative" are quite different. Our objective should be to provide students with transparent, durable tools that they can use in life outside school, not to make up clever assignments that tell them what to think or that force them to write from false premises, like making ad copy for Atticus Finch's law office or an Internet social network page for the characters in *Romeo and Juliet*. Low-quality assignments place the thinker in a constrained space of meaning, and higher-quality ones

Assignments That Support Teachers' Agendas

- Everyone, make three sketches of the main characters in this novel.
- For homework, please place quotes in this chart. The book's themes are listed down the side and specific chapters are listed across the top.

Strategies That Support Independent Literate Lives

- Sketch whenever you notice yourself trying to picture something in the next couple of chapters.
- I notice, as you talk, you are trying to plug parts of the story into particular big ideas. Let's try making a chart.

instead hand over a tool and allow the student to invent ideas while remaining concentrated on the actual experience of reading. We are going to concentrate on the high-quality activities, teaching students to use a range of externalizing strategies to support their own authentic response to literature and other texts. First, let's examine a range of possible devices for thinking.

Talking

Even though the entire next chapter will be about talk, we glance at it briefly in this context, so that we can see the ways other tools always fit within a broader conversational context. It's easy to talk, so we can do more of it; compared to just about everything else, it's effortless and motivating. And like the other thinking devices we'll discuss here, talk is an activity that can help us think new thoughts. Britton (1982) quotes the nineteenth-century writer Heinrich Von Kleist saying:

> Whenever you seek to know something and cannot find it out by meditation, I would advise you to talk it over with the first person you meet. He [*sic*] need not be especially brilliant, and I do not suggest that you *question* him, no: *tell* him about it. . . . Often, while at my desk working, I search for the best approach to some involved problem. I stare into my lamp, the point of optimum brightness, while striving with utmost concentration to enlighten myself. . . . And the remarkable thing is that if I talk about it with my sister, who is working in the same room, I suddenly realize things which hours of brooding had perhaps been unable to yield. . . . Because I do start with some sort of dark notion remotely related to what I am looking for, my mind, if it has set out boldly enough, and being pressed to complete what it has begun, shapes that muddled area into a form of new-minted clarity, even while my talking progresses. (Quoted in Britton 1982, 140)

Everyone has had this experience—finding out what you think through the process of expressing it. So talk provides one easy, transparent, and ordinary means of externalizing thinking and thereby creating it. Sure, it's common enough for people to talk to *themselves* when the situation allows it, but students are aided by actual conversational partners—someone to talk *to*. As always, we have several structures available to us: pairs, small groups, and whole class. The most efficient way to get the most people talking at once is by organizing students into pairs, and thus partners afford the most ample resource of talk as a thinking device.

While listening to another person's ideas can also be a helpful form of mediation, we're focused here on *talking* as a tool, and it is in many ways the speaker who gets the most out of such a conversation. So the point isn't to use partners to make sure certain weak readers "get it" by having partners explain their text to them. It's to give all readers opportunities to think aloud.

Readers can talk to think in support of any of the particular kinds of thinking I discussed in the previous chapter. They can talk in order to *envision*, or to *anticipate* what is likely in the rest of the text, or to fill in with *interpretive* comments those things the author is not saying. They can talk through the personal *memories* that begin to arise but don't quite become clear before speaking, or they can construct their *critique* of the social world represented in a text by beginning to articulate it. If the whole class is spending a few days inquiring into the kind of thinking I have called *listening*, then the teacher might ask everyone to talk with a neighbor about what they heard in their mind's ear as they read a section of a shared text, or to talk with their partner at the end of reading time about when they noticed themselves needing to work at listening in order to hear a text. If a teacher is conferring one-on-one with a particular student who seems to need to build up the habit of *relating to characters*, the teacher can get the kid talking about how he's relating to the people in this text, first during the conference, and then perhaps continuing with a partner as the teacher moves on to confer with others. Capitalizing on talk as a tool for thinking, in sum, involves searching for opportunities to install purposeful but explorative talk into many different structures and seams of a class.

> ### Talk That Supports Particular Kinds of Thinking
>
> - *Envisioning*: "At first, I wasn't sure what the room looked like, but when it said the sunlight was shining through the skylight, I started thinking that . . ."
> - *Interpreting*: "I was thinking that it was going to be about how people are always so stupid in new situations. But that wasn't as true of the other characters. Mostly, if you thought about *all* the characters, the point seemed to be more about how people need each other.

One special form of talk deserves a little more description here. It has gone under several different names, from "think-alouds" to "say something" (Short, Harste, and Burke 1996). The key feature of this activity is that talk occurs as a fairly frequent interruption in the reading process. Students read a little bit of text—perhaps a few paragraphs—and then stop and talk about what they are thinking before reading on a bit further and stopping to talk again. I tend to call this practice *interruptions*, because I think that best describes how it feels and why it is effective. Though most people do not read this way as a regular practice, they do sometimes. If my wife and I are in another country, looking at text beside a museum object, we read this way, stopping to figure out what the text is saying, especially if we don't know the language well. People often "read" sports events this way, offering running commentary on the action in order to share it, mediate it, and arrive at common understandings of complex events. People sometimes read instructions for assembling furniture this way, reading a bit and then saying something to their partner about what the hell it means. So we do it when we want to arrive at common understandings and there is some risk to adequate comprehension (or a risk to furniture that stays put together).

The thinking device of *interruptions* is especially supportive of students who have not developed enough of a habit of *monitoring for sense*. If a reader has to say something about a section of text a few seconds from now, he had better be attending to what the text says and had better be getting some ideas ready to say in response. The activity forces readers to lean forward with respect to meaning, to make something actively of what they are reading, and that is just what is needed for some students who tend to let meaning roll by them without really thinking about it. Even for students who understand most of what they read, at times when they are attempting to get better at a particular form of thinking, like *interpreting*, frequent interruptions can keep them working on it and retrying with each successive new beginning.

Indexing: Underlining, Marginalia, and Sticky Notes

One of the most common and simple things that people do to support their active thinking as they read is *indexing*, by which I mean marking places in the text with ink or with sticky notes. Experienced readers often mark places that seem important, something to come back to. It's a scholarly kind of tool, because it takes the text as an object of study—as something to discuss, rethink, perhaps write about later. Many people who read a lot mark books even when they read them independently. The physical action of marking important sentences or passages helps us to construct understandings, makes us choose actively where our attention should go. And when we can't mark in the book because it doesn't belong to us, we use sticky notes; sometimes we write on them, often we do not.

These things may seem obvious (especially since readers of this book may very well be underlining or otherwise marking these pages right now—please underline that). What may be new is the idea that a reader can use sticky notes in support of a particular, focused kind of thinking. Sharon decides, for example, that in the next chapter, she is going to pay special attention to *calling other texts to mind*. She grabs a stack of sticky notes and begins reading, adding a sticky to each place she notices herself thinking about other texts. Once she gets started, it starts to seem like she can use the notes almost continuously, because now that she's thinking about it, other texts—books, movies, shows— come to mind almost continuously. Without using the tool of indexing this way, she would be vaguely aware of the intertextual resources she is drawing upon, but the use of the tool makes that particular kind of thinking visible, muscular, and interactive. The same process applies to any other kind of thinking.

Sketching

Sketching is another tool for thinking, one that is common in the arts, design, architecture, engineering, the sciences, and many other areas of life outside English class (Whitin 1996, 2005; Moline 1995; Wilhelm 2008). Like writing, it involves the making of signs—those squiggles that stand for something else— to mediate thinking, and so it too can support the thinking readers do in collaboration with texts (Short, Harste, and Burke 1996). Making a sketch in support of envisionment, for example, Besim uses the page and the evolving sketch to think through what he is really seeing in a particular scene or description. Drawing a scene in a hospital waiting room, he thinks through who is sitting in chairs and who is pacing in front of them, decides that those seated are not in adjoining chairs. He realizes that the teenage boy's head is still bleeding throughout all the dialogue and that the younger boy can't take his eyes off the father, monitoring how angry he is at his two sons. These details are not in the words of the text, which is mostly dialogue. But they are Besim's contribution to the story world, an essential part of a reading experience. By sketching them, he makes this envisionment more conscious and fully developed. He sees more because he sketches; the hand and the page create what happens in the mind, as much as the other way around.

Sometimes students—of any age—complain that they "can't draw" and therefore, they say, this tool can't work for them. The trouble is, they have mistaken for a performance what should be understood as a thinking device. They are not drawing for a museum when they sketch to think, any more than they are writing for publication every time they write to think. Moreover, when people say they can't draw, they usually mean that when they make a horse, it doesn't look like a real horse in the world. But, of course, that ignores most of what the world has known about art, at least for the past 150 years, if not forever. There are lots of ways to see and represent, and they aren't all about creating a 2-D replica of what the eye perceives in life. People, animals, places can be represented in many ways, lots of which don't necessarily resemble real life; and when they don't look representational, we can think even more about what they mean. If the head is huge, then what's that about? If one hand is bigger than the other, what could we make of that? If people just start sketching to think, they eventually find a style, whether scribbly lines or freeform blobs or circles and boxes, that can help them think things through. At the same time, I do encourage people to avoid representing human figures as stick figures. (You may be getting used to me arguing against myself in this chapter.) That's not really what they envision when they read, and the abbreviating of stick figures fails to invite them to consider clothing, hairstyle, physical attitude, and lots of other things that would be awfully helpful in visualizing. In other words, some conventionalized drawing strategies are more like labeling than describing, and they in fact get in the way of really seeing in the mind's eye. That misses the point.

Sketching, however, does not only serve envisionment. Like other thinking devices, it can mediate multiple kinds of thinking. In the example above about the hospital, Besim was clearly thinking about the characters and their relationships, thereby working out his relationship to each of them. A reader can also

How Many Thinking Devices?

No class needs to attend to too many tools at once. It's fine to focus on just around two, three, or four thinking devices in a particular class. Letting students get good at a few is probably more important than taking on a large number.

use sketching to reconstruct memories evoked by the text, drawing not what's in the text but what's in her memory. I've seen readers make drawings that metaphorically explore interpretation. Asking a reader to try sketching the most important image in the story, the one that says the most about the whole point, is a request for an interpretive claim made through sketching. It may be stretching things a bit to say that sketching could support any sort of thinking, but it can mediate a range that extends well beyond visualizing what is going on.

Charts and Diagrams

Charts and diagrams provide two more visual tools for thinking, though they are visual in a different way from sketching and in fact differ significantly from one another, as well. Diagrams might be understood as images of concepts and relationships; some people call them *concept maps* or *mind maps* (Buzan 2000). What many teachers call *webs* would also be one kind of diagram. Figure 7–1 provides a diagram of some ideas from this chapter. By contrast, charts are usually matrices that bring multiple questions or criteria into dialogue with another set of multiple items (whether other ideas or a series of instances, such as texts). Figure 7–2, for example, is a chart that represents ideas in this chapter, specifically, the ways particular kinds of thinking can be mediated in varied thinking devices. Figure 7–3 represents a comparison between little bits of the novels *Hunger Games* (Collins 2008) and *Catching Fire* (Collins 2009), without any real plot spoilers. Like sketching, indexing, talking, writing, and reading itself, charts and diagrams are useful in a wide range of domains—academic, practical, social, and personal.

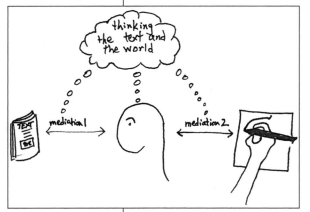

FIGURE 7-1 Diagram: Mediation and a Reader's Thinking

By *diagrams*, I obviously don't just mean the Venn diagrams that are supposed to show common elements from two separate sets. To me, those are often a little too simplistic. They also provide the least space in the overlap, right where all the important stuff goes. I certainly don't mean, when I say *diagrams*, teacher- or publisher-produced "graphic organizers" where students are asked to plug in values for preestablished boxes and lines someone else has already made to represent textual elements and their relationships. Those are low-quality because they create learned helplessness and dependence, in addition to being boring, insulting, and often just wrong. I mean, rather, *teaching students to diagram*—to develop ways of representing the relationships they are thinking about.

	Envisioning	Listening	Interpreting	Critiquing
Indexing	Placing a sticky note where you witness a strong image.	Underlining a sentence where you have to work to hear how it sounds.	Putting a sticky note with one key word where you have a hunch about what this text is all about.	Adding a sticky note to pages where you find yourself thinking about fairness and justice.
Sketching	Sketching a moment that you found hard to picture.	Sketching possible sources of sounds in a scene.	Sketching the most important image in this text.	Sketching the people in a scene, showing who's powerful in what ways.
Diagramming	Diagramming the relationships among the types of images you see as you read this text.	Diagramming the intensity of the voice of the text at different points as you read.	Mapping the relationships among different big ideas at work in this text.	Diagramming the groups represented in this text and which of them exert more or less power.
Performing or Enacting	Casting a scene from the text with a few other readers and acting it out, paying attention to what you have to imagine.	Rehearsing several times a read aloud of a text, marking the words that need emphasis and getting the melodies of sentences just right.	Planning a performance of the most important scene in this text so that it shows why this is so important.	Improvising a scene in which the less powerful characters in this book challenge the more powerful ones. What would happen?

FIGURE 7–2 Some of the Thinking Devices Discussed in This Chapter in Relation to Some of the Kinds of Thinking They Can Support

	The Hunger Games	Catching Fire
Reading problems	Adjusting to the strangeness of the world, noticing when things are invented rather than just things I don't know	Remembering Hunger Games and what the details mean; catching up to what is new in her life
Noticing about this world	Official language, limits on movement, oppression	Brutality, unreality, more intense oppression
Places	Home, woods, Hob, town square	Woods, Hob, home, big tour
Katniss political position	Unknown, invisible, powerless	Famous, still powerless
Early hunches about themes	Policing of feelings, attitudes, actions	Possibility of rebellion, insurgence

FIGURE 7–3 A Chart for My Thinking in Just the Beginnings of *The Hunger Games* and *Catching Fire*

Meredith makes a diagram to support her *interpretation*, with a central shape that represents a big organizing idea she sees in the text, the idea that after the storm, things would never be the same, even though days seemed kind of normal. She draws lines as streams feeding into it from shapes representing moments in the text when she began to grow that idea, such as one for the day after the storm, when the weather was fine, and one for when the character ran out of dog food. She labels the streams or connectors between the moments and the idea as hunch, building idea, eliminating alternatives, and confirming theory. The act of building the diagram makes the intellectual work of theory building more explicit, and that may even make this habit of mind more transferable for her into other contexts.

I have worked with students, too, who used diagrams to trace their listening, envisioning, or relationship to character, representing how these perceptual experiences of the text changed as they moved through the reading experience. In one-to-one conferences, as a way of externalizing social critique, I have asked students to diagram the social worlds in a text, making it visually clear which groups had power and how the other groups responded to and resisted that power. It is even possible to make a map of the ways one's expectations shifted as one moved through a reading experience, representing the moments of surprise, of most intense predicting, and of confirmation. Because of its abstracted and flexible nature, diagramming can support just about any kind of thinking.

While diagrams represent abstract concepts, charts bring sets of ideas in relation with one another. Along the left side is one set of factors and along the top is another. Each item from one set talks to each item from the other. In support of *relationship to character*, a reader might put characters along the top and then, down the side, name sections of the book. Filling in the chart accounts for how her relationships to various characters changed across time as she read. In support of *interpreting*, a reader might line the top of the chart with big ideas she's making and put events from the story down the side, to see whether and how the plot supports that potential theme.

Charts can be especially useful for thinking *across* texts, because they ask the reader to apply the same criteria to multiple instances. If we list a number of different texts down the left side of the chart and particular questions or categories across the top, then every cell of the resulting matrix invites us to think about the texts and the criteria. Thus, charts are especially useful in supporting intertextual thinking—what I named in the previous chapter *calling other texts to mind*. Particularly during independent reading, I want to teach students that moving from one book to

> ### Multilingual Note
>
> Reading, talking, and writing place heavy weight on the one area where students who are learning English can be at a disadvantage. Inviting response in modalities that don't involve English vocabulary can be a help to their reading. Sketching, enacting, and diagramming let all students think together in activities not as dependent on the English language.

another creates a text set (Short, Harste, and Burke 1996)—a journey of thought that builds ideas across time and through the reading of a collection of texts. Even if texts are not by the same author or in the same genre, the reader should be making connections across them: that's a big part of what it means to have an intellectual life. A chart can provide a way of externalizing and supporting this building of ideas across texts.

Enacting/Performing

Another set of media that support thinking in response to text is less confined to pen, paper, and wrist movements and instead engages more of the body, voice, and physical space. *Performance* involves voicing the text as it is written—essentially rehearsed reading aloud. *Enacting* scenes, on the other hand, involves selecting and acting out passages of dialogue and physical action from a narrative, or improvising ones that are implied but not actually shown in the text. Both are ways of embodying, though each makes something different possible, and within each of those categories are varied strategic possibilities.

Performance

In a sense, every time someone reads something out loud, they're performing that text. There could be a large audience, an audience of one, or just the audience of the reader's listening self. It's unfortunate that in school settings, especially those with younger children and those with struggling readers, the performance is so often focused on getting every word correct. In that case, the kind of thinking the performance supports becomes one of concentrating on each individual word. That's bad, because attending to individual words often prevents people from attending to meaning as it adds up across phrases, predicates, and overall statements. Words don't usually *mean* one at a time.

Performance is especially useful in work on *listening* to the intonation of sentences, which, as I said in the previous chapter, actually helps construct meaning in language (Worthy and Broaddus 2002). Consequently, performing also requires that the reader think about meaning on several other levels. A reader can support a particular kind of thinking in reading by choosing to orient a performance around that thinking. For example, you could perform a

Types of Performance

In every case, it's the preparation and rehearsal that are most important, not the actual performing.

- Oral performance—an individual plans a read-aloud, including mood, tone of voice, words that need emphasis, character voice qualities
- Choral reading—a group plans an oral performance, combining individual voices, unison voices, and vocal effects to underscore the meanings they see as important
- Reader's theatre—a cast performs a scripted version of a text like a radio play, including actors in roles, sound effects, and a narrator
- Chamber theatre—a cast performs a fuller theatrical adaptation of a text, usually without a narrator

text as an exploration of an *interpretation*. Or you could perform it with attention to *relationship to character*. Like the other thinking devices I am discussing in this chapter, performance is a tool that can serve multiple purposes in a reader-thinker's experience.

Enactment

Enactment, compared to performance, focuses more on the action of text and less on the language. Enacting a scene from a story allows, even requires the reader to step into the 360-degree world of a text, to make the dream flesh. A reader chooses a scene that she would like to think more about, and she gets together another person or two in order to put that scene on its feet—act it out with their voices and bodies. They find a place where they can do the scene (admittedly, sometimes tricky), and they try it. It's one thing to read about a character saying to another that she never wants to see him again, and it's another to experience a person looking at you and saying that. Doing so gives the reader a chance to notice what she would like to say back to the other person and then perhaps look back at the text to see whether the character responds the same way she does. Taking on the identities in the book and embodying their experience intensifies the reading experience. One can enact a scene paying careful attention to *envisionment*: looking around while the scene is going on and pretending you can see details of the place that you hadn't thought of while you read the first time (and that are not given in the text). Enacting a scene, a reader sometimes realizes that this book is like a certain sort of movie she has seen before, because of how the dialogue sounds spoken aloud. So this kind of enactment can be done in support of *listening, envisioning, relationship to character*, and *calling other texts to mind*. It can also produce new *autobiographical memories*, as the scene becomes more real to the reader, and this thinking device can also support *interpretation* and *critique*, because it makes the reader think about what is really going on in the text and provides a means to examine power relationships as they are embodied by characters.

It's pretty easy to imagine how performance and enactment could work when a whole class is reading a text together. The teacher can sponsor it, either in the whole group or in small groups. People can break up and spread out to rehearse their scenes. For reading clubs or small literature circles to take on enactment is also pretty easy to imagine, since multiple groups around the room are already talking about different things. It's somewhat harder to sponsor spontaneous enactments in independent reading, just because there are a bunch of people reading in one room.

TECHNOLOGY NOTE

You could call any of these tools—even writing—*technologies of response*. I focus here on low-tech tools, but some digital tools could also be useful. There is easily available, free or cheap software, for any platform, in which students can draw, diagram, chart, and record performances. Watch that the software is not more restrictive than necessary, especially in diagramming software, which can result in much lower-quality diagrams than students can make freehand. Consider podcasts for rehearsed read-alouds and for reader's theatre performances, videos for enactments.

Shoshanna is reading *Catching Fire*, which has lots of physical action in it, and she decides the best way to figure out what is happening in one scene would be to act it out with a friend (something her teacher showed them to be possible a couple of weeks ago). When, where, and how is that enacting likely to happen? One possibility is that the teacher would provide a time for part of a period, once a week, when people could choose a scene—either written or implied in their texts—that they'd like to enact with partners. Until that day, Shoshanna will just have to plan the enactment—picturing just what she'd like to enact and how it should go. Another possibility, which depends on space, is that Shoshanna understands that she and her scene partner could go into the hall or a room near the classroom—somewhere out of direct observation by the rest of the class but available to teacher checks—in order to try out a scene for a few minutes. But because all enactment and some performance strategies require simultaneous participation by a group—something that no other of these thinking devices demands—it is likely to be better served by the teacher arranging appointments for all interested students at a particular time.

For more about performing and enacting as ways of responding to literature, see Bomer (2006, 2007), O'Neill (1994, 1995), and Wilhelm (2008).

Examples of How Students Have Acted Out Text to Good Purpose

- They improv, trying to understand the motives and feelings of people in important scenes.
- They run through a scene, remaining true to the text's details and trying to envision exactly what happened, especially in a scene with a lot of physical action.
- An event only implied in the book, or one that occurs offstage, comes up in discussion, and they act it out to fill in what is missing and see how it might have happened.
- They enact a scene from one reader's analogous autobiographical memory, and compare it to the scene in the text.
- They choose and rehearse the scene they view as the most important in the whole book, and their enactment explores the ideas that they think make the scene important.

When Is a Strategy Not a Strategy?

If you think about it, what I've written here could be viewed as a machine for producing assignments. You've got a text, you pick a kind of thinking, combine it with a mediational tool—and presto!—you've got yourself an assignment. You're reading Chapter 4 in *Of Mice and Men*, and you ask the class to make a chart about the shifts in their relationships to the characters in the scene as the chapter proceeds, with Beginning, Middle, and Later along the left side, and three characters they think are especially important in the scene across the top. In the matrix, students are to jot notes about how they feel about each character at that point in the chapter. As far as it goes, that's OK. It's not so cute and thoroughly designed as to crowd out student thinking entirely, dancing the teacher's steps, and there is enough ambiguity in the task so that the learner has to make decisions to get it done. Still, the kids are obeying, not thinking

Ways to Introduce a New Thinking Device

- In a minilesson—explain it, do it in front of them, and then ask them to try it.
- In a conference—in response to the student's thinking, extend the kind of thinking she is doing by asking her to try out a thinking device, then ask her to share with the class at the end of the period or the next day.
- In a reading club—in response to students' conversation, ask them to take on the challenge of this new tool for extending their thinking as homework, and then ask them to share with the whole class the next day. Generalize the strategy to the class so they know when and how to use it.

strategically. This assignment, in fact, is not a strategy for the students who do it. It's a strategy for the teacher—a means of solving the problem of what to do in fourth period on Tuesday or how to get the kids to think about their shifting relationships to characters in this particular book. But it's not a strategy for reading.

A strategy is only a strategy when someone decides to use it to accomplish something or to solve a problem. A reader decides to intensify some aspect of her experience, so she chooses a tool that can do the job. She's reading *Of Mice and Men* because she chose it, which changes her whole relationship to the reading event, and she is trying to sort out how she feels about the characters, who in this chapter, have multiplied pretty fast. So to help sort this out, she makes a chart, noting how her mind has changed at different points. *Now* it's a strategy.

Making the chart as a class could also be a strategy—under similar conditions. Talking about the book, we realize we think differently about the characters. So we make a chart together to help us recognize and think more about those interesting differences. But if the chart is just a strategy to solve the teacher's problem, then the only strategic thinking students will be doing is about how to get through what has been demanded of them.

Throughout this chapter, you and I have been entertaining ideas about how we might hand over to students strategies that help them think in response to reading. Of course, these strategies are just as valuable in science or social studies, in redesigning a living space or planning a publicity campaign, in organizing for political purposes or for financial ones, as they are for reading. Learning to be generous with muscular effort, breathing fully and making something even if it is not Great Art, is part of living, making, producing, participating across many social forms of life in these times. The most basic of these thought-producing machines is talk—which almost defines human connection. And talk is the subject of the next chapter.

CHAPTER 8

Teaching Toward Great Conversations

People learn to think by participating in conversations (Vygotsky 1987; Wertsch 1991). Every way of thinking we have as individuals was introduced to us through our membership in particular groups with particular ways of talking. The more experienced members of those groups brought us into those ways of thinking by positioning us as a certain kind of participant. Our ways of thinking are born as we get ready to say something—even if we don't actually get it out. We think as an answer to others' thinking when we talk, and we use those habits even when we think on our own (Bakhtin 1981). It's extremely important in a literacy classroom, therefore, to be deliberate about talk, to think carefully about the forms of participation we create as we structure talk, and to induct students into thoughtful ways of participating in academic discussions, ways that can help them build new thinking so that they become not just better participants in discussions, but better thinkers.

We live in an age when work gets done through collaboration. People have a shared object—a project on which they are working together—and they have to bend their minds—their own and one another's—toward a common way of thinking about the object. They have to disagree in ways that permit the collaboration to continue—neither trying to destroy an opposing view or to make their own perspective invisible. They have to venture tentative ideas, even lame ones, just to get the ball rolling. They have to say "Yes, and . . ." to their collaborators' initial, lame ideas, so that something better can be built among the team. Collaborating successfully involves ways of listening and talking, strategies for connecting, and ways of building ideas from a sequence of turns at talk. There is certainly no reason to think people are born being able to do these complex tasks.

English teachers are used to thinking that the study of literature involves lots of discussion—in groups of varying sizes. Sometimes, one student reads with another in a partnership, and the partners make meaning together of what they read. Other times, students read in small groups—reading clubs, or literature circles—and while one purpose of these groupings is that their talk facilitates comprehension, engagement, and growth as readers, they also are settings for the development of control in conversation. And, of course, most teachers at least sometimes share books with a whole class—either by reading them aloud to the class or else having everyone read their own copy. Whole-class discussion, too, can (and really should) become a setting for the development of higher-quality discussion.

Talk is not everywhere the same. When people talk, they are not only trading information or just saying what they're thinking; they behave in patterned ways. Talk at a particular family's dinner table has patterns that are different from talk in the hallway of a workplace, which is different from talk in a legislative body or a psychotherapy session. And talk in school is a very special instance of talk, an instance of which we need to become more aware, in order to open up new possibilities and identities in that space. First of all, talking is what people in schools do. Schools are talk factories; it's our chief product (Cazden 1988). And perhaps because of that, it can also be one of the most contested and stressful activities in teachers' and students' lives. In schools, talk is policed and controlled, and who gets to do it is a mark of status and privilege. If a teacher says to a parent, "She's a real talker," it's not meant as a good thing. Walking down hallways in many schools, one is much more likely to hear "stop talking" than "talk more."

There has been lots of research on talk in school (and lots of other settings), and one of the things we know is that there is a default pattern in classroom talk, in which the teacher asks a question, a student responds, and then the teacher asks another question (Mehan 1979; Cazden 1988). This pattern may not always be bad (Mercer 2000; Wells 1999), but it can often result in students guessing what the teacher wants, rather than really thinking in the ways we would want them to when the teacher isn't around (Nystrand et al. 1997). We need to examine the patterns we create as teachers, to make sure they're serving to bring students into thinking practices, into collaborative practices, and into ways of thinking about themselves that are intentional, thoughtful, and confident about taking intellectual initiative.

Nothing is more supportive of developing comprehension and interpretation than good conversation about text. The character of the conversations in a reading classroom is, therefore, its most important feature.

Leading Discussions

The centrality of conversation to comprehension and interpretation means that the teacher has to stop, for the most part, functioning as the center of all the talk, the manager of everyone's utterances, and release participants to control more of their own conversation. Of course, in whole-class discussion, that can be complicated, because there are lots of people bidding for the floor at once and other people reticent to speak up in front of such a large group. That is why whole-class discussion shouldn't be the only structure for conversation. In fact, if you think about it, talk in the whole class is the most inefficient way of distributing talk. One person speaking, twenty or thirty listening. By contrast, with partners, you could have ten or fifteen speaking and the same number listening. For a teacher to get the most benefit out of talk as a tool for thinking, it's necessary to let go of some of the control of speech.

Still, even within whole-class discussions, it is possible to create expectations that can produce more thoughtful conversations rather than guessing games. One place to start is just not asking questions to which you already know the answer. When I find myself looking at text with students and asking something like, "So what is a term for a comparison that equates two different things?" I just stop myself and either choose a more open-ended question (one to which I don't know the answer) or else just state whatever it is about which I'm clearly wanting to remind them. In this situation, I could just ask them to say what else they see in this writing, and if metaphor comes up, then so be it. If it doesn't, then maybe I should remind them. If I really need to take this moment to tell them about metaphor, then I'll do that—in declarative statements, not through a guessing game. Once we break this pattern and commit to asking questions that are really questions, questions with answers that can surprise us, then students shift their participation to be real shared thinking rather than filling in of blanks. But until the teacher makes that shift, conversation is going to be locked into a form that limits thoughtfulness and positions students as less than they can be.

Once we have made that shift toward more authentic ways of speaking, we can do other things to improve our ways of leading a whole-class discussion. We invite more thoughtful and energetic conversations when we:

Open with a broad invitation to readers to say what they are thinking. It's often little more than a shrug and "What struck you in this text? What could we think about together?"

Give it to the readers. Believe that this conversation is about them building ideas together, with their teacher as one participant in the conversation, not the only agenda setter. Everyone here should have as strong an agenda as the teacher does with respect to the questions and topics we should address about the shared text. Expect that they do and treat them as if they do.

Engage ourselves in participant talk rather than always procedural instructions. If we don't watch out, we will sound like a teacher just giving directions instead of a fellow reader sharing our thoughts about the text. And if we do that, where will the students get an adult image of educated conversation? We need to demonstrate for them what a good turn sounds like, so we need to talk as we want them to talk. So we stop always saying, "OK, good point. Anyone else?" That's not what we want them to do! We need to say, "I was thinking, and this may not be something anyone else thought, but I was thinking that they seemed even more lost when they got back home than they were when they were out in the city." Then stop and let someone respond to our ideas.

Listen and maintain awareness of the students' point of view. If we are trying to get them to perform for us, to answer our questions and build our argument, we're really not thinking from their perspective about what this feels like. We need to reach around in our mind's eye and see the classroom from the back. What would make it possible for a quiet student to speak now? What would make it difficult? What does it mean that this boy keeps filling every silence? Who hasn't been able to get into the conversation?

Eliminate the evaluation part of the initiation-response-evaluation (IRE) talk pattern common in schools. After a student speaks, it's not necessary to tell them that their speech was good, or to ask for another student to talk. Tell the students that you're not going to do that, and let them take turns. Some people try to eliminate hand raising as well, but I find that uncertainty about who has the floor can be anxiety producing for students, whether children or adults, and that it's probably not worth it. I can silently recognize hands to facilitate orderly turns without becoming the hub of conversation. Some teachers call on several people in a row, or keep a list of people who will speak in turn, to allow people to relax about getting the floor.

Build ideas together. The trouble with a list of speakers is that it prevents one utterance from building upon the one right before. The goal of an intellectual conversation is for ideas to develop that none of us could have constructed alone. That means that an idea has to remain in the center of the conversation for long enough to grow it. Usually, I begin leading a discussion by jotting down notes of the points students bring up, with the person's name who launches the idea into the room. Then after about six ideas have been nominated, I say them back to the class and ask which one we should take as a starting place. I say that we'll probably be able to get to all of them and that they're probably related underneath, but let's choose some idea to work on together for now. Someone says, "How about *x*?" Someone else nods or agrees, so I say, "OK, *x*. What are you thinking about that?" And we're off.

Invite and sponsor connections. It's a good idea to teach students explicitly that building upon what someone else has said is a positive, constructive move in conversation. To make explicit reference to someone else's point and then respond to it is a way of building an idea, either by extending the other person's thinking, agreeing with it, or differing from it.

Keep asking why. Sometimes, the best way of expanding and grounding what a student offers is to ask *why*—why she thinks that about the book or about life, why the character feels the way she does, why the author would want to bring that up. And when a student makes a monosyllabic claim, like "Yes," or "I disagree," then some version of the question *why* is a reliable way to get them to say more. And just one questioning of why may not do it; it may take a few *why*s to get to some real meaty discussion.

Pull on differences to draw them out. Good conversation usually involves negotiating the things that members of the group see differently. If everyone is just saying, "Yeah, yeah," there is not much to discuss. So a teacher can help build a conversation by pointing out the differences in the positions different students are taking, and extending the implications of those differences to other parts of the text or into life. This move is not just a participant turn, but a corner in the conversation, where the teacher raises the level by saying, "OK, Tonya is asking us to think about the role of parents in someone's life. She's saying that they should always support their child. Maybe that's different from what Wallace was saying a little while ago, that the parents need to limit what their child can do. What do you think this book is saying about that?"

Make trouble and get students comfortable with it. One of the killers of good classroom dialogue is students' reticence about noticing the differences in their positions. Certain cultures, including perhaps the dominant culture in the U.S.A., prefer to smooth over differences and create a false consensus. But going for consensus in dialogue can often just repress minority views and diverse perspectives. The norm of everyone agreeing just makes the people who think differently shut up. By asking for difference and holding it as the center of the conversation, as the space in which good thinking is built, a teacher can help students accustom themselves to participating in civil discussions where differences are visible instead of hidden.

Leading more thoughtful and inquiring whole-class conversations will establish in students an expectation for how talk can go and a hunger for the great feeling of being in a good discussion, thinking with great intellectual energy and seriousness with a group of people. Many readers of this book got hooked on those kinds of conversations at some point. It wasn't necessarily the books or the reading or the writing. It was the great talk about all of it that hooked us on the intellectual life. That's the addiction we could offer our students.

The point of discussion in English language arts class, in other words, is not just to process the books or ideas about language or writing. It's largely to build habits of talk and dispositions toward inquiring conversations that students can carry over into their educated, literate lives. That means that having a great discussion about *House on Mango Street* is just a first step. We need ways to hand over the building of good conversation to students so that they develop for themselves the same toolbox of opening, questioning, sustaining, and developing through talk.

Teaching About Conversation and Toward Independence

If we are to teach toward students being able to build their own good talk, then we have to set up structures that provide an opportunity for them to make decisions about conversations and to develop habits of acting and responding in the midst of the flow of discourse. To talk is to negotiate socially, and the teacher's presence makes much of that negotiation optional. If the adult will save the social situation and rescue the conversation, then the students are not positioned to take responsibility for their interactions. They may be learning to be students, but they aren't learning to create conversations. Moreover, the experience of responsibility for smaller-group structures prepares people for more competent and responsible participation in larger-group structures—a principle that applies not just to talk in classrooms but to participation in a democracy (Pateman 1970; Putnam 2001). So if students can become better at conversation in clubs and partnerships, their participation in whole-group discussion may also grow.

Because it is oral language, improvised and continuously flowing, conversation is tricky to see, to learn about, and consequently, to teach. When we're in a conversation, the thing we are making is continually moving and shifting, like a river. It's not like a text, staying still so we can look at it and look again, layering ideas onto it. A conversation feels invisible and nearly out of control.

To work on it, we need to make conversation visible. First, we need to talk about conversations after we have them, turning their memory into something we can revisit. What were the sections of that talk we just had? How did we move from one section to another? What was the tone of that conversation? What actions helped us to build ideas? What were the ideas we developed? By reflecting on conversations after they happen, we turn them into stories, and experience starts to become something more like text. When people start perceiving of conversations as more like texts, they can start to take control of the moves they make in talk.

Another strategy for making conversation more visible is to use technological tools to record it and review it. Students listen to an audio recording of a particular section of conversation or watch it on video, along with perhaps reading a transcript of the conversation. Frozen in time, the talk becomes more like a text and more investigable as something that has been constructed by the group.

Through both reflective conversations and technologically frozen discussions, a class starts to develop a way of talking about talk, of naming the moves people make as they begin and finish a topic, as they transition from one thing to another, as they disagree and as they wind down to a silence. They discuss things like whether it's OK for people to be quiet for a while, just thinking, in the middle of a conversation. They have a reason to consider using writing or sketching as a way to renew individual thinking so that the conversation can be restarted. In other words, once talk becomes an object, something that can be studied, people can become students of it.

Most likely, as soon as they start to study it, students will start to realize that different people perceive of conversational moves differently (Agar 1994). There is not a single predictable consequence of either an extended silence or a statement of disagreement. Conversation is one of the most detailed sites in which culture is enacted, and since people come from different cultures, we can expect significant variation in their responses to spoken actions. People from different social backgrounds feel differently about all of the following: overlaps in talk, interruptions, the length of pauses between turns, ways of getting the floor, how long a turn at talk should be, how many times a person should speak in a conversation, explicit disagreement, the degree of deference owed to the teacher and to other members of the class, and just about everything else about speaking and listening. What is more, even within a particular cultural group, women and men (generally speaking) may be acculturated to expect different things from conversation. And then, of course, there are individuals, each of whom is a member of these generalizable groups and also different from other members of the same group and may in fact not fit into sociolinguists' categorizations. So speaking in a diverse group of people is a minefield, and people are inevitably going to offend one another a little bit from time to time. Sure, teachers could avoid conflicts by just taking over all the talk, but then what would students learn? The better route is to let them own the difficulties of speaking and then to teach into those difficulties.

I'm going to discuss some things to teach about conversation in thoughtful, academic contexts. They aren't necessarily rules for all talk in all contexts, and they won't necessarily come naturally to any particular group (though they may seem white and middle class to many students). They are ways that are often valued in communities of people who are inquiring, and so they are useful to learn in classrooms like the ones I'm describing here. They are not culturally neutral, but they seem to be helpful norms in permitting the widest diversity of voices to be heard and the most substantive collaborative construction of ideas.

What Is There to Teach About Talk?

As with the other tools for thinking we discussed in the previous chapter, teachers usually introduce new ideas, lessons, and strategies for conversation through minilessons distributed across the times when students are actually working, in partnerships and small groups, to create good conversations. They are also useful in attempting to grow the quality of talk across discussions about a whole-class text. In the rest of this chapter, I will offer some of the things that people I know have found useful to teach, sometimes as a particular day's minilesson, but more often as a string of minilessons across several days.

Getting a Conversation Started

Often, one of the hardest moments in a conversation is the very beginning—the move from silence to talk, the move from no content to shared content. And a conversation that begins in a way that doesn't invite the participants to think *together* will have some trouble getting back on the right track. Participants are often intimidated by one member acting too certain at the beginning, or beginning to speak in a way that others don't really understand yet, or starting too far down the road in their own thinking. The speaking person may have good ideas about the text itself but could harm the development of a good talk, because others aren't able to find a way to get on board. So in the beginnings of good conversations, participants often entertain an open sort of wondering, casting about for possible things to talk about.

That means that readers in conversation are sometimes willing to say first what's easiest to say, even if it seems obvious. They know it helps just to begin to establish some shared thinking about the text. It may seem odd to say it, but a group needs to develop a shared realization that, even though we each read separately, we have the same text in our minds. This is an especially fragile sense among people who are used to struggling to understand what they read. Arriving at a shared construction of the text world is not trivial. Even for very powerful readers, hearing exactly how someone else perceived what was going on, even at a pretty simple level, can provoke thinking about the different ways they saw the same part of the book.

> **Minilessons for Opening Conversation**
>
> - Wondering
> - Casting about for topics that others will think interesting
> - Saying something unsure but easy to say
> - Stating the obvious

One thing to recognize about a conversation over a book is that, if the readers are actively making meaning as they read and think, then people come to the conversation with some points to make, some cards to play. This one is interested in the character who seemed mysterious and isolated; that one is building a big idea about a sense of belonging and home. To a certain extent, each wants to play her card, not to listen to the other person's idea. To prevent everyone from moving in different directions then, the opening moves of a conversation may involve each one saying whatever they brought to the table, and then agreeing together on one of those ideas as a place to start. Sometimes, groups have found that listing the initial ideas on a sheet of paper, then circling the one that is presently the focus—literally, on the table—can be a concrete, clear version of this process of getting started.

> **Minilessons for Selecting and Focusing**
>
> - Spotting potential significance
> - Making a case for the significant things to build
> - Naming a topic as what is on the table

This discussion so far has been about the first turns of a conversation, the tentative opening moves. At this point, the readers have nominated several potential topics of varying interest and potential. If someone has said, "I didn't get whether Ray was younger or older than his brother" and another has said, "Younger," then there's not going to be much deep negotiating of meaning from that starting place. Conversants need to be able to tell which possible topics are going to produce better thinking and talking. When a conversation goes well, the readers have succeeded in spotting the potentially *significant* ideas on which to build their conversation.

After the initial casting about, after they have recognized the more significant ideas, they name a topic as being "what's on the table." This move from broad surveying of possible areas to the selection of one particular place to dig is a fundamental move in any inquiry, and it's something at which students can get better with our support. While it's true that a casual conversation with friends can range freely and loosely from one topic to another, an intellectual conversation for building ideas needs to be somewhat clearer about its central topic, so that everyone can participate in the construction of the shared idea. The move of naming that topic and getting everyone focused on it is crucial to the purpose of the discussion.

Generosity with Thinking

When conversations go well, participants are generous with their thinking, offering it freely. I don't mean they necessarily blurt out every thought that comes to mind, but while they discuss a shared focal idea, they don't just hold their thoughts silently about it. They get a bit of an idea and then just start speaking and see what comes out. They trust, in other words, talking as a medium of thinking. Start talking, and some thoughts will happen.

For that to work socially, the other members of the group must take on an accepting attitude and not punish one another for generously offering ideas. There needs to be a very high level of tolerance for statements that seem obvious, as good enough to build on. The group has to be almost grateful just to have words in the air with which to think. In every good thinking community I've been part of, this attitude of acceptance has been a central ethic, though it rarely needs to be articulated. It does need to be talked up with young people, however, especially if they are not used to having people take an appreciative stance toward their conversational turns.

Participants in inquiring conversations are willing to speculate playfully about interpretations, to throw out ideas that "may sound crazy." They may even use those words at the beginning of an utterance. Ideas don't have to be fully cooked or well supported in advance of sharing them; the group can help figure out what to do next with the idea, where to take it. They may even decide to drop it; the speaker doesn't have to decide that for them in advance. (A section below addresses the need for groups to be able to deal with difference in perspective.) What one offers to a group can and often should be considered sacrificial, brought just to contribute to conversation, even if it ends up getting taken apart.

For a conversation to go well, participants often need to pose problems about the text and about their conversation. That's what the group will work on, the slow untangling of problems. So good conversation is not just stating certainties or pontificating; it's identifying the gaps that readers need to fill in and working those through. Problems may be posed about the conversation, too, such as suggesting that the group seems to have spent a lot of time on this one aspect of a book, perhaps asking one of the quieter people to offer an idea they haven't yet talked about. Sometimes, the posing of problems can mean formulating thoughtful questions for the group, though not all problems need to be stated as questions. I discussed the importance of investigable, interpretive questions in Chapter 6, and here we are applying that same strategy to conversations. When one becomes conscious of one's own questions in reading, then one typically tries to put together potential responses to the question pretty quickly. In a group conversation, a reader may offer the question to the group, as a way deliberately to get *them* thinking about the problems, which is also a way of making the problem even more knotty for himself.

> **Minilessons for Generosity**
> - Valuing the experience of talk
> - Offering thoughts freely
> - Beginning a turn with half-baked ideas and developing them through talk
> - Acceptance toward others' offerings
> - Playfully speculating about meanings
> - Posing problems about the text
> - Formulating thoughtful questions for the group
> - Balancing fidelity to topic and flexibility for connections
> - Inventing strategies for thinking and preparing

Participants need to learn to strike a balance between being faithful to a topic and being flexible enough to develop ideas. On the one hand, the group has declared a particular topic as being on the table. On the other, one way people make new thoughts is through connections to other things, which are not on the table. Because of this tension, it's common among groups to hear both wanderings far, far away from the topic that was accepted as the conversation's center and also students saying, "That's not what we're talking about; you're off topic." Those two likely events represent the extreme poles in this tension, and these groups just need more balance. Neither is all wrong. There must be some tolerance for lateral moves in thinking, because sometimes a conversation moves to a marginally related topic and then comes back to the topic with new insights from the other area. But as I have said, without agreeing that something is central and the group's commitment to develop that idea, there can't really be collaborative thinking.

Good groups are inventive about strategies for thinking, talking, preparing for discussion, and solving problems. If students realize they have been talking a lot about a particular character and think they have divergent ideas about what she is like, then they assign for the next conversation that everyone will make a sketch of what she looks like and write a page in her voice to show how she thinks. Or, realizing that their meetings often begin with everyone wanting to talk at once, they institute a procedure, a regular part of their agenda, where they write for three minutes before beginning. Though the teacher may offer, in minilessons, particular strategies for response to literature or for conversation, there needs to be an explicit valuing of students developing their own strategies, not just obeying the teacher. Groups are complex and very different from one another, and there is no size that fits everyone. The only precise way of helping students get better at collaboration is to ask them to invent approaches that fit who they are.

Overall, participants' generosity with their thinking and offerings to the group demonstrates their trust that meaningful conversation is intrinsically beneficial. It means that they don't get "done" and sit there not saying anything to each other. Of course, that happens at first, and it happens when someone in the group is in a foul mood. It often surprises me how often it happens with college students who, in many cases, have never been asked to sustain an intellectual, curious, open-ended conversation, at least not in school. I often have to teach my university students how to keep going for even bursts of fifteen minutes of talk. The expectation needs to be explicit, that conversation keeps opening to new ideas, new questions, new activities to generate problems, and new connections to other experiences. As this disposition toward talking to think develops across time, there should be increasing evidence that students value the experience of being in good conversation and want to keep it rolling.

Awareness of Others

In many ways, the most basic lesson for students learning to create conversation is that participants need to really listen to each other and think together (Barnes and Todd 1995; Hynds and Rubin 1990). Here is something that is pretty common to see when students first begin working together in collaborative groups. They know they're supposed to tell what they were thinking in response to this chapter, so first one kid makes a short statement. Then the next kid says, "OK, so what I thought? Was . . ." Immediately after, the next student in round-robin rotation says his piece, and so on until each has spoken, at which point, the students announce, "We're done." This isn't collaboration, and it isn't really much of a dialogue, because each person is just reporting into the air their individual thinking, without being messed with or transformed by the thoughts of others.

In order for thinking to be collaborative, when one person talks, the next person takes their utterance as a point of departure for new thinking. They don't just go on to say whatever they would have said if the first person had never made a sound. There is nothing necessary or natural about this unfortunate pattern in student talk: it's just another language by-product of the way students are usually positioned in school. Talk is understood as an individualistic performance, not a medium for emergent, collaborative thinking. You talk when you know the answer and not before. But they *learned* to talk in this nonlistening way, and they can learn to attend to one another's contributions and build upon them.

Another snag in conversation occurs when some people are uncomfortable with silence and they rush to fill every pause. I remember when I first started participating in very heady conversations and there would be a long pause while everyone was thinking, I felt like someone was mad or something had happened. To introduce an alternative to this steady flow, perhaps it's a good idea to allow, in whole-class conversations, occasional pauses, time for people to think quietly in the same space, rather than acting as if we are responsible for keeping a steady stream of sound going without cease. We can also teach explicitly that maybe it's OK in good talk for people to go silent for a few minutes. Maybe that silence is a sign that everyone is thinking toward the next possible central topic to talk about. Maybe it's a good moment to write—or maybe if we just be still for a minute and relax, something new will come up for the group.

Members of good conversation groups, after all, are specifically aware of others in the group as particular readers and writers, how they think and what they need to be at their best. That's why it's almost always best for students to choose reading partners and groups only after they have gotten to know themselves and one another as readers or writers for a time. If their decisions are based on information like that, then they're likely to be better groups, more attuned to the characteristics of these specific members.

It's also important to teach students that thoughtful group members demonstrate a sensitivity to others being able to get into the conversation, especially quieter members who have trouble getting the floor. They notice that Andres is shifting his weight back and forth in his seat, and they ask if he's got something on his mind. They perceive I-Shih's intake of breath and ask if she'd like to get in here. It's actually unskilled for group members just to keep talking turn after turn when there are students who need a longer pause to feel like they can take the floor. Explicit conversations about who talks most and who needs to get in more often are a necessary part of a curriculum for collaboration. This question needs to be applied not just to individuals but to social groups: how do length and frequency of turns at talk vary between male and female and among different cultural backgrounds?

Minilessons for Social Awareness

- Really listening
- Thinking together
- Accepting pauses
- Knowing members as readers and writers
- Noticing others' attempts to talk
- Asking follow-up questions
- Responding to what the group needs

TECHNOLOGY NOTE

If students have access to the Internet when they are not together in school, their reading clubs or writing response groups may be able to maintain contact between face-to-face meetings. For example, instead of bringing the homework they have assigned their group to the meeting, they can post it onto blogs, a wiki, or a social networking site that the group shares. That way, when they come to the conversation, they have already begun intertwining their thoughts. Some research has found that people online, in writing, respond more to the detail of others' contributions than they do in oral discussions.

Turns can take lots of different forms, not just the opinion announcing that students might assume at first. Participants in great conversations often ask each other follow-up questions to clarify that they have understood. Sometimes these questions are challenges to the speaker, and sometimes they are ways of extending ideas. After a question and then the speaker's response, the questioner often says how he was thinking about the topic and why he asked the question. This move, asking questions, is observable evidence that conversants are engaged in real dialogue with one another, not just performing school talk.

Building Ideas, Making Connections, Developing Thinking

The work of a conversation is to develop thinking together. In good conversations, participants keep the topic on the table for a good while, in order to build thinking. Their time horizons are longer than less experienced participants, and because they understand inquiry and mediated thinking, they know that if they give generously of their thinking, topics aren't easily exhausted.

Skilled conversants also rely on connections and comparisons that everyone in the group can entertain. They refer frequently to things that are shared, such as the text, experiences, and shared notes. One thing that makes the text so important to a good discussion is that it's the common ground. Everyone has his own memories and ways of thinking, but what we have together is this book. To help others consider our ideas, we need to show them the exact place in the book from whence our thinking grew. We need page numbers and quotes. The group also may have made some shared notes that make easy touchstones to help everyone know what the group is talking about. They have shared some experiences, as classmates and as reading group members, and those experiences provide another point of possible comparison. They cycle back, returning to previous topics they have discussed before, not because they are incapable of moving forward, but because by returning to previous topics, they can claim common knowledge from which they can extend into new thinking. In some communities, it is pretty common for young people to talk in a cyclic way, rotating in and out of topics again and again, layering them each time with more thinking (Gilles 1993). It's different from the way writers typically build meaning in a text, one heading at a time, but it's a congenial and relaxed way of orally building thoughts together. When students are together for long enough stretches of

Minilessons About Building Ideas Together

- Keeping the topic on the table for a long time
- Making frequent reference to page numbers
- Making shared notes to record emerging ideas so you can return to them
- Referring to common experiences
- Going back to previous topics that connect to this one
- Referring to past conversations about other books

time (and that is best for their chances of building good conversations), they can refer to past dialogue, connect this talk with the one they had about another book, another character, another student's piece of writing. Each of these connections taps into a well of shared content and creates new resonance for the present conversation.

Dialogue About Difference and Changing Minds

Where there are multiple people thinking, there is difference. As I said in the above section about leading discussion, though, it's sometimes the case that people in conversation get used to ignoring difference if it's not very objectionable. And usually, it's just not that big a deal if someone thinks differently from me in a novel, so why bother pointing it out? But people who are going to be in good conversations need intellectual negotiation, need dissonance, need difficulties. So good conversants recognize the difference in their perspectives and interpretations. That's what they are looking for, and that's when conversation starts to get good.

Though it will take emotional work for many students, part of learning to be in quality conversations involves becoming comfortable with disagreement. For some people, it can feel like their value as a person is questioned if someone differs from them in viewpoint. But the only way a good discussion is possible is if these points of divergence become visible; that is, if people explicitly differ.

At the same time, some students like to become competitive and combative in their style of talk. I've seen groups of boys who seemed unable to move away from a pounding-the-table debate style of discourse. That, of course, can be yet another way of not really listening to one another, and it can oversimplify issues by making everything into a for/against binary. Instead, they need to learn that the other members of the group are not opponents, but that they are inquiring together, trying to look at something they share, shoulder to shoulder, not just forehead to forehead. Disagreement needs to be part, but not the totality, of most good discussions.

A related but different habit that conversational partners need to develop is using language to soften the edges of their disagreements. Sometimes, people do this by complimenting the other person on their thinking, naming specifically what they like about it, and then going on to say why they don't see things just that way. They may thank the person for giving them the idea, and then go on to express the opposite opinion of the other person's. They may use phrases like "I see why you'd say that, but . . ." or "I don't see it exactly the same way because . . ." or "I don't know . . . I'm just not sure about that, because. . . ." They may also try restating the previous speaker's point, to make sure they have it right and to reassure the person that they have been heard, and then go on to explain why they think differently. If the phrasing I have given here just doesn't sound like them, then a good conversation with the whole class might be figuring out the kinds of words they can actually imagine themselves saying that could help make sure my partner still feels valued even while I am disagreeing with him.

People whose contributions support great talk know how to go against the grain as a strategy for helping the group think further about the topic. They stir up controversy in a conversation, turning against the easy flow so that people have to consider multiple possibilities. They may announce this by saying, "Let's just ask ourselves if it might be the opposite." Or "Let me play devil's advocate for a minute." These performances of challenge allow the group to entertain more perspectives, even if the group members tend to think much the same way at first.

Minilessons About Differing and Changing Minds

- Recognizing and naming the differences in interpretations and perspectives
- Being comfortable with disagreement
- Avoiding addiction to debate
- Going against the grain in a conversation
- Changing your mind on the basis of evidence and reasoning
- Compromising for consensus on procedures
- Softening the edges of disagreements
- Hanging together even if it's uncomfortable

As a matter of conversational ethics, members need to be able to change their minds on the basis of evidence and reason. If they are really inquiring together, they need to be able to search for the most persuasive possibilities available, not for being proven right. The experience of changing one's mind should be extremely common in meaningful conversations, and to walk away from a conversation not having been transformed by it should be perceived as a failure to really engage and a failure really to participate in what the conversation was all about. If everyone isn't changed by a conversation, then they're not really building thinking together. For that reason, some of the best assessment questions about real conversation are things like "What did someone say that really surprised you today? Why was that a surprise, and what new things did it make you think?" Or "In what ways did your mind change across your conversation today? What did you do to make it change, and what did others do?" Asked repeatedly across conversation appointments, these kinds of questions can be deeply instructional.

Everyone does not leave a conversation thinking the same way about a book. But when a group is trying to figure out what to read next, or what response activity will be the best preparation for their next conversation, or what the agenda for a particular meeting will be, it's important that the plan just be good enough for everyone to get on board without refusing or resisting. For such practical decisions, an understanding of consensus is helpful. Consensus refers to a group coming to a decision that will not be everyone's first preference, but isn't so horrible to anyone that they can't abide it.

Accomplishing this means that participants must be able to compromise when necessary. But again, I'm talking here only about consensus on little, practical matters; building consensus is not necessarily desirable for discussing ideas and meanings.

Finally, part of learning to deal with difference involves understanding that each member will remain a participant, even in rough times. I may feel a little hurt that no one liked my idea, and I may even cry or yell, but I'm still a part of the group. I don't walk away just because there was difficulty. What could be a more useful life lesson for our students?

I know I make a lot of arguments in this book that this or that is very important. But it seems to me that collaboration, learning to be together with ideas, is as important as anything else. Naturally, it's not just part of English but of all disciplines in school. Still, talking about literature, aiming for good and meaningful discussions, is something most of us grew up thinking a central part of English language arts. Learning to be in dialogue is learning for life, learning to have partners, relationships, and communities.

CHAPTER 9

Writing That Supports Readers' Meaning Making

Before going too far into uses of writing that may support reading, I want to return to the argument against myself I began with regard to reading response activities in Chapter 7. All reading experiences do not need to be accompanied by writing. We should not build English classes where every reading event has to be commodified into a product that can be graded. It makes many people hate reading when we do that. As with other forms of mediation, *supporting thinking* is what writing about literature should be for; too often it is assigned only for the purpose of manufacturing grades or because that's assumed to be the way we must do English.

In my own literate life, I almost never write in response to novels or poetry, though I read them all the time. I bet the same is true of you. Occasionally, something in a piece of literature will get me thinking and I'll go to my notebook and write. But that's pretty rare—even though, probably, compared to most people, I am a facile writer and spend a lot of time doing it. For most students, freighting a reading event with writing just makes it harder, more laborious. At least some of the time, reading should be lighter and easier.

That said, I'm now going to describe ways that writing may support different kinds of academic thinking in response to reading experiences. Some principles will be just the same as those that govern the use of sketching and other forms of mediation we explored in Chapter 7. But because writing often has a special role in school, we will extend our discussion in several ways.

Writing to Think

By far, the most important use of writing in support of reading is its role in helping the reader think about the text—not for a grade or to please an audience—just to figure things out. Whether located in a journal, a writer's notebook (described in Chapter 10), an email, a blog, or a dedicated reading response journal, writing can give readers an opportunity to find out what and how they are thinking in response to a text. And the fact that the reader is writing can help him extend and concretize thoughts, rather than leaving those thoughts liquid and fleeting. This is writing intended only for the person doing the writing, not for an audience, and we will consider how it can work in several different ways.

Many teachers find that this sort of writing-to-think seems to belong in a reading notebook, a separate tool from the writer's notebook we will discuss later. It will be easier to think through this decision once you know the purpose of a writer's notebook, but briefly, the writer's notebook is a kind of journal about a wide range of topics, and it can serve as a launch pad for more extended pieces of writing undertaken for readers. Some people want students to feel an extra-strong sense of control and power in keeping their notebook and don't want to ask them to write about their reading in those notebooks. Other people think that some of their students' best thinking might occur in response to literature, and so it will be useful to have that thinking available when they are looking for writing topics. To some people, it seems clearer and more intuitive to have these tools separate—a reading notebook for reading and a writer's notebook for writing. To others, it seems unnecessarily complex, they get tired of students saying "should this go in the writing or reading notebook," and they like the idea of having a single, elegant tool. These are important considerations, and there is no right answer. My personal favorite answer would be to teach students to make this decision for themselves, just as everyone has to make decisions about their tools for their learning lives, but I do understand that, for most people, an approach that entertains that kind of complex diversity in a classroom would seem like a management nightmare.

Either way, there will be advantages and consequences to the decision. If there is just one notebook, it does compromise, at least on occasion, students' sense of ownership, and when kids are looking for a topic, there may be lots of stuff in their notebooks from their reading, stuff that doesn't relate to the topics they really care to write about. If there are two notebooks, then there will be personal responses to literature that include valuable memories and reflections, and it won't be near the other such entries in their writers' notebook if they are preparing to write a memoir or piece of fiction. There will also be times when students ask whether something should go in reading or writing, and you stand there flummoxed. You can't win. But then again, you can't lose either. For now, the point is that the writing-to-think needs a place to accumulate if it's going to be useful in more extended projects.

Writing for Audience

There may also be times (probably less frequent) when writing for other readers can bring forth further extensions of thinking. Writing about literature, like all writing, can be powerful with a real audience in mind. By "audience," I do not mean a teacher's judging eye. I mean people who have some real reason to be curious about what this person has to say. When I write about my reading for an audience, I'm communicating with others, whom I already know think differently. To do so, I have to select what I want to say from among diverse options, focusing my message toward the things I most want to get across to these particular people. I make a first draft of the text, just making sure I have a sense of the purpose of what I am making, but not trying to get every detail exactly right from the beginning. And then I do extensive substantial revision, with an eye toward my purpose with respect to this audience and also a vision of quality writing. This writing for a real audience of other readers is qualitatively different from someone responding to "write a five-paragraph essay about how Jem and Scout's relationship changes."

So we have writing to think and writing for an audience. These two kinds of writing can be related, as phase one and phase two, with writing for an audience based on ideas developed during the writing-to-think phase. Writing to think (phase one) is valuable even without leading to work for an audience; phase two without phase one, not so much. In what follows, we will look at several different reasons why readers might write. We will first consider writing as a tool for mediating thinking in a reading experience, as we did with other tools. Then, we will think about how writing can serve discussion, providing preparation for conversations about books. After that, we will see how these same processes

Writing in Response to Literature

1. Writing to enrich a reading experience
   a. Writing in a notebook, in the midst of reading, to support kinds of thinking from Chapters 5 and 6
   b. Writing a report for an audience, after a reading event, to share the results of that inquiry into the reader's thinking

2. Writing to participate in discussion
   a. Writing in a notebook to think through what I could talk about with others
   b. Writing talking points to plan my exact contributions

3. Writing to analyze a literary work
   a. Writing to notice themes and patterns in the work throughout the reading
   b. Writing an argument for an audience, making the case for one of those critical ideas

4. Writing literature in response to literature
   a. Writing personal and aesthetic responses to literary works throughout the reading experience
   b. Making works of art from the personal material that literature brought to mind

might work in a more traditional approach to literature that focuses attention on the literary work itself and attempts to make an argument about it. And finally, we will explore what happens when students are positioned as *makers* of literature and they write *from* the literature they read, the way poets and authors do, making literature in response to literature. For each of these reasons to write, we will consider both phases—writing to think and writing for audiences.

Writing to Support the Experience of Reading

Writing is an especially versatile and fluid tool, as it can support just about any form of thinking. A reader can write in order to *visualize*, by writing what she sees in transaction with the text, developing, as she writes, a more detailed and fleshed-out envisionment. One can write in support of *interpretation*, making hunches explicit, tracing them through a reading experience, gathering evidence and connecting it to interpretive ideas. Readers will *expect* more thoughtfully because they undertake to write their predictions. A reader's initial, glimmering notion that *this text is kind of like another* she's read can become more explicit, the things that connect them brought out and thought through, if she writes in order to extend her thinking. The writing makes thinking happen. And it does so in the medium of words—the same material with which the reader is working while reading the text.

Writing to Concretize Mental Actions

When students write to think, the concern—for the writer or for the teacher—should not be on conventions or forms. It's not about commas, because this is writing for the writer, and the thing that matters is that the writer stay focused on meaning and not get distracted into surface features. It's not about topic sentences for the same reason. It's not about supporting paragraphs, because we want writers to accept their first thoughts as a point of departure and perhaps wander well away from those initial ideas as new ones develop through the motion of the pen. That's how we see that they are thinking—going on a journey to a new idea—precisely because they do not adhere to their first thoughts but instead write in order to change their minds.

Writing to Support the Experience of Reading

Writing to think: As you move through the text you're reading now, write a couple of times a week to support a particular kind of thinking: envisioning, listening, interpreting, relating to characters, etc.

Writing for an audience: Drawing from data in the above entries, write an account of how that kind of thinking went for you across this reading experience, including how this experience fits with how reading usually goes for you.

Used in this way, writing is a strategy, rather than an assignment. When writing is a strategy, the writer is trying to accomplish something beyond the writing itself—in this case, trying to use writing in order to build ideas in response to a text. When writing is an assignment, the writer's attention is taken up in trying to respond to the authoritative demands of the assignment itself: how long is it supposed to be? What exactly does she want? When writing is a strategy to support what students are already thinking, something that they have to do, but without a particular assigned task, then it can more closely resemble a self-sponsored writing moment outside school. (See Figure 9–1.)

Writing serves thinking best when it mirrors and supports the reader's own development of patterns and themes, rather than the teacher's. Getting a question from someone else exempts me from tuning into my own mind and asking myself, "What am I thinking as I read this?" But that is exactly the ques-

FIGURE 9–1 Writing to Support Thoughtful Thinking

A Pattern That Might Help Writing to Support Thoughtful Reading

You're going to be writing about how [this kind of thinking] goes when you read. First, just read [the text] and notice your thinking, especially when you [do this kind of thinking]. You'll look back and write about specific times when you [do this kind of thinking] in a few minutes.

1. Look back at what you just read.

2. Point to a place where you can remember doing this particular kind of thinking (whatever is the point of the investigation . . . envisioning, listening, relating to a character, getting a hunch about the big idea [interpreting]).

3. Just barely mentioning that part of the text, write a few sentences about what you were doing in your mind when you read that part.

4. Say a little bit more about that.

5. Look for the next place in the text where you remember doing this kind of thinking.

6. Write about what you were doing in your mind there.

7. Keep looking back at the text and writing about moments where you were doing this kind of thinking. At least two more times.

8. Write a little about this: Is this what you usually do when you read? Can you think of times when this kind of thinking went this way before? Have there been times when it was different?

---

tion whose answer students construct as they write. At first, of course, students are not necessarily facile at thinking about their own thinking, or naming it. To them, what's in their mind may exactly equal what's on the page of the book, and therefore when they write, they just summarize the text they're reading. But if they have been learning about varied mental actions, using other thinking devices to support them, and if the class' conversation has given them chances to give accounts of their thinking in discussions with peers and the teacher, they they're more prepared to write about their mental actions and use that writing to extend them. This writing captures their ideas—because it helps to form those ideas—at a particular moment in the story of this reading event. While reading Chapter 1 of his novel, Gary writes his hunches about what this novel is really trying to say—thinking through the first event, the opening sentences, and the title—allowing the act of writing to support emergent *interpreting*. He writes then, while reading Chapter 3, about those hunches that seem to be confirmed as the book rolls along, and about the theories he has discarded. Across the room, Monica writes into her development of *envisionment*. Across the reading of this novel, she will make frequent entries in her reading journal about what places, things, and people look like. The writing, in these cases, is not about the text per se, but rather about Gary's and Monica's mental activities to make the text real to themselves.

Writing for an Audience About the Experience of Reading

In a classroom that functions, as I suggested in Chapters 3 and 4, as the Center for the Study of Us as Readers, students become adept at thinking and talking about what makes them different from and similar to one another as readers and writers. They have also become interested in the details of one another's experience—partly because hearing about how different people are from you is so freaky. You just can't believe anyone would like doing *that*. Thinking about others, if it's understood as human difference, is just another way of defining and understanding yourself. Such a class, therefore, provides an interested audience for students' writing about what reading is like for this particular individual.

Based on the frequent writing-to-think Monica has done on envisioning in her notebook, she uses those entries as data to study her envisioning process—how this experience went for her, with a focus on a particular kind of thinking. How did her envisioning change across the book, and what was it like by the end? How does this experience with her mind's eye compare to how things usually go for her? The paper will be about the book, in a way, but it's more about how Monica read the book—the story of some of her thinking through the course of reading—not everything she thought, just how she envisioned, because that was the kind of thinking on which she chose to focus. Writing it for an audience of classmates who have not read that book will mean she needs to de-emphasize the book itself, because reading about a book you haven't read could be either boring or frustrating because it gives away the plot. What is interesting is Monica, the human reader, this person we all know, what she was trying to do as she read, and how that went.

It should be clear, too, that this kind of writing is every bit as academic as an argument about a literary work consisting of thesis plus supporting evidence. This kind of writing—descriptive, employing data collected across time from which the writer must draw themes—is like anthropology and other social sciences, as well as some kinds of research in natural sciences. It's hard work, and I don't think we should do too much of it for reasons I have already explained, but I think it's at least as valuable as a kind of academic writing as the forms that seem so inescapable in the usual English curriculum. And this kind of writing draws more explicitly on students' own thinking and the resources they bring to the reading event. As such, it has often seemed significantly more engaging to the students who do it.

> ## Multilingual Note
>
> Keep in mind that writing long prose in response to reading long prose and lengthy discussion is a lot of English for multilingual students to cope with. Consider options for response activities that demand less English language. Keep imagining yourself moving to a new country, culture, and language and having to stay all day in the modality that is exactly what you don't know (though there are lots of things you do know and would like to be recognized in this class).

Writing to Prepare for Discussion

Writing can also be useful in reading literature when it serves as preparation for discussion. Often, when we ask students to talk in class or a small group about what they are thinking in response to teaching, they are jerked from silence and solitude into public speaking with no steps between. Writing (or sketching, charting, indexing, or diagramming) can provide an intermediate step between silence and a higher-risk speaking situation, a chance to mediate some thinking without looking stupid in public.

Writing to Think Through What You Have to Say

Before beginning to think about exactly what to say in a discussion, a reader may use writing as a way of figuring out what she *could* say, prior to committing in public to a particular set of points. She just writes to figure out what is on her mind. Writing to think provides an opportunity for trying out her initial thoughts, so that she is less often tempted to end a turn at talk by saying

"Oh, never mind, it's dumb." For an example, after reading the first chapter of Ishmael Beah's *A Long Way Gone*, I write:

> We know that he's going to see war, but the book starts off talking about how far away the war is, and everything seems fine and normal. It's a different country than mine, so it's not that it's normal like my life, but it's relaxed and nothing special is going on. The sky is blue, and kids are learning rap lyrics and joking around with their families. When suddenly, in the middle of all this ordinary stuff, there are people shooting people, it seems completely bizarre. And so sad, because you feel the loss of usual life, and the ordinary things people were trying to do.

That kind of writing helps me to move from a fairly muddled group of impressions upon my initial reading toward being able to focus on a couple of ideas about that section. I move from the complexity of the whole chapter to something more manageably simple, though as I discuss it with others, I would expect it to become complex again, in a new way.

Writing to Plan Points for a Discussion

Once students have some thoughts that they have named to themselves, they can turn those initial ideas into some prepared points for a discussion with a small group or the whole class. Since the publishing of this kind of writing really comes through *speaking*, this is the nearest we get to writing for an audience. It's not that they should develop their ideas fully before presenting them to an audience. It's just a good idea for each participant to have some kind of agenda when they come to the group. So I could make these points for a discussion of the first chapter of *A Long Way Gone*:

- Life seeming normal
- Things people are trying to do - projects
- War is bizarre to everyone it happens to.
- It makes me almost unbearably sad that this happy life is going to be lost.

Now I am more ready for a conversation. I don't have to say all those things, but at least I won't sit down with my friends and then start looking for something to talk about. Though this is written with an audience in mind—the people to whom I might say these things—it's not written out in prose, because it's just meant to serve as a reminder to talk naturally about these things I have already thought

---

Writing to Prepare for Discussion

Writing to think: Immediately after reading, write as much as you can as fast as you can about what is on your mind in response to the text.

Writing for an audience: Right before starting your conversation, reread the writing you did after reading. Prepare at least two points you would like to discuss with the group (or your partner).

through. I have opened my thinking *toward* others, even before I get around to talking to my fellow readers.

Writing *About* Literature

As English majors well know, in much academic work, people make texts in response to other texts. There are a few domains outside school where this practice is common, such as in the writing of legislative aides, judges, certain kinds of attorneys, of publishing companies and others in the literary world, and of course, of critics and scholars. Indeed mostly, writing about text is academic, and it's not especially practical in most domains of life. But across the curriculum in middle school, high school, and college, it is sometimes useful for students to write about a text—so that they are forced to deal with ideas that were not already present in their own heads—so that they engage with what is new or different from them. How can a thoughtful process of writing, one that includes writing to think and writing for real audiences, support this kind of writing?

I would not want to be understood here as advocating the writing practice that most of us know from traditional English classes, where students write formulaic thesis-support arguments about a work of literature. Who are they arguing with? Why are they all fighting with no one? Why is that the way to write in extension of reading? With that kind of writing, students are not actually communicating with anyone, but they're not really writing to think either. They're too concerned with being explicit about their claims and their relationships, with providing evidence, and with maintaining a cohesive text that avoids any digressions into new thinking. So they're not really using writing to think or to communicate, just to comply. We can do better.

Writing to Think

First, as students are moving through a reading experience, say with a novel, they have responses and ideas at different times. Writing through those ideas in a notebook, allowing some of their intuitions to develop as they go, provides a way for them to grow their own interpretations to defend in critical essays, rather than simply writing in response to teachers' questions. It's not that they have to be totally on their own—the teacher is continually participating in discussions, posing questions, wondering aloud, offering interpretive hunches. Some students will pick up on these as seeds for their own interpretations. But becoming a reader who can develop a reading, things to say about a book, involves learning to pay attention to your own mind and to look for ways of seeing this book that others haven't noticed yet—rather than just obeying and supporting someone else's ideas all the time. So building ideas over time, gathering evidence as they go, students can use a notebook as the starting point for critical essays they will write for an actual audience.

Writing to Discuss and Argue

When students read literature together, they engage one another's differing ideas about why the people in the story do what they do, about what the author is trying to get across, about the ways things in this text work together, about how this text is like and not like other texts we know. The environment of ideas is all about difference. Sometimes, the difference produces arguments, sometimes negotiations, sometimes just appreciation about how weird one another's thinking can be. But participants in an academic discussion need their thoughts to be considered legitimate and justifiable, and so they provide reasons why they think their arguable thoughts, and they array evidence to demonstrate that their perspectives are grounded in the shared experience of the text. It's not always about trying to win, but it *is* about trying not to seem crazy.

> ### Writing to Argue About a Text
>
> *Writing to think*: Write frequently about the theory you're building about what this text is mostly about, the ideas you notice yourself attracted to, especially the things you think other people don't have a handle on as you participate in discussions. Collect the evidence from the text that shows you're not crazy for thinking what you think.
>
> *Writing for an audience*: Write to the other readers of this text, using the evidence you have collected in your notebook to show why your thoughts about this text deserve their careful consideration. Make your case as clearly and persuasively as you can for your fellow readers.

Audience

Since audience-oriented writing is going to be situated in the class' or group's ongoing oral discussing and arguing about a book (or other text), the writing has to be directed toward that audience. Writing an argument for a teacher to evaluate is just pretending to make an argument. In order for it to be socially real, the student needs to be thinking about the person whose mind he means to change, the other student who said in class an unjustifiable contradiction to his point. Teaching students to make arguments, to justify points and reason through the relationship of evidence to thesis, is much more concrete and socially realistic if they are writing for the other students with whom they have already been discussing, or others who have been having a similar discussion in another class.

Models of Critical Essays

If we want students to be able to write critical essays well, we need to show them some examples of them. One of the dysfunctional ironies of English teaching is that we constantly ask students to read stories and poems and then write essays; so they never are able to draw what they learn as readers into their work as writers. (Chapter 12 deals more extensively with using models to teach writing.) These models are very hard to come by, however, because the kind of critical essays we have in mind are substantially different from things like book reviews, which assume that the reader has not read the book being discussed. Because critical essays assume readers are familiar with the text they are discussing, they include more detailed analysis about the language, structure, and story world, and less of a summary. The difficulty of finding quality models means that this genre of writing may not be the place where it is most congenial to teach students the craft of writing. Rather, it is an induction into a practice of interacting about texts and textual evidence. Since that is so, it's good to keep our instructional goals lined up with what's practical and to focus assessment of this writing on our purposes in teaching it. Teachers sometimes solve the models problem by showing students small portions of published literary essays from journals like *The Believer*, certain essays in *Harper's*, some book-related blogs, and online repositories like *Modern American Poetry* or *The Modern World*, showing reviews that are as close as possible to the kind of argument they'd like to see students make. They also show student work from previous years, and that's sometimes the most useful sort of model for this kind of in-school writing that only imperfectly matches up with the texts of other domains.

Process/Thoughtful Revision

So a notebook has permitted students to gather evidence and figure out an argument they will construct. And a social environment of negotiating meaning with other readers provides a bed of thought and an audience to argue toward. Models of literary essays provide an overall image of a successful text and a demonstration of small bits of technique. Still, the process of writing the essay itself must still be conscious, deliberate, and thoughtful. Though Chapter 12 deals more fully with the process of writing for readers, it will help to think briefly about it here.

The first attempt at an argument is often as uncertain as a toddler's first steps—wobbling, ambiguous of direction, happy just to stay upright regardless of where the writer ends up. Most academic writers make a first draft still in the process of discovering what they can believe themselves, not from a position of certainty. They need to return to the original text and see if they have it right. They sometimes change their minds entirely. They worry about which example will actually say what they want to say. They move from the draft back to the notebook, back to the text, and then back to the draft. They cut unpromising points and try new ones. They decide whether the argument works best with their strongest point first or the strongest one last, and then they often put their second strongest point in the other position, burying the relatively weaker ones in the middle. There are lots of decisions about how the parts should be arranged, what the content really must be, and how to move the reader's thinking from one section to the next. These decisions are never self-evident, even to experienced writers, and they certainly aren't things that kids should be assigned to do at home alone without guidance. If this form of writing is worth paying attention to, then it needs thoughtful assistance in class.

When students are writing about texts, people are tempted to provide formulas that they believe encode forms expected in college, or that they just see as helpful patterns to support inexperienced writers. Unfortunately, nothing is more damaging to students' prospects as college writers or their genuine academic thinking about a text as prescribed formulae for writing. Five-paragraph essays, rigid patterns like intro-body-conclusion, or metaphors like a sandwich are attempts at algebraic thinking that create a variable x substitutable with any content. But such forms fail to represent accurately the real work of composing, especially the composition of texts designed to persuade others. We know from research that writers do their best work when they are able to focus on *content*— on what they are thinking about and what they would like to say, and finding a form that allows them to say it (Perl 1979, 1990; Presley et al. 1998; Sommers 1980). Assigned formulae distract from that content and ultimately render invisible the social process of reasoning with an audience.

Writing *from* Literature

The most literary way for students to write in response to literature is to produce their own poems, stories, memoirs, and other literary texts as their responses, in just the ways that poets, novelists, and literary journalists do. When a poet reads a poem or novel, she doesn't necessarily jump to write a critical essay about it; in fact, most poets would do so only very rarely. Their writing in response to reading is the making of poems. Since we want our students to think of themselves as actual writers, not just as students, we should invite them, much of the time, to respond to literature in the ways their mentors would do.

Writing to Think: From Literature to Life and Back Again

Reading literature, from this perspective, is less an analytic task and more a matter of making oneself personally vulnerable to what one reads—growing as a reader by becoming able to be more deeply affected by literature. Writing, then, can be an answer, a personal one, involving one's life history, values, important relationships, and conversations. The responding writer speaks from

Making Literature in Response to Literature (see also *Time for Meaning* [Bomer 1995])

Writing to think: Immediately after reading for the next few weeks, write what the text makes you think about, what it reminds you of from your own life. When you write in your notebook at some other times, call your reading to mind to get your thoughts going.

Writing for an audience: Look over your writing in your notebook and see what that content wants to become. Is it a memoir, a poem, a story, an argument, an essay? Accept the genre that seems right for the content, keep thinking about those ideas and feelings, and design a particular kind of experience for your readers. Test it out on readers as you go.

home. That's not to say that this kind of writing would necessarily always be confessional, a revealing of secrets. But it does presume that one will write in response out of a real feeling of having been moved—because one approached the text with the expectation of being moved.

After a stretch of time responding to literature in these ways, students reread what they have written, just as they do entries about topics not inspired by literature (see Chapter 11), and look for things that might become a piece of verbal art. I often ask students to look at these kinds of responses and ask themselves, "What does this want to be when it grows up? A poem? A memoir? What would happen if it became a short piece of fiction? Should it be visual, like a graphic novel, a picture book, or a drama? What could I do with this?" Their own raw material, the thoughts they have in response to literary works, becomes the beginning of a new literary work—an answer in kind.

Writing Literature for Audiences with Literature as a Model

Moving to craft a work of literature, especially of a kind the writer hasn't had much experience making, the writer immediately has a new set of questions—how do these go? Forthcoming chapters about writing will discuss how students learn craft, but here, as we think about ways students respond to literature, we should briefly consider some of the uses of reading in the making of a literary work—the ways the poem keeps on giving. Discussing the writing of literary essays, I suggested that it was essential that writers have an opportunity to read the kinds of texts they would make. In writing literature in response to literature, however, the models for good writing are right there in the texts that provoked the thinking.

Chapter 12 deals with an extended process of organizing the study of texts empirically, with attention to genre, structure, voice, and other technical dimensions of writing. (I also have an extended discussion of making literature in response to literature in *Time for Meaning* [Bomer 1995], especially Chapter 6.) I will point out here that I'm not really referring to a quick process of reading a poem and then immediately imitating it. Rather, I mean a deeper experience of reading across time fiction, poetry, and other genres so that thinking and feeling can accumulate in a notebook until the time when the writer draws on that deep well to make something beautiful from that material.

People Who Make Things

Teaching Writing as the Design of Meaning and Relationship

" I speak of these people, and I speak to you because I cannot help it. It gives me strength, almost unbelievable strength, to know that you are there. I covet your eyes, your ears, the collapsible space between us. How blessed are we to have each other? I am alive and you are alive and so we must fill the air with our words. I will fill today, tomorrow, every day until I am taken back to God. I will tell stories to people who will listen and to people who don't want to listen, to people who seek me out and to those who run. All the while I will know that you are there. How can I pretend that you do not exist? It would be almost as impossible as you pretending that I do not exist."

—David Eggers, *What Is the What: The Autobiography of Valentino Achak Deng*

CHAPTER 10

Writers' Notebooks: Tools for Thinking

Farid is writing about the pump motor he worked on last weekend in the basement of the building where he lives. He's remembering exactly what he did and how he figured out which part he would need, as well as considering other possibilities for what it might have required. As he writes about the pump, he thinks a little more explicitly than he did over the weekend about just how it uses electrical energy to move water. A few seats away, Jessica is writing in her notebook about her favorite singer, one who is not popular among her friends and who, consequently, sometimes causes Jessica some embarrassment. She writes about how weird it is that liking a singer can signal that you're somehow not as cool of a person as someone else. When she first started writing today, she was almost embarrassed to write the singer's name in her notebook, but the more critical her attitude becomes, the more energetically she claims her preference. Lydia, meanwhile, across the room, is sketching an elaborate cartoon that populates the entire page with little people waving and saying quirky, funny things. A balloon floats across with a couple aboard having champagne, toasting the little people below. In this world she's making, people are wittier, classier, and happier than they usually seem to be in real life, and everyone has something to say. It's kind of like this class, in fact, where students are more visibly thoughtful than they might usually seem in school, and everyone has something to say.

I've learned that composing is not just one thing—not just a matter of writing to please the teacher. When planning a class, I have to consider at least two broad, different though related categories of writing. There has to be writing in which the kids address a real audience other than me, the teacher— when they think about clarity of expression and craft across a process of revision. That kind of writing will be the subject of the next chapter. The present chapter is about the other crucial kind of composing: writing to think. It is about teaching students to write for themselves, to write in order to find out what they have to say, how they feel about things, where they stand, how they are different, and what teams they're on. It is about writing to discover, rather than writing to communicate—though in a way, even discovering is not right, because a writer's meaning isn't just out there waiting to be found; it's got to be built. It's writing to construct thought. I introduced this concept in discussing writing in response to reading, in Chapter 9, and this chapter extends the idea of writing to think as part of a curriculum focused on composing.

We began considering the ways writing could support thinking in reading, but I believe it's not enough just to write in response to other authors' texts. Part of a school curriculum should involve asking kids to pay attention to their own thinking, to notice when they have a thought, when they begin making an idea. Though in many ways, we always think with others, always making our ideas and words in response to others', students' thoughts do not only occur in response to things their teachers put in front of them. They think in dialogue with a wider world, with more diverse voices, and so school should teach students to construct ideas into that richer conversation, following the trail of their own attention, not only to respond to ideas presented to them by authority figures. At least some of the time, students should create language as the initiation of a stretch of conversation, not just as a response.

Have you ever noticed that, if a student in school pays attention to her own thoughts, we say her mind is wandering? She's considered off-task because she is not giving over her thinking to someone else's words. Instead, especially in English class, we need to teach students to attend to their thinking, to develop and extend it, to control their attention and direct it to matters of significance. This can't be accomplished if students are always waiting, waiting, waiting to be told what the topic of the day will be.

Students' writing-to-think is not necessarily all personal, but it often is— because of what kids' lives are like. Many or most of the things they care about are, naturally, personal, and so if they pay attention to their own thinking, then they are often drawn to areas of life usually overlooked in the school curriculum. So students choose to write about things that come to mind often for them: people important in their lives, interests, activities, personal expertise, memories, plans. In a sense, the notebook runs the border between the private and the public—a place where things that are still inside can try out their legs outside, where thoughts at least start to become known to the writer, even if they aren't ready to be known by an audience yet. All writing works this way—thoughts, even academic ones, begin where even the writer cannot see them and become gradually more public as they develop toward audiences.

Naturally, since this border is being brought into school, there will be concerns about disclosure—for kids and for teachers. Students do need to understand that writing to think in school is not an invitation to reveal their deepest secrets—those need a private hiding place (such as a diary with lock and key or an anonymous blog—though no writing, on or offline, is completely safe from others' eyes). Too much focus on issues about privacy can actually make a writing environment seem less safe, more continually on orange alert, and might urge students not to engage in the disclosure of what they are thinking that is at the heart of writing.

This chapter focuses on writing that is, more or less, the writer talking to herself or himself, and the container—or better yet, the tool—I will describe for supporting and extending this type of writing is the *writer's notebook*. One advantage to writers' notebooks is that the pedagogy associated with this tool allows writing-to-think to connect to the other kind of writing—crafting texts for audiences. That is a big piece of what makes a writer's notebook different: it's not just a journal, which could be seen as an end in itself. It's not a dialogue journal, which is a place where the writer communicates with other students or with the teacher, writing messages back and forth. In other words, though there are other possible tools and pedagogies for writing to think, the writer's notebook is distinguished by its relationship to more extended, revised projects written with particular purposes and audiences in mind. Consequently, with a writer's notebook, the point is to live with a consciousness of possible writing topics and ways of thinking, to rehearse all the time for potential public announcements.

I learned about writers' notebooks in the late 1980s, when I was part of a community led by Lucy Calkins at Teachers College Reading and Writing Project in New York City. Lots of fine educators there contributed collaboratively to the development of a careful pedagogy, a way to fit what we knew about writers into classrooms. What I write here is my version of that pedagogy. But, of course, we didn't make up writing-to-think or the keeping of a notebook. We were influenced by exhibitions of famous writers' notebooks and journals from across literary history in the New York Public Library. We read the substantial traditions and scholarship about all kinds of journals by scholars ranging from Donald Murray to Vera John-Steiner, and we also read authors', artists', and scientists' accounts of the ways they used notebooks in their development of ideas. When we learned about writers who did not keep notebooks, we tried to understand the inner processes they undertook to prepare for writing, things it might be helpful to have externalized for novice writers in classrooms. In the end, a notebook pedagogy was, for us, a way of making complex processes of inquiry more concrete and manageable for teachers and their students—not an orthodox model of the one and only writing process.

For one thing, a writer's notebook is meant to change the way the user pays attention to the world. The writer notices more because she has a notebook and a responsibility to write in it. She has a problem to solve—what to put in the notebook today—and the solution to that problem involves tuning into her own thoughts—noticing when she has them, becoming aware of their relationships, and following them where they might lead. Because the notebook is easy to carry around, she gets used to noticing her thinking in many different parts of the day, many locations, the way an artist with a sketchbook notices the curve of a branch or the juxtaposed textures of asphalt and concrete. She starts to notice, and to write into the seams of her day; she develops a writing life.

Materials

It's not that there's something special about the notebook as an object; really, writers' notebooks are just pages stuck together. The device is not the point—what matters are the practices that teachers and students engage in when they say they are working with writers' notebooks. Still, though there is no particular thing that everyone calls a writer's notebook, a teacher has to make some decisions about materials from the outset. Some people have decided to ask their principal for funds to buy all their students composition books, which you can usually find for about a dollar, and that way, they know everyone is going to have a notebook with them on the launch date. Plus, they find that, when they collect these notebooks to review them, they stack nicely. Teachers have often encouraged students to decorate these notebooks so that they make an identity statement about the writer, about what is important to them, how they want other people to see them, and the kind of writer they would like to become this year.

Other teachers bring in an array of notebooks—composition books, sketch books, hardcover journals, and whatever else they can find—with small and large paper, colored and white, fat and narrow lines—and ask students to handle the different types of notebook and talk with a partner about which would best suit them each as writers. Some students need something small, that would fit into a pocket, and finding that will make the whole difference in whether or not they ever carry it around. Others would feel so cramped by a small notebook that they'd never get any momentum built up in their writing. Some need paper without lines because sketching or other visual media might often be part of their composing process. There is much to be gained from this kind of tailoring of the tool to the user. The trick is that the writer needs to have the whole notebook in class every day and that

it must be portable enough for the writer to take advantage of caught moments on the go—in a waiting room, bus, kitchen, or the back seat of a car—to capture small threads of thoughts that might grow into something more. At the moment, I still think that a paper notebook is the best thing for that. But people are different, and it's always worth keeping an open mind to what practices writers might invent. For my own writing life, the default position remains a moleskin notebook pretty similar to one Hemingway might have carried.

As I stated in Chapter 9, one other thing that has to be determined is whether students' writing in response to literature and about their reading lives will go into the same notebook as their other writing. My own tendency has been to focus, to reduce the number of tools I ask students to use, and to bring their thinking about their favorite book up close to their thinking about people in their lives. But I, as a writer, do have different notebooks for different purposes, and there might be good reasons to have a reading notebook separate from a writer's notebook. It's something to think through and perhaps try in different ways.

Launching

One way or the other, the students get notebooks, and the day arrives for launching them. Let's call it Tuesday, so that they can get a reminder on Monday to bring the notebooks with them the next day. Tuesday's minilesson is going to carry over, as most minilessons do, for at least an additional day or two. The content of that minilesson needs to be a balance of making it feel easy to write and making the work in the notebook feel like an extension of the students' agendas, rather than compliance with an assignment. The last thing we'd want to do in notebook work is give one assignment after another so that students learn to wait upon the teacher to find out what they'll do in their notebook. The point of the notebook is for it to become an instrument for thinking, self-sponsored by the users themselves. But early on, we have to show students that they have things to say, that they can trust their own minds, and that what they come up with will be acceptable to us as their teachers.

A teacher has to establish a balance between (a) giving students lots of space for decision making and (b) providing enough support so that they don't feel abandoned and empty. That balance is crucial throughout the teaching of notebooks, and the key is to make students responsible for making decisions, but to teach actively what they need to know to make good decisions. Teachers have launched notebooks with varied attempts to achieve this balance. Here are three of those ways.

1. Launch by teaching students that they have stories to tell.

Some writers are intimidated by the blank page, and this can be especially true when confronted with all the blank pages in a whole notebook. So one useful way to launch notebooks is by helping students feel full of their own material. Many teachers have done this by starting with oral storytelling. This is an especially good beginning for students who are learning English as an additional language and for any students for whom writing has sometimes been difficult.

When I do this, it basically goes like this. I remind the students about how sometimes, when you're talking with a friend, you tell a story and then that makes your friend remember a story. Then your friend's story reminds you of another one. And you go through the conversation like that, with one story giving birth to a story in the other person's mind, for quite a while. I say we're going to try to get that started in our talk today. Then, I tell a story, something from when I was younger than they are now, something I think they may be able to relate to. I see if, in the whole group, maybe one or two of them will share a story that comes to mind, from me having told that story. It's always possible with adolescents that they'll be too shy to speak up at this time. But sometimes, a couple of them will, and they're often much better storytellers than I am (it doesn't take much), and it helps to get the class going. Then, I ask them to break up into small groups of three or four people sitting near them (or people with whom they're comfortable talking) and start swapping stories. I narrated this procedure in detail in *Time for Meaning* (Bomer 1995).

2. Launch by teaching students to be responsive to whatever is around them.

Getting started on a notebook entry is a matter of placing attention wholly on an available thought. Any thought will do, including just accepting a topic from something in range of sight. A writer needs to be able to look around a room or out a window, see something, accept that as good enough, and start writing. It's a practice, something one gets used to doing, and it's another good way to get students started in notebooks. This launch can be facilitated by just trying oral versions of the things one could start thinking in response to objects or vistas at hand—an eraser, a floor tile, the view out the door to the hallway.

3. Launch by teaching students to write in order to think.

I've said that notebooks are all about writing to think, and so aiming directly for that goal is yet another potential first step. Most writing teachers do this with some version of what Peter Elbow called "freewriting" (Elbow 1998)—writing as much as you can, as fast as you can, without stopping, for a specified period of time. You don't worry about correctness or anything except getting your pen ahead of your head—leading thinking with the writing itself. With a whole class, I usually explain the idea, then demonstrate it for them on a document camera or chalkboard, and then say, "Ready, set, go." I say they're going to write for ten minutes, though I usually take pity on them after about eight. Almost everyone writes the whole time, and many write more than they have ever written, just because they kept going. As you would expect, lots of what they write is repetitive and maybe even meaningless, but what they learn from doing this is that writing can just be a behavior—just something you do, whether or not you feel like you have something to say. In fact, you can write in order to find out what you have to say.

Whichever launch a teacher chooses as the first lesson about writing in notebooks, there is almost always a need to reteach the same strategy for another class or two, and then to move on to other forms of writing-to-think, so that students don't define notebook writing as consisting exclusively of either memories, writing from the environment, or freewriting. Their notebooks will be more useful to their writing lives and the projects they will develop if they learn a variety of kinds of entries. Plenty of further notebook lessons will be discussed later in this chapter.

The Language(s) of Notebooks

In notebooks, writers usually employ language that is not particularly audience-directed. Because the purpose is to think and not really to communicate to others, there may be even more elliptical language than that which is used among family members. When notebooks are part of school, the close intimacy of the references may be compromised, but it's still not appropriate to expect a notebook to read as if written for a general audience. The language may be informal, near to everyday spoken language, and in fact, allowing students the space to explore the written potential of everyday speech is one of the ways they may be able to develop a sense of voice—the memory of the human, breathing body that sometimes stays in written language. In the interest of thinking, what is most important is that the language adheres to the way the thinking lives. If the thoughts are most accessible in language similar to that which is used in the student's home, then that is the appropriate language style for writing to think about that subject.

Naturally, this point is especially important for multilingual students. Their different languages probably belong with different identities, relationships, activities, and therefore, thoughts. They can be different people and think about different things in their multiple languages. Spanish may be home, and English the language of friends. They may have a tribal language as well as Arabic for religion and English for popular culture. They may use different varieties of English with different communities in which they participate, so a notebook might include entries in academic English alongside entries in African American English, Appalachian English, Chicano English, Cajun English, Pidgin, or Creole. It's good for students—and their teachers—to understand the ways language is tied to location. So they need to try lots of experiences to see how their languages and their familiar mental territories relate. It's true that this necessarily means that their English teacher sometimes won't be able to understand what they have written in their notebook, but the conversation, which the teacher can understand and even lead, can be more about how these multiple languages work in the student's intellectual life, rather than about the specific contents of every single entry.

Overall, the notebook, for all students, should be a place for experiments in language. It can be a place to try on new ways of saying things, just to see what ideas are like when they sound fancy or simple, pretty or ugly, when we sound like ourselves, or like the people next door, or like people from a long time ago. Writing in a notebook is an opportunity to see, without much

Multilingual Note

We should encourage our English-dominant students, too, to try out the international languages they are learning in their notebooks. If a way of saying something in Spanish occurs as students are writing, I think they should try to switch codes and see what happens. Maybe they will just mix particular phrases, even perhaps individual words, from their second or third language into their English for a while. Maybe there also will come a time when they could try on the newer language for an occasional entry and see how their thinking feels when they do. A literacy education in the world we inhabit in the twenty-first century should include frequent reaching toward multilingualism and openness to global citizenship.

social risk, what it is like to bring forth the diversity of possible voices within the writer.

Practices

Once a class is underway with notebooks and pages are filling with writing, a number of minilessons and conferences can serve the practices and habits of keeping a notebook. Keeping a notebook is not "just writing." It is something people have to learn how to do, and many of the things that make a notebook work as a thinking device need some explicit explanation and support.

It often surprises me, for example, how often it's necessary to teach kids that they should begin their next entry either right beneath the previous one or on the next sequential page in their notebook. It reveals how unaccustomed they are to thinking about their own writing/thinking as something for which they would have any future use. Their stance is: I'm just writing this out of compliance with your demands. What difference does it make what page it's on? Because of this sense of compliance, it's important not to teach this or any other notebook practice as a rule, but rather to explain the function and use of the practice in a writer's life. There are several reasons why it's important to write notebook entries sequentially. One is because you want to know when you start an entry that you have plenty of blank pages behind this one to finish it in a way that lets it keep going and make sense. You don't want to suddenly come upon a page that's been written on. Another is because you want to be able to see your journey through days and weeks of thinking in this book, and the order of pages lets you follow that route. Furthermore, there may be a need to index all the places you wrote about one thing, say, the dog you had when you were in kindergarten. If you're going to find those entries, they need to be in predictable places, arranged by date (in sequence) or by page number. When we address those kinds of concerns, we are paying attention to the notebook as a technology.

That brings up some other conventions of notebook keeping: dating entries and numbering pages. Dating entries is especially important, because of the functions stated above, and also because it permits the writer and the teacher to see how frequently the student is writing in the notebook. If I look through my notebook and see there are big gaps between entries and that the entries are scattered sparsely across weeks, then that has to tell me I need to get my life right. For some students, numbering pages can also be a useful habit. I'm not sure that it should be required, but it can be awfully useful once there are quite a few entries in a notebook, for being able to make an index in the back so the writer can know the page numbers on which she can find all the entries about that dog. This kind of indexing is a low-tech way of creating links among parts of a text, in a way that has long compensated for hypertext (computer writing with clickable links among parts) not having been invented yet.

One practice that makes notebooks useful for thinking is the habit of returning to things you have written about before and saying more about them. Just because you wrote about a topic once does not mean it's finished. This is an essential lesson for an intellectual life that is all about building ideas, themes, evidence, and arguments across time. In order to facilitate that kind of returning, recursive, layering thinking, it's helpful to teach students to leave some serious white space strategically placed in their notebooks. That might be accomplished by writing with very wide margins, or by leaving the back of every page blank for returning to think again. Or by sometimes just leaving a big blank area, because they know they're going to have more to say later about this idea. Sometimes, leaving lots of space actually encourages writing, because even if they can't think of much to say about it now, getting that down creates the opportunity to return and think some more about it. Figure 10–1 provides some of the intellectual moves that help writers say more about something they have already written, and Figure 10–2 provides some practical conventions of notebook keeping that can invite those kinds of thinking.

Because all the pages of a notebook are the same, what you write can get buried in there. To help establish visible connections among entries in different spots in the notebook, it's helpful to show students that they can use sticky notes, color-coded page edges, marginal notes that index topics, and other strategies to identify and connect entries visually. Emphasizing these concrete practices has effects beyond practical convenience; it teaches students that one important habit of mind is to make connections among the ideas you have on different days, in different settings.

Teaching these practices with notebooks, the point is for writers to employ them purposefully, not for teachers to just assign them to the whole

FIGURE 10–1 Ways of Layering Meaning in a Notebook

Ways of Layering Meaning in a Notebook

Ask yourself: Why?

Ask yourself: What is important about that?

What other events does this connect to?

When was another time I felt the same way?

How far back did this go?

What exactly did this look like?

These are the most important words in that entry—and here is why . . .

This sentence is a fast and short version of this next whole entry . . .

Technologies of Layering Meaning

1. Write in the margins.

2. Decide how you will leave space for layering meaning:
   - Leave bigger margins
   - Leave blank the whole right half of each page
   - Leave blank the facing page (backs of each page)
   - Leave empty space at the bottom of the page, or just a corner of it

3. Return to entries by writing on sticky notes you can put onto the entry.

4. Use sticky notes with codes to connect entries across pages.

5. Develop a coding sheet for your notebook, in the back, where you keep track of a set of codes and pages that help entries connect.

6. Quote yourself by putting a sentence or two from a previous entry at the top of a page and writing from that.

---

class. When I do a minilesson on a strategy like using sticky notes, the idea is not necessarily for everyone to immediately start doing that in the same way. Rather, it's for each student to start thinking about what entries in the notebook might be connected; the concrete actions are just an embodiment of that motive, the habit of thinking.

Management

Workshop Every Day

Since this work with notebooks involves sustained engagement in a particular form of literate activity, day after day, a workshop structure is most appropriate (see Chapter 1). That is the structure that allows the focus to be on students' ongoing work as writers, with opportunities for the teacher very actively to teach—through minilessons, conferences, and student sharing—into what students are doing. The teacher can be freed from constantly giving instructions about how the class is going to go in only one way—by making the class run in the same way every day, by making it predictable. That means, during this stretch of time that kids are learning to keep notebooks, the class is dedicated to a daily writing workshop. Not just Fridays. Not twenty minutes of the class. The whole-class time (or about half of it, in a block schedule) is writing workshop.

Teaching Stamina and Concentration

Picturing a class full of kids getting themselves writing and continuing to write through a half-hour or so of allotted time sets off anticipatory alarm bells for many teachers. They picture kids stopping writing, smacking their friends in the shoulder, getting up and wandering around, climbing up onto the windowsills. In some ways, this is a reasonable concern, even though the evidence is strong that students act the ways we expect them to. It's reasonable because most of our students have never been taught how to stay with work, especially writing, through moments of difficulty, inattention, distraction, and fatigue—and keep working. It's important, then—one of the most important things we can take on—to teach students stamina, concentration, and focus as writers. Teaching such basic things aren't just what we have to do in order to have a class that operates smoothly (though that's part of it). These are also intrinsically important educational objectives—every bit as important as habits of learning new words, or interpretive practices in response to literature. In a writing workshop, classroom management is not some perfect system of absolute control of students—it's teaching. It's teaching about how to keep writing, how to make your material matter to you, how to get reengaged when your mind drifts.

A writer will back away from writing for so many reasons. Because she doesn't believe that the material she has is valuable, interesting, or rich enough to write about it. Because he thinks of something more interesting to him than the paragraph he's in the middle of. Because something outside (like a friend sitting nearby) distracts her. Because the lead breaks on his pencil or someone's nose nearby sounds funny when they breathe or a random memory of a television show flits across his mind's screen. It is not possible to prevent distractions. What is important is that every writer have ways back to what she was doing—pathways of renewed concentration.

Conferring and Recording

In a writing workshop focused on notebooks, the teacher spends most of her time circulating and conferring with individuals. While students work on their notebooks during class time, the teacher circulates and talks with individuals. She talks with Hector about his entries about soccer, leading him to reflect on how he feels during the games, what his struggles in practice mean to him, and leaves him thinking about how he might go back and layer reflection into the margins of several entries on that topic. Vanesa's entries in class are a couple of pages long, but the entries she makes outside class are only about two sentences long, and the teacher helps Vanesa consider various times in her week that might lend themselves to more sustained notebook writing so that some of the outside entries can look more like the in-class ones. Each conference meets the student where she is and seeks to extend what she is already doing toward a greater degree of thoughtfulness, fluency, ambition, or discipline.

Especially when students are writing in notebooks (though many other times as well), conferences are, for the teacher, largely about listening (Anderson 2000). The teacher is there to create a bridge between silent, inchoate impressions and language, then between what is easy to speak and what may be harder to write. Many teachers have found it useful, upon kneeling beside a writer, to ask, "What are you thinking about today in your notebook?" The idea is to get the student to immerse her mind in her material, rather than as a task she has to get finished. The student starts to speak, something that is easy to say, and in dialogue with a thoughtful adult, the material becomes perhaps a little more elevated toward the literary, more interesting, interpretive, and significant. We create a conversation focused not, at first, on the page, but on the writer's language and thinking right now. The student doesn't need to tell everything they know, and the teacher will have to keep this pretty short in order to keep circulating around the room.

As the writer talks, the teacher listens to see what strategies from the next chapter in this book (Chapter 11) come to mind as the student talks. The teacher announces to the student that there is something he'd like the writer to try. He explains the strategy, perhaps quickly demonstrating an abbreviated version, and then asks the student to try it right here on this notebook page. He may stick around to watch her get started, but if he's been sitting here a while, he'll need to get moving. The whole conference takes, on average, about five minutes—some longer, some shorter—so that in a given writing time, the teacher is able to confer with six or seven students.

After each of these conversations, the teacher makes a note about what she and the student just talked about; that way, she can connect the next conference with that student to the one that came before, rather than just offering isolated dribs and drabs of advice across time. She can also remember to check back in with Vanesa in a couple of days about how the project of finding slightly longer writing times is going, or can get to Hector before he starts the next entry to remind him to think of the inner world or reflective meanings in the events he recounts. Conferring, then, is not just a means of instructing but also part of a management system, organizing and raising the quality of student work at the same time as the teacher organizes her own time and attention.

Homework

Most teachers who work with notebooks assign them as a standing homework assignment for the whole year. Notebooks are meant to be a tool for developing students' writing lives, and figuring out how this tool can fit into the rest of their lives—all the parts that are not about writing—is a big part of building a writing life. To figure out the details of the assignment, it's a good idea to consider a range of purposes and kinds of writing in the notebook. On the one hand, the notebook should be a place to collect momentary impressions or ideas, fragments of fact or thought that might prove someday useful. On the other hand, it's important to an intellectual life that students learn to sustain their thinking on one topic, during one particular writing session, not just dash off quick thoughts. So at least some of the time, say, two or three times per week, entries should be written in twenty minutes to half an hour of sustained writing.

But homework in secondary schools needs to be balanced across classes and subjects, and sometimes groups of teachers get to the point of diminishing returns—the more homework is assigned, the less commitment and engagement they'll get from students. It's always worth considering the overall ecology and time management being asked of students. Perhaps in some cases, expecting shorter, caught entries outside class and longer, more reflective ones in class is a decent balance.

Occasionally, I have been tempted to think that if kids carry their notebooks around with them, they'll lose them for sure. Often, though, if I examine this assumption, I realize that it is not really all the students who pose this risk: just certain kids in each class. If I'm right about that, the best solution is probably one tailored to those students who have the most difficulty keeping up with things, rather than locking all the students' notebooks in the classroom and losing the possibility of portable, on-the-go writing that fits into the varied contexts of students' lives. So maybe some students can leave their notebooks in the classroom and have separate little notebooks—maybe just pages folded and stapled together—to take with them for a few days at a time. That way, if they get lost, it's not as tragic.

Encouraging Variety

When I first began teaching with notebooks, my chief problem with kids' writing was that they kept making diary-type entries over and over—just summaries of the day's events. Think about what that meant for developing topics toward crafted pieces for audiences—a factual record of Monday, Tuesday, Wednesday usually was no way for themes or obsessions to emerge across time.

Most likely because my students had been taught some previous school year to write that way in "journals," each day was a separate summary, often with little meaning making or built connections. In addition, my intended sort of experimenting and reaching for growth could not arise out of an inflexible pattern like this—we needed more variety.

We began, each class as its own community of writers, cataloguing the range of different types of entries we had already thought of to write. I got some from books about journal keeping, though I tried to be very selective about what I would call a type of entry. I wanted a "type" to be something that someone could do again and again, that someone else could try—not a clever idea, not an assignment, but just a type of notebook entry that almost anyone could try on without an assault on their peculiar taste or topic preference. Figure 10–3 provides a list that I have culled from hundreds of conversations with kids about the kinds of entries already in their notebooks. I don't know that every class needs a list. People are pretty inventive without them. But at least such an array of possibilities might feed someone's imagination and a writer's decision making.

One special possibility to keep in mind is writing in response to literature. As I discussed at length in Chapter 9, literature can provide a meaningful and important stimulus to thinking, and writing can be a way of mediating that thinking. Many students' best entries have been written by bumping off a text they read, taking up feelings, associations, and themes from the literary work and applying them to personal material or the concrete and social world around them. Often, literature tunes the writer's ear to more complex sentences than they might have written otherwise, and there is to the thinking a more exalted feel than might seem easy to get while thinking about the conversation in the hallway between second and third periods.

Reading, Responding, and Grading

If the notebook is to be written for the writer's thinking and not with a very strong sense of audience, the experience of being read and judged needs to be minimized. This is, of course, tricky to pull off in school. It's difficult to assess writers' progress in becoming a keeper of a notebook without becoming the audience for what they write or a judge of the quality of language that was never intended to be read that way. One strategy is to delay looking at the notebooks, at least for a few days. There is really no reason at all to try reading every entry as it is produced, and even once a week probably creates too much audience presence in the writer's mind. Collecting one class' notebooks every other week or so is probably sufficient, and setting up classes on a two-week

FIGURE 10-3 Possible Types of Entries

What Kinds of Entries Are There? Just a Start . . .

- Identity statements and reflections
- Observations—things I notice in the world
- Questions—things I wonder about
- Thinking about what events might mean
- Response to things I read
- Response to things I see
- Drawings, sketches
- Entries as diagrams or charts
- Clippings from websites, magazines, news
- Photos I want to write about
- Images that stick in my mind
- Lists
- Experiments with long and short sentences
- Kernels of stories or play scenes—notes toward ideas
- Ideas for fan fiction about my favorite shows, books, or movies
- Kernels of blog posts, microblog tweets, or status updates
- Stories my family tells
- Memories
- Last night's dreams
- Entries that are really chains of ideas about different things
- Entries in my second or third language
- Descriptions of places
- Descriptions of objects
- Descriptions of people
- Experiments with poems or other genres
- Experiments with different languages or voices
- Experiments with multimodal design
- Free association
- Revisions of prior thinking
- Returns to previous topics
- Lists of future topics to write about
- Information
- Fragments of manifesto
- Quotes
- Overheard conversations
- Imagined conversations
- Dialogue with parts of myself
- Things a particular person has said to me
- Interviews
- Caught poetry and found poetry
- Decision making
- Plans and goals
- Celebrating victories
- Reflections and lessons about writing processes

rotation allows a manageable workload for the teacher. After all, the students are writing every day in class, right there in front of the teacher. We're conferring, checking in, monitoring progress in more ways than just when we collect the notebooks. When we do collect them, the purpose is to review accumulated entries, not individual ones.

Once they are collected, what are we evaluating about notebooks? We're trying to understand what this writer thinks a notebook is for, how he has conceptualized its use in a writing life. The real substance of our response will come through conferences, and we often will already have held important conferences with the writer well before grading the notebooks. It's in conferences that I'm most likely to tell the writer about the possible metaphor I see in one entry, or the way one entry reminded me of a picture book, or that I'll think with the writer about opening up the iceberg of content beneath the surface of what she has said so far.

In many cases, it might not be either necessary or desirable to grade the notebooks. I'm including a discussion here about grading for the huge majority of teachers who will be unable to avoid it, either because they just need grades in the grade book, or because their students just won't do work that doesn't get grades. As I wrote in *Time for Meaning* (Bomer 1995), there seem to be three criteria for evaluating the quality of what students are doing in the notebook. *Volume* is a criterion that asks whether the notebook has enough writing in it—especially whether it has the amount that the teacher has said is required. *Variety* refers to the degree to which the writer is trying different kinds of thinking and writing in the notebook, and the nature of those "kinds" is the subject of most of the next chapter. *Thoughtfulness*, as a characteristic of notebook writing, means the extent to which the writer goes beyond the givens of a topic to say something *about* it and uses reflective or meaning-oriented language. In the rubric in Figure 10–4, I have also used the criterion of *Specificity*, which I define there as the "extent to which you are collecting concrete specifics and using them in your reflection." These criteria help me define the sorts of feedback I need to provide in order to help the writer get closer to what I have in mind.

To come up with a grade, it's always important to remind yourself that the grade is really a judgment, not a "measure." If I had five piles of notebooks, one with the work that was really impressive, one with work that was OK but not amazing, one with work that was kind of bad, one with work that was terrible, and one with work that was basically absent, I could almost always toss a particular notebook in one of those piles without too much difficulty, especially if I had been clear about the criteria. Those piles are all that A, B, C, D, and F mean. It involves complex judgment. It's not subjective, but it's not quantitative either.

Figure 10–4 shows a rubric that uses such criteria as these. Rubrics are not always helpful, because they can communicate aspects of writing as if they were completely different and because sometimes the most important things are not easy to fit into that structure. But if a teacher had already determined a rubric to be absolutely necessary, the one shown here might be helpful.

	Beyond Expectation	Meets Expectation	Does Not Yet Meet Expectation	Work Is Insufficient to Judge
Volume— Expectation for the number of times you write in the notebook				
Variety—Extent to which you are try- ing new kinds of thinking in the notebook				
Thoughtfulness— Extent to which you are reflecting, connecting, and abstracting				
Specificity—Extent to which you are collecting concrete specifics and using them in your reflection				
Overall—Quality of use of this tool				

Observed uses of notebook:

Tool for thinking _____ Source of topic_____
Experiments in writing _____ Collection of information _____
Journal writing _____ Development of topic_____
Returning to ideas and layering _____ Workbench for writing _____
Other: _____

FIGURE 10–4 One Possible Rubric for Writers' Notebooks

For most teachers of writing, the most important form of response comes through conferences, not writing all over student papers. Too often, we English teachers fall into a culture of grading-as-teaching. But grading is not the most important form our teaching takes. While feedback to writing can be helpful if the writer chooses to learn from it, it's much more helpful to be assisted in the midst of the writing process, guided as one makes decisions, coached in connecting one action to the next.

When the goal is writing to think, however, it may not always be obvious what the decisions or actions would be. What should students learn about writing as a tool for thinking? What kinds of things might be indicators of quality in notebook writing? The next chapter provides some answers to those questions.

CHAPTER 11

What Is There to Teach About Writing to Think?

What students do when using writing as a tool for thinking will vary widely. Even so, minilessons about writing to think strategies can open up possibilities for students that may support thoughtfulness in many varied contexts. What follows are a bunch of fairly specific things to teach about writing to think. In most cases, it will be necessary to teach strings of three or four minilessons to adequately explore any one of these ideas. Just saying them once for ten minutes won't be sufficient. And since each of these could take several days worth of teaching, what's represented here would be more than could be taught in the first stretch of time in which notebooks are getting going. They might be things to teach across a whole year, or a particular teacher might just focus on a few that seem important and appropriate for the students he is teaching.

Teaching Diverse Types of Notebook Entries

Accepting What Comes

In as good a description of writing to think as anyone ever wrote, William Stafford discussed "the importance of just plain receptivity." Certain of the world's richness and that it would "give and give," he described his own process this way:

> I get pen and paper, take a glance out of the window (often it is dark out there), and wait. It is like fishing. But I do not wait very

185

long, for there is always a nibble—and this is where receptivity comes in. To get started I will accept anything that occurs to me. Something always occurs, of course, to any of us. We can't keep from thinking. Maybe I have to settle for an immediate impression: it's cold, or hot, or dark, or bright, or in between! Or well, the possibilities are endless. If I put down something, that thing will help the next thing come, and I'm off. If I let the process go on, things will occur to me that were not at all in my mind when I started. These things, odd or trivial as they may be, are somehow connected. And if I let them string out, surprising things will happen. (Stafford 1978, 18)

Stafford comes to this conclusion: "For the person who follows with trust and forgiveness what occurs to him, the world remains always ready and deep, an inexhaustible environment, with the combined vividness of an actuality and flexibility of a dream" (Stafford 1978, 20).

Starting with Little, Nearby Things

I remember teacher and author Vicki Vinton once saying that writers aren't people who have more ideas than other people. Instead they are people who have learned that you can start with anything—the coffee cup in front of them—and follow it to something meaningful. It is an extension of Stafford's acceptance that, at moments when going inside your head won't yield an impulse to begin, you can engage with something easily at hand. I want kids to know how to glance around the classroom, see a cinder block or a map or the branch of the tree out the window, and just start writing about that—descriptively or narratively or scientifically or metaphorically—whatever seems easiest. But I also want them to allow that initial suggestion to bloom into sustained thinking.

Reaching into Memory

Memory of our lives and experiences is, of course, a rich source of things to write about. Most of us haven't even really thought about most of what has happened to us. An important source of notebook writing is a habit of reaching back into memory. Just cast your mind back. What memory comes easiest to hand? Receive it, and get writing—see where it takes you, see how you reconstruct that memory by writing about it, see how it becomes material in your hands. So as I write this, I'm trying it, and here's the first memory that occurs to me:

> Every holiday season in Texas, there are boxes of grapefruits
> that are harvested in the Rio Grande Valley at that time of

> year. It always reminds me of how my grandparents always had those, gifts, I think, from my grandfather's coworkers at a farm equipment factory, and the fruits were individually wrapped in tissue paper that had Christmas designs like poinsettias. They were so orderly in their uniforms and rows in the crates, and it was so satisfying to hold them and unwrap them, but as soon as I did, it was kind of disappointing because then you just had a plain old grapefruit and the box wasn't as perfect anymore.

That's not a memory of a big event, or an embarrassing moment. It's just a little corner of memory, something I happened upon when I looked back. It may not be a great thing to write about, but I just reached back, found that, accepted it, held it, and started writing.

Thinking Toward Writing

One of the benefits of daily, regular, predictable writing time is that students can write when they are away from their tools—that is, they think about what they may write about when they do sit down to write. They use their thinking life to get ready for the writing moments. It's a good idea to call their attention to this, since they don't all catch onto the habit at the same time. We might as well make explicit that, when you're sitting around waiting for something, when you're traveling from place to place, when you're trying to sleep or bathing, when you're watching television, you can also be making mental notes of things you want to write when you get back to your notebook. Toni Morrison said that she does a lot of her writing when she is washing the dishes, and many writers throughout history have talked about the ideas that come to them when their hands are busy but their minds are free.

Thinking in Words

Another form of mental rehearsal is less about topic than about language. We need to ask students to think, more of the time, as if they were writing. Thinking in sentences, fixing the sentences as they go, spending more of their intellectual life engaged in language that sounds like writing. So it's not just thinking "what I'm going to write about," but "how I'm going to say it." This form of rehearsal is almost like practice at writing itself, and it begins to tune writers into the inner voice to which writers must attend in order to produce text.

Asking "How Am I Feeling?" and Then "When Was Another Time I Felt This Same Way?"

Though just writing about today's feelings can be too much like a diary, thinking from present feelings to a different but analogous time can be a way of exploring themes, ideas, or patterns. As soon as you have two incidents, there must be some more abstract idea that connects them, and thinking through the connection is a way of becoming more reflective.

Thinking About a Person

Sometimes, writers feel like they have run out of topics, because their sense of what might be a topic is narrower than necessary. It's possible to sustain lots of inquiring writing by focusing on particular people – their personalities, physicality, stories, and relationships. Lots of people's thinking, moreover, is intrinsically social in nature, and they draw power from thinking about other people—what they are like, what makes them who they are. Also, most readers use their experience of real people in thinking about characters, and students might therefore grow as readers of literature if they develop more complex ways of thinking about the characters in their own lives.

Beginning with a Story and Flipping Toward Ideas

A typical move, not only in notebooks but also in memoirs, essays, short stories, and poems, is for the writer to recount an event and then to flip to a reflection that might include abstract ideas or lessons learned from that event. For adolescents, making this move requires that they develop some control over when they are thinking concretely and when they are thinking in abstractions. Following my little narrative above about the grapefruits, I could flip to a reflection on how sometimes it's not the flashy and impressive gifts like record players and bikes that last. Or that perhaps the memory remains because of the combination of senses I recall, the smell of the grapefruit, the feel of the tissue paper unwrapping from the individual globes. Or it might be a reflection about taking pleasure from orderliness. The point is this shift from the concrete to the abstract.

Beginning with Ideas and Finding Stories

This move is the inverse of the one described immediately above. Sometimes a writer wants to write about an idea, an abstraction, like love, war, or emotion—a desire that I have noticed is a typical point of departure in some adolescents' notebooks. When a writer starts with an abstraction like that, part of the work of writing is to look for a story that helps to extend, enrich, and complicate the idea. Sometimes, doing so is a way to follow up on the flip I described above, from story to idea. You may start with a story, then flip to an idea, then find another story about that idea. So if I went from the grapefruits to orderliness, then I'd search my mind for another story about taking pleasure in order, such as visiting the Kimbell Art Museum in Fort Worth, where a relatively few exquisite art objects are arranged perfectly so that the whole experience is one of crystalline clarity and unobstructed reception of beauty.

Moving Between Concrete Specifics and Reflections

The moves described above between narrative and abstraction are similar to the relationship between particulars and global ideas. Even when the entry is not a narrative, it may begin with a single particular. A writer begins thinking, for instance, with a particular fact. Darius saw on a TV program about slavery that Southern whites would sometimes cut off a black slave's index finger if they found out he could write. Beginning with that fact—which is, of course, a hugely significant fact in itself—he wrote an entry reflecting on the fact that no longer could the African American write about what had happened to him, he could not point a finger; his ability to accuse was chopped off. Or a writer begins with a direct observation of an object. Yolanda wrote an entry just about the surface of the table in her kitchen, about how its nicks, stains, and burns made her think of the shared experience of her family's life. She moved back and forth between the concrete object she described and the abstract idea of a shared history.

Other students like beginning with global concepts. Joe, for example, was interested in thinking through right and wrong, but he was especially interested in what it means if something is considered "wrong" by some people but not by others. He had never really thought of wrongness as relative before, and he wasn't sure he liked the feeling of thinking this way, because it challenged the moral certainties he'd been brought up with. In his entry, he moved back and forth between the idea of "wrong" and specific instances that might be universally wrong, like killing people, versus those that did not seem to rise to that level at all, like talking in school. Almost every kind of writing has to deal with this relationship between concrete specifics and abstracted ideas. That's because so much of our thinking, especially that which is valued in academic contexts, also relies on this relationship.

Writing into the Fact That the Present Contains the Past and the Future

Here is a minilesson I recently taught on this kind of writing-to-think in the notebook.

Today, I want to show you another way of thinking and writing about topics in your notebook. I've noticed sometimes, some of you—and I've noticed this about myself, too—will sometimes write about something that happened today, and it's like today is in a box. The topic today has no connection to the past or to the future. And there are times when, of course, that's fine. That's all you really want to do. But I'd like to show you how you can think of more stuff to say about a topic, by following it into the past and future. It's like taking today out of the today box.

Earlier, I was writing about sunglasses, about how I have to have them if I'm outside because bright light bothers my eyes, and how I have several pairs because I need to be able to find them when I go someplace. If I just had one pair, I know I would be in trouble lots of times.

So if I want to follow that topic into the past, I could think about when I got my first pair of sunglasses—which I think probably was in middle school, maybe even high school. When I was a little kid, we never wore sunglasses, even though the sun was just as bright then as it is now. We also never wore sunscreen—we were just out there exposed in the intense South Texas sun. So that's one way I could scoop up history with this topic. Once I start thinking that way, I could decide to look up something about the history of sunglasses. Like when you see images of people from really olden times, like the eighteenth or even nineteenth century, it doesn't seem they ever have sunglasses on. When did people start wearing them? Why did they start then? I could think about my parents' and grandparents' sunglasses, or about their vision. Or I could think more generally about the history of my own eyes. So, that's the past.

I could also follow the topic "sunglasses" into the future. Let's see . . . How could that go? [Here, I sort of write in the air with my finger, to let them see what I'm saying is writing an entry.] "Since my eyes have gotten more sensitive to bright sunlight as I have gotten older, I guess that will keep up as I get even older. I probably will always need sunglasses, and they will probably look less cool as time goes on. Maybe I'll keep wanting the designs I'm used to, the ones from today, even though eyewear fashion will move along. It's pretty likely that I'm not going to be as cool one of these days." Or instead of thinking about MY future with sunglasses, I could try to think about how sunglasses might change as the future goes on, about what might be true of sunglasses when my great grandchildren are adults, or even later. It just gives me one more way of thinking about sunglasses.

So the point is, you could take an entry—really any entry, and write about that topic by looking at its past and its future. Because any moment—this moment—has a past in it, and it already contains possible futures. Thinking like that can help you have lots of good ideas for your writing in your notebook. If you can think of a way to try that today as you write, please do. Tomorrow, at the beginning of class, we will hear a couple of your examples. I'll look forward to seeing what you come up with as I move around the room and confer. Let's get writing.

Writing Only with Your Eyes

Sometimes writers discipline their attention only to what they can see. They write an entire entry that is purely visual, not reflecting on it, not attributing anything to what they see, just writing in a purely visual way, almost as if they were trying to draw it with their words. Many writing teachers have thought of this as writing from observation (e.g., Hillocks 1975) and it connects well with the sorts of writing that are essential to science and art, anthropology and technical writing, as well as literary writing.

Writing Only with Your Ears

In this type of entry, a writer composes through trying only to hear the sounds of language, only valuing sound as the way of making the decision of what to say next, making it sound interesting, making it sound a particular way—clunky, jazzy, jerky, mellifluous—even if it doesn't quite make sense. Just following the sound of language. It's a way of working on voice and of working on the habit of listening to language, building more entries created only with the writer's ears. It might also mean attempting to write about an event by focusing only on what the writer heard during the event—the sounds of the setting, people's voices, the noises the actions made. Focusing on these cinematic dimensions of sound can tune the writer into the sensual experience of what they are recounting.

Writing Toward What Is Significant

Often a writer starts writing about something that is not, in and of itself, particularly a big deal. We're just writing about what's in front of us, something that happened today, or some memory that comes to mind. We're not claiming it's the most important thing in the world. A very valuable habit of mind is learning to find our way to the question: what's important about this? How is this significant? Even it if is not intrinsically significant, we try to give it significance, we try to build significance around it. It is not a matter of discovering significance that's already there; it's an affirming, an argument for the significance of this thing.

Writing Toward What Is Trivial

In some ways, this is the opposite of the above, but in some ways, it's just another way toward significance. You take a topic, even if it seems very serious, and try to find what is trivial, silly, or funny about it. It's a way of undermining or subverting the usual way of thinking about importance. Oscar Wilde has a character in *Lady Windemere's Fan* say that "Life is far too important a thing ever to talk seriously about it," and this quality of finding the trivial in the serious was one important facet of some of his art, as well as much comedy writing.

Taking Little Mentionings and Extending Them

Sometimes as we reread our notebook, we might find something that we have just mentioned in passing. That something can become the basis of a whole entry of its own. Like in the entry above about grapefruits, I mentioned Christmas with my grandparents. I could write an entire entry about Christmas with my grandparents, or a whole entry about their house, which are things that I glided past in that entry. I mentioned the smells of the grapefruits, and I could write a whole entry about the smells in my grandparents' house. Every text has subtopics that do not receive emphasis, and the same is true with any entry in a notebook. Consequently, notebooks are stuffed with little twigs of potential development. What we are really teaching is that small slivers of thought can be developed, so then the pages of a notebook are stuffed with a seemingly endless potential for meaning.

Compressing Entries into a Single Entry

Another strategy in the notebook is to bring together multiple entries into one idea and write about that idea in a single entry. A student may have written a notebook entry about a musician he likes; and then another about being able to clean his room only if he has music on; and then another about attending a concert. Bringing those three entries together into a single entry about the role of music in his life allows him to synthesize his thinking about the topic. It's one way of making a new entry, and it may even yield new kinds of insight and suggest new subtopics to develop in yet more entries.

Layering Thinking and Potential Ideas

One really important strategy in notebook writing is to return to previous entries and layer meaning onto previous thinking. That may mean writing more sentences into the margin of an entry, stapling a new page into an entry, writing on the facing page, or starting on a new notebook page and just indicating the relationship among pages by using sticky notes. Any of these concrete strategies invites the writer to write back to herself, to layer meaning across different times, writing first when you are one person, and then again later when you have become slightly different.

Writing from Multiple Perspectives

There might have been an event in the hallway last year. Two guys got into a fight. So the writer tries writing the same event from each of the two guys' perspective, then from the point-of-view of a teacher who broke it up, then from the perspective of one of the guys' girlfriends, and then from the viewpoint of a student who just stood there and watched. Not only the attitudes and responses, but the entire way of telling what happened changes as one moves across these perspectives. The details that matter change, the sequence, and the emphases.

The topic one examines from multiple perspectives might also be an idea or issue, rather than an event. A student interested in immigration and citizenship might take up the issue of undocumented immigrants and write it from varied perspectives, in order to try and understand how different people feel about it. Such thinking might help to develop openness in thinking, breadth of thoughtfulness, but it also is essential in the reading and writing of literature and is at the core of being able to construct careful arguments in writing, anticipating the viewpoints of those who think differently.

Probing for Issues of Fairness and Justice

Writers who are attempting to develop critical and civic literacy tend to examine everything they see for issues of justice. When they notice something that seems unfair, they write about it as a matter of justice. When they notice that some people have privileges that are denied to others, they use that as an opportunity to complain and reflect in their notebooks. They develop a habit of writing a few sentences in most entries about the power relationships that are so often in the background of our lives, even if the structures of power weren't the first thoughts that occurred to them. Topics like race, gender, class, and language ideology are always present, if we just shine a light on them. It should be a regular habit to create entries that consider these issues (Bomer and Bomer 2001).

Imagining Actions to Answer What You See in the World

In order for students to develop into participants in a democracy, notebooks can be used to orient their minds toward action in their lives and communities. They can walk around with a notebook, alert to the thought that "someone ought to do something about that." When a problem persists in a community, when someone is being harmed, or when those in power are not receptive to the needs of their constituencies, then those events can be recorded in a notebook and can lead to the development of a vision of action, a plan for something that might address these social problems (Bomer and Bomer 2001).

Writing Like the Best Book You Ever Read

Sometimes, for a stretch in my notebook, the language will become flat and pedestrian. Even though the purpose of the writing is only to think, the quality of the writing may make a difference in the way one thinks. So sometimes to try an entry that sounds like literature, that sounds gorgeous, can be an effective strategy for developing a new vision of a topic.

We might think of literary writing as a tool, one particular use of language that can affect how your world appears to you. The writer decides, "I'm going to write this beautifully," and that commitment can re-angle thinking in an artistic way. A minilesson that might support this would involve reading a passage of some beautiful writing from a novel or story that students may already be familiar with, and to ask students first to look for entries that sound like that in their own notebooks. Then the students listen once more to the example and try today, regardless of the topic they are writing about, to take on some of that literary beauty in their language.

Using Questions to Pursue Ideas

One way of writing an entry is to write all the questions one can think of about the topic—especially the interesting, investigative, interpretive questions. The obvious ones that have a correct answer will not do as much for the writing. Questions that ask the writer to dig for meaning about the topic are ways of thinking, and can be supportive of both inquiry and the spirit of wonder that surrounds our engagement with complicated material.

Intentional Strategies Versus Assignments

By and large, notebooks are locations for students to work on self-control of the literacy that allows them to name experience, construct identities, and imagine powerful social positions. That means that students must feel, overall, that they have control over their notebook. It may not be the kind of "ownership" that allows them to say "Get off my property!" to anyone who approaches, but they do need to feel like this is a tool they can use for purposes they initiate outside the teacher's authority.

For that reason, it is important for teachers to realize that the notebook is not a place for all the one-shot assignments that you can't otherwise give yourself permission to make. I have had extensive conversations sometimes with people who describe complex things they have their students do. I often say something like, "That sounds interesting and might be valuable for someone. But I have to wonder whether doing that is more important than developing a writing life where the writer has some sense of agency." Then the teacher replies, "Oh, I agree; I just have them do this as a notebook entry." I reply that I hadn't understood and the conversation goes on. Then a few minutes later, it becomes clear that there is another very clever and insightful notebook assignment, and then another. Pretty soon, it sounds to me as if the notebook is the place where all the assignments she used to make are still accumulating.

I want to suggest that this might be a mistake, because it takes the very tool that was going to permit a conduit to exist between the student's self-sponsored, outside-school literacy, interests, experience, and thinking and the academic work of school, and it draws a boundary around that tool so that it in fact is part of the school world and not living on the boundary the way it might have done. Furthermore, in order for a notebook to serve as a springboard for more extended written projects, to provide a laboratory of potential ideas and voices, to serve the larger writing process in the most helpful way possible, the entries, as much as possible, need to have been intended by the writer.

Notebooks and the Writing Process

One of the things that makes writers' notebooks what they are, something different from most people's journals, is that they feed deliberately and systematically into pieces of writing made for readers—essays, articles, stories, poems, websites, posters, picture books, blog posts, academic papers. Because they are safe places to produce thinking as content, they help get the writer full of things to say, which can then be shaped into crafted, revised texts directed outward to the world. They allow the writer to find a topic—or a topic to find the writer—by reflecting a recent journey of thinking.

They then provide a space for further thinking about that topic—development of the ideas and content that might end up in a first draft. A notebook is a workspace for testing out possible arrangement or organization of the parts of a draft yet to be written. Drafts exist *outside* the notebook, so that the notebook itself can still be a workbench for possibilities, sections that aren't ready for the draft yet, notes and information, reflections, revision ideas, and ideas for the writer's next piece—as well as the same sorts of captured reflections, memories, and news from the world that the writer was collecting before starting to craft a text for readers. The notebook is also a place for recording helpful tips about editing—those examples of using *that* and *which* I want to remember, or the list of words whose spelling I seem always to guess wrong. And it's a place for reflection on how this process went—before the writer plunges back into collecting from her attention to the world, in preparation for the next project. Figure 12–2 (p. 220) depicts the writing process as a cycle, driven in part by the use of notebook writing to think, reconsider, plan, reflect, and organize the process.

Choosing a Topic and Writing More About That Topic

Once students have ten or fifteen entries and are catching on to the ways a notebook can help explore their life and consider possible interesting topics to exploit more fully, they can choose one topic and commit to developing it. For a few students, this might not even be much of a change, since they have mostly been writing about the same topic or two from the beginning. But for

FIGURE 11–1
Strategies for Gathering
Entries About a Chosen
Topic

Strategies for Gathering Entries About a Chosen Topic

Some of these might already be in the notebook, and others might help writers sustain thinking about the topic they have selected.

- Memories of [the topic] in your life
- Ideas and thoughts about what's important about [the topic]
- Reflections and feelings about [the topic]
- Concrete facts and information [the topic], and then reflection on that information
- The way [the topic] fits into the lives of people connected to it
- The history of [the topic]
- Descriptions, from direct observation of [the topic]
- Objects that would be in a museum about [the topic]
- How different people think differently about [the topic]–and what arguments they could have about it
- How [the topic] makes me think about fairness and justice
- The science of [the topic]
- The motivations and purposes of [the topic]
- How [the topic] affects my life

---

many, this move from expansive exploration of many different things to a committed inquiry into a single topic will be a significant shift.

Usually, teachers have students spend a period or two rereading their notebooks in search of a topic that stands out to them as interesting, as worthy of further thinking and writing for a larger audience, as having potential to be like a published text the author admires. They may have written about it a number of times, or might only have mentioned it once in passing, or may now see that they have written around the topic without actually ever stating it. But the topic they choose to develop should have a relationship to what has gone in the notebook previously—partly in order to assure that future exploratory work in the notebook is undertaken with some serious realization that notebook writing is all possible fodder for more extended writing intended for readers.

Having narrowed their attention to a particular topic, writers spend a few days making entries just about that one topic—in assorted aspects, from varied angles, and at different levels of depth. Figure 11–1 lists some of the lenses writers have used as they return to the same topic again and again in order to develop ideas toward a draft. It is still writing to think, but this is more focused, driven by the needs of inquiry and development of a topic. And this writing to think provides the material that can be marshaled and transformed into a draft of something written for readers, a process to be explored further in the next chapter.

CHAPTER 12

Pointing Students Toward Audiences

In the last two chapters, I discussed writing as a tool for thinking, and in this chapter and the next, we will turn writing outward, toward audiences. Of course, I'm not suggesting writers stop thinking just because they start writing for readers. Through the whole process we explore in this chapter, writers are thinking and rethinking about the content of their work as well as the design of their text. But they are making more of their decisions socially, by thinking about their reader—what a reader will or will not know at this point, the information or argument that needs to be built in some sequence, what information they want to withhold until later, the arrangement of parts that will be most pleasing or shocking. They're still involved in the topic and substance of their writing, extending the material they began building in the late notebook work described toward the end of the last chapter, but they're attending, too, to someone else's future thinking.

The notebook is like a backyard, and when a project comes out of the notebook, it's like language coming out the front door into the world, greeting the neighbors, calling on friends, complaining to members of the community, and asking people in power to make things better. This transition in the function of language is aided by a shift in materials as students begin drafting—sheets of paper that could be handed to someone else take the place of the notebook, which seems, by contrast, almost attached to the writer's body. What is made on those sheets of paper could take many forms. They may be works of art—poems, stories, comic strips, and essays that are made to create aesthetic experiences for readers. They may be packages of information—feature articles, pamphlets, and posters designed to teach readers. They may be forces of influence—arguments, leaflets, websites, and letters that are designed to change people's minds. They may be turns at participation in intellectual or academic discussions—arguments and explanations intended to make both the writer and the audience more discriminating about ideas, more understanding about issues that have not yet been recognized in the conversation. When writing for readers, we are making a particular something—a kind of text crafted in a specific way in order to achieve a purpose with respect to the people who will read it. We write to take action, to accomplish something, and knowing the purpose for which we are writing is essential for making all the shaping decisions that actually form the text (National Council of Teachers of English 2004).

An understanding of the importance of purpose and audience makes clearer why it's simply not enough to write at the demand of a teacher in order to be judged according to how well the writer accomplished the teacher's purpose. Often, in those situations, some students don't write well or make quality decisions because they aren't really doing anything; their purpose is just to get a good enough grade. Even those who do write well under those conditions aren't learning to be writers, just reinforcing their status as someone's student. After all, the text they're writing isn't about getting a good grade, and so the purpose for which they write doesn't interact with the content to create the structure, language, and reasoning. To become writers, students need experience thinking about an audience, believing in a purpose, planning a text that could achieve that purpose, and designing a work process that will produce that text.

Prior to a Draft

Let's think about the story we're asking writers to live out. They have collected a number of notebook entries about a topic, and so now the topic is richer and more complex in their minds than it was when they first thought about it. There is more stuff in it, more parts to it. Consequently, there are now more decisions to make in order to turn this mess of material into an experience designed for readers—decisions about which part will come first, how all the stuff inside the topic will be arranged, the sound this text should have, and many others. This turn toward a draft, in other words, requires substantial reorientation of thinking.

Many students still see writing as simply performance on demand. (Where would they have gotten that idea?) And consequently, those students may not yet have developed understandings of writing-to-think or writing-as-a-social-action-toward-readers. It's still just something they have to do in school. Why, they will ask, should they have to write something again, outside the notebook, when they already did it—on these pages right here that they could easily just tear out and hand you so you could give them the grade. They think this way because, at least when they write in school, they don't yet have a purpose with respect to their audience.

At this point in the process, writers need to be pretty explicitly aware of what they intend to do to an audience with this piece of writing—their purpose for publishing. They need to decide what they want their audience to understand, know, believe, and feel, how they want to affect or change the people who will read this particular piece of writing. Yes, they are still doing it in school, but that's not the purpose that will shape the piece; a writer needs a proactive intention. Some teachers have student writers, as they turn the corner toward making a piece for readers, write a short statement of purpose—perhaps just a few sentences as a notebook entry saying what they are trying to do to whom.

As part of this sense of purpose, a writer needs to have others in mind—an audience to whom she is speaking, and that person or group out there helps, from very early on, to shape, constrain, and develop this piece of writing. I don't mean that there's some audience member who comes and directly tells the writer how to write; I mean that the writer decides how to write by thinking about what the audience member knows, wonders, feels, values, expects, and believes. In that way, the audience partners with the writer not just at the end of the process but also at the beginning. To establish that presence in the writer's mind, there needs to be a real audience on the way.

So one of the key types of planning writing teachers do involves putting their student writers in touch with audiences. Even very early in the writing process, the teacher should establish the date for a publication event. People do lots of different things for these sorts of events, including:

- a website going live;
- people coming to the class to hear a reading;
- people coming to view the writing displayed as if in a museum;
- the exchange of work with another class;
- a multimedia event with voice recordings, video, and other forms of publication;

> ## Multilingual Note
>
> We shouldn't automatically assume that the appropriate language choice for every piece of writing will be English. Multilingual students are multilingual because they have potential audiences in different languages for the things they have to say. *Una poema para mi abuelita* should be in Spanish; a letter to my cousin in Bangladesh in Bengali. It's really not that difficult to teach and evaluate the process, thinking, habits, and decision making writers go through even if they are writing in a language the teacher doesn't know.

- posting the texts under glass in a school display case;
- publishing a class magazine, of which every student gets a copy;
- circulation of such a magazine among other interested adults in the community.

By announcing, as students come out of their notebooks, that November 30 our website publishing these pieces will go live, the teacher makes clear how this writing is different from notebook writing. She also claims a new role with the students. Where she might have been the authority requiring writing of the students for herself to read and judge, she now is more like the director of the play, getting kids ready for the audience who is the more important arbiter of whether the work is interesting or not. Sure, the teacher will be giving grades, but even that will be an evaluation of how the students appeal to their real audience. For the rest of the writing process students will put themselves through, the teacher will be by their side, coaching into their work, rather than sitting across the table demanding something.

Once writers have built up content in their notebooks and articulated a purpose and audience for writing, the context is ripe for teaching students how to develop a vision and plan for their texts. What will it be like overall? What feeling should it give the audience? How should readers perceive the writer, the kind of person she is? To accomplish those things, what tone will it take? Cheerful, serious, expert, inquiring? Given the audience, in what language should it be written? Though the answer may often be English, it will not always be. What level of formality should it use? Thinking through these kinds of questions will help the writer draft, and this kind of planning in advance will later help a writer consider what to revise, where he may have drifted from the plan. (Then again, of course, the drifting might always be right, the plan wrong.)

At about the same time, a writer must make some structural decisions. What will be the first part of this text? What will come next? What's one possible sequence of sections? What are two more possible sequences of sections, and how would ordering the parts those alternate ways affect the meaning? What is the role of visual elements in this text? What kinds of images need to be made or collected? How should this text be designed in order to achieve its purposes? These architectural decisions serve the purpose, audience, and overall vision of the piece, and writers usually should not just accept the first structure that occurs to them and start writing. There is much to be gained by figuring out what the sections might be, and listing them in different orders, imagining

A Productive Moment for Collaboration

One of the moments in the writing process when students can most easily and productively think together in groups is during the phase when they are still planning a draft and developing a vision for it. Later, after they have a draft, defensiveness and resistance can make response groups somewhat more difficult.

how each structure would change the meaning of the text it represents.

With a vision and structure for the piece in mind, the writer may also develop some plans for the way she'll go about composing this piece—a specific project plan. This plan addresses the sequence of actions the writer will carry out. What will she actually write first? It should probably be whatever section is easiest and will go the fastest, though there are some people who will throw themselves into the hard parts right away. When will that first section be done? What will be the order of working on the sections, and when will the whole draft be completed? The order of work may, of course, be very different from the sequence of sections in the text's organization. Who might she ask to read it and provide some feedback? What are the days set aside for revisions? These timelines, if the writer is anything like me or most writers I know, will change as things move along. But asking students to plan out a process is one way of making sure they understand there will be a process, that there needs to be time to revise, to rethink the design, to clean things up. The details of the writing process don't amount to one thing that is always the same for all situations; what a writer does across time is specific to a particular occasion, purpose, or audience.

As I discussed in Chapter 3, one important dimension of writing is project management, and so orienting students toward breaking down and sequencing the tasks involved in composing a particular project is part of the teaching of writing. To make regular, adequate progress in getting something written, writers need to have a clear idea about the very specific next thing to do all the time, so that they don't get lost in a confused muddle where nothing's happening because it's all too big. Being organized and planned in this way is certainly not a guarantee that things will get done, but it makes it more likely. Throughout a writing process, the writer needs to be setting deadlines and goals for the subparts of the task of making the text. That's an important habit for school, for college, for career, and for life.

Teaching Drafting

As students begin actually writing the piece, it's important to do some work on the concept of draft. Especially the first time through the process, there should be at least a couple of minilessons just working on the attitudes and

Chunks in a Different Order

I'm writing about my grandmother, and I have figured out four chunks of this piece. See here how rearranging the order of the parts suggests quite different texts.

1. what she looked like	1. seeing people who look like her
2. her laugh	2. what she looked like
3. her cough from smoking	3. her cough from smoking
4. seeing people who look like her	4. her laugh

Each of these arrangements would create a different piece, but I don't have to draft the whole thing to see how each might go. Just the order of the parts suggests a whole different feeling and meaning.

understandings that make it possible actually to get something out that can be revised. To understand the concept of draft, students have to grasp that writing is not something you do in a single pass, like vacuuming a floor (though even that might not work well in a single pass, unless you're just not all that committed to clean floors). A draft is something pulled forth quickly, so that the maker can see what he has and begin interacting with it, rethinking in response to this emerging object, making ideas and changing his mind as the draft evolves. The first moves in creating a draft, therefore, need to be venturesome but easy gestures, and the wrong way to do it is any way that slows down those initial moves. Young writers (and older ones, too) need to learn that it is OK to be unfinished and in process; they need to be comfortable with being in the present, in the midst of the making, rather than rushing toward the future when all of this writing stuff is over and done with. They need to learn to convince themselves that no one is listening in to their drafting, that there is no risk of saying something wrong. We want them to learn that it is alright to make something that is not yet good—that in fact may never get good.

Writing Conferences During Drafting and Revision

One-to-one writing conferences—usually just around five minutes long—are one of the most important sites of teaching while students are writing for audiences. They begin with the teacher interrupting the writer to interview him about his purpose and what he is working on right now. Once the teacher really understands where the writer is coming from, she decides on one single lesson to teach this writer, one that may be useful not just for this piece, but potentially for a whole writing life.

Making quality things, it turns out, is not simply a matter of having high standards; it's more a matter of strategically lowering one's standards when it's time to make a first move, and also being able to raise them progressively across the revision process. To have high standards in the end, most people must lower them in the beginning. In essence, the concept of draft depends upon an understanding of the concept of revision, and vice versa, because both concepts mean that once your thinking is outside your skin, you can lay over it qualities, features, goodness, and coolness. All those things can be absent when you first begin. So it's safe to come in.

This drafting is not simply an act of recopying from the notebook. In a writing classroom, it is very important that writing never become a mindless, boring, rote activity, and copying is mindless, boring, rote, and unnecessary. If there is a small section, a few sentences that came out nearly perfect in the notebook, there is certainly no reason not to use them, and I can't imagine a writer in the world who would not do so. That much copying might be acceptable, or else the writer might photocopy or scan those sentences so that hand-copying is not necessary. Overall, however, the material in the notebook is going to be transformed as it is rewritten into a text designed for readers.

For most writers, drafting involves some attention to tools and technologies. In a classroom, it is usually important, for instance, that drafting happens on paper outside the notebook. (It's fine for the draft to be in a different note-book, but the writer's notebook itself needs not to be the location of the draft.) There are two reasons why this is best. First, it makes concrete the very impor-tant shift that happens when the writers go from talking to them-selves to talking to an audience. Where a notebook is almost part of the writer's body, a piece of paper can be handed to someone else. Second, the move to sheets of paper allows the notebook to remain useful as a tool for thinking without being gummed up by a draft. If the writer begins a draft on Tuesday in a notebook, then when Wednesday morning, he has a thought that would be a good note-book entry, where's that thinking going to go? In the middle of the draft? If, however, the draft is outside the notebook, then the writing life can continue without completely being overwhelmed by the draft, allowing the writer to get down new ideas for topics and future pieces of writing. Most of us have lots of ideas for future pieces while we are drafting and revising—anything to avoid the present work! Since the draft is on loose sheets of paper, most teachers have students keep them in a folder that is stored in the classroom.

The paper for drafting can be anything, but for some particular writers, it might be helpful, psychologically, for the paper to be headed for the trash can. I have spent some time looking through the papers of children's and young adult authors in the Kerlan collection at the University of Minnesota, and one thing that struck me was how often people used the backs of things and little unimportant slips of paper to get writing going, especially in very early drafts. Katherine Paterson wrote the initial idea for *The Great Gilly Hopkins* literally on the back of an envelope. Judy Blume, Karen Hesse, Nikki Grimes, Scott O'Dell, and others all began works admired by thousands on the backs of scrap paper. I don't like writing on the backs of things, but I have pads of very flimsy recycled yellow paper that I use liberally to get the writing going, forc-ing myself to write the things that are obvious and easy to me until I get engaged enough to begin writing on better paper. I shift often among different materials to signal different things to my brain—anything to make it easier. And that is the key to drafting, doing whatever it takes to make the content flow and become engaging to the writer.

I have known teachers who had well-intentioned directives for drafting about skipping lines on drafts or writing in pencil. Such a policy would be more appropriate if the only revisions writers make are correcting a few mis-takes. But that's not the kind of revision we're going to value, especially early on. Substantial revisions are not going to take place on the skipped lines, and

TECHNOLOGY NOTE

Some students feel they write best on computers, and many adults like me are sympathetic to this claim. Computers are valuable tools, though their usefulness deteriorates if they prevent stu-dents from being able to work dur-ing class time! I do plenty of composing at a computer and also plenty of writing on paper, printed drafts or just blank pages, away from electronic devices. It helps my concentration to shift my tools. Flexibility with tools is impor-tant in our age, and students should learn to print a draft and keep working away from the com-puter, to compose on paper and take that back to the computer.

they're not going to be achieved by erasing a few words. Furthermore, asking writers to think about the teacher's rules for drafting is a good way to make sure they are overly concerned about judgment and authority entirely too early in the writing process. The correct materials and procedures for drafting are those that make a draft flow for this particular writer, and every writer is going to have to experiment to come up with the magic mojo to trick that content out of herself.

Teaching drafting, it is usually important to teach velocity. While many writers do think of themselves as slow, we're trying to help students build a concept of drafting here, and the habit of getting something down quickly and calling it a draft is helpful to that agenda. Faulkner compared writing to building a house in a strong wind—you just have to get things nailed down. That's the feeling I have about teaching drafting. I want students to know that if there are hard parts to write, they can just skip those and work on them later in revision. And I teach that in a draft, you can say things that are easy, even if they're wrong, and just fix them later in revision. It's all about making the draft possible.

Despite all my attempts to keep things easy, I, as a writer, sometimes become lost in a draft, losing my sense of direction or even the slightest idea about what could come next. I start to become passive, standing in the middle of the woods looking at the bark on trees, not moving anywhere. I see it in students, too, when they seem stuck, uncertain, or insecure about what they're saying. My strategy as a writer, and so the main thing I know to teach kids, is to go to a different, even more worthless piece of paper and make a list of the next few things I want to say. So for the draft of this section of this book you're reading right now, I have, on a slip of yellow paper, these words I scribbled in planning the content of the paragraph just above this one: "speed / skipping hard parts / saying easy but wrong w/ intent to fix." For this paragraph, I see: "notes, plans as you go—like <u>this</u>." These little slips give me someplace to look when I just don't have the heart to keep speaking into silence. I glance at them and then just obey what they tell me to do.

I have tried to emphasize here the tentativeness of drafting, the sense of something to come, the belief in possibility as yet unrealized that makes revision not only possible but inevitable. When students resist revision, it is sometimes because they haven't actually drafted. Instead, they have written the text as they think it should appear. Because most of us don't do that very well, what they have written still needs work. But they don't have the will for the work, or

Minilessons During Drafting

During the phase of the process when students are drafting, the teacher delivers minilessons just five to ten minutes long, at the beginning of class. These lessons provide some of the kinds of advice I describe here about drafting, and they can also be a first round of descriptions and demonstrations of the key features of the genre in which students are writing (see the appendix for some ideas about these key features). These same teaching points will need to be revisited and deepened when the writers are revising.

the intent of doing it. So in addition to a commitment to the topic, a complex knowledge about the topic built up in notebook work, a particular set of design decisions from among many, engagement with revision also demands a particular attitude and task definition when the writer is drafting.

Teaching Revision

I see teaching revision as teaching the practice of freedom. Maxine Greene (1995) tells us that freedom involves the ability to imagine that things could be otherwise, and that same act is what revision involves as well. A writer is able to look at text and imagine it otherwise. That imagination comes from experiences at making text different, as well as experiences reading texts that work in lots of different ways, with many varying structures.

In this section, I'm going to discuss ways of giving writers more experience with revision, first by just trying stuff with their earlier drafts. To teach revision to a whole class, it can help to offer strategies for throwing the whole thing up in the air and seeing how it lands differently. Then, I'll discuss some important differences between early revision, when deep levels' content and structure are still under construction, and late revision, when the writer moves her attention toward the surface of the language. After that, we'll move into a section on editing, which involves clarifying and cleaning up the reader's most immediate interface with the text and its meanings.

Thirteen Ways to Support All Students' Revision Without Reading Every Student's Paper

Often, teachers think that the only way they can support revision is to read every student's work and then offer suggestions for ways to make it better. That is, of course, one way to support revision, one that is very specific and individualized but also pretty slow and labor-intensive. Moreover, it doesn't necessarily teach each student to be an independent decision maker as a writer who revises her work. We should prioritize each student getting used to trying new things with his own work, engaging in the practice of imagining his text otherwise—and by *imagining*, I mean *writing*. So we need to loosen students' sense of the inevitability of the text as it is now. That's why many good writing teachers teach students ways simply to make their piece different, trying something out that can perhaps open up possibilities they haven't yet considered. What follows is a list of revision strategies—actions that entertain possibilities, things writers can try, especially if they don't have a specific idea about how to improve their writing.

1. Fold this draft up and put it in your pocket. Without trying to remember the old draft, just try writing it again in a new way.

2. Put boxes around the different sections of your piece. Maybe even cut it into pieces. Write more for the parts that are too little. Decide what parts stay and what parts to cut. Try out different orders for the parts.

3. Draw some part of your piece (or make a chart or a diagram) and then try adding some of what you thought about as you drew.

4. Get up on your feet with some friends and act out parts of your piece. Pay attention to things you notice that you could add to your draft. Talk about how everyone feels doing the acting and what kinds of thoughts and feelings you could add.

5. Change the genre of your piece. Try it as a poem or a memoir or a piece of nonfiction. See what new thoughts come as you mess with the topic that way.

6. Read your piece out loud to someone with whom you feel comfortable. Pay attention as you read and imagine you're the person you are reading to. Notice what is hard to understand and might need more explaining. Notice the places where you might say more. Notice the good little bits that you might be able to do more of.

7. Have a friend read it out loud to you. Notice places where they have trouble saying the sentences out loud. That could be a clue that the words there don't flow that well.

8. Take something that you just mention in your piece and write two pages about it. Take something that you have a lot about and see what happens if you just say that part quickly.

9. Come up with ten different ways to begin the piece. See how it would be different with each of those possible beginnings. You could also do this with endings.

10. Once you have made a draft, try outlining the piece five different ways to see what different structures you can find for it.

11. Try changing the way the piece sounds, or the voice it talks in. If it's plain, make it fancy. If it's fancy, make it plain. If it's careful, make it reckless. If it's stuffy, make it loose and funny.

12. Call someone and tell them about your piece without looking at it. Tape yourself doing this so you can add in some of what you say.

13. Put this piece away and work on something else for a while, then come back to it and see what you think later.

Once a writer has tried one or two of these revision strategies, she will, in many cases, have two or three different versions of the text she was making (or at least the beginning of it). The versions may suggest different purposes that could be served by the same ideas—two completely different texts. But more often, one will seem preferable to the writer's present purpose, with the other offering some details that could improve this draft's effectiveness. The writer's next task becomes integrating the best qualities of the two drafts.

Teaching Purposeful Revision

While the above strategies are helpful in just loosening a writer's grip on the first draft, they're not quite the same thing as the purposeful revisions that writers undertake when they are crafting a piece for publication. These more common types of revisions involve the writer responding to his emergent vision of how the text can get its job done. It's not that it's fixed in advance, some ideal version of the piece; if it were, the writer could just write the ideal one and be done with it. Rather, in the act of composing, the text takes shape in dialogue with the writer's developing understanding of what it can be and do. No matter how thoroughly a writer has planned a text, it still evolves in the writing as language leads thinking in sometimes unexpected directions.

Throughout the writing process, writing conferences are an important mode of teaching. When students are engaged in this purposeful kind of revision, there is sometimes in these conferences a temptation for the teacher to make decisions *for* the writer, essentially writing the piece using the student's hands. I'm not shy about making fairly strong suggestions to students, but I try to leave them in control of their writing even as I help them think through the decisions they have to make. What is most important is that they take on the process of decision making in revision for themselves, so I need to temper my strong opinions with respect for their agency, to reign in my expertise with questions to help them think through their purpose, audience, aesthetic intentions, motives, and reasons. For this reason, conferring with writers later in their process of making something can be like a dance in which the two partners take turns leading.

Generally speaking, writers begin by shaping the large, deep structures of a piece—the substance of what they are saying, the order of parts, the completeness of the explanation. There is not much point in fixing the sound of sentences that are going to end up cut or rewritten entirely, so those kinds of surface details wait until the larger meanings are just about set. Gradually, as they feel ready to move on from the substance, or as a deadline begins to approach, writers then start to look at the surface structures—transitions, cohesion, sentences, diction, conventions of written grammar, punctuation, and spelling. It's not necessarily that the stages of attention are completely separate. A writer who hates the sound of the sentence she just wrote is likely to change it so it feels better, just as noticing a typo, most people will backspace to correct it. But in the earlier stages of revision, the writer's attention and sense of task is focused on the larger chunks of meaning, and later on, his attention moves to the details of sentences and words.

The writing process isn't really a production process like a factory; rather, the words writing process simply refer to a description of the tasks to which writers' attention goes at particular stages of working on a text. Because many people have, throughout their history as writers in school, had their attention focused mostly on surface features, we'll spend some extra time on strategies for early revision.

Teaching Early Revision as Reopening

Many teachers find that students resist revising. That's not surprising, in a way. Sometimes that's because they prefer their text the way it is now to the way someone else thinks it could be. Sometimes it's because once a text is written, it feels like punishment to have to rewrite it. Sometimes, it's just because it's extra hard work. These positions are likely to be especially strong among students who haven't had the work in notebooks, designing, and drafting that I have discussed previously. But at least one big reason students resist revising is that they don't know what to do. It's confusing to look back at finished text and try to find a way to reopen what feels closed, to find space for thinking in what appears to be a crowded page.

Early strategies for revision are concerned with ways to reopen the text, to develop content, and to find the best arrangement of sections. Each of the strategies I list here could be a stretch of minilessons, since any of them is probably too complex for many students to pick it up in only a single minilesson.

Select and Expand. All writing involves choosing particular things to include and other things to leave out. Sometimes, in an attempt to be complete and thorough, to "have enough," writers will dump things into the draft that just aren't that important. Or, sometimes in the speed of drafting, they don't allow their momentum to slow with concerns about what is most important and what can be left out. Other times, a writer doesn't decide about the big, governing idea in this piece until she sees the draft. In early revisions, the writer selects and develops the ideas or parts that are most important and cuts things that don't serve the emerging point of the piece. The principle is to say more about the really important parts, and to allow those parts to crowd out and push aside the things that now clearly don't belong.

Develop Significance. Because early moves in the process of writing a piece are all about acceptance, it often happens that an initial draft contains ideas that are still small and rather insignificant—an anecdote about a particular day, a few fairly obvious responses to a text, a point that seems as yet trivial. Often writers can feel this: the writing so far is just not about anything important. The whole process I have described up until now helps to make sure that the topic and the content really are important to the writer, but that importance may still be implicit in the material and not yet in the language so that readers could share in it. The writer needs to build up the significance that is available in the content, needs to know more explicitly why and how what she is talking about is important. In most expository text, this importance needs to be explicitly explained to the reader. In narrative text, it can be more obliquely communicated, but the writer needs to have a grip on why this matters and what matters about it. Sometimes it can help to take the notebook back out, write at the top of a page Why is this important? and write a page or two in response to that question. Some of those sentences may turn out to be useful, but at any rate, the thinking will help to focus the design of the text and how it speaks to the reader in conveying that significance.

Move to Something Related. It's sometimes possible to expand the territory of a piece of writing by moving to another topic, another story, another text that is nearby, right next door, to the one that launched the piece. Including more than one point of focus can just widen the thematic territory of the piece. Say I begin with the idea that music has helped me with all the major decisions of my life, that particular albums or songs are associated with major turns I have made. I could move to a topic right next door to it and expand the focus of my piece: say, the way music has also been a focus of important relationships to me. If I were having trouble growing the first idea, then expanding it slightly to include the second is a way to keep developing the bigger theme of music as giving my life an emotional center. Sometimes, a little move like that can loosen a writer's tight grip on a limited topic and can allow a more freely flowing writing process and freely moving text.

Show and Tell, Scene and Summary. It's often said that good writing comes from showing, not telling. Sometimes that is true, especially in narratives and some poems. And often, if a student has written that her mother is so nice to her, or that two people's whole relationship was depressing, it's pretty clear that finding a way to make those ideas more specific, clear, and visual would improve the writing. But it's also the case sometimes that a writer begins with an outside story—a scene with dialogue, for instance, or an objective account of what a text has said—and what is needed is more explanation of what the writer or the character is thinking. Good writing usually involves a combination of showing and telling, and it's useful in revision for writers to take stock of where they have shown and where told, so that they can make sure these different modes are complimenting each other. Similarly, it's a good idea in narratives to make deliberate decisions about scenes and summaries—detailed scenes in which characters talk, behave, and have facial expressions minute to minute, and summaries in which the narration strides quickly across time. Varying these ways of writing is another way of loosening up the writer's—and ultimately the reader's—experience.

Perspectives, Disciplines, and Voices. In many ways, revision strategies return to the kinds of thinking that writers may have done in their notebooks. The strategies in Figure 11–1 of the previous chapter, designed to help writers develop and complicate the content of their pieces, also can serve to reopen the piece for substantive revision after a draft. Among them, I listed a consideration of how people think differently about the topic, which can mean either opinions or the distinct perspectives of varied people in a scene or discussion. In revision, it can also be helpful to give voice to a different perspective, sometimes also answering that perspective to reinforce the writer's main point. Similarly, many writers ask what different voices might be available in the material about which they are writing. I discussed exploring how the topic might look from varied disciplines—what science might say about it, how it involves quantitative thinking, what the history of the topic is, how it connects to the thinking visual artists do. Those varied disciplinary perspectives can also be very useful in early revisions as ways to develop content further—as long as they do not cause the writer to drift too far from the center of gravity being developed in the draft.

Revisiting the Design Vision of the Piece. One very useful form of revision is to return to the plan for the piece and see whether that plan still seems appropriate or whether it needs to be redesigned. Sometimes, the most helpful outline a writer can make comes after an initial draft that is improvised and discovered without prior restraints. The outline is, in that case, a way of naming the sections that came about in spontaneous thinking while writing. Then, those newly named chunks can be rearranged, developed further, cut from the piece, or transformed. But once again, the ability to identify sections of a text and make decisions about those sections is essential to a writer's work. Revisiting other aspects of the design is also an important revision strategy—the relation-

Peer Response as Usability Testing

It helps to think of peer response as design testing, rather than an evaluative conversation about whether the reader thinks the piece of writing is good or not. In design testing, the maker attempts to understand how the user interacts with the crafted object—in this case, the text. That means the reader needs to think out loud as she reads, saying what she's honestly thinking but not making evaluative comments geared toward changing the piece. The author takes notes on her observation of the reader.

- Where does the text seem to be working for this reader?
- Where does the reader's mind wander away from my purpose, and is that something I want to revise to prevent?
- Is the reader affected in the way I intended?
- What did she say that I didn't expect, and how can I learn from that?

ship of visual elements to the text, text features like headings and pull-out boxes, and title.

From a design perspective, nothing beats getting the responses of a few users—readers—as they read. This user testing is a common strategy in software design and other design and engineering fields in which the point of the work is ultimately to serve someone else's activity or thinking. The writer should find others to test-run the piece and ask them to think out loud as they read through the text, rather like we described readers doing in Chapter 7. How are they thinking? What confuses them? When is it clear? Are they doing what I would want them to do, having the experience I'd like them to have? The writer takes notes on the observed reader's experience of interacting with the text, and uses those notes in developing the next iteration of the design. Some students who don't necessarily thrill to the identity of "literary author" enjoy thinking of their writing as engineering. You're making a machine, seeing how the user interacts with it, and then remaking it in order to give the user either more choices or fewer choices, depending on the kind of experience the maker wants the user to have.

Open Physical Space. One thing that makes revision hard sometimes is that a page already seems so crowded, it's hard for writers to imagine the space into which they can write a new section. When I'm writing, I often just find a spot where it feels like there could be more text, and I put "insert A" there, then write "insert A" at the top of a piece of paper and start drafting from there. Getting a sense of openness from the clean page allows me to gather momentum on the section that needs to be written. If I don't feel that sense of space, I just can't seem to summon the prose. The same thing can happen with a computer. Even though one could always just insert the cursor and start typing, for some students there might not seem to be an inviting space right in the middle of existing text. One easy strategy is to insert a bunch of returns in order to make a large white space into which they can compose. But for some reason, it also helps some writers to open a new document, even in a new software application, and compose there the chunk to be inserted. And sometimes, as I have mentioned before, it's helpful to shift away from the digital device and compose on paper, then return to the computer to enter the new text. The shift in environments permits a different kind of thinking and a sense of open space that can build momentum for a new burst of text making.

Sequential Readings. Revision can be served through a series of purpose-focused readings of the text, so that the features the writer wants to include can be layered into the text as attention is focused on them one at a time. Each reading is devoted to a particular feature related to the writer's purpose in the piece. She might read once for completeness, once for structure, and once for voice. Depending on the type of writing, a writer might do a reading for humor, suspense, image, or mystery. Doing this, the writer only has to hold one feature in mind while reading, looking for a spot to develop that feature in the text, and that makes it easier to consciously manage that particular aspect of this text. I sometimes make a checklist of features I want to build into a particular piece, and just do sequential readings during which I do my best to build up those features, one at a time.

These early revision strategies are useful for new explorations of meaning, for reopening text, and for developing further what the writer wants to say. They come to an end either when the writer is satisfied with the content, or more typically, when it's getting pretty close to time for the reading audience to receive the text. Once the text is stable, it's worth moving nearer to the surface in late revision and editing.

Teaching Late Revision

In what I am calling "late revision," writers think even more deliberately about their audience, bringing more clarity to their meanings and thinking moment by moment about the reader's experience as they move through this text. Though one can't always help having new ideas, for the most part, the large chunks of content can remain as they are from now on in this production process. Big new ideas might be best saved for the next project, so that this one can come to completion. I don't mean that as any kind of absolute rule, but often people are prevented from finishing things because they keep changing their minds, and while it's good to have an open and generous mind, it's also good to know how to close. To help, there are a few ideas teachers can bring up that can move writers' attention toward the language itself, still remaining thoughtful about meaning.

Writers need to learn to examine their paragraphs and sentences as units of information. One way they can look at each paragraph is to ask whether it's really earning its keep, carrying the load of information it should. Some should be cut, some combined with neighboring paragraphs, and others broken into two or more separate paragraphs. They can be any length, from a single word to pages long, but writers should have reasons for designing their paragraphs as they do, and they should make sure that their reasons are considerate of their readers. Though I was taught in school that they have to have three sentences, that, like many things I was taught, just isn't true. Instead of thinking about a particular formula, writers should consider how design decisions about paragraphing will make the experience of reading as clear as possible for readers, avoiding anything that might distract the reader from the meanings the writer wants to convey.

Other Changes Fairly Near the Surface

Each sentence within a paragraph should be scrutinized, too, to make sure it is carrying enough information to stand on its own. With young writers, it is often helpful to combine the information in multiple sentences together into a single, longer, more fully populated sentence. There are sentence-combining activities that can help to get this across (Killgallon 1998), but far more important than activities that rehearse external behavior is the development of the concept that each sentence should do real work in carrying the information this text is about. Even as we teach students to make longer sentences, we also need to teach them to pare out words and phrases that aren't doing much. Uncluttering sentences, weeding out unnecessary words, is another way of making sure sentences are hardworking, and figuring out which words could be cut requires equal awareness of those that could not be cut, as a butcher distinguishes fat from muscle. Because we English teachers love attention to language so much, it's probably important to note that we can't spend forever on this; the writers are headed for audiences here.

Still, one of the reasons it's important to teach about sentence awareness in the context of writing is because sentences don't operate in isolation. Rather, each sentence reaches back to the ones before it, hooking this new meaning on those already established in the reader's mind. A paragraph is not a list of sentences; it's a cohesive set of ideas that build to larger concepts. So writers, once their content is set, need to look across sentences and see if the relationship between each one and its predecessors is clear. Transition words can often help, but this development of cohesion isn't just a matter of sprinkling words on the surface of sentences; it involves the writer thinking through one sentence to the next and building the idea of this sentence on the previous one, logically and clearly. When sentences are disjointed and listed, the fix may involve adding some sentences in between, adding transition words or phrases, or rethinking the logic of what is being said here. Each of those three strategies can make a good minilesson topic in a stretch of days at an appropriate phase in the writing process.

In this focus on sentences and their relationships, we also have an opportunity to bring students' attention to the sound of language, a way of working that may be especially appealing to students whose thinking is more musical. Whether or not a particular writer enjoys the music of language, some of his readers may, and so it is still a worthwhile object of attention. We have discussed supporting readers' attention to the sound of text (see Chapter 5), and explicitly connecting to reading experience and to examples of literature can help

TECHNOLOGY NOTE

It *seems* a natural and simple use of computers in writing just to have students type up final drafts on a computer and then correct mistakes with the help of grammar- and spell-check. But just as that is a fairly surface-oriented concern in the technology of pen and paper, it's also a pretty superficial use of digital technology. It may be a little bit better than *no* contact with computers, but it doesn't really teach students what they should learn about digital composing—that text and how they are made can be transformed substantially by new technologies (see Chapter 14). Word processing, especially late in the writing process, does not come anywhere near addressing the new forms of literacy we should attempt to engage in our teaching.

students develop an awareness for this dimension of language. Sentences do not have to have come out lovely in the draft to be made lovely for readers; now is the writer's chance to pay attention to them. In individual conferences and in minilessons, teachers show students that, when you write, you are creating a sound in your readers' mind. They ask student writers to consider what sound is best for the kind of meanings they want to convey and the relationship they want their readers to develop to the text. Writers need to listen to each sentence's rhythm and melody as well as to the piece of music it creates as it connects to the previous sentence and the next one. Listening to sentences end to end in time this way, adjusting phrases and the order of their parts, is like editing recorded music.

So late revision overall is a focus on the medium-sized units of meaning—paragraphs and sentences—a focus that still attends to meaning, even if in smaller units. Editing, which we will consider next, extends this focus toward the reader's expectations, bringing conventions—the social contract about written language—into the center of the writer's attention.

Teaching Editing

In the editing phase, writers turn their minds to conventions—the expectations of their readers about how sentences go, where punctuation appears, the use of words, and how words are spelled. For many mature writers, all the attention to sentences that I described above as late revision would have taken care of most misplaced modifiers or subject-verb disagreements. Moreover, for adult writers, there is sometimes an institution full of people who pitch in to make a writer look good. (The sentences I'm writing will be checked not only by me but also by my wife Katherine, my editor Kate, a production editor, and a proofreader, after which I will check them yet again.) Student writers in classrooms, in contrast, are notably underresourced, a fact worth keeping in mind while moving through a classroom process of producing finished texts.

Editing, a writer has to look at text and set aside most of its deeper meanings in order to sharpen attention to the surface. She has to hold a complex filter up to the text—one that compares every feature to her generalized memory of how published text looks and her memory of a collection of different explicit prescriptions about spelling patterns, grammatical patterns, the uses of punctuation

Promises and Pitfalls of Peer Editing Groups

Another spot in the writing process where response groups may have interesting and constructive conversations is during editing, when students can inquire and reason through alternatives for surface features like syntax, punctuation, word choice, and spelling. These conversations help writers construct new theories and investigative questions about the details of language. However—and this is important—there is no reason to think that these groups will produce perfectly edited prose. In fact, in their inquiring and experimenting, partners may help introduce new unconventional forms.

marks. She has to recognize things in her own text that she hasn't noticed even through successive revisions. This final reading for conventionality of the text cannot really take long, because once the writer has read through, noticing and correcting the surface-level patterns she recognizes as deviating from conventions, there isn't really anything else to do in this phase of the process.

Consequently, teachers often attempt to increase the number of things to which students can attend, the number of patterns they might recognize and address, during this brief phase. If a teacher thinks most students need to direct their attention to a particular pattern—say, commas around parenthetical elements—she teaches a minilesson about it. She then asks the students at that time to add it to an editing checklist, either in the writer's notebook or in the writing folder that holds students' work-in-progress. An even more important use of these checklists is that each writer adds to it those patterns to which he especially needs to attend.

As the teacher confers with students, she overlooks much of what she might think to say in order to focus the writer's attention on only one language pattern she'd like him to learn to recognize, and that is the pattern that is added to the student's editing checklist—as a reminder for this piece and future pieces. An editing conference is not an occasion for editing the whole piece aloud, because that volume of detail would be overwhelming for anyone. The point of the conference, like all conferences, is to shine the writer's attention on one single point about writing that heretofore has been in shadow. To teach too much is not to teach at all, because it miseducates about attention, asking the reader to hold so many things simultaneously in mind that no learning can occur.

Because attention is limited and because the opportunity to attend to surface conventions during editing is relatively short, teachers have to perform some triage about the things to which they will ask writers to attend. In considering the language rules we will bring to our students, we need to consider first whether they are really even rules. Most of us walk around with ideas about rules and mistakes we got from our own teachers, whether or not they are true. Figure 12–1 lists some rules that are not rules—things we might spend needless attention worrying about—that we should work to clear out of students' way, not reinforce in their minds. These have been discussed in scores of books and articles by linguists. A recent book that is very clear about how these fake rules came to be and why they aren't really rules is Crystal's *The Fight for English* (2006)—see especially pp. 107–30.

> ## Multilingual Note
>
> Many students who come to English later in life may always write with an accent, and there is no reason to look down on people who write with an accent because of their knowledge of multiple languages. Though it's important to make them aware of the patterns in their writing, like, say, placing articles in places they don't belong while leaving them off places they do, it's equally important not to so fixate on those patterns that it's all we ever talk to them about. They may never get the articles, and readers may always be able to tell that they are multilingual: that's not a bad thing. We need to make sure they're also gaining access to all the other important things to learn about writing.

FIGURE 12–1 Writing
Rules to Let Go

Let go of rules that are not rules.

We can stop worrying about:

Split infinitives, as in *to boldly go*. Not an error.

Ending sentences with prepositions, as in *It was something he wouldn't put up with*. Also not an error.

Beginning sentences with conjunctions, as in *And it was still hot*. Just not an error.

The use of *I* in academic writing. There is nothing wrong with it, and scholars in the humanities and social sciences do it all the time.

Sentential adverbs, as in *Hopefully, we'll be going soon*. Though some people talk about this as a mistake, it's not. The adverb modifies the whole sentence, and we have lots of those kinds of modifiers—*lately, usually, happily*.

The repetition of *said* in dialogue. Most readers don't attend to these words, just who is speaking, and that's as it should be. So varying them self-consciously with *uttered, exclaimed, shouted* is just distracting.

Fragments. They do not make a piece of writing a failure and can sometimes be the most effective choice for a particular sentence.

Another aspect of this last-minute readying for public performance is the design of the appearance of the piece. Every written text is a visual object as well as a linguistic one. For many genres, such as graphic stories, comics, websites, posters, and pamphlets, the visual design of the piece has to be part of the initial planning and all the drafting and revising. But for texts that are primarily print, editing and design may go together. It will be here that students make final copies as neat as they can be if they are handwriting and that they make final decisions about fonts, margins, spacing, and other visual elements if they are printing their texts out from computers. When all these final moves have been completed, the curtain rises.

Teaching Students to Finish and Begin Again

For all of this work toward readers to be meaningful, as I said at the beginning of this chapter, there has to be an audience. Otherwise, there is no real cycle of communication, no one listening and no one responding. Publication is what makes the process meaningful. In order to extend publication to multiple audiences, it's also a very practical lesson to ask students to plan a few efforts to circulate their piece to additional audiences. How can they get more people to see what they have written? What is the route from the hands of the first readers to other groups of readers? How can they get it onto more computer screens, bringing more attention to the perspectives they wanted to put into the world? I will say more about circulation in Chapter 13.

By the time they publish, our student writers have gone quite a journey, from a topic that is just a glimmer in a notebook's eye to a crafted piece to response from readers right back at them. This whole experience was designed to teach them about writing as a process, about themselves as writers, and about how texts work. Now, what does each writer think she or he learned? How would they name these learnings? Hey, why don't we ask them! It's a good idea for writers to spend some time reflecting in their notebooks on the process they have been through, discussing such questions as:

How was this experience of writing different for you?

How did it resemble other experiences you have had?

What will you be keeping in mind for next time, to make sure you're wiser in your process?

How did writing interact with other activities this time, such as talking, reading, or researching? How is that like other times, or how is it different?

It's always the learner's assessment that is most important, because it's that self-evaluation that the learner carries into the next experience, that sets the learner's intention for the next effort.

In response to the learner's statement about her own learning through the process, the teacher can add his own perspective on how well the work went in this cycle. For grading and responding, it's important to be explicit about the criteria by which the grade is determined, though that doesn't mean circling or correcting every nonconventional mark on the page or filling the margins with comments meant to justify the grade. The criteria should be clear to the whole class, and they should be exactly the few things the teacher has been discussing over and over in minilessons and conferences. What needs to be communicated to the students is the degree to which their work on this piece of writing shows attention to the criteria they were meant to engage during this cycle of writing. This can be done equally well through rubrics or through more open-ended notes or comments (see also the next chapter and the final chapter).

Secondary English teachers think a lot about grading, and often, it does feel like a big part of what we do. But we also need to remember that grading does not equal teaching. Furthermore, when a writer has finished a piece of writing, that's not the best moment to teach him what he needed to know to write it. If we have students writing in front of us in class so that we can interrupt their process, conferring as they make decisions, we can actually teach them to be better writers rather than just assigning writing and then grading it, trying to squeeze some instruction into the very last part. In that case, grading is a more manageable task—just a communication to students about how well it's been going. Assessment, the more complex, descriptive, qualitative activity of understanding and recording who these learners are and how they are growing, is a constant and ongoing process, situated within our every interaction with groups or individuals, and it is much more worthy of our attention and efforts.

The whole process I have described in this chapter and the last can be conceived as a cycle, as diagrammed in Figure 12–2. I introduced this cycle in *Time for Meaning* (Bomer 1995), and it has turned out to be a useful way of thinking about an English language arts curriculum, especially those parts of the curriculum that focus on students making things. It begins with students bringing their lived lives into the classroom, proceeds to collecting in the notebook, passes through selection of the topic and design of the piece, and then traces the parts of the process I have described in this chapter. What makes it a

FIGURE 12–2 Writing Cycle

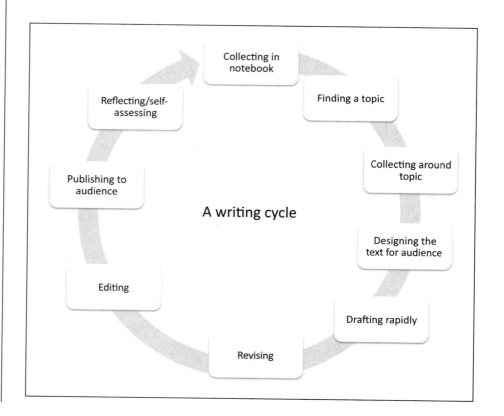

cycle is the assumption that students haven't arrived at the end of the process when they have published and reflected. Rather, they return to their notebooks, because there's an assumption in a writing life that the writer is always getting ready for the next project, always living with writing so that it makes her more attentive, more thoughtful, perhaps more reflective. The fact that the notebook is always there waiting means that no one is sitting idly once she is "done," because what the class is about is constructing an ongoing writing life, not finishing an essay and turning it in.

The idea of this familiar process being a cycle also underscores that the process is employed for lots of different kinds of writing—writing about literature, as I described in Chapter 9 (which may be making more sense now), and also writing in varied genres, as we will examine in the next chapter. The cycle helps us think about what remains the same across a school year—the kind of process writers should understand how to go through—and also those things that change—the forms and purposes students take up in response to different learning invitations their teacher offers.

CHAPTER 13

Empirical Inquiry into Qualities of Good Writing

Being a maker changes a person's eyes. When you're building bookshelves at your place, the set in your friend's house looks different. The layout of a vegetable garden in another state is meaningful and intriguing because of the decisions you made about the arrangement of your own back home. And writers notice how texts are put together—the deliberate design decisions made by the authors of published texts. Working on my own short story, I notice Toni Cade Bambara's decision about the point of attack in her story. I look at how she moves from one scene to another, because I have to solve that same problem of taking my reader from place to place and moment to moment in my story; I see how she mentions physical traits of the characters without interrupting action. I only have eyes for those things because I'm making my own story.

Sure, someone could point those things out to me if I were not shaping my own story, but it would be like a mechanic walking up to me while I'm cooking and showing me the sump and piston rings in my car's engine. My response might be something like, "What do you want from me?" We English teachers, and those who write standards for us to teach, often value students learning about how texts work—the difference between exposition and narration, the importance of setting, decisions about characters and plotlines. We want students to notice the arrangement of feature articles, that they move through logical categories rather than through time, that they often have headings that announce what the next section will be about and sometimes even tell the reader in one sentence what's going to come in the rest of the article. There's plenty of reason to believe that understanding the architecture of text can make reading experiences more deliberate, strategic, and rich. Plus, the way texts work is just good knowledge to have. Trouble is, that kind of architectural thinking is really optional when reading, and only fascinating to a few people.

When a reader is trying to make meaning of the substance of a text—focusing on content—formal concerns aren't foremost. Most of the time, when we are focused on teaching reading, we want students to let the language be a window they look *through* to the world on the other side. We want them involved in the meaning of the text and attending to not so much the words on the page as the world beyond the page. But when we look at writing like writers, we ask them to attend to the glass of the windowpane itself: the text structures, sentences, phrasing, words, choices in arrangement and style that create an impact on readers. When a whole classroom is writing short stories or feature articles, therefore, that community is a much riper context for studying textual architecture—the context of making things.

Teaching students to write *well* means helping them become acquainted with particular ways with words that are valued in literate communities and building their habits of seeing those qualities in writing. Students need to be able to see quality in the texts they read, to notice and admire it, and also to find words to talk about it. Becoming aware of what is in someone else's already-written text allows people to take a step toward controlling those qualities in their own writing.

Of course, it is tempting just to tell them the qualities of good writing, as abstract principles. And that's what many people do; maybe we all do at certain times. We say that a good piece of writing is organized, or that the organization should be logical. We announce that good writing is detailed, never mind the fact that there are many different kinds of detail and heaping all of it into one piece of writing is impossible—and if it were possible, the result would be unreadable. The difficulty is that these kinds of words can be less than completely helpful because they just become mental clutter, things the writer is trying to remember even though the phrases themselves don't produce an image of quality or a real feel for excellence.

Rather than merely dispensing ready-made characteristics, teachers can support a writerly consciousness that is more internal and generative, more appropriate to the mind of a maker. This maker's mind is more concentrated on the content, the image, the feeling, the idea, and the very particular language that gradually comes to name the writer's thoughts. It's a kind of analysis that is most truthful and accurate when it is situated within a text's meaning and intention. Teachers can help writers develop this consciousness by helping students learn to examine published, crafted texts empirically—to read like writers. Like any craftsperson, when a writer looks at other people's writing, she often notices the way it is put together, the craft decisions that make it up. Once she knows how to do this, when a writer is reading, she is able to use that experience to get better at writing—for the rest of her life, hopefully, across contexts in which very different textual features are considered high quality.

An Example of Empirically Examining Published Text with Attention to Craft

I'm going to take a look with you at a little section of a feature article by Terry McDermott called "Parental Advisory: Explicit Lyrics" (2003). It's from a book called *Da Capo Best Music Writing 2003* (so I'm not the only one who thinks it's good), but it's originally from the *Los Angeles Times* and, at least at the moment I write this, it's just a Web search away on the Internet. It's also on McDermott's website, tmcdermott.com. There are very interesting things about the first couple of pages, but I'm going to just summarize the beginning and look at the first major transition in the text. The beginning details the origins of the famous rap partnership N.W.A., how they began in 1988 recording together and put out a record called "Straight Outta Compton." See what you notice the writer doing on the opposite page.

I'm quoting only 240 words, but there are a lot of crafted moves in there. I won't try to describe all of them and will leave some for the reader to find, but I'll point out a few things I notice. To begin with, I notice a few places where he has a list and the first word of each item is repeated, even though it's not, strictly speaking, necessary: the list of *too this, too that* near the beginning, the list of *so this, so that* in the next long paragraph, and the list of *hip-hop this, hip-hop that* in the paragraph after the heading. He could have just said "too crude, misogynistic, and violent"; "so perverse, nihilistic, and forbidden"; and "hip-hop records, fashion, film, and attitude." It would have been faster and more efficient, and many style manuals, copy editors, and computerized grammar checkers would have recommended that he do it just that way, eliminating the repetitious modifiers. But let's assume McDermott is both right and purposeful. To understand the craft from the writer's point of view, it will help to think about what it achieves by writing it the way he did. Sure, maybe he did it instinctively, but we're interested in looking at it as craft, because the only way to develop instincts like that is to build a habit of noticing things. So if this

Parental Advisory: Explicit Lyrics
by Terry McDermott

The record contained no hit singles. In most of the country, nothing from the record was played even once on the radio. It was too crude, too misogynistic, too violent. MTV, which had by then established itself as the primary gatekeeper of popular culture, refused to play N.W.A. videos.

No radio, no television and no publicity.

"Straight Outta Compton" sold 3 million records.

The music it contained was so perverse, so nihilistic, so forbidden, politicians—then and still—elbowed each other out of the way to condemn it. Highbrow critics couldn't find language strong enough to critique it: they went further, questioning whether it was even music at all. It's barbaric, they said. Hide the women and children; bar the doors. Too late.

Gangsta rap was in the house.

Locking and Popping

The content of youth culture today is, to a significant extent, hip-hop: hip-hop records, hip-hop fashion, hip-hop film, hip-hop attitude. It is the only genre of popular entertainment that cuts consistently across class, ethnicity, gender and age. Just as rock music was a vehicle for the countercultural attitudes that provoked social upheaval among the middle classes in the 1960s, hip-hop in general and gangsta rap in particular have carried urban underclass sensibilities to the wider society—which has reacted with equal parts enchantment, imitation and outrage.

But in the first half of the 1980s, people in the Los Angeles-based record industry saw hip-hop as an East Coast fad.

decision was strategic, then I'd say he did it for several reasons. For one thing, precisely because it wasn't the fastest way—this way slows the reader down with the repetitive word. Also, the repetition draws attention to the rhythm of the words. Repetition like this is also a feature of oral language, and so this choice gives us a sense of voice—makes us recall the memory of real human bodies breathing and speaking and our own human body resonating and hearing sound. Furthermore, each of these lists is representing a social reality—something people keep talking about. The repetition could create a sense of many voices speaking out there. It also accumulates much more potently than a simple list, because the repetitious element makes the reader aware that things are piling up. Having noticed it, I could perhaps try something like it in my own writing, if I could ever be so purposeful, so inventive, so bold in my stylistic choices. Hey!

I also notice those two single-sentence paragraphs in a row:

> No radio, no television and no publicity.
> "Straight Outta Compton" sold 3 million records.

These two sentences, one really a fragment, sit isolated and stark naked on the page. Again, what is the purpose, if it's purposeful? He could have attached it to the previous paragraph and written, "Even though it had no play on the radio or television and no publicity, the album sold 3 million records." It seems to me that, once again, there is rhythm at work, and that starts to seem significant, that in an article about hip-hop, rhythm is an important element of craft. Even more, perhaps, these two sentences juxtaposed this way without explicit relationship force the reader to infer the connection and therefore to see the paradox and irony in that relationship. The album was ignored. The album was triple platinum.

Of course, that wouldn't work in a book like this.

See what I'm doing?

I next have to point to the sentence about the politicians, because it made me actually laugh out loud. There, he's taking the more general notion that several politicians spoke out against the music, and he is making that idea visual—a sight gag of these people physically elbowing past each other to condemn it. And it's specifically a group of people he means to make look ridiculous—politicians who use music and pop culture to score points with certain groups of voters they think will agree with them. Having noticed that, I could choose to do it somewhere in my own writing, rather than obeying the dictates of the standards writers who line up to plunk down one tome after another, full of categorized and subdivided distractions that pile up and obscure my view of real quality in the writing I read.

Though the heading itself in the middle of the quoted passage would be something else to notice, I'm going to skip to the passage just below the heading for the next thing I'll discuss. I notice though that before the heading, the writer was narrating a story, telling what happened next, after the heading, he shifted gears and started explaining something more general and abstract. That shift is a typical and very crucial move in feature articles, the move from the opening narrative into an expository passage. He's telling a story, and at a certain point, he just stops the progress of the story and explains some background. He has to decide where to break the nar-

Multilingual Note

Students who are learning English as an additional language will best be able to perceive the kinds of reading-writing connections that pertain to text structure, overall design, titles, beginnings and endings, explicit transitions, manipulations of time—anything that doesn't require attention to detailed idioms or intricate combinations of words. So fixing attention on diction or juxtaposition of words would tend to make the study of craft more difficult for them.

rative (at the album's release), and what idea he wants to explain (the impact of hip-hop more generally), and in this case, he uses the heading to help with changing gears. These are major structural decisions that are unlikely to appear in a list of prescriptions for good writing.

Indeed, almost nothing we have looked at in this passage would be all that likely to appear on such a list. It's almost impossible to imagine one that includes: unnecessary repetition, single-sentence paragraphs juxtaposed in opposition, farce as ridicule, and shifting modes. Away from the workings of a particular text, they wouldn't make much sense. And that's the thing about qualities of good writing in real text—it all depends. It depends on genre, meaning, purpose, attitude, audience, and the character of the author. It's possible to say some things that are, more often than not, worth trying to do in writing, and Figure 13–1 outlines some suggestions for those who might find such a list helpful. But as with most things, it's easiest to be very accurate when we are actually looking at a specific case rather than just pronouncing generalities.

For teachers of writing who have active reading lives (I'm sure that's all of us), the world is full of opportunities to develop our resources for teaching. Every text we read—whether it's a novel, magazine article, website, catalogue, or song lyric—might be a source of teaching. We fill our books with sticky notes so we can find the pages that might be useful to students. We mark passages,

FIGURE 13–1 Qualities of Good Writing

Common Characteristics of Good Writing

This chapter argues against teaching qualities of good writing as a list of abstract principles, and yet here I am presenting just such a list. I expect there might be much critique and loud complaining about what I'm doing right here, what a hypocrite I am and so forth. I hope so. Go right ahead. But I also predict that some people would like a little boost into thinking about quality in writing and might benefit from some suggestions about what to look for. Here are some things that people often admire in good literary writing of many different genres:

- Images in words
- Sound patterns in words
- Reminders of the human voice and embodied experience
- Reasons why—a sense of searching and striving for deeper meaning
- Inner and outer meanings to things
- Pointed connections to varied texts, experiences, and disciplines
- Texts that are deliberately designed or organized to provide the reader with an experience

scan articles into our computers, and take photos of pages with our hand-held devices with the intention of using them. Our own reading and writing lives are our most important resource and the world is full. Of course, sometimes we don't even remember all the passages we have marked, but still, the practice of noticing is the most important thing to bring into the classroom with us. Teachers need to leave time for their own literate lives in order to be able to make these moves responsively, on the spot, in response to students' noticings and, in fact, in response to their writing (see K. Bomer 2010).

Teaching a Pattern of Noticing, Describing, and Imagining Possibilities

It has sometimes helped to teach a pattern of attending, a heuristic, to support students' noticing of craft in writing. Figure 13–2 provides one example, and I will discuss it here. Whenever I ask students to read something, I want them first to attend to the text's meanings and how it speaks to them. I have been in workshops where people read a story aloud and asked us to listen for the verbs, and when it was all over, I really didn't know what the story was about. To do the same thing to students whom we also are teaching to be more attentive readers seems undesirable. So the first step is to attend to meaning and their response to that meaning, even if only briefly.

The second step is to look back through the text for a place where you can tell the writer was doing something on purpose. It may be a pretty part, or it could be a surprise, or a mysterious part, or some other spot that *sounds* special to you. It's about the words and sentences, not necessarily about *what hap-*

FIGURE 13–2 Studying a Writer's Craft

Studying a Writer's Craft

1. Respond initially to what it says to you.
2. Point to a place where you think the writing is good.
3. Describe (don't label) what the writer is doing there.
4. Speculate about what might have been in the writer's notebook in order to write that.
5. Speculate on the sorts of revision the writer might have done there.

---

pens in that part of the story. In that same question, I ask students to point to the words, because I want to make sure that what they're going to describe is somewhere in the actual language of the text, not an overall, vague quality that they wouldn't be able to emulate if they wanted to. I also want to push them away from readerly statements like, "I liked the relationships between the characters," which may not really look like the craft of language. Instead, I want them to think about the text from a writer's perspective: How is it made? What is she doing?

In the third question, I ask students to describe what the writer is doing there. I'm not asking for labels, like *simile* or *personification*, but rather a description of how the student thinks the words are working to produce a particular effect. I'm not interested here in students being able to apply official literary terminology. In fact, I ask them to stop worrying about those words, because those terms can actually limit what they see in text. They're so busy trying to remember which one is a simile and which a metaphor that they're not really thinking about the literary object in front of them. If attention goes to these terms, it moves away from admiration of the text and analysis of how it is working. It's trivial mental clutter and a distraction from really rigorous academic work. Where the terminology fits, I may use it in front of them so they have a chance to pick it up, but I do not want to turn the practice of reading like a writer into an exercise in matching a received term to a received example. Instead, I want them to see it strange, to look and look at what the writer is doing until it becomes interesting, to look at it like scientists look at the phenomena they are studying, before they have come up with a hypothesis, really seeing and describing. Developing that sort of descriptive language may aid in students' control of those features of text as they write. At least they can see them and name them, and producing them may be related.

In order to keep focused on the writer's perspective and process, I ask students to think about what might have been in the writer's notebook that would have allowed her to write that part. Finally, I also ask them to think about the sorts of changes to the text that might have been predictable if first the language came out in a blah and ordinary way and then the writer made it better.

Let's try this on another short piece of prose. At the top of the next page is a passage I marked in Richard Ford's novel, *Independence Day*, where I thought he had clearly crafted his writing, where I felt like I could tell it didn't just come out like this; he really wrote it this way on purpose.

Independence Day
by Richard Ford

On the beach, beyond the sandy concrete walk, moms under beach umbrellas lie fast asleep on their heavy sides, arms flung over sleeping babies. Secretaries with a half day off to start the long weekend are lying on their bellies, shoulder to shoulder, chatting, winking and smoking cigarettes in their two-pieces. Tiny, stick-figure boys stand bare-chested at the margins of the small surf, shading their eyes as dogs trot by, tanned joggers jog and elderlies in pastel garb stroll behind them in the fractured light. Here is human hum in the barely moving air and surf-sigh, the low scrim of radio notes and water subsiding over words spoken in whispers. Something in it moves me as though to a tear (but not quite); some sensation that I have been here, or nearby, been at dire pains here time-ago and am here now again, sharing the air just as then. Only nothing signifies, nothing gives a nod. The sea closes up, and so does the land. (Ford 2006, 151)

Though I admire quite a few spots in this little passage, I'll go ahead and drop my finger on the words, "Here is human hum in the barely moving air and surf-sigh, the low scrim of radio notes and water subsiding over words spoken in whispers." What I notice here is that the words sound like what they mean and that the actual sounds in the words—the breathy *h*'s and hissing *s*'s—help me hear, in my mind's ear, the beach and the way people's voices and radios sound there. Apart from this sound-sense, this sentence is actually a series of these auditory images strung together, and it all comes together in my mind to make the soundscape. So Ford had to tune into his memory of how a beach sounds and write meticulously what he heard. I could imagine that he might have written the sentence as a longer description and later realized he could bring the sounds into such close relationship by squeezing them together into one sentence. He also may have written, "I hear people talking, radios playing, and the sound of the waves," and then reworked it into this more musical and specific version. (And even if he didn't, I would probably have to do it that way. Furthermore, even if Ford is able to write that way in a first draft now, it's after a lifetime of toiling away in the middle of sentences.)

If I imagine what might have been in his notebook, it is certainly possible, even likely, that he actually went to a beach and looked around and listened, in order to get these perfect, telling details. He might have had reflective entries about how places sometimes seem familiar, though they don't recognize you back and when you go back to them, they aren't the same as they seem in your memory. Ford has often said that this novel and its predecessor were born from hearing the voice of the main character in his notebooks, and so we know he had notebook entries with this sound and sensibility in there.

A little passage like this—even one not nearly as beautiful—can easily occupy fifteen minutes of attention or so, and students usually come up with observations and insights that I could not have predicted. Of course, as I've said, it's much better if the passage is from a text that the students already know because they have read it or heard it and have discussed it and made meaning of it. The task here is to shift from thinking like a reader—someone who is interpreting and seeing what they can make of something given—to a writer—someone who has to wrestle with language to make the text sound the way it sounds and say what it says. This kind of reading is not just "this is what it says to me," but an examination of craft and an imagining of the writer's activity in producing it.

As I mentioned in Chapter 5 about reading, it's important to push students further once they have a convenient handful of words and phrases they know you want to hear ("snapshots and thought-shots," "I could see it in my mind"). Too easily, these become ways of not thinking, of just labeling with fossilized terminology. To avoid that, it's helpful to push further, to act, in fact, like you can't understand what they mean when they say these terms (even though you may have introduced some of them), and to ask them to move past labeling and see text anew, just as they have to see their world when they write in a notebook.

Understanding Genre Studies

This way of reading can work for any kind of text—poems, short stories, social networking genres, blogs. And because genre—or kind of text—organizes so many of a text's features, it is very often convenient to inquire with students about text qualities within a unit of study on genre. In a genre study of this kind, students make connections between their reading of published texts in the genre and writing their own texts of a similar sort. Here, I will discuss some ways of using genre studies to organize empirical inquiry into the way texts work. In Chapter 17, I will talk about planning a year, including genre studies. (I also discussed genre in Chapters 7–10 of *Time for Meaning: Crafting Literate Lives in Middle and High School* [Bomer 1995].)

> ### TECHNOLOGY NOTE
>
> Ordinary people who participate in digital culture rely on the strategies outlined in this chapter all the time. Someone wanting to sell their proofreading services or their pottery decides to put up a website and looks around at the sites of others offering similar services for design ideas. An engineer who begins a blog looks at the kinds of posts that others with engineering blogs tend to make, choosing the types of content, tone, post length, and design features that would seem to appeal to this audience, even as she also looks for a way to be different from everyone else. A student participating on social networks notices that a certain friend always gets responses to her updates, and he studies that person's updates for clues about what provokes that kind of attention. We're all actively using others' texts to teach us in this changing environment.

We should consider first the sorts of things that are reasonably considered genres and are appropriate for this kind of whole-class inquiry (see appendix for a listing). A genre, first of all, is a broad category of text, and for our purposes here, is best thought of as a form, not a type of content. Though many English professors, publishers, booksellers, and librarians use the term *fiction genre* to describe novels and stories such as westerns, romance, science fiction, detective stories, and so forth, that is not how I am using the term here. It seems to me that, for compulsory English language arts classes, it is a pretty intense imposition of taste to require that every student produce a western. Here, I would consider all of those to be subgenres of fiction narratives—varied types of content that go into fiction. And because we are talking about young people writing in school, I consider *fiction* to mean short stories. (Though some young people do want to write novels and of course may do so outside the official curriculum, the writing of a novel doesn't fit easily into a genre study in a classroom.)

In addition to short stories, poems are obviously a genre, as are picture books, comic strips and cartoons, and posters. These are forms you can spot from across the room, without even being able to read their content. Memoirs are a genre, and though, in a reader's mind they are often very similar to short stories, the writing processes can be so different (mostly remembering and reconstructing versus mostly inventing) that they are well served as separate genre studies (with an acknowledgment of the overlap as part of the teaching).

Several expository forms make good genre studies, and they are especially important to teach, since they are close to forms of academic writing even as they are also common among people who make texts outside of coercive school environments. When I use the term *essay*, for instance, I'm referring to the form that Montaigne invented around Shakespeare's time—meditations that turn an idea this away and that, journeys of thought that try out a concept or family of ideas—and this genre is very close to the kind of writing many students do in their writers' notebooks. It is not really close at all to the creature made in schools and called by the name *essay*; that thing (when it's not formulaic and reduced to something that's not even composing and resembles no text produced outside school) is really an argument.

Arguments are, indeed, another good genre for study, and I think it is useful to distinguish among *public arguments*, *policy arguments*, and *textual arguments*. *Public arguments* are designed to bring the general public around to a particular view or set of behaviors. *Policy arguments* attempt to change rules or laws that are official parts of community life. *Textual arguments* are about the meanings of texts, and they use parts of texts themselves as evidence for their claims. Much academic writing in a range of disciplines consists mostly of textual arguments. While it might be possible to do a genre study that considers all three kinds of argument, it also might be useful to teach them separately, making it possible to consider the different demands for evidence and emotion and the varied ways a writer has to assume a specific persona that will work for this particular purpose and audience.

Feature articles are kinds of texts one often finds in magazines and newspapers. They are written to appeal to a general public, not necessarily people with a highly motivated interest in the topic, so they have to be written in an engaging and approachable style that connects new information to things with which the reader is already familiar. This is the kind of writing about information that is most congenial to the study of literary craft and high-quality prose style, even as students do the quasi-academic work of collecting, analyzing, and organizing information, developing an angle on their topic, and designing a text that works well for readers.

Digital environments have produced several genres that may be related to some of the more traditional forms I have named so far—blogs as arguments, blogs as memoir, social network updates as notebooks or essays, microblogging as poetry or short fiction. But in online environments, there is an emphasis on participation—on the dynamic, constantly changing content rather than on the craft of making something permanent. Consequently, a study of writing to participate in the digital world might be treated not so much as a genre study as an inquiry of a particular literacy practice, along the lines of *writing for social action* (see comments about a unit on this below and in Chapter 17). Still, static websites do exist, and they would still work as a genre study. And there is no doubt that new genres are emerging in the social world of the Internet.

To be clear about what we are doing in a genre study, it's important for a teacher to make some decisions about what can be taught especially well with that genre. These central purposes might be common in that genre and sometimes provide useful insights into writing in other genres, too. The appendix provides examples. If you have ever read the Best Essays or Best Poetry collections from various years, you know that the features of a genre can't really be limited to particular characteristics. I'm not suggesting here that they can; I'm just trying to identify things that can conveniently be brought into focus as students work in a particular form. These teaching foci can also become criteria for assessment (more on that in Chapter 17).

Grading and evaluating in a genre study, I look for the characteristics not just in a final, published piece, but the evidence across drafts that the writer has been paying attention to that area of our shared inquiry. I'm evaluating

Releasing Writers' Energy and New Knowledge

Every unit of curriculum in a writing workshop is not a genre study. Students need at times to be responsible for their own decisions about the genres in which they will write, and in a certain sense, one can only assess the impact of a genre study when students make their own decisions about genre. There are other possible foci for a unit of study in writing, such as revision, writing partnerships, use of a notebook across a process, and writing for social action.

the evidence that the student has attended to the elements I have attempted to teach, not necessarily the degree to which I think they are good or right in the final draft. That's basically because, first, sometimes writers inadvertently revise good qualities right out of their successive drafts because they are still working on being able to control the features to which they are attending. And second, the purpose of a universal, compulsory education is not to get everyone to produce "perfect" arguments or poems but to provide everyone with understandings of how texts work and habits of manipulating elements.

As I've said, genres are large categories. They are not assignments that specify both form and content. They are not algebra equations with everything given except a few little variables. Poetry is a genre; poems about springtime and "where I'm from" are an assignment. Essays are a genre; This I Believe essays are assignments. Feature articles can be a genre study; "ten places to see while you are young" is an assignment. There are times when assignments are appropriate, such as when we ask students to make a notebook entry about places at home where they might try to write next week. Such an assignment makes sense because the investigation of writing spaces within a literate life is an important bit of content in our teaching. But genre studies that involve sustained inquiry into form and craft are best kept open to student-developed topics.

Though "myths" and "folktales" and "legends" have reappeared recently on certain lists of standards, they are not really genres in which writers just sit down to compose. To become what they are, they existed orally for centuries before anyone turned them into written texts. I would consider it somewhat miseducative to undertake them as genre studies per se, though of course many writers have borrowed themes, plots, and characters from them for short stories, poems, and plays.

There are other genres of text that, though they are fine as genres in the world, aren't ideally suited to a shared form for a class. Often, the main reason they don't work is because the students aren't really positioned toward a real audience that motivates this kind of writing. For instance, it doesn't make sense to do a genre study on laws, because the students are not in the position of lawmakers. Similarly, if there is no business in which they are actually trying to sell something, advertisements will at best be pretending and not socially meaningful. If everyone in the class isn't going somewhere, then travel writing will not work as a genre, no matter how much the teacher loves reading it. It's useful to ask, therefore, whether the students are actually situated to be able to speak with authority and purpose in this genre, and whether an audience is in fact going to read these texts the students produce as they would read the texts of a professional. In the case of aesthetic genres like poetry and short stories, the answer is yes. In the case of many other practical genres, the answer is no. (For more guidelines on choosing genre, see *Time for Meaning* [Bomer 1995], especially Chapters 7 and 10.) Readers might also benefit from thoughtful, inquiring readings of Katie Ray's book *Study Driven* (2006) and Heather Lattimer's *Thinking Through Genre* (2003). Tom Romano and others have also explored multigenre writing, which is a different way of becoming clear about genre, even as it invites students to lay down one genre alongside another in a single piece. He introduced the concept in *Blending Genre, Altering Style* (2000). Another important variation on genre studies, in which students choose to explore independently a form of writing with which they have had little experience, is detailed in Fleischer and Andrew-Vaughan's book *Writing Outside Your Comfort Zone: Helping Students Navigate Unfamiliar Genres* (2009), though obviously, such a unit of study supposes an ongoing curriculum that is at times attentive to genre. These possibilities present teachers with a wide array of ways of studying genre with students, and here we will continue to examine the planning of a whole-class genre study that helps organize inquiry into the craft of published texts as a resource for writers.

Planning a Genre Study: What Goes In

Publication Date and Event

It may seem strange to begin with the last thing that will happen, but in planning a genre study, it is a pretty good idea to schedule some publication dates in order to provide structure to the time, to plan the study's duration by determining when the audience will arrive. As I suggested in the previous chapter, that sense of audience allows a class to become more like the school play, or like a sports team, with the teacher in the role of helping students get ready for an audience that needs to be pleased, informed, entertained (rather than actually *being* that audience). The presence of an audience focuses each writer on a purpose and motivates both revision and editing. A publication event may be the moment the website(s) go live or the day a class magazine is ready for distribution. It may also be an event when another class comes in, to view posters up in the hallway, to browse among the feature articles arranged artfully on tables covered in colored butcher paper, or to hear performances of poems.

It can, of course, be intimidating for some writers to think about an audience reading their work, so a teacher has to know his students and be deliberate about when and how much to talk about the audience. Perhaps the best timing for this conversation is not while students are in notebooks or are first visualizing or beginning their drafts, though certainly, the time has arrived once revision is underway. The publication event, at the end of the process, can be the engine that drives everything that leads up to it. Having people hear what you say and speak back to it completes the socially reciprocal cycle that is at the heart of all communication.

Writers' Notebooks

Since a notebook contains the material of potential drafts, each genre study must involve students going back into their past notebook entries to see what is already there as a potential topic. Rick's entries about riding bikes will look different if he is getting ready to write a poem than they do if he's looking for a topic to research toward a feature article.

Moreover, for a week or so, it is almost always important that students begin keeping a notebook in a manner that befits the genre they are getting ready to write. A poster designer's notebook will have things in it (sketches, boiled down slogans tried different ways) than a poet's (phrases that sound good, images captured in words, entries written with line breaks). Feature articles require actual research, and the notes, along with reflections in which the writer makes facts meaningful, go in the notebook. Each genre has its form of preparation, its equipment for quality, and notebooks therefore provide the writer's initial moves toward taking on the kinds of thinking that are valued among people who make that kind of text. (See Chapter 10 for more on notebooks. Also see *Time for Meaning*, Chapter 3 [Bomer 1995] and *For a Better World*, Chapter 7 [Bomer and Bomer 2001].)

Wide Reading and Self-Selected Mentor Texts

While students are becoming insiders in particular genres, teachers try to provide a couple of different kinds of reading experiences. Shortly, we will discuss close and intensive reading of a few texts in order to examine how they are put together. Here, though, I want to argue for the value of inviting students to read widely in the genre, finding instances of it in their own lives, choosing texts about topics that appeal to them, and selecting one or two examples of the genre as mentors for their own writing.

There are several goals for this extensive reading. First, it permits students to explore the diverse options available within a particular genre—the range of topics, strategies, styles, and emphases that are still open to the writer even when, say, poetry is named as a shared genre. Second, it allows them to test the boundaries of this particular genre, thinking for themselves and with one another about whether a particular text could be counted as a poem and why. Being able to make distinctions among genres is part of the point of a genre study, and so discerning whether an example is inside or outside the category is an important kind of conceptual learning. Third, reading widely allows each student to more clearly develop an image of what this genre looks like. If students are looking through magazines at home and in the classroom, searching for examples of the sort of text we are studying, that means they're holding a textual shape in mind and testing it against different possibilities. Students developing a memory of that shape—the nature of the genre—is part of the goal of a genre study. Finally, giving them a chance to range widely in selecting interesting instances of the genre is how they will have a chance to develop favorites, to find at least a couple of examples that aren't repulsive simply by virtue of having been selected by their teacher.

Immersing a class in lots of examples is sometimes pretty easy. It's not hard to fill a classroom with poetry anthologies and give students time to browse, share, develop some favorites, perhaps even copying (or cutting and pasting) some into their notebooks. Websites and videos, comics and cartoons fill many students' lives in lots of ways, so it takes no particular effort to immerse students in those genres. Though short stories are slightly more difficult, over the past couple of decades, we have seen the release of several dozen collections of short stories, thanks in no small measure to the efforts of Donald Gallo, who has edited most of them, it seems. To immerse students in feature articles, essays, and arguments, however, requires more effort at hunting down examples on a wide range of topics, in a style and at a level of difficulty that makes it possible for students to both understand their meaning and imagine themselves as a maker of one of this kind of thing. Still, whenever possible and practical, immersion is an important goal, and from extensive reading, it's useful for students to choose their own mentor texts and look in them for the detailed strategies writers have used to craft a reader's experience, so they can try some of the same techniques in their own writing in the same genre.

It's just really not enough for us to lead students in admiring particular parts of texts we have chosen for them, even though that mentoring is important. They may become competent at engaging in those conversations, being good students, but there's no reason to think that they have then learned how to undertake this kind of perception and analysis independently. The point is for them to be able to learn to write from reading when we are not around to sponsor and support it; otherwise, what's the point of all this? So we need to hand these habits over to them. This concept of handover is especially important in all aspects of teaching (Bomer 2007; Edwards and Mercer 1987) and in order to accomplish it, we need each individual to notice and trace his own admiration of writing. We do this when we ask students to collect quotes and favorite passages in their writers' notebooks, annotating them with their noticings and observations about what makes this part so good. They may clip and save with both paper and digital devices, in English and other languages they know, developing habits of saving admired passages—admired because of their writing, not the content—in files on computers and handheld devices. And just as we ask them to name in ordinary words and describe as accurately as they can what the writer is doing and to speculate on how the text got that way when they read with us, we should ask them to do the same kind of thinking independently in their notebooks.

A Few Touchstone Texts

At the heart of a genre study are two to four texts that the teacher and students return to again and again to figure out the decisions necessary for writers in this genre to design deliberately. These may include an example or two found by students, but it's most important that the teacher be purposeful in choosing these. These are the texts that will provide examples of the elements of craft on which the class will focus in many minilessons. They don't necessarily have to be the best examples ever made, and some mediocre texts or even some that seem less than brilliant can be instructive for writers to study in developing understanding of how the craft works. It's also more important that these particular students find them engaging than that they be classic or award-winning masterpieces admired by academics. As I emphasized earlier, the first lesson of any text is its power to matter to readers. Therefore, it's usually best for texts to enter a writing workshop via a reading workshop, or some setting in which students have had a chance to talk about the texts' author meanings, the worlds represented, and the sense we as readers can make of them. Then, when they talk about craft, architecture, and the surface structures of texts, that technical thinking serves a meaningful function.

Using touchstone texts is far more efficient than looking for a new example for each lesson, since choosing new ones would mean that the students would have to read it and think about it before the class could attend to particular elements of craft in question. Taking out a text with which the students are already familiar, the teacher can, in a particular minilesson, quickly zero in on the relevant part of the text, without sacrificing students' connection to the context, meaning, and background. Moreover, students might learn the deeper, more lasting lesson, that a writer is never finished with a text just because she knows how it ends. If you look in the appendix, you see that I have named four objectives for poetry. If a teacher took up those four objectives and then chose three poems, examining how each objective operates (or does not) in each of three touchstone texts would require about a dozen minilessons. Repeating the objective with different examples is one way to sustain attention to the same element of craft for a longer time. And it does not require a large number of texts to produce a varied, while focused, set of minilessons.

Inquiry into the Craft of That Form

The point of these minilessons with mentor texts is not to lay down the law about particular ways all students must write their poems, arguments, or posters. Rather, it's to take up the craft of this genre as an inquiry. To inquire into craft means looking at a line of a poem and asking why the poet might have broken the line right there, how that could be seen as a choice, a craft move, and how it might have been revised to get it that way. What would it mean, we encourage students to reflect, if *you* had created a line like that? Why would you do it that way, or why might you change it to a different way?

Inquiring this way provides students with the opportunity to become insiders as makers of a particular kind of text. As their drafts and revisions emerge, then we investigate those, too, as design experiments—the trying on of craft elements to see how they work with readers. Therefore, even though I have discussed assessment and even rubrics, it's important to me that genre studies not become merely prescriptions of written technique or formulaic certainties—and it's important that they not provide yet another way to find certain students deficient. Instead, they should be opportunities for wonder, for open-ended explorations of possibilities, chances to innovate and negotiate quality rather than merely imitating and obeying.

Extensions and Contractions

Curriculum in Today's English Classrooms

" Because the kind of advance planning heretofore engaged in has been so routine as to leave little room for the play of individual thinking or for contributions due to distinctive individual experience, it does not follow that all planning must be rejected. On the contrary, there is incumbant upon the educator the duty of instituting a much more intelligent, and consequently more difficult, kind of planning. He must survey the capacities and needs of the particular set of individuals with whom he is dealing and must at the same time arrange the conditions which provide the subject-matter or content for experiences that satisfy these needs and develop these capacities. The planning must be flexible enough to permit free play for individuality of experience and yet firm enough to give direction towards continuous development of power. "

—JOHN DEWEY, *Experience and Education*

241

CHAPTER 14

Teaching Toward Participation in Digital Culture

To point out that we're all seeing new forms of text is not to reveal any astonishing surprise to anyone. Websites, blogs, message boards, video games, software programs, multimedia texts, and cell phone text messages have rapidly become pervasive in most middle-class people's lives over the past decade or so.

And as many people have pointed out again and again, young people are already at home in this layered textual environment, often more so than their elders. Usually, young people adopt new forms quickly, learn to use them purposefully, and begin transforming them well before many of their teachers are completely aware that the new text forms even exist. Their speed and flexibility has made some youths more experienced than many of their teachers at the new forms of text and new practices of literacy.

Still, all young people do not have equal access to these practices, and those who have always been disadvantaged by literacy practices (the poor and others who are socially vulnerable) are likely to be left out of the newly emerging environments. Moreover, certain traditions of literacy are also important to bring into these new environments, such as evaluating the reliability of a source and critiquing authors' perspectives in the interests of a fair and just world. So despite youths' well-known motivation to play with new devices, there is still a need to teach into their enthusiastic practices.

What I will here call *new literacies* refers to the whole set of textual practices that have grown up around changes in technologies, especially the personal computer, the Internet, gaming, and video (Kist 2005). These practices are changing so rapidly that writing a book chapter about them is probably a bad idea, but here I am. Despite my reticence to write a dated book, to ignore these changes would be to misrepresent the literate world we and our students live in. Though some of the practices I'll describe are as old as literacy itself, new technologies and cultural trends are intensifying some aspects of language and literacy and adding to the repertoire we all need to move comfortably through our literate lives.

Teaching new literacies can't just be about teaching students to use particular electronic devices. When I was in school, teaching us to use technology as part of our literate lives would have meant teaching us to use typewriters, film projectors, film strips, and the big three television networks along with good old PBS. I suppose it might have involved cameras and laminating machines. And I'm not a particularly old person. Machines change, and people have to know how to adapt to new hardware and software.

What's more, it is entirely possible to use machines and keep right on engaging in the same old literacy practices. The Accelerated Reader program, for instance, uses computers simply to give students low-level comprehension tests. That's not new literacies; it's old literacies on computers.

New literacies are practices—ways with texts—ways of doing reading and composing. And though they are "new" by virtue of their emergence as practices in a digital environment, they are ways of operating that can also be extracted from that kind of environment. New literacies can be unplugged.

Whenever we talk about literacy and technology, we need to remember that literacy is a technology—or it involves a collection of technologies. Writing with ink on paper is a technology, and a reader of a book, turning the pages, flipping back and forth to cross-reference something, is a user of a technological device, too. My argument in much of this book has been that our approach to those rather old technologies

The NCTE Definition of New Literacies (National Council of Teachers of English 2010b)

Literacy has always been a collection of cultural and communicative practices shared among members of particular groups. As society and technology change, so does literacy. Because technology has increased the intensity and complexity of literate environments, the twenty-first century demands that a literate person possess a wide range of abilities and competencies, many literacies. These literacies—from reading online newspapers to participating in virtual classrooms—are multiple, dynamic, and malleable. As in the past, they are inextricably linked with particular histories, life possibilities, and social trajectories of individuals and groups. Twenty-first-century readers and writers need to:

- Develop proficiency with the tools of technology
- Build relationships with others to pose and solve problems collaboratively and cross-culturally
- Design and share information for global communities to meet a variety of purposes
- Manage, analyze, and synthesize multiple streams of simultaneous information
- Create, critique, analyze, and evaluate multimedia texts
- Attend to the ethical responsibilities required by these complex environments

(but young in comparison with speech) is less thoughtful, flexible, situated, and powerful than it should be. We often do the old technologies badly, and we can do the new ones just as badly. What matters are the practices we induct students into.

This is good news for schools—essential news. Even affluent schools will probably never have the hardware, software, and support staff necessary to keep up with the changes that occur every year and a half or so. I spend way too much on electronics, and I don't come anywhere near keeping up. Schools aren't going to spend as much as I do. But the affluent schools will come much closer than schools with students from economically disadvantaged homes. It is not unusual in such schools for all the computers to be broken, frozen, missing pieces, or otherwise unusable. And there are often nowhere near a sufficient number for students actually to function on them, to get serious work done, or to develop independent habits in digital environments. It is important to use any resource available to give students some access to the online world, to genres like podcasts, to video production. But my point is that those resources will not be sufficient—teachers need to know how to think beyond the device and to understand practices.

So what do I mean by changing practices in literacy?

Changes in Literacy

Everyone is a publishing company.

First of all, because of the enormous changes in digital technologies, every individual is now a publishing company. In the past, most authors had to rely on typesetters and professional designers to create the look of a text and to make its elements appropriate to its content. Over the past thirty years or so, every individual has gotten used to formatting documents, choosing fonts, determining color and size, and designing the overall image impression that texts make on readers. It's also downright easy to add full color photos, design features, diagrams and charts, video, sound recordings, and interactive elements to the texts that we compose, sitting in our pajamas at home. In fact, it's much easier for individuals working in digital environments to have something like color images than it is for a publisher like Heinemann to do so, since print runs of color photographs are much more expensive than loading a photo into a website (which is essentially free). All of this means that every individual with a computer can do what required a financed and fully staffed operation to accomplish a few years ago.

Everyone is everywhere.

From the invention of writing through the development of the Internet, it has become increasingly possible for people's thoughts to be expressed where their bodies are not. Now, it seems that it's possible for any individual to be everywhere at once. From their cell phones, people can upload a statement to a Web page and nearly instantaneously, people around the world can access it. If my friend moves away, I can still know what is "on her mind" by just checking her status updates on social networking sites. It means that I can reach out to anyone I want, anytime I want, rather than going through elaborate publication and distribution plans for paper texts. It also means that others have access to my attention, and that my reading time has constantly competing demands, in ways that are unprecedented in human history.

Text is fast and easy.

It is so quick and easy to produce texts with digital devices and to get them to our intended audiences that we often forget the labor involved in text production in years past. Now, we don't even have to tolerate the friction of a pen against paper. Our fingers fly over the keyboard, and zip-zap, a text is on its way. Composing is still difficult work, but to an increasing extent, our audiences are just not willing to wait for a pokey composition process to get a text done. We can cut and paste, reproduce and borrow, lift a snippet and develop new thinking from it, collect information from a range of resources, access a huge array of perspectives on a topic, and read libraries full of research at a near-instantaneous rate. Our reading may be limited by our own speed of processing, but it no longer includes even a car drive to a library in many cases.

Every text is connected to other texts.

The Internet is a worldwide network of computers, and the writing that has developed in its environment is a similarly global network of texts. And as a network, its parts are connected, not isolated; that is, every text is connected to other texts. Texts are actually composed to be connected; links are built right into them. They speak for themselves, but they are explicitly located in connection or dialogue with other texts, and sometimes, they are

> ### TECHNOLOGY NOTE
>
> I am describing an environment and a set of practices in rapid development. Since I am doing so in a book—an artifact of print culture—it is very clear that by the time anyone reads this, these things will have progressed beyond the state I am describing. The most important thing we can do with our students with regard to the constantly evolving nature of literacy in our age is to keep inquiring alongside them about what is happening, not to be the winner of the "name the newest practices" contest. Where would one find the finish line for such a race, after all?

only intelligible if the reader follows the links, reads some of the other texts, and then comes back again to the first text. This means that our reading and writing experiences with texts are no longer closed within the beginning-middle-end structure of a single, unified work. This development has great implications for literate structures and processes, as well as the human relationships they shape.

Purposeful reuse is part of the process.

Because texts are so connected, and because people have the power previously reserved for publishers, and because accessing, copying, and creating texts has become so easy and swift, an environment has developed in which individual texts don't seem to be as completely owned by any single author or publisher. There is more reuse, more borrowing, more transformation of existing content as part of a composing process. This isn't completely new either: people have for centuries quoted, copied out passages, and traced images. But as every teacher knows, the ease of copying has increased to a transforming extent over the past quarter century. Many people are familiar with mash-ups, mixes and remixes, and digital photo manipulation, as well as software functions that help us copy whole sections of text, images, and video for later reuse. There is, of course, much contention about everything from copyright protection to plagiarism, but these literacy practices are with us and are inescapably part of the digital landscape in which we read and write.

Five Changes in Literacy

Everyone is a publishing company.
Everyone is everywhere.
Text is fast and easy.
Every text is connected to other texts.
Purposeful reuse is part of the process.

These five transformational trends have important implications for the ways people create and interact with texts. Because everyone is a publishing company, the process of composing becomes more than ever a process of visual design, which necessarily means that reading involves understanding, interpreting, and critiquing the assumptions of others' designs. Because of the speed and ease of making texts and because they exist mostly in connection with other texts, we now write into a participatory network, with each of our contributions more explicitly tied to others' turns. The increase in speed, along with the fact that everyone is everywhere means that each of us engages with literacy in a crowded and complex world rather than the extended, relatively solitary times that have often been associated with literacy in the past. Those new realities will organize the literacy practices I'll discuss as this chapter moves along.

New Realities in Our Literacy Practices

We transact with purposefully designed, visual texts.

Designing

As I stated before, ordinary people sitting around in their pajamas now regularly produce their own finished documents, making decisions that were once the territory of publishing companies. With so many options available to writers, we can now see clearly that every text is designed. There is a background with a texture and color, a particular font, size, and color for the print, decorative features alongside print, images that carry meaning, embedded video, music, or other sound playing. The text may even be delivered entirely via a sound or video recording (currently called *podcasts* or, sometimes for video, *vodcasts*). In digital environments, all of these things are extremely easy to do—and getting easier.

Sometimes, a writer may choose to make a text look "plain," and that's a design, too. A setting, such as school, may require a standardized design—black ink on white paper with headings on the tops of pages—and that decision now speaks as loudly and clearly as an innovative one. (And it's worth wondering what that message is, and why a school might insist on sending it.) The arrangement or organization of a text is also an aspect of design, a set of deliberate decisions that predict the experience the reader will have—just as much as a Web designer predicts users' experience of a site. As Wysocki and Lynch write,

> **New Realities That Shape Our Literacy Practices**
>
> We transact with purposefully designed, visual texts.
>
> We transact with texts by participating in a network.
>
> We transact with texts in a crowded and complex world.

"Arrangements arrange the pieces in a composition, but they also arrange our needs, expectations, and desires. Take seriously the needs, expectations, hopes, and desires of those who read your writing or use what you design" (2007, 47). This emphasis on the readers and what their use of the text will be like becomes central in thinking of composing as design. How and where will readers be engaging with this text? What is likely to be their body position? How will they hold the text physically, and how will that condition their way of responding to it?

These design principles apply very obviously to digital compositions, like websites, slides for presentations, and digital documentaries. Indeed, people who compose extensively in digital environments are focused at least as much on the visual and material design of a text as on its language, and they understand that the overall look and operation of a text is part of its meaning.

However, like everything we will discuss here, these principles apply as well to nondigital texts—those that appear on paper, in handwritten or printed ink, on skin, wooden signs, or the sides of buildings. Each notebook entry can have a design, if the writer intends it. Each piece written for readers should be designed and tested on readers, then revised not just in language but in its visual and material elements. To go further with this idea of composition as design, one that could help us rethink composition in important ways, let me suggest Anne Wysocki and Dennis Lynch's book *Compose Design Advocate* (2007).

We transact with purposefully designed, visual texts.

Designing
Composing with images
Using sound and movement
Redesigning
Attending to materiality
Planning delivery and circulation

Though actual designing is the main point I want to push here, it's also important that students learn to respond to design, to think about what it says and whether its claims fit with other dimensions of the text. If a text has a very clean and rational look to it, an astute and critical reader should weigh those design elements against the text's linguistic content, to be on guard against a cool appearance that dresses up muddy, wasteful, or indulgent thinking. Being critical, as we discussed about reading, involves being able to resist a text's power, and that's certainly as true of visual and material elements as it is of words and sentences.

Composing with Images

In digital environments, many texts include images or may even be built around images that do more work than the text itself. It is easier than ever before to include images in texts, and so they have an increasing presence in all kinds of compositions, including academic work, personal literacy, political discourse, and interpersonal interactions. We use photos, drawings, and other media to complement or extend meanings. It has become a regular expectation for websites, posters, blog posts, and other common genres to include a picture. To do so, an author has to either find or create one that is logically appropriate, as well as emotionally, politically, and personally fitting for the purpose, audience, and meaning. Like the choices a writer makes of words, the selection of an image contributes to the formulation of what you mean. Pictures are rejected for a wide range of reasons—the car is from too early a period, the black people are at the margins of the photo, the person's face looks glum, there is too much of the green that won't look good with the blue border we have. Images often suggest some kind of power relationship, some point of view, some identity, and these meanings will either be right for the whole text or not. That requires that writers build habits of thinking visually—of considering elements of visual composition as part of a vocabulary of meaning.

Since visuals have become an increasingly important part of literate practice, it really won't do for English teachers to pass off responsibility for this modality to art teachers or to say that they'll wait to engage images until the art teacher can be involved. First of all, these visual elements in composition aren't necessarily "art"; they are images integrated into all texts. Secondly, the whole point is that writing and images are integrated into a single text. Since the students have to learn how to do both, it seems reasonable that the modalities need to be integrated into a single teacher as well. Someone especially expert at visual media might serve as a resource, but that shouldn't exempt the English teacher from dealing with visuals.

It's not only the making of visual texts that requires attention in our curriculum. It's arguably even more important that students learn to be critical readers of images, able to interpret their meanings, take those meanings seriously as deliberately designed, and critique their assumptions. Images may be especially persuasive precisely because they purport just to show us the world rather than making explicitly verbal claims. A picture is worth a thousand words, the cliché goes, but all those words may be lies. When human beings are represented in images, certain genders, races, attitudes, and social types are represented as dominant. That should be noticed, and readers/ viewers should be able to think carefully about whether such a representation is accurate and fair, or whether it contributes to a stereotype that freezes individuals into particular social positions by reinforcing everyone else's assumptions about them. So even as they are becoming writers with images, our students need to become readers of images, applying many of the same sorts of thinking they do when they read texts.

> **Other Critical Questions to Ask of a Visual Text**
>
> What is the point of this picture?
>
> Who benefits from that point being made?
>
> What assumptions about power are represented?
>
> What social groups are represented as central or dominant in this image?
>
> What social class perspective is reinforced in this picture? What is the role of money?
>
> How might this picture be revised if it were to be remade in the interest of justice?

Using Sound and Movement

Part of the design of a document may include sound. Some Web pages have music, voice, or sound effects when the user does a particular action. Planning the sound that appropriately accompanies text, or carries meaning on its own, is a form of literacy. We think immediately of this as part of media literacy— the ability to be critical participants with television and film. The craft of affecting viewers, even manipulating them, with music that tells them how to feel about what they see, has been developing for a century in film and longer than that in the theatre, where opera became the first art form to integrate as many modalities as we deal with in contemporary digital contexts. Digital texts sometimes integrate this craft with traditional print forms of writing, so that a digital text might have music accompanying videos, static images, and print. I'm not just talking about putting one's favorite song on a website. I'm talking about sound—sometimes music, sometimes voice-over, sometimes a sound design like you'd find in a film—that is actually integrated into the meaning of a text. Electronic artists have led the way in these advanced forms of text, and you can see some examples at The Electronic Literature Organization's website (www.eliterature.org/).

Looking at the texts on that website, one learns that some elements in a text may move. The transitions between slides or pages, the movement of animated text, the inclusion of video and other moving elements in a page—all of these call for choreographic or cinematic thinking, the design of movement. A transition can be sudden or gradual, can remind the viewer of a physical phenomenon in the real world (a windshield wiper, a spinning cube) or just the shifts of a dream. Animated text can seem playful and silly, or it can be poetically graceful. An embedded video can serve as an illustration of what is described in the text, but it's often more effective (as is the case with images in a picture book) as an extension that further develops meaning, contributing ideas that are not in the words. Most often, perhaps, such videos actually serve as parallel texts that lay thematic content alongside the writer's ideas in print. What is most important here is to realize that sometimes, writers in digital environments need to think about the meaning of movement, the way a choreographer or theatre director does, just as they need to be thinking like a sound designer or musician. Composing multimodally draws upon more different parts of the writer's being.

Redesigning

Even though people are making new visual images, music, and moving images for Internet-based composing, it's still more common for writers to draw upon the vast reservoir of existing images, music, and video and to redeploy those resources into their own texts. Making texts, in other words, often involves purposeful redesign, which is also called *mash-up* or *remix* (Knobel and Lankshear 2008; Lankshear and Knobel 2003; New London Group 2000). Composition in digital environments involves taking pieces of what other people have done (or what the writer herself has done) and reusing it for a new purpose, to serve a new meaning. Images, fragments of text, connections to previous writing, pieces of recorded songs may be combined to create something new—like a written collage. Digital technology has just intensified what has been a practice in art for centuries, especially the twentieth century (think of Joseph Cornell's boxes, his sculptural collages made of found materials, and the reuse of many texts in *Ulysses* and "The Waste Land"). Hip-hop culture produced sampling and remixes (at first using turntables and later digitally sampled snippets from famous musicians' hits); the online video culture that presently coalesces around YouTube has produced mash-ups. And the principles of redesign have become extremely common among individuals writing as bloggers, designers of personal websites, and many other Internet genres.

This remixing practice hardly needs teaching, if we just get out of the way. Working with digital tools, students will be very happy to drag images into their own pages and link to YouTube videos. They will need instruction, though, on ways to edit images and cut snippets of sound files (sometimes converting them from one format to another) in order deliberately to use pieces of texts in a new work. Often, tools to do these tasks will be available at no cost on the Internet, if the school network will allow software to be downloaded. In a school that has sufficient resources to do this kind of work, there are likely to be some students who have been doing it at home and will have some strategies, though this level of manipulation of files will need support for most people.

In low-tech environments, we can just invite students to stick other texts to their own, either literally or figuratively. To be ready to participate in digital culture, students need to adopt the agenda of finding images, sound, and video that can accompany their text. They can find those resources as ways of thinking about what they are writing, even if they don't have the technology to manipulate the resources into one digital text. They can also invent ways of attaching them to their writing, either through simple citation, by physically cutting and pasting, or by setting up headphones playing music at a physical location where they display their finished writing. These activities were fairly common in writing classrooms before the Internet, and the fact that they have since become digitized doesn't make them completely out of reach for classrooms that are not as privileged with machines.

Of course, the practice of redesign, common as it is in Internet environments, leads inevitably to worries about copyright. Many teachers tend not to want to ask students to make things that actually turn them into outlaws. On the other hand, fair use guidelines do cover most educational uses of copyrighted material (though it won't apply to things permanently posted on the Internet), and students can learn about Creative Commons licenses, in which photographers and others have given advance permission for the reuse of their work. There is no solid answer to these issues, because it is contested terrain in the world of intellectual property law and emerging artistic and literate practices. The most educational answer is, as is so often the case, to teach about the conflicts (Graff 1993) and not to allow corporate bluster to keep us from acquainting our students with important new composing practices (Hobbs 2010).

Attending to Materiality

Texts in the new forms of literacy often call attention to the way they are made, or to the things that the user can do with them. They point to their own

251

material existence, and they call for the user to interact with their parts. The materiality of school assignments through the twentieth century could be taken for granted. Students would turn in their compositions either in notebooks or on loose-leaf paper. Newer technologies and expanded options, however, have made writers and teachers pay new attention to the material options writers are invited to consider in constructing textual objects (Wysocki 2004).

Because digital texts seem to be made only of ideas and pixels, their makers seem even more self-conscious about the pieces they are made of and sometimes even provide an illusion of substance—sheets of paper, chalkboards, other reminders of the body's interaction with material forms of text. Digital texts are material, too, of course, relying upon electrical signals, light of a particular intensity, means of projecting color. And these elements that might, during the age of print, have been the concern of a publishing elite are now everyone's business.

Developing awareness of materiality away from the computer involves having students think about the size, shape, weight, and configuration of the literate objects they make—and planning them so that the user moves them around in meaningful ways. I have worked with Melody Zoch, Ann David, and Hyounjin Ok to develop a unit of study that gets students making new literacy texts out of ordinary, concrete materials (Bomer, Zoch, David, and Ok 2010; Bomer, Zoch, and David 2010). We integrated this new literacies work into a unit of study on memoir, and we just heightened the possibilities of multimodality, design, linking, and attention to materiality. Many students made their memoirs out of boxes, slips of paper, scrolls, windows the reader could open, flip books, spaces for the reader to write back in response. Thinking deliberately about what their texts could be made of allowed students to take up the practices of high-tech composing with low-tech tools.

In high-tech environments, students can learn to strategically, explicitly direct the reader to click in particular places, or else they bury their links in the interactive surface of the text, forcing the reader to hunt around and find them. They can plan the texture of their pages and what materials in the user's experience this text should invoke. They encode into their texts self-conscious attention to their construction and the substances of which they are (and are not) made.

Planning Delivery and Circulation

Designers of texts (also known as authors) in contemporary environments think about the form in which this text will reach the reader and how the reader is going to use this thing—where they will be when they read it; how the text is (or is not) going to move around with the reader. Will this be a PDF file that users download from a website, or will it be a sequence of html pages that readers click through? The experience for a reader receiving those two texts is very different, and writers have to think carefully about which form says what they mean. A PDF is more of a commitment for a reader, easier to print out but slower to load in a browser. An html file, which appears in a browser window as a Web page, is quicker and sometimes more colorful and interactive, but more transitory, a bit more cumbersome to save and archive. Should this text fit into a small window or would it be better as a large layout that readers scroll across? Would it be better if a recorded voice read the introduction aloud as soon as the page loads, with music behind it, or should the text be silent and up to the reader to voice? Should some of the text be represented as a video, even if it's essentially read aloud like the news, rather than as print?

These are issues of delivery, as Aristotle called one of his canons of rhetoric. He was talking about a different communications technology—the delivery of speeches. Then "delivery" wasn't that interesting during the age of the printing press, the five centuries or so that have been called the Gutenberg parenthesis because the print age brackets off concerns, like delivery, that were more interesting in oral cultures than in digital ones (Pettitt 2007). Everything during the Gutenberg parenthesis tended to be delivered in pretty similar ways—as a bound set of pages. Now, with so many decisions involved in the way texts come to readers, delivery is back.

Teaching in low-tech environments, it should be clear from the foregoing discussions, does not exempt students from thinking about delivery. How should this text come to readers? As a poster on the wall? A play enacted on a stage? A handheld pamphlet? A scroll or folio? The fact that students aren't making such decisions in digital environments does not deny them access to the thinking; only their teacher can do that.

In digital environments, composers are also very conscious about how the text is going to move from one reader to another (or how the readers will come to the text). The circulation of texts is a matter of special concern to anyone in a contemporary environment who wants their writing to have a substantial public impact (Matthieu and George 2009; Trimbur 2000), though how a text will make its way through networks of readers is a concern as well for poets, bloggers, cartoonists, fiction writers, and essayists. Bloggers, for example, know that, to get readers, they can post comments on others' blogs, use their social network updates (microblogging) to direct readers to their entries, and work actively in varied strategic ways to increase their traffic so that readers will encounter their ideas. If we want our students to develop practices that make them effective participants in digital culture, we need to keep track of current ways people are circulating their texts and make those ways explicit to students.

We can attend to circulation in low-tech environments as well. What is going to bring people to read a poster hanging outside the classroom? What adjunct signs in other locations could point to that poster? How will a pamphlet be handed out in a way that is going to get people to actually read it? Who do we want to get it, and how can we most effectively get it into the right people's hands and keep others from diverting it away from its intended audience? How many copies do we make of the class magazine, and how can we get other teachers and community members interested in subscribing to it? What resources (as in money) will we need for being able to produce that many copies? Would it be better as an email? Every organization has these questions to consider, and we should teach students as writers to plan for the circulation of their own texts, too.

We transact with texts by participating in a network.

Composing Responsively

Since everyone is writing into a network, there is a more explicit sense that readers are responders, and writers get ideas about what to say because of what they have just read. Reading with an expectation of answering and writing in response to others' texts is certainly nothing new; in many ways, it's the nature of scholarship. But in digital environments, there is a nearly universal expectation that readers are responders. Even online newspapers (which, as of this writing, still exist) have space beneath just about every article for readers' comments. In an online reading environment, one participates much more by writing back than could ever have been the case in a printing press world. That means that the world that is emerging at present calls upon literate individuals to compose responsively.

Many typical classroom practices support this habit, including much of what has appeared in this book up to now. Teaching thinking devices to invite students to respond to what they read is one way. Another is asking students always to consider themselves as writers, so that their notebooks are full of responses to the world around them, including other people's texts. In addition, to pump up the responsivity of the classroom environment, we might need to get students responding to one another's writing more often. There may need to be sections of the classroom wall covered with butcher paper and sticky notes in which students carry on dialogical writing about academic and personal topics, as adjuncts to their writers' notebooks, which can be much more isolating and solitary. It may be useful for students to use one another's notebooks as springboards for writing in their own notebooks, by swapping notebooks for the first five minutes of writing time before getting started on their next entry.

When we have students writing in digital environments, it's important that they be responding to one another, taking the teacher's response out of the central position it too often occupies, and making students more dependent on one another to know the effect of what they have written. Of course, in order for this to have an effect on the writer's composing process, they'll have to know from the beginning of their writing process that the publishing environment will include space for others to talk back, people from inside and outside this classroom.

We transact with texts by participating in a network.

Composing responsively
Composing with velocity
Linking
Composing fragmentary, decentered texts

Composing with Velocity

One of the main features of newness in literacy is that texts are produced more rapidly and are instantly out to readers. You write something and click "Publish" and there it is for all the world to see. Compared to the slow, laborious processes of composing in print culture, this speed makes a writer's writing and someone else's reading of that text almost simultaneous. Bloggers like Andrew Sullivan post ten to twenty times per day, sometimes just a sentence, a quote, an image or video, but sometimes something very nearly like a short essay (Sullivan 2010). That means that not everything he writes is going through an extended process of revision and editing. He is, most of the time, doing what James Britton called "shaping at the point of utterance" (1982, 139)—designing his text once and for all as he says it the first time. He is publishing his first draft.

I believe revision is an important thing to learn about writing, for many reasons I detailed in Chapter 12. At the same time, we need to recognize that extended processes of revision are part of an ecology where a manuscript is being sent to a publisher, not always where a writer is publishing directly to an audience. Moreover, if you are trying to participate in the discussion in a comments section of a blog, you'd better get your response posted quickly or no one will ever see it, because the conversation will move on to something more current. In a digital world, not all texts have extended shelf lives. Consequently, there is a constant tension between speed and carefulness. One wants to think well, to sound good, to be persuasive, to assemble reasons and evidence, to seem educated. Yet one needs to get the thing out, too. Dealing with the need for velocity has to be part of students' literacy education, therefore. Of course, as long as a good deal of their writing experience consists of being prepared for one-shot writing tests, there will (sadly) be no shortage of this kind of composing, whether or not it bears much resemblance to the conditions under which people write rapidly on the Internet.

Linking

As I have been describing, the fragments that comprise texts in digital environments are connected not by linear transitions (like this sentence) but instead by links. Indeed, links are a kind of argument, evidence, subtext, and allusion. They are a much higher-quality citation practice than traditional forms of citation, because a click takes the reader directly to the reference, evidence, or expansion of the writer's idea.

To write with the conscious intention of connecting explicitly to other people's words is not brand new, but it is new for it to be the assumed way of writing everyday texts. Among forms current as I write this, blogs and certain kinds of wikis are often understood to be built as collections of links within prose. Often, a link—the desire to point something out in a different text elsewhere on the Web—is the originating idea for the post or fragment. The sentences are really built around that initial link. As an extension of writing the text, the writer either inserts additional links as the sentences unfold or he goes back through the text before posting to see if there is anything else that can become a link, sometimes for evidentiary purposes, sometimes just whimsically—because linking these words to this picture will be funny.

For low-tech teaching, these changes may mean teaching students to focus on objects that help them change the channel in their own minds. In memoir or poetry writing, if students bring in objects and then look at one object in order to write about it, then change to another object, there is a kind of mental hyperlink they click that moves them from one domain of thought to another. It's useful to realize that this is what links do—they change what you're thinking about. We also need to give more attention when students are writing in notebooks to the connections they can find across entries, and even to connections between their own notebook and those of others in the classroom. Using sticky notes within notebooks, with one- or two-word labels that name the topic on a particular page and connect it to another spot in the notebook can, if we bring out this theme, be connected to the new literacy practice of building writing through links.

For our opportunities to work on literacy with high-tech devices, it is important at least some of the time to get students to create their postings or entries on the Internet around links—not as a digital version of text that might have appeared in print culture.

Composing Fragmentary, Decentered Texts

In order to understand what's changing in the structure of texts, it's useful to think a bit about how texts have worked in the age of the printing press, from the fifteenth century to the present. Mostly, a book, article, or essay has to stand on its own, apart from other texts. There may be references to other texts, even quotations, but readers assume that the text they hold in their hands has a certain amount of closure and completeness, bounded by its own beginning and ending.

These days, because a text is composed into a network, an individual piece is just a fragment of a complete line of reasoning, which is extended in the links to other texts. Though there are plenty of exceptions, Internet-based texts that take real advantage of the network features are intended to be partial, incomplete, and subject to replacement later on. A text is relatively fragmentary and decentered. As a result, texts are structured like webs, not like linear narratives or arguments we're used to in print culture (or even speech). A reader makes her way through a set of text fragments by designing pathways of interest, intention, and curiosity, often slipping free of a particular author's control before even finishing the whole thing. That means a reader has to learn how to form cohesive thoughts out of texts that are not always structured with the kind of cohesion that experienced readers have become used to. And writers have to think in small units of loosely joined parts, like shapes on a Calder mobile.

For us as teachers, such changes may mean that, in addition to all our attention to teaching students to make elegant transitions across the sections of their expository writing, we also have to show them how a text can work without such transitions, with the pieces just hung together with links embedded that might connect to several other possible pieces. We certainly need to be teaching them how to read across text and form ideas that are not bounded within the pages of a single book or article.

If we are actually using digital tools in our teaching, then it's important not to use them simply as publication machines to make traditional forms look prettier. Rather, we need to teach students to plan their texts as small units with a complex pathway structure, more like mapping a journey with interesting possible side trips than planning a traditional paper.

We transact with texts in a crowded and complex world.

Managing Attention

Living in the information age means that there is information everywhere, constantly pushing at us. There was a time, a few years ago, when if you couldn't remember the name of that actress in that movie, you just had to wonder for years until you saw the movie again. Now, we don't wonder anymore. In fact, we have to push most information away in order to pay attention to any of it. That means that every person in a digital environment participates in an attention economy (Goldhaber 1997), where attention, rather than information, is what is in scarce supply. It's very important to learn that each of us has a limited supply of attention, and we have to plan where and how to use it. As more information is available, our problem becomes how to find the information that is truly useful to us, access it at the right moment, and avoid all the information that is not useful, that is merely a distraction.

People will often say that they are multitasking when they're not quite paying attention. And it's possible to multitask on some things; you can eat a sandwich, file some papers, and talk on the phone at once, for instance. But that's because eating and filing don't demand much continuous attention. For tasks that are more cognitively demanding—like reading, writing, talking, listening to a lecture—there really is no such thing as multitasking. What people call that is usually really switch-tasking—rapid refocusing from one task to another (Crenshaw 2008). Every switch of focus, however, has a cost. It takes both time and mental energy. There is no substitute for being rapt, engaged, concentrated, even in digital environments. It's just harder to achieve because so much of the world is available to us at once. Outside the digital world, such a state of being plugged in is a rarity, and it's safe to say that many students have not often experienced it, at least not when engaged with text. We need to talk to them about the experience of full attention, or *flow* (Czikszentmihalyi 1990), and let them know that that is what they are after, then help them make progress toward it.

As a teaching agenda, attention management requires that we draw students' awareness to the ready distractions of not just the Internet and cell phones, but of friends in the hall and across the room, interesting stuff out the window, and the myriad other distractions in school. We don't require a virtual crowd to be distracted, since we have an actual crowd right here. Mind you, I'm not talking about students paying attention just when their teacher talks. Sometimes they don't do that because they really don't want to, or because the teacher is in fact boring, and not because they are easily distracted or have difficulty returning to a focus once they have departed it. I'm talking about being able to focus on the work they have chosen to do—reading, writing, sustaining focus on projects. For that kind of focus, they will be receptive to teaching. For "Pay attention to what I'm telling you," teaching about attention would just seem self-serving.

It's extremely important, first of all, for writers and readers to be engaged in the *content* of what they are dealing with. If they have been distracted into the form of the task or the surface of the text, then distraction is going to be much more of a problem. They need to know that in order to remain engaged and to reattach themselves to what they're doing, they should think about what the book is *about*, not how many pages are left in the chapter. To keep writing, they need to fill their mind with what they are writing about, not with handwriting, paragraphing, or what the grade is going to be.

Secondly, one advantage to literacy is that, when your mind wanders, the text is still there, right where you left it. It's possible to get going again just by backing up and reading a bit before you left off reading or writing. Thirdly, we need to create an ethic in classrooms where it's not taken as rude or antisocial to be uninterruptable. One difficulty in the world at large is that people really don't want us reading or writing right now; they want us paying attention to them. Learning to resist the pull of face-to-face engagement is hard, but it's necessary for a writing or reading life.

Managing one's own attention is essential to any complex task, and so it has become an obsession for people whose work involves digital composing—whether that's writing text or writing code. Follow any long-term discussion about getting work done in cyberspace, and you will see people worrying about attention, concentration, sustaining work on important projects, and an array of positions on the notion of multitasking. William James wrote a century ago that "My experience is what I agree to attend to. Only those items which I notice shape my mind—without selective interest, experience is an utter chaos. Interest alone gives accent and emphasis, light and shade, background and foreground—intelligible perspective, in a word" (James 1890). And as important as it was a century ago, it's hugely more salient now and is likely to be an inescapable part of a literacy curriculum from now on.

We transact with texts in a crowded and complex world.

Managing attention
Managing activity
Archiving
Strategizing processes
Collaborating
Evaluating content

Managing Activity

One of the important uses of writing in the midst of complex projects is to manage one's own activity. To-do lists, next actions, project plans, calendars, and contextualized prompts help composers move planfully and productively through their work. When a writer sits down to work on a particular day, it really helps if she is clear about the next well-defined, achievable action. I take this idea of well-defined *next actions* from David Allen, whose book *Getting Things Done* (2002) is hugely influential among people whose bread and butter involves making steady progress on complex tasks. If a writer is confused about what he needs to do next, if his task definition stops at *just keep working on the piece until it's finished*, then it is much harder to get started each day. It's much better to be able to say, for instance, "Begin the section on how the house looked." Telling yourself that the task is just to begin is one way to avoid procrastinating (Fiore 1989); once people get started on something, it's usually easier to keep moving. Dividing long-term, complex tasks into achievable, bite-size chunks is one habit in managing activity that is possible to teach student writers;

it's basically a very thorough kind of task analysis. While it's no sure way of completing those little tasks, at least it makes them clearer.

It's also important for writers, or anyone else, to write things down as they come to mind. You realize that you should add a section on how the house looked while you're writing the story of how they came to live in that town. Because you need to stay focused on the present task, there needs to be a ready place to write this other task. How about a writer's notebook? While you're eating dinner, the lettuce in the salad makes you think of the garden at the back of the property, and you grab your notebook to remind yourself to throw that in there, too. Then, at least once per week, it's important to assemble all the little caught ideas and put them somewhere else in the notebook, so that when you actually sit down to write, your tasks are there for you to look at and then just obey.

This use of literacy—planning, reminding oneself of the things one wants to do so that an agenda can have legs—is one of the most practical ones in a literate life. Most of the teachers, leaders, and graduate students I know, despite their considerable success with school-based literacy tasks, still struggle with their lists and systems of getting things done. It's not that there should be a single way for everyone, or that there is an answer that will work for all students in a given teacher's classes. I wouldn't advocate imposing a single system on every student, because any user can subvert a system. Rather, like so many things about a literate life, management of activity needs to be an inquiry the class undertakes together in order to provide resources and focus attention so that individuals can work out what makes sense for them.

Archiving

In an information-rich environment, participants have to know how to save a lot of pieces of text, image, and sound, and to retrieve those bits for purposeful work. Developing habits of saving, storing, and retrieving, habits that are predictable to the user, is becoming increasingly important, especially as it becomes easier to save everything. There are several phases to this practice. First, the user must regularly have the impulse to save things that seem interesting or potentially useful, while at the same time being selective enough so she is not saving everything in the universe. Developing this filter takes some experience, and we should expect students not to be very good at it right at first.

Second, the saved things need to be put away in a place that is easy to get to; otherwise, they'll sit in disordered piles, either figuratively on the user's desktop, or literally, all over his bedroom. If the system of storage is too fancy or takes too long to get ready or is a big mess, then the user is likely to avoid filing, which means things won't get put away. Things being put away is important for several reasons—not just a motherly injunction to clean one's room. For one thing, visual clutter creates distraction from the passionate and important work upon which a writer needs to focus. In addition, the point of archiving is the ability to retrieve the stored material and use it for inspiration, reference, and redesign.

Clearly, this is not a curricular agenda that should be limited to digital tools. The terms *clipping* and *filing* in digital environments are metaphors for the concrete activities involving scissors and paper. And even when people do use digital tools, they still, at least at present, have paper archival requirements. But digital tools multiply the possibilities for archiving and therefore the problem of storage. In either environment, it's another crucial dimension of a literate life in a digital culture.

Strategizing Processes

When someone undertakes a new project, she has to figure out tools and processes that will move her from start to completion. In digital environments, this means, in part, determining what software one needs to do a job. Can it be done with the usual word-processing program? Does it require drawing? Would it help to array the information in a dynamic matrix like a spreadsheet? Do images need to be edited or pieces of music or video cut? What can be used most cheaply to get that done?

Whenever I start a new research project or a new piece of writing, I think through what I'm going to need to do in order to build the content and store the data for the work. I use several different database applications, depending on the nature of the analysis, the way I want to be able to see pieces of data in relation to other pieces, and the people I'm working with on the project. Sometimes, I use a solution that is cheaper, sometimes I need exactly the right process in order to get the work done. Many people engaged in complex tasks in a digital environment have to evaluate processes and tools in a similar way. And when collaborating, sometimes the versions of software programs need to be taken into consideration.

When working away from electricity, one still needs to get—or make—the tools that will help to get this specific job done. Making a notebook, preparing a folder, lining up an interview—any of these may be part of the work of creating the workspace in which the job will get done. And the fact that I use digital tools doesn't mean I don't do these things, too. Most people use a combination of digital and paper tools and processes. That's why, once again, when students tell me they'd rather write on their computer at home, I tell them the good news that they'll have a chance to learn something here about working between page and screen, something they'll often need to be able to do, by printing a draft for each day and bringing that to class. Situations, including this one, often demand it. Being able to plan the tools and processes that fit with one's practical conditions at the moment is part of being technologically astute.

Collaborating

As technology helps to close the distance between human beings, fewer and fewer texts are composed by a single author. In organizations, businesses, politics, and the arts, collaborative composing is the usual means of getting things written. Web-based documents, such as those (presently) on Google, make it possible for two authors to work on a single document, to keep up with the most recent revisions, and to comment to one another about ideas, even simultaneously. While there are plenty of writers still working on their own on the Internet, digital tools have made collaborative writing much more common than it has ever been before, and they have made more visible and powerful the collaborative processes of producing finished text that up until recently would have been known mostly to professional writers, editors, and designers. It is much more common for a community to come together around everyday texts now than has been possible in the past.

Collaborating on texts involves different skills than writing alone. One's attitude toward a draft should be tentative and full of expectation of revision even when writing alone. But a draft that's going to be revised by someone else needs even more of an attitude of *just throwing it out there to be destroyed, transformed, and amended.* Furthermore, one learns, writing with someone else, to be very grateful for an early draft, just as something to work with, just so you don't have to start from nothing. Even if you end up changing almost all of what the other person wrote, it's still part of the process that they moved you from silence to speaking. At the same time, in order to keep collaborative energy moving forward, it's sometimes worthwhile to reign in one's own impulses to change material if it could possibly be considered good enough to remain as it is. One's actions help to determine whether one's collaborators feel like continuing to work. Though that lesson may only be learned from experience, it's worth pointing out to students who are working on a project together.

One common way of collaborating on writing is first to plan the sections together, then for each person to be in charge of drafting a particular section, which is then revised by the other author. There will probably need to be a conversation sometime after the first revision to talk through discrepancies in the writers' judgments. If writers meet for a few days to plan the text, then work independently, then get back together to talk through differences, then they will, in most cases, be well on their way toward a completed text. There are of course many processes for collaborating, but this one provides a way of working together without getting completely gummed up in talk about every single word that is to be placed on the page.

Even in online writing communities for fan fiction and other self-sponsored writing (Black 2007; Lam 2007), adolescents have become accustomed to putting a draft out for comment and using the widely distributed thinking of a literate community to help them design texts that will appeal to a reading public. Classrooms have much to learn from such environments, and yet similar kinds of structures have been part of serious writing classrooms for decades. Many teachers have already begun to create more collaborative environments, at least more social spaces for writers, long before the Internet was the Internet. As with many of these practices I have been describing, a digital culture provides a new way of looking at many things that have already been common literate practices.

What is very new, however, is the degree to which students can, in a very short time, collaborate with fellow writers at a great distance. There is no reason for students in Florida not to be collaborating with students in Alaska or Singapore, as long as teachers can create the contexts and the common purposes for writing. I've heard Kylene Beers say that our students should be collaborating with someone in a different time zone. That seems an especially good idea if the time zone is quite a few hours different, since it means that once the Florida kid has worked on the text, the Alaska kid can pick it up about half a day later, and then the Singapore kid later still. By the time the Florida student returns to his text, two collaborators have taken their turn. Such an experience brings a globalized world up close, and truly takes advantage of technological developments—without that much specialized knowledge about devices and software.

> ## Multilingual Note
>
> Both Lam (2007) and Black (2007), cited in this section on collaboration, have shown the ways that multilingual students in particular are able to learn productively from the relatively informal but still quite rigorous feedback they receive over the Internet from those who critique their fan fiction. It helps that the feedback is from peers engaged in the same kind of project, that it is in writing, and that it is productive of revision. In the possibility of global collaboration I describe here, it would seem obvious that multilingual students' resources would naturally be valued.

Evaluating Content

Digital technologies have helped to produce an increasingly participatory culture, including a political process that asks for more than just a vote from citizens. People can and do speak out about particular issues or politics generally. Increasingly, ordinary people have a voice. That sounds good, but ordinary people also include those with undemocratic, racist, sexist, and socially violent views. Because everyone is speaking out, because there isn't even the institutional filter there used to be on what gets published, it's more important than ever for students to judge the social and political perspectives of the texts they read and to consider the other perspectives that might be available.

In digital environments, we have to read with the knowledge that the world of texts is full of people advocating particular positions. Sometimes, their advocacy is more important to them than the informational quality of what they say. Users of literacy must be well informed about the characteristics of high-quality information, and they should attend to evidence, reputation, authority, credibility, reasoning, and the explicitness in the text about its purposes. They should also be able to apply some critical lenses to any text, and the next chapter will further develop this notion of critical concepts as lenses.

Literacy as Participation

I have called this chapter "Teaching for Participation in Digital Culture," and not something about technology skills or twenty-first-century literacy for a reason. Literacy is participation, and the most important features of new literacies involve acting in response to and in concert to others within digital environments and the cultures they produce and foster. To become a more literate person involves extending oneself into ways of doing in particular environments, and in our era, literacy is most importantly expanding in online environments. That means that the forms of literacy we teach ought to make such participation available to increasing numbers of students. But as I have argued, participation is not mainly about switching on and operating electronic devices; rather, it concerns particular habits with text.

Literacy also involves participating in other contemporary environments, as well, and a high-quality curriculum in English needs to orient students to some of these environments. Chapter 15 will examine participation in the study of language itself, the discipline of linguistics, a study that can itself have democratizing impact, as it shows people how to think about others and their language, even when it diverges from one's own language or that of people in power. After that, in Chapter 16 we will look at ways of helping students become powerful participants in a system that threatens to disempower them—the accountability and testing system—as we examine some approaches to testing that may be consonant with the values for which I have argued in this book—values that have been important in our profession for a century. Finally, in the last chapter, we will attempt to bring things together in a chapter about planning an entire school year.

CHAPTER 15

Making More of Grammar: Studying Language Like Linguists

There is a subject in school that is as filled with the drama of raw power, status anxiety, and cliquishness as the most intensely competitive adolescent peer relations, where who counts, who's more important, who's in and who's out, is the essence of the material. There's a subject that's actually *all about* style and seeming cool. This subject also requires an understanding of particular social groups' resistance to prevailing styles and opposition to dominant groups, their members' efforts to display their distinction and signal their belonging to one another. It's a subject that asks questions about competing groups—about youth and age, haves and have-nots, about tensions among races, about the histories those groups carry of violence, exclusion, and silencing. This ought to be the most interesting subject in the whole school, directly appealing to familiar concerns and anxieties of young people seeking their place in the world. This subject is language itself, when we tell the truth about it—grammar as if it mattered. And almost no one ever studies it in school.

It's the argument of this book that young people—our students—already have access to the forms of knowledge that are most important in English class and that when we build subject matter on that existing knowledge, it can develop in directions that are motivating and ultimately more useful to people in their real lives. Such an approach, I have argued, is more respectful of students and so creates more productive relationships with them and makes stronger identities available to them. It also comes closer to the heart of the subject matter of English as we practice the discipline in the present day, in ordinary lives and in the academy. This same argument applies as well to the study of language when we accept everyday language as an object of study, acknowledge language variation as interesting and valuable, and respect and build upon the knowledge of those everyday practices and differences that students bring with them to school.

Most people think of language study in English class as a discipline that disciplines your way of expressing yourself, a study of grammar some people call proper, a reformist program to replace the grammar students usually use, the one with which they identify, with the one their English teacher likes better. No wonder students don't approach it with eager curiosity. When traditional grammar comes to the fore, English class becomes students' most despised subject. Most people do not find it engaging—partly because it's technical, partly because it involves looking closely at words and sentences in ways we usually take for granted, and partly because it carries a moralistic cast that seems to want to standardize parts of people that they would prefer to remain diverse.

So it's a hazard to linguistic education that, though many students dread this kind of language study, many people who go into the teaching of English enjoy talking about language, looking closely at it, and feeling superior about it. What if we explored ways of doing the first two, talking about language and looking closely at it, but just removed those overweening power moves of superiority and domination? What if we helped students to see the differences in language communities and the power relations that sometimes try to wipe those differences out, often by erasing the language of the nondominant groups?

Grammar study has too often been a political battle between races, generations, and levels of privilege. What's worse, the teaching of grammar as a means of correcting patterns in speech or writing may not even do any good. Braddock, Lloyd-Jones, and Schoerr wrote in 1963:

> In view of the widespread agreement of research studies based upon many types of students and teachers, the conclusion can be stated in strong and unqualified terms: the teaching of formal grammar has a negligible or, because it usually displaces some instruction and practice in actual composition, even a harmful effect on the improvement of writing. (37–38)

This and subsequent studies and reviews of studies (e.g., Hillocks 1986; Hillocks and Smith 2003) concluded the same thing. The usual kind of grammar instruction—exercises out of a book or on worksheets, drill and practice in class—don't succeed in standardizing students' language. (Though as Brown [2009] points out, that may be because of bad teaching more than because it's especially unhelpful to study language.) Those findings have led many, mostly progressive, English educators to say that there is no reason to study grammar, because it just doesn't work. Other educators, who may style themselves as conservatives, just don't care about the research and try to guard the citadel of English correctness with grammar instruction anyway. Both sides of this usual framing about the teaching of grammar, however, assume that the outcome would be prose without any nonstandard language patterns. But maybe that isn't the only possible purpose in studying language.

The effort to standardize language is overall a misguided enterprise. The field of linguistics—the study of language—is not about telling people their subjects and verbs don't agree or about forcing people to distinguish participles from gerunds. Linguistics is about describing and analyzing language as it occurs in the real world of speakers, listeners, texts, and readers. Only in middle and high school English is the study of language reduced to a prescriptive, undemocratic, neurotic attempt to standardize everyone's syntax. It does not have to be that way.

Surface Features and Global Communication

In a globalized economy, workers had better get used to embracing language diversity and a softened sense of what is tolerable in communication. In an Internet-based literacy environment in which people read texts from across the world, a generous spirit of "correct enough" is the only appropriate lens.

It is also a mistake to think that, since direct instruction about grammar won't "improve" writing, then studying language is a complete waste of time. There are other reasons to study language in school besides the standardization of writing and speaking. I'm not making this up. An NCTE resolution passed in 1994 put it this way:

> Language awareness includes examining how language varies in a range of social and cultural settings; examining how people's attitudes vary towards language across culture, class, gender, and generation; examining how oral and written language affects listeners and readers; examining how "correctness" in language reflects social-political-economic values; examining how the structure of language works from a descriptive perspective; and examining how first and second languages are acquired. (National Council of Teachers of English 1994)

Looked at this way, language study is clearly valuable. As citizens in a democracy, students need to learn ways of thinking about language variation that will allow them to respect other citizens across differences. They need to learn to think about language variation in order to understand the intelligence and value of linguistic patterns different from their own. For students from linguistic minority communities, that might involve learning about the patterns of their community, learning to value those patterns, and also learning to see the difference between those patterns and ones in a different community. That might even provide them with control of which language patterns they employ in different contexts.

It is also important that students from dominant groups learn respect for diverse forms. It's not enough just to sit comfortably with one's privilege; an educated person is one who understands the world from more diverse perspectives and entertains more difference in style. An educated person knows how to think about linguistic diversity.

There are, therefore, significant political and moral agendas in teaching students how to think about the role language plays in people's real lives. This is part of the organized knowledge of our discipline, and English language arts class is the place where students' dispositions, attitudes, and ideologies about language are being fashioned. We ought at times to think about it explicitly.

How can the study of language become engaging? And how can it be undertaken on the basis of students' existing strengths, as constant and capable users of language, rather than on a deficit perspective that focuses on errors and gaps? First, engagement is obviously more available when students are studying themselves and other people who are significant to them. If grammar represents a relationship between oneself and one's world, as Lesley Rex and her colleagues suggest (Rex et al. 2005), then studying it that way might motivate interest and sustained engagement. Second, language study is also more engaging when it has some drama in it—that is, when the curriculum offers the very real differences and conflicts that are in fact a major theme in the ways language works in the real world. Third, the language that students study—if the study is to be engaging—needs to be natural, authentic language in use—not factory-made "examples" of predetermined rules.

Perhaps most importantly, as with most instances of learning, language study will be most engaging, and therefore most helpful, if it is undertaken as inquiry rather than a series of correct or wrong answers—with questions that lead to new questions and wonderings that remain open and unfinished. I will say more about a possible process of inquiry after discussing the *what* of language study—some of the possible topics that either a class or a particular student might take up.

Topics for Real Language Study

Here, I provide a few brief descriptions of the kinds of topics that are both interesting and deeply valuable for language study. In some cases, a teacher might well decide to take one of these topics as a whole-class unit of study. In other cases, a brief description of the problem identified by the topic might get particular students interested in choosing that topic as an independent or small group inquiry. Even then, perhaps there would be a shared whole-class inquiry topic, with individuals, partners, or small groups taking on related topics or other language-related inquiries. In that case, the multiple structures for participation— each student a member of a large group the teacher leads plus the designer of her own inquiry—allow the teacher to demonstrate ways of investigating that students can then take back to their more self-directed work. That way, they are receiving explicit instruction but still taking on the topics that matter most to them and learning to be language inquirers. Interested readers can find other topics and discussions in Andrews (2006).

Code-Switching

Any given person uses different languages with different communities. But multilingual people use distinct lexical languages (like Spanish/Vietnamese) and they switch among them not simply to match the dominant language of the person to whom they are speaking. Their reasons for code-switching some-times also have to do with a particular feeling that is captured in the switch, or because of the meaning resources available in the other language, or as a way of being playful and creative in their expression. A study of code-switching would draw upon the habits of speaking in various contexts where students think people will do lots more of this switching. Obviously, one needs multilingual students in order to be able to do this study, and so this is one of the many ways that their multilingualism can become very explicitly a resource for the class-room. It is also possible to use the term *code-switching* to talk about the different social languages people move across in their lives, like their languages that fit into work, religious community, and home. This switching across discourses could also be an object of study.

Dialects

People who speak a dialect with their families, such as one distinctively of Brooklyn, or one of Mississippi, or one in which their African American family feels at home, also code-switch. Dialects can in themselves be a powerful lan-guage study. The point is not to disparage one dialect or another but to see the intelligence and stability in the alternative language forms. It's important to realize that the dominant language, sometimes called Standard Written English, is a dialect, too, just one with more power than most of the others. To study dif-ferences among dialects, students could collect language from people outside the school and bring it in for analysis. They could, of course, also use themselves and their classmates as informants and make recordings of them telling stories or engaged in conversation with various partners. For more on studying dialects in classrooms, see Jordan (2003), Smitherman (2000), Wheeler and Swords (2006), Wolfram (1998), and Adger, Wolfram, and Christian (2007).

Contrasts Among Different Languages' Patterns and Rules

Another way that multilingual students' knowledge can be an essential resource is through comparative studies of the ways their languages work. If there are students who speak Spanish, Chinese, English, and Urdu at home, then the patterns in their languages, brought into relation with one another, can help everyone become more conscious about structures in their own language. Because the contrastive analysis is based on the languages of actual students in the room, it is more interesting than it would be if it were of language samples chosen by the teacher. So the placement of modifiers, the ways things become past tense, the locations of verbs in relation to their objects, the variations of the notion expressed in English as "doing," the untranslatable idioms, the forms of politeness and formality all become useful categories for comparison, along with many others of which these students are already aware because they think all the time about the differences between their other languages and English.

> **Multilingual Note**
>
> In addition to all the direct benefits of language study, it also provides a place in the curriculum where multilingual students' resources are directly acknowledged and valued. For that reason, it might even be a good idea to plan a brief language study relatively early in the school year.

Contrasts Among Different Writing Systems

In the four languages I listed above—Spanish, Urdu, Chinese, and English—there are three different writing systems. A study of the writing systems known by people in the room—how they work and what they look like—could branch out into a more general study of writing systems. For students who have had schooling in their first language, making these connections and distinctions is very important, but it is also interesting even for monolingual students to become more aware of how varied writing systems work. If the multilingual students don't know much about the writing system, their parents may, and the student may be able to learn just enough about it to become the local expert.

Contrasts Between Oral and Written Language

Speech and writing do not sound the same, even for the most highly educated and literate person. Transcribed natural conversation or even performed storytelling doesn't bear much resemblance to planned and ordered text. There are important differences, and they can become the object of study. In speech, for instance, a shared physical context often makes it possible to have the same thing in mind without making it explicit what one is talking about, whereas in writing, one has to establish more shared context very explicitly. In speech, there are multiple ways of emphasizing and shading words (as I described in Chapter 5 when discussing listening as a kind of thinking), through intonation, stress, phrasing, gesture, and facial expression. In writing, we use paragraphs, font styles, and other visual clues, but they don't necessarily correspond to the paralinguistic features of talk. Spoken sentences have looser, looping structures, more shifting subjects, relational or interpersonal markers, and are often held together by repetition. There are lots of interesting contrasts between speech and writing, and an understanding of those contrasts might be helpful in getting students to understand why, in writing, they have to work hard at certain features.

> **Language Study in Dialogue with Specific Students**
>
> The precise topics most appropriate in a language study will depend in part on who the kids are and what resources they bring. Are there speakers of many languages in this class? Are there big Internet users? Are there people especially interested in topics like work or children? Regardless of the particular topic, though, the ways that power and language are braided together will be inescapable themes in the inquiry.

Language and Power

An investigation into the relationship between language and power would examine the gatekeeping functions of language and the specific locations in which particular kinds of language are either more or less influential. By investigation, I don't just mean speculating about job interviews or workplaces, but actually collecting language samples from them and seeing what is and is not true about the common claims people make. This study could also investigate the attitudes, feelings, identities, and relationships that particular language patterns create. In any particular region, there are fixed and strong attitudes about certain low-status speech forms or languages, whether they are connected to a particular race, a class, or a signal of an urban or rural background. These attitudes are sometimes called *language ideologies*, and the beliefs about language held by a range of different people in a community would be fruitful to explore. Just asking a wide variety of people what they think about Spanish, for instance, will produce lots of data about language ideology. Of course, another kind of study of power and language would be an investigation of political language—the words that government officials use to talk about problems or policies—and the degree to which it is accurate or honest. These types of critical examinations of language are ways not just to make students aware of language, but to prepare them for participation in a democracy.

Early Language and Literacy Learning

Many students will be interested in the language learning processes of younger children, and this is yet another kind of language study. It involves studying how babies learn to talk, not simply by doing library research, but by recording samples of language from infants and toddlers in interaction with their parents. Little children learn language as part of fitting into the things people in a community do together. They say "bye-bye" and "thank you"; they ask for more. Their approximations of the language—attempts to say things that are not quite the ways adults say them—are valued and, in many families, remembered forever. Students with younger siblings, cousins, or neighbors become resource-rich in such studies. Another form of early childhood language study would be an examination of how young children read and write. That kind of literacy focus could form the bedrock for reflections on our own processes of reading, writing, and learning.

How People Learn New Languages and Literacies

Another language study would inquire as to the ways people go about learning new languages and the ways people who know multiple languages use them. Do people learn oral and written language at the same time? What is school or course learning like, how does it help, and what are its limits? What are the nonschool ways of learning a language? What makes it easy or hard to learn or use a language? Observations of people using multiple languages or new languages would be part of the data collection, as would interviews with adults and young people about their experiences. In some cases, writing samples might also provide interesting data, especially where the language requires learning a new writing system.

Related to this inquiry, but also quite different, would be the study of how people learn new forms of literacy as those forms change. Who has learned texting and uses it regularly? Who has not? What motivates the difference? Who designs their own website or makes YouTube videos or participates in the innovative spread of memes on the Internet? What new forms of literacy are required when people change jobs or take on a new role in a union, political party, or professional organization? A study like this provides students with rich insights into the varied roles of literacy in people's lives, and how that role changes across a biography.

Language and the Internet

The Internet has been a major force for rapid language change, and studying the ways language is being transformed by what people do with digital technology provides another interesting and important topic of study. For one thing, the Internet is the most important source at present of neologisms, or new words, in English. Each year, new words enter the dictionary, and many of them arise from technological environments. But it's not just the words of the Internet that make it important; the ways people are using it matter, too. The manner and degree to which pictures and words accompany each another in digital environments is another potentially rich study. People on the Internet have also invented new ways of spelling, new abbreviations (many of which are even already archaic), and new kinds of voice. Studying the particular style of writing engaged in by varied communities online is another potentially rich topic for language study. A huge sample of language is available to everyone on the Internet, some of it even clean! And that resource is one to which many students have access and in which they have interest.

Sounding Right and Sounding Wrong

Another important topic for study would involve students recording their miscues, the times when they are reading aloud and they say something unexpected, different from what is written. They can then go back and mark their miscues in the text and write a little bit about what they see across those instances. This activity is called a Retrospective Miscue Analysis (Goodman and Marek 1996), and it's a very helpful way of getting students to think about their reading process and revalue themselves as readers. What makes it especially valuable as a language study is the investigations of the syntactic cueing system, that is, the fact that competent readers (indeed most readers) will usually miscue by substituting a word that sounds right—one that could go there in the sentence. In other words, they will substitute the same part of speech and the same specific type of a part of speech. If by chance they substituted something that could not go in that spot in the sentence, and if they were at all paying attention, it would sound wrong to them.

If you take selected words out of a sentence, most people will replace those blanks with words that will work syntactically. Take, for instance, this sentence, from Jean Fritz's book *Homesick*: "There was lots of _____ to be made among the _____, but it was _____." I have given this example to rooms full of people for years now in talking about the syntactic cueing system. People tend to put these words in the first blank: *love, happiness, money, blood*. They're not all equally good answers, but they are all nouns. They have to be nouns

> ### TECHNOLOGY NOTE
>
> Because new words and ideas travel fast on the Internet, new words and expressions enter common use much more rapidly than they ever have before. And because it's often possible to document the first use of the term on the Internet, people can claim authorship for particular neologisms, where before, at least in common oral usage, that wouldn't have been possible. Examples of recent neologisms include: to google; crowdsourcing; meme; blogosphere; social network; e-reader; personal learning network. If you are reading this book several years after it first came out, you will see how transient the language really seems, since most or all of those words may seem absurdly dated.

because they are the object of the preposition *of*, and because there is no noun coming later than the blank, so it has to come here. It's a special kind of noun, too, a collective one, because there has to be lots of it but it has to be singular because the verb is *was* and not *were*. Now no one is ever aware of all of those constraints on their choosing of the appropriate word, no one has to think that way to produce a possible word for the blank, but the constraints and rules are there nonetheless. We know how sentences have to go when we have competence in the language, and we will not fill that blank in with something like *running* or *blonde* or *happily*. Studying the ways this works with real reading events and student-designed exercises like this one is a useful avenue into both the reading process and an examination of syntax. And what do you notice about how you could fill in the other two blanks?

Everyday Metaphor and Interpretation

Attention to natural, everyday language allows students to pull up close to certain language forms and practices that are also a part of writing and reading literature. It's impossible to say much without employing metaphor. In the first sentence of this paragraph, quite without realizing it, I used *natural*, *everyday*, *pull up close*, and *a part of*, all metaphors in the sense that they are comparisons, not the literal thing. It's easier to see metaphor when it's bigger and more explicit: "she's so sweet"; "big as a house"; "you're golden." (You'll notice that I don't think anything is served by distinguishing metaphor from simile. What's important is that they're the same, not that they're different. A simile is a kind of metaphor and it's just no big deal that it uses *like* or *as*.) A brief study of metaphor in daily life can be useful in connection with a unit of study on writing poetry.

In order to understand those metaphors in everyday speech, you have to interpret. But that's not the only kind of interpreting we do. We constantly have to fill in where speakers assume a shared context; we restore what is not stated explicitly in people's utterances. I discussed, in Chapter 6, the fact that interpretation is a necessary part of language, especially if one understands inference as one form of interpreting. We think we know someone's point, from the context of what they are saying, from their tone, from the words they do say, so we fill in what they mean. Students can collect instances of interpreting from everyday life and language and bring them into class for analysis, categorizing types of interpreting from the instances they collect. A brief study of interpreting in everyday life can provide a useful entrée to a deeper study of interpreting in

Language and Gender

Language variation traces all lines of difference, even gender. Some students might be interested in studying the language patterns of males and females, and to avoid essentializing boys and girls, the varied *kinds* of males and females in a school community. It will also vary across ages of men and women.

reading. It can also be useful right before a unit of study on poetry writing, because the kinds of indirection and gaps that poets use to draw readers' thinking toward their poem are just extensions of this everyday manner of speaking.

Language Study as Inquiry

Taking up language as a topic for inquiry, the class' objectives are to increase students' language awareness; to promote a critical language awareness of power relations; to explore the process of inquiry; and to develop democratic attitudes about language variation.

As with other forms of inquiry, questions about language lead not to finished answers or right/wrong distinctions, but rather to new questions about social relationships and the ways they are fleshed out in language. The point is to keep wondering, and to have one's conceptualizations remain open and unfinished. The whole idea is for everything to become more troubled, less taken for granted, and more explicitly engaged in a conflict of perspectives. What kills inquiry is the total dominance of one perspective, especially like the prevalent one in our culture, where there is understood to be a proper way of speaking and writing and everything else is just wrong.

An inquiry into language should proceed with respect for the intelligence and appropriateness of all language forms within their communities of use. It should be based on empirical observation of people actually using language, with special attention to everyday speech in students' communities outside school. It's an investigation that seeks difference—that tries to understand how people accomplish things with language, how their choices about how to say things reflect specific functions. The question isn't whether things are being said right or wrong but how language is functioning for a particular individual within a specific language group.

This kind of language investigation requires the collection of data from real speaking people. The data should usually be audio recordings of instances of natural language (people saying things in real contexts for their own purposes), brought into the classroom for interpretation and analysis. Students should try to collect instances of language that are in some way typical, and they should be able to explain why they chose to record this particular instance—what they thought it would show and why they think it is not just one weird example but can be seen as representing something more generally true about language in the group they are studying.

Inquiry Strategies Across the Curriculum

An inquiry approach is not only what students are doing in English class. It may be that other teachers in their schedule—physics, global studies, math—are also using an inquiry model of instruction. To help students learn habits of inquiring, it would be a good idea for teachers to highlight the connections across their experience, and perhaps even use some of the same terms and processes.

One activity that has been especially useful in classroom studies is contrastive analysis (Wheeler and Swords 2006). This analysis usually involves first making two columns, with each column representing the ways of saying something in a particular group. So one column might be labeled "Standard Written English" and the other "Chicano English" (the most common name for the particular English language forms of many Mexican-American communities). The two columns permit a side-by-side comparison of how each language community works. At the bottom of the same page, Wheeler and Swords leave space for generalizations from the instances compared in the two columns. One of the virtues of this approach is that it makes clear that both language forms are competently expressing the same thing, and it also asks students to be able to tell the difference between the forms and to think about the contexts in which either would be most appropriate. Respect for differences is a foundational assumption, since the point is to understand how people who speak differently say the same underlying meanings in varied ways.

In order to fill in that part in which they generalize about language patterns, students will have either to already know, to look up and learn, or to invent terminology to name what they see. It may be the first and only time they actually want to know the names of things in a sentence. As always, it is best for students to develop the concepts and ways of describing them before getting a label to attach to them. The teacher's use of terminology should be selective and purposeful, serving to build concepts and meanings, not viewed as an end in itself. The point of this study is to engage students with interesting investigations of substantial, important issues in language use, not to provide lessons in parts of speech.

As they look across their language samples and the patterns they can see in them, students need to build bigger interpretations, developing theories about the patterns they see in their language data. Each researcher or research group should periodically write about, "This is what I think I am seeing here," and then go out and collect new data in order to test those guesses. After another stretch of data collection and rechecking their analysis, researchers may be ready to present or publish their findings. If they are writing about community languages, with respect for difference, then members of the community may be an interested audience for these pieces of writing. Alternatively, students may find language-oriented websites that would be interested in their findings. If groups have chosen topics with an eye toward entertaining or impressing their classmates, then a presentation of some findings to at least a section of the class might be useful. One efficient way to share findings in a whole class of individuals is for them to do large posters with their overall findings, perhaps with a handout containing major points. By dividing the class in half and making half presenters and half audience, it's possible for each student, standing by her poster, to present several times to classmates. Then the groups switch roles as presenter and audience.

Weighing the Relative Importance of Language Study

We are nearing the end of a book whose curriculum, if one tried to teach all the material contained within its covers, would take several years. No one English class will contain everything I have written here, not even all the things I have claimed to be very, very important. How could we weigh the importance of language study in a balance that includes reading and writing for varied purposes and audiences? How does it compare in worthiness with preparation for participation in a democracy by writing for social action and reading with critical eyes? How does it measure up against an agenda that considers the role in people's lives of emerging digital forms of literacy?

To be sure, there have been times in my career when I would not have highly prioritized a unit of study about detailed attention to language. But more recently, I have begun to think that an agenda of educating for democracy makes language study more important than it would be if I thought of it as nothing more than correcting students' patterns of "errors." I do value an effort to create a world in which the powerful do not feel justified in ignoring the voices of those they dominate because of the particular grammatical and diction patterns in those voices. I still think students becoming strong, independent, purposeful readers and writers with active literate lives is much more important, and it's such a high expectation that it requires most of our attention.

Language as the Medium of Democracy

To have a democracy, people have to be able to say what their lives are like, and others have to be able and willing to listen carefully so that decisions can be made for the common good. If some voices are determined in advance to be unworthy of listening to, just because they have language patterns that differ from the dominant group, you can't have democracy.

But there might be ways in which attention to the meanings of the surface of language could aid that larger mission, by tuning students into language itself, perhaps even helping them to tailor their own messages for appropriate audiences. They might see the language in the novels and other texts they read in a more appreciative light. They might also arrive at more democratic dispositions toward language, valuing the diverse ways people have of speaking and thinking that all those voices are worthy of respect.

Some might become interested in the field of linguistics and pursue language study in their further education. Considering the number of people who pursue linguistic analysis across the disciplines, in not just linguistics but psychology, philosophy, anthropology, education, communications, political science, and, of course, English, it is not unlikely that this study will prepare them for certain areas of higher education, considerably more than would a Shakespeare play or unit on mythology. It is extremely likely to prepare them for careers in a multilingual society and a globalized economy. A systematic way of paying attention to language and a disposition to value linguistic difference seems very important to a person making her way in the real world of business, science, and many other vocational areas.

It may take a relatively small amount of time, especially compared to the actual reading and writing agendas, but there is significance in the study of language, and at the very least, the kinds of study I have been discussing here make for a richer curriculum than one in which students are pointlessly distinguishing between gerunds and participles, underlining the subject once and the predicate twice, or circling the subjects and verbs that do not agree. There is important learning available for our students, and we should not waste their time.

CHAPTER 16

Working Toward Tests Without Insulting Students' Intelligence

This chapter is about tests. I'm going to argue that it's not necessary for tests to ruin all of a teacher's hard work for real literacy learning—or all students' efforts to construct identities and practices that position them as powerful readers, writers, thinkers, and citizens. Though we live in a time when tests have done much harm to curricula in many places, not all teachers have experienced it that way. Some people are finding ways to teach thoughtfully and well, even in the midst of high-stakes tests. Let's think about how.

Preparing kids for tests, we adults in schools often run as fast as we can in the wrong direction, focusing narrowly on mechanical responses to test tasks and conditions. We might think, for example, that because students can only have two sheets of paper out for planning on test day, working in a notebook would not be practical, since it has more than two pages. We might think that because writing tests provide prompts, students need always to be writing to assigned topics in constrained segments of time. That thinking is unnecessarily narrow and substantially weakens students. Students should learn real things in the curriculum, and the strengths they develop will help them with the test. If you are taking a reading test, it does help if you can actually read. If you are a strong writer, a writing test is not particularly daunting. In the few weeks before a test, narrowing tasks so that they more closely resemble the test may in fact be helpful. But to close the curriculum for much of the year is to deny students an education, because a test-prep curriculum is not focused on making students the most powerful readers and writers they can be.

Moreover, the closing of the curriculum does not happen in equal measure to all students. If you belong to a group that has been historically disadvantaged in the school system—if you are African American, Latino, American Indian, or poor—you are much more likely to have a 100 percent test-prep curriculum, thereby being denied an education that is good for anything—college, career, life, or meaning. That is because the adults around you (very likely to be white and middle class) become fearful about your performance on the test, and they reduce the curriculum so that you have far too little extended time with text to get better at reading and far too little experience at tuning into your own thinking or writing for audiences to become strong and confident as a writer. Instead of subjecting students to this desiccated curriculum, we should instead emphasize the capacities demanded by tests—such as really understanding what you read—and work through a high-quality curriculum to offer them.

Demands of Tests and High-Quality Literacy Experiences

Let's take the example of writing. In a sense, tests (those that require actual writing) do demand some capacities that are also strengths that all writers must possess. These are basic potentials that each test taker must summon in order to perform well. If teachers pay more attention to these aspects of a test's demands, and less to the more superficial and mechanistic aspects of a test's task design, then perhaps it will be possible to help students do better on the tests while not sacrificing their development as writers, readers, and thinkers.

In this section, I want to suggest three strengths that every writer must develop for tests, which also are essential to writing development in general. For each of these strengths, I will suggest a couple of classroom conditions that help to build it.

Three Strengths Essential for Tests

Fluency

Tuning in to thought

Responsiveness

Fluency

Fundamental to becoming strong as a writer is the ability to get writing flowing, to write with momentum and ease. This easy power is called *fluency*. It requires that the writer feel that the activity of writing is no big deal, not something to be resisted or blocked. The writer must have a disposition that it is OK to put down thoughts and let them lead to the next thought, a belief that what occurs to her is good enough to go with. It is an attitude of acceptance, a decision before the fact to take what your mind offers and to keep putting your thoughts outside you onto paper.

Paradoxically, in order to have high standards, a writer must be able to lower her standards, at least at the beginning of the writing process, when it is time to get some text on the page. If one begins with high standards or a narrow conception of quality in writing, then one is likely to be weakened by indecision and doubt and insecurity, and consequently become unable to produce.

Writing tests require fluency. More than getting the form exactly right or every phrase felicitous, writers must be able to generate text with ease. Many people have difficulty doing so, and most poor writing is poor first because it is undeveloped. Even problems with sentences sometimes arise out of too much hesitation and stalling, because the writer loses the thread of the sentence and shifts direction in the middle of it. Fluency helps reduce the demands on the writer's memory and makes writing a little more like speech. But mostly, a habit of writing with flow permits students just to get started and to keep writing, even through their uncertainty and insecurity. With enough experience getting themselves started and sustaining their concentration, they develop stamina and an ability to make rapid decisions rather than being frozen in ambivalence.

Helping students to build fluency as writers requires particular conditions in the classroom. The first conditions are negative; that is, certain things have to be absent from the classroom environment. First, you can't have criticism of early drafts. Second, you can't have students just guessing what the teacher wants. Third, you can't have writing formulas like five-paragraph essays forcing students to think about the structure of a finished product before they've even figured out what to say.

Instead, tools like writers' notebooks allow students a place to develop fluency without worrying about an audience's response to their writing. When teachers work with these tools, they teach students strategies for thinking on paper—how to get an idea and sustain it, how to say more about an initial blip of a thought, how to write lots of different times about one topic, what to do when you can't think of anything to say, how to move between global ideas and particular details. These are the insides of a writer's thinking, and they cannot be captured by formulas. Notebooks create a safe environment for experimenting, trying things the writer isn't sure he can carry off yet, and for solidifying gains in development—for doing something well, over and over, with increasing power.

Classrooms that promote fluency also must have a particular relationship to time. Writers learn to be generous with their thinking when they are able to create in their minds a sense of an open expanse of time, in which to think about one detail for a while before going on to the next one. In order to create this sense in their minds, writers must have had experience of it in the material world. Therefore, writers must have worked on writing across significant spans of time, sometimes working on a single piece for, say, four weeks, every day. And they must have had regular, generous time in class to work on it. Giving students lots of time to work on something outside of class, as every teacher knows, just compresses several weeks' worth of expectation into a night or two of frenzied scribbling. Fluency is not created in desperation. It comes from a generosity of activity that only plenty of time can afford.

Tuning In to Thought

To be able to get started writing, one has to be able to tune in to one's own thinking. A writer listens to herself in order to find the thread of thought she follows as she makes sentences. In a world full of many divergent voices, it is not always easy to get quiet enough to listen to what is in our minds. But without this settling and quieting and tuning into one's own thought, one can't find a voice, can't develop sentences, can't elaborate ideas, can't create a line of logic.

Obviously, you have to be able to find your way to your own thoughts in order to build your initial ideas—the bare bones of what you have to say. But developing those thoughts, the skill of elaboration, also requires that you be able to connect to your inner world. Let's say you're writing about something that happened to you when you were a child. You say that you felt embarrassed. There it sits on the page, the phrase, "I was embarrassed." How do you say more? The writer has to be in the habit of reconnecting to the memory, going back inside and creating the answer. Paying too much attention to the questions, or to strategies, or to structural formulas can just get in the way of the real reservoir of thought to which the writer must attend.

To be strong on a writing test, the test taker must be in the habit of gaining access to her own mental world. She reads a question and decides on a basic answer. But that basic answer does not give sentences, does not spin itself out into text. She has to find her way to a thinking voice. And yet, schools are not necessarily friendly to this move of tuning into one's own thoughts. As I have said before, when students are paying attention to their own thoughts rather than those the teacher is speaking or assigning, we say their minds are wandering.

In classrooms where students are encouraged to pay attention to their thoughts, however, a few things will be the case. Students will be asked often to choose what they write about, taking responsibility for their process from beginning to end. Working with their notebooks or journals, they will ask themselves often, "What is on my mind?" They will become much more familiar with their inner territory, the thoughts they are likely to write about with ease. Even when they write for readers—or for a grade—they are expected to make many decisions about what their topic is, what to say about it, and how the text should go. Having to solve the problem often, and having a teacher's guidance in thinking it through, gets writers used to the most important aspects of any writing task—those that involve the actual construction of thought.

Responsiveness

I've already introduced the idea of responsive composing in the chapter on new literacy practices; it might be somewhat surprising to see it here in a chapter on testing, too. Some of the most prolific (and widely read) writers working at this moment are the online bloggers who write small essays, sometimes several times a day, about news, books, and cultural events. One of the things that amazes me about many of these people is the way they have something to say about everything. They have cultivated responsiveness, or answerability. Whatever they read or see, they make a response to it. Nothing leaves them speechless. We may not necessarily desire such qualities in a companion, because if you're driving down the road, and your passenger feels a need to respond to your every move or that of every other driver, it is a little exhausting. But in writers, this is a good quality.

A response is not something that comes upon you and takes hold like a seizure. It is something you make. And it is much harder to make a response one time than to become habitually responsive. For people working with adolescents, it is not hard to imagine what it is like for someone to be unresponsive. Presented with something, they may say "It's OK," or "Fine," or "Boring," and stop right there, having made the consumer's thumbs-up or thumbs-down judgment to which their culture has accustomed them. Being responsive, however, is really not about being evaluative. It's about making an answer to what is being said to you—understanding it and saying something back. A reader and writer must understand himself to be in dialogue, constantly, with all the texts he encounters, and being responsive just means taking your turn in that dialogue. Today's writing tests demand an instant response to a quote, a work of literature, an imaginary rhetorical situation, or a prompt. People who scratch their heads and think, "I don't really think anything about that" are in trouble in these situations.

To support responsiveness, teachers need to think about how they teach reading and content in general. If students are always being confronted with text that is understood just to be authoritative and the final word on a subject, then how are they being invited into a dialogue? The assumption, rather, needs to be that any text they read is just taking its turn, and every student is responsible for taking a turn in response, developing things to say back. That means the teacher isn't telling them what the text means and then quizzing them on their "comprehension" of these prefabricated meanings. Rather, it assumes that meaning arises from each reader's participation in the conversation.

In such classrooms, talk is different. Students are asked frequently to talk to a partner or in small groups, because, by simple mathematics, such arrangements permit more people to be talking at the same time, and therefore call for more responsiveness. Even when there is a whole-class discussion, the students are continually constructing whole responses to one another, not trying to read the teacher's mind in order to answer questions to which he already knows the answer. The conversation is more like a real talk among equals and less like the kind of discourse we have come to expect in schools. The significant change we want in students' minds will come as a result of real change in the kinds of conversations in which they have participated.

Chunking and Manipulating Chunks

The enduring popularity of the formulaic "five-paragraph essay" is due to some teachers' concern about students' ability to organize their writing. We know that students must think of their subject as containing different parts, and then they must put those parts into an order that will seem thoughtful and logical to a reader. Ironically, formulas like those people often teach actually prevent students from learning to organize writing, because they place the organization prior to the ideas or the structure of the argument itself. Remembering the kinds of sentences that are supposed to go in an introduction becomes a distraction, a good way to underperform on the assessment. Instead, students need to learn to see the sections in their material, to think about their reader, and to order the sections so they are the way you would say them if you wanted someone really to understand. Organization involves social thinking, not the kind where you apply a ready-made formula.

Becoming Test Insiders

Most teachers are aware that tests are not really measuring what they purport to assess. In a real sense, they actually measure the degree to which the test taker's assumptions correlate with those of the test maker. Work awhile with students who underperform on tests (score lower than our observations of their abilities should make us predict), and you'll see that they read the questions as intending something different than the questions were meant—usually something more straightforward and honest, though sometimes more indirect and interpretive. They don't notice that there is a trick to the questions, that there are answers that are made deliberately close to right but just a little off. What they need is to learn to think more like insiders in the world of test construction. Luckily, we know how to do that!

We know how to make students insiders in the world of a particular type of text. We have seen students become poetry insiders, fiction insiders, feature article insiders, Web design insiders, through their work in genre studies. To help students understand the functions and motives of the language on tests, it can be productive to lead a short genre study on tests (K. Bomer 2005; Calkins, Montgomery, Santman, and Falk 1998). If the focus is reading tests, students browse through a bunch of test forms (particular test booklets) that show the range of different kinds of reading tests and the items (test questions or tasks) that go on them. I like to throw a huge pile of tests onto a table and invite students to browse through them and see what they notice in them. I want them to see tests not as something fearsome that controls their fate but as a dime a dozen, common as can be, which they are. I want to position the students as powerful, intelligent analyzers of these kinds of texts.

TECHNOLOGY NOTE

The huge volume of sample test items available online provides a wide array of examples for students to study. These are not hard to find. Students' categorization schemes will reveal their understandings of how tests work.

Then, it is useful to narrow the focus somewhat toward the particular item types that are common on the test they will take. Seeing these particular kinds of questions as a choice made by particular writers allows students to see that the test is not natural, is not God peering into their minds to assess how hard they have been trying. Every step in this study is designed to equalize students' sense of efficacy (confidence in their own abilities and knowledge) with respect to the test. Particular men and women made this test in this way by means of a series of choices, and those choices have particular theories and intentions behind them. Productive discussions can develop thinking about why our particular test makers have chosen these kinds of questions instead of the ones they did not use. Students need to understand in detail the ways those questions are crafted—how the stem works, how the multiple choices are chosen. How many possibilities are there? How many of those need to seem like they could be right?

As with other genre studies, students have eyes for craft when they are makers. They need to be writing test questions themselves, administering the test to friends as the friends think aloud, so that the test writer can see how this question is working. Trying to stump their friends, they look more closely at published tests to see what level of trickiness is fair, the specific kinds of distractors (answers that might seem right but aren't) that test makers are likely to use. They can become more competent at figuring out what a test maker is thinking if they are test makers. Though this should be a short unit and is not worth a huge section of the year, it can help to reframe students' relationships to tests during a test year, especially if these students tend to be vulnerable to underperforming. This way of working toward test efficacy engages students in a kind of thinking that fits with a good curriculum, rather than relying solely on rote practice as a preparation for a test—a pathetic and deadening curriculum.

Marshaling Familiar Material

It can be very costly for students to assume that they have to generate all new content for a test prompt. When they have been in a writing classroom all year, building up many things to say in writers' notebooks, there is text inside them that is well rehearsed, whose structure they already understand, for which they may even have turns of phrase they think really work. When a test question is very general, such as asking for a time in their lives when they felt a particular way, or asking for them to take a stand on a controversial issue, they may very well have material that is already in the thinking territory from which they have written several times. They need to know that they could use that material; it's not cheating. In fact, it's what writers, scholars, and successful students do all the time—they reuse their thinking and content repeatedly for particular purposes and audiences.

What might be new for many students is that they need to be able to take on an assigned angle or theme or spin and apply it to their own material. If asked to write about a time when they saw someone go through a big change, then they need to angle their material so that it emphasizes the theme of people changing. If asked to write about the most exciting day they ever had, they can use the same story, just with the slant of how exciting it all was. Asked to "Discuss some issue of personal, local, national, or international concern and its importance to you," why would a student who'd been keeping a notebook need to sit there dreaming up an issue of concern? What else would they have been writing about all that time? These kinds of topics are meant to be empty so that students can fill them with whatever they have. There is no reason on such a test, therefore, for a kid to be sitting there trying to come up with new material. For an extended discussion of this type of preparation for writing tests, see Katherine Bomer's *Writing a Life* (2005), Chapter 9.

Proofreading Tasks

Some tests whose makers claim to be writing tests ask students to choose from four options to adjust the surface language of a given passage so that it is correct in the minds of the test makers. Though there are sometimes poor choices in these tests, they are basically asking a student to recognize the ways language structures appear when they are published. Spending a year practicing tasks like this is the wrong approach, because it actually exposes the student to much, much less published language than would be the case if we just had the student actually read books. Whatever gets students seeing conventional language the most is what will be most helpful, and independent reading will have people looking at the most edited text of any activity we can devise. Since the specific task is to replace the language that has been identified as problematic with language that the test makers view as preferable, proofreading the work of other writers would also be a valid but more authentic approach to preparation.

Test Boot Camp

I have discussed so far several ways of thinking about the connections between an excellent literacy curriculum and an assessment and accountability regime, and I've argued that aspects of an inquiring and rich curriculum make students stronger users of literacy who are likely to do better on tests than people with a stripped-down curriculum of test prep. There comes a time, however, when we have to acknowledge the unusualness of the literacy practice of taking a test. Unlike anything else, it is designed to trick the reader/writer. Unlike anything else, it is designed for no purpose other than to judge the reader/writer. It has tightly controlled, predetermined tasks that are supposed to be done under strict conditions of time, body posture, and work conditions. It takes some getting used to.

About four weeks or so prior to a test, it's probably a good idea to enter into a mode of thoughtful practice in which we acclimate students to the test environment. All literacy practices have contexts, and tests have a very specific sort of context. Students need to see how they respond to that context, reflect on those responses, and attempt to adjust in the light of that reflection. The tone of this boot camp should be light—not at all like real boot camp—and even more than other parts of the year, this unit can be gamelike and easygoing. The class can look at test problems together and think through strategies of approaching them. But it is also important at this point for students to feel the isolation of the test environment and to then talk about how their thinking went when they encountered the same kinds of problems they had discussed as a class. It is also important that the time scale be as close to that of the test as possible, with writing time limited to a single sitting at least some of the time, even if students will have longer than a class period to take the test. The conditions need to be formalized like those on the test, and very importantly, students should, the very next day, if not sooner, talk and write to reflect on how they had to adjust their minds to feel strong in that environment. Though they are preparing for a form of literacy that can sometimes penalize excessive interpretive thoughtfulness, they can approach it in a thoughtful and reflective manner so that they're not getting a poor education in how to stop thinking and just follow instructions. Entering what is sometimes like a dystopian world, at least they can be the hero of the story.

Test Anxiety and How to Make It Worse: Positioning, Efficacy, and Stereotype Threat

Every teacher has known students who are capable readers and writers in situations when they are engaged in learning about a topic they care about; the students know the audience for their work, and they have ordinary support structures surrounding their engagement with text. But in a test situation, they freeze up and cannot seem to demonstrate the very capabilities observable just last Thursday. Several things have been suggested as explanations for phenomena like this. Test anxiety is an emotional state, a stress response, that some people have to tests—as if someone has put a gun to their head and demanded they sing "America the Beautiful" and because they are so freaked out, they can't remember any of it or even which America song that one is. Only some people really experience test anxiety to the extent that it affects their performance, especially ones who become excessively worried about a negative evaluation and if they perceive the assessment as beyond their capabilities. In the midst of a test, by focusing on those tasks they find difficult or don't know, people often start to think of the test as too hard for them, and they increase their anxiety response to the test. Anxiety is decreased by feelings of strength, efficacy, the belief that one is equal to the assessment (Cizek and Burg 2006).

Another, more specific reaction to testing has been called *stereotype threat* (Steele 1997). This term refers to the tendency, for example, for a woman to score lower on a math test than a man if they take the same test at the same

Multilingual Note

For students who are likely to have trouble with the language of the test, it is even more important than ever that we prepare an appreciative case on their behalf, showing the range of intellectual and linguistic knowledge they *have* mastered. This argument against a deficit perspective is important for principals, parents, and the student himself.

time. The notion of stereotype threat is that, because much of society stereotypes females as being less successful at math than males, the possibility of fitting into the category threatens the woman in such a way as to make her do less well than she does in another social setting. These studies have shown similar patterns for African Americans and Latinos, who, taking the same test as a white person at the same time, will often score lower, as will white people when taking a math test at the same time as an Asian. Aware of stereotypes that place them in society, people may fail to demonstrate their capacity, if they are aware of themselves being compared with a group believed to outperform their own on this particular task.

Test anxiety and stereotype threat are very different, but we can think of them as related beneath the surface—both being cases where people can't show what they could do in a test situation because of the way they respond to how the testing event positions them socially. A test is a social and political event—power is being exerted by some group on another. And people have responses to that kind of event. Testing situations cast people in particular roles, give them a story to play out, and the meaning of that story is especially loaded for some groups. Identity comes into play in testing, very powerfully so, as it does in everything to do with literacy for adolescents. There is an emotional dimension, therefore, to achievement as it is measured on testing, and the consequences are pretty much what any thinking person would expect. If students lack confidence and believe that a situation threatens how others will see them, they will be less able to concentrate and perform. It is, therefore, fairly easy to force students to perform in a way that lives up to low expectations or a community's worst fears.

If we were evil people, mad scientists who wanted to make test anxiety and stereotype threat worse, what could we do? We could exacerbate the identity and emotional effects of testing by doing things like those listed in Figure 16–1.

By contrast, we can attempt to mitigate the effects of the test by taking a pretty matter-of-fact stance about it. I suggest this even if we feel worried about it. People have remained calm in much more dire conditions—war, famine, mass migration—so if we keep it in perspective, we should be able to educate without the giant, distorted stress level one sometimes sees and without the warped curriculum that comes about as a result. We also mitigate the effects by demonstrating to students, with evidence of their own eyes, their own strengths as readers and writers. We don't have to offer empty praise or pep talks, just show them what they are already capable of.

Throughout this book, I have argued that an appreciation of the assets students bring to school is the appropriate meeting ground for the teacher-student transaction. Deficit perspectives, by contrast, see students as lacking the

How to Make Tests Have the *Worst* Possible Impact on Students

- Hype the importance of the test, something pretty easy to do when there are consequences attached to it.

- Talk a lot about the test being unimportant, communicating the same level of concern about how students will do and also letting them completely let go of any desire to do well.

- Communicate your own anxiety about whether students will do well.

- Talk a lot about people and schools who score well on the test, using them as models, or even critiquing their privilege.

- Practice helplessness before the power of the test, by simply practicing taking the test all year and creating a curriculum that mimics the test tasks.

- Offering endless political critiques of the testing regimen in which students are helpless.

- Tell students to get plenty of rest and a good breakfast, because on this day their physical well-being actually matters.

skills that the school is supposed to provide, and such perspectives therefore blame the victims—the students, their families, and their communities—for their own maltreatment in a society that is often classist and racist (Bomer, Dworin, May, and Semingson 2008, 2009; Dudley-Marling 2007; Dworin and Bomer 2008; Marx 2006; Valencia 1997, 2010). Testing as an enterprise tends to draw educators into deficit perspectives. It is designed to bypass the learner's own assessment of their strengths and resources, and find out what is absent underneath.

Too often, both teachers and students buy into a myth that tests show the real truth about intelligence, ability, and achieved knowledge, taking test results at face value. If there is concern (fueled by high-stakes testing regimes) that a particular student may bring down a group's scores, then everyone starts regarding that student as deficient and trying to fix him. Like most adults, adolescents do not always take well to being fixed by people who think they are deficient, and the cycle continues.

Instead, a teacher or school should take on the sustained project, in partnership with the student and his family, of documenting personal, familial, and community strengths, knowledge, and resources, and helping him draw upon those assets toward valued forms of literacy. The test should not interrupt that process, but instead, test results should be situated within a context of all this other work. Does the reading test score fit with the teacher's conference notes and observational records and the student's own documentation about her independent reading? How does the student's writing on this test look alongside his writing done in the context of a supportive and respectful curriculum? And how does the account of competency line up with what we know from our continual assessment of the student's reading and writing life outside school, especially as we have been working to grow it across the year?

The material assembled in response to such a question can prepare a teacher to advocate for a student when the assessment system can be shown to be inaccurate. The most important audience for this advocacy is the student himself: to provide him with evidence about who he really is. A second audience is the student's family; in order to have high expectations for his academic potential, they need to see the best work he has produced, so that they stay sure that school is a good place for him. A third audience is the school and district administration, especially those people with the power to make decisions affecting this student's progress in school and general well-being. And, of course, we teachers need to collect evidence for making a public, political argument if we want to be able to show legislators, the media, and the public in general what we know: that tests are not as innocent as we want to pretend they are in the simplified discourse of policy making.

CHAPTER 17

Planning a Year

Here, at the end of this book, we come to one of the first things teachers do every year—planning the year's journey. To make decisions about parts of the year—chunks in this composed world—is to commit to the things a classroom community will pay attention to. Though there are a distressing number of districts and schools in which teachers are neither required nor permitted to make curricular decisions about their own classrooms, most teachers go into this profession because of the promise of composing meaningful and satisfying experiences with kids. The world is full of ideas in this regard, some of them good (some not). Indeed, there are more good things to do in a year than any teacher could really do in ten years. Even in this one book, there are more things than anyone could do, and composing a year always involves selection, development of some themes, setting aside of others.

This chapter is about such composing, a guide for guiding, and it will offer first some general ideas of planning, then more specific guidelines for beginning-of-year units, thoughts about the relationship of reading to writing, possibilities for units of study, and a few other suggestions about passages in the year's curriculum. We'll end with some considerations about the total text of a school year and the relationships among the parts of that text. I won't discuss everything possible in an English curriculum, or all the ways of thinking about that curriculum. Rather, I'll provide some ways of composing a whole out of the particular kinds of teaching I have described earlier in this book.

We need to acknowledge some important limitations to all of a teacher's planning. There is no sure or correct path, as teachers have known for hundreds of years. Therefore, we always have to take care not to mistake the map for the journey, to borrow John Dewey's metaphor. What produces an education is the minutes students spend engaged in meaningful activity with their teacher and other students, not some technically correct sequence of lessons. Those minutes include much more than the sequence of points or actions that the teacher has planned. They include relationships of a particular character; identities the student is invited to assume; the tone of the interactions in a community; the forms of talk employed; and many other elements that are, to most students, more immediately available to attention than is the teacher's idea of the planned content. These social and political realities of schools, "the tacit teaching of norms, values, and dispositions that goes on simply by their living in and coping with the institutional expectations and routines of schools day in and day out for a number of years" (Apple 2004), is what Apple has called the "hidden curriculum" (13). And it is important to keep in mind the intensity of these constants as we attempt to plan a year that might, especially for the students who could most benefit from an alternative, create some new possibilities and break these everyday chains. We should try to do no less.

Speaking of power and politics, we need to think for just a minute about state standards. Too often, people confuse standards with curriculum and think that everything listed in the standards needs to be lined up and taught to students one by one. But getting students engaged in the ways I have described in this book would usually not only meet states' standards but go well beyond them. A school year is a composition, a kind of story and a kind of argument. Trying to include everything that some committee could come up with is a recipe for incoherence and unfocused flailing. I would argue, as I have throughout this book, that, even as we address the political dimension of our work in conversations with other teachers and administrators, we must make instructional decisions that make sense in the lives of real students.

If a particular teacher's curriculum is loaded with required texts, that's not a condition created by the state standards. It's much closer to home—usually English department colleagues. In that case, the curricular work is political work—a process of persuading colleagues of the need for more space in the shared curriculum, more varied roads that can arrive at a similar set of goals with respect to students' literate capacities. Teaching always involves educating people outside the classroom almost as much as those inside. That work is never complete, and everyone who does anything good in teaching has to do it.

Throughlines: What Remains and Develops Across the Whole Year

In earlier chapters, this book has focused on many things that remain in place and develop across the year—kinds of thinking and tools for thinking; processes of reading and writing; forms and functions of talk; attention to literate lives; teaching students to manage their attention and activity. This chapter is about things that change as we move across the year—seasons of inquiry through which a class moves across time—chapters in our collective story. At times, these seasons are ruled by attention to writing (as in genre studies, for example) and at other times, they are governed by agendas related to reading (as in a unit devoted to independent reading). Very often, reading and writing work together in these units; this is especially true for those times when writing is in the driver's seat and reading is invariably riding along. I have argued previously (in Chapters 7 and 9) that writing may at times need to recede almost completely in order to make reading as light and fleet as it can be for people who need to develop fluency and stamina in reading. In other units of study, such as genre studies, reading and writing can be brought together, with one or the other leading the way. This is very good news for people who teach one forty-five-minute English class per day that must address reading, writing, and literary knowing.

Certain underlying processes, assuming the teacher makes these connections, form lines that connect through the changing units of study across a year. Students are continually learning, for instance, to revise their textual designs in the interests of readers and to listen to the sound of written language, though sometimes the curricular unit is focused on poetry (a genre study) and sometimes on reading partnerships (a social arrangement for reading). The writing cycle repeats multiple times across the year, sometimes when students are writing memoir (in a memoir genre study), sometimes writing in response to literature (perhaps in a unit where students are reading in clubs or literature circles), sometimes with no assigned genre but with attention to the craft of sentences (in a unit of study on sentences). That repetitive structure is what makes it a cycle—and what makes it possible for student writers to learn from writing experiences, applying learning from one experience to the next cycle.

Across the whole year, teacher and students must also continually bring their attention back again and again to

Things Teachers Plan to Remain Fairly Stable Across the Year

- Sense of community
- Kinds of thinking
- Specific tools for thinking
- Cyclical process of making texts for readers
- Good conversation
- Reading and writing lives
- Self-management of attention and activity
- Forms of literacy emerging in digital environments
- Critical perspectives
- Democratic participation

the students' constructions of their literate lives outside school. There need to be frequent invitations throughout for a student to reflect on himself as a particular literate person with a reading life and writing life that are situated within all the relationships and activities they care about. That agenda is obviously incomplete if confined to a few weeks, and it is, after all, the point of the whole enterprise. None of this English stuff is of any significance unless it is taken up in the life and habits of the individuals we hope to affect.

Planning a year's course also involves attending to other throughlines as well. For example, the teacher has to plan the tools and technologies that will be available to students across time. What will be the tools that students will use long enough to build habits? Will there be a single writer's notebook or separate ones for reading and writing? What will be the habits the teacher expects students to build in the use of computers and the Internet? Is there a role for handheld devices and mobile computing in this classroom, and if so, how will such tools work across the year to build habits of use, rather than being a single, isolated experience and therefore perhaps not even worth that much time? Though almost any plan for tools and technologies will require revision as the year proceeds, most principled practitioners think carefully about what their students will use to think and publish, even as they expect to revise.

Relatedly, I think teachers should, as I argued in Chapter 14, think through the new literacy practices to which they will pay the most attention as throughlines throughout the year. Pretty much every unit of study, every aspect of literacy education, should be angled toward the transformed practices that are occurring in a digital world. As I have said, that definitely does not mean that everything needs to be done on computers. But the ways our practices are changing need to be monitored and discussed frequently with students. It seems especially essential to think about multimodality and design as aspects of every composing and reading activity. While it may be possible to do a unit of study on some aspects of changing literacy practices, it is an area of attention that should carry through the year as well.

Teachers who are committed to pursuing social justice through the teaching of literacy will also want to be sure that attention to issues of power and justice are threaded through the year. While the overall thrust of the approach outlined in this book is one that attempts to make more voices heard and hand control and efficacy over to students, it is possible to work on such agendas without ever really asking students to think critically about the structures and institutions in society. If conversations about race, class, gender, and sexuality

TECHNOLOGY NOTE

There are two ways to think about technology across the year. One is to teach a couple of tools, such as writing in hypertext on blogs and designing visual documents, and to repeat those across the year so that students' ability to use those tools deepens. Another is to focus on a range of purposes and functions for literacy that are not about technology per se, and to use selected technologies to support students' explorations of those literacy practices.

For students learning English as an additional language, the stable elements of a curriculum are especially important. They are likely to be repeated enough for them to develop well-grounded and flexible vocabulary in discussing those elements. They provide stable elements in a world full of changes and sometimes confusion. In addition, they are deeper structures, less reliant on ever shifting collections of words, so they draw upon strengths, assets, resources, and knowledge our students bring to the table.

What Changes Across the Year?

- The texts we read
- The genres we explore
- Special areas of focus for our collective attention
- The addition of elements that will become stable themes
- The literacy practices that create the leading edge of learning

are not visible and explicitly inviting, they do not exist, and by their absence, they endorse the power relations of the present. It takes attention to these themes for students (or their teachers) to really begin to see them and work on them. I have discussed thematic units that might bring critical concepts to the fore, and I have mentioned a unit of study on writing for social action (see also Bomer and Bomer 2001). But no one who is committed to this agenda will feel comfortable leaving it boxed inside a single unit of study.

In addition to these deep themes in content, some practical structures we have discussed in previous chapters also repeat across the year. The workshop structure and all the habits of independence that make it work productively are useful for many different kinds of content. Even though I have admitted (in Chapter 1) that it's not the only valuable structure in teaching English, it is still the most useful, predictable structure for times when students are making things or when they are reading independently, with partners, or in small groups. Consequently, workshop is something that is stable, even as attention shifts across the year. Even as stable and cyclic structures hold steady, however, they seem different, taking on varying tones and hues, as teacher's and students' attention moves deliberately across the varied foci of a curriculum.

Now let's turn to what changes across the year. First, we will consider a few different possible beginnings to a school year. Then, we will examine a few different kinds of units of study as the year progresses. After that, we will explore ways of thinking about how pieces of the year come together to comprise a whole, and we'll end with my proposals for what a year in a high-quality English class should foster in students' abilities, understandings, and attitudes.

Units of Study: Seasons of Inquiry

A unit of study is a stretch of time in the school year in which the teacher has made a decision to attend to a particular focused objective or domain of inquiry. For students, each unit of study is a temporary context for being a certain kind of reader and/or writer, and so it carries a possible new identity—such as those of poet, reading group member, or involved citizen. And a unit of study permits students to become insiders in particular literate practices or kinds of texts. Some units, done thoroughly, might take a fairly extended time, like eight weeks. For example, it is difficult to speed through feature articles, especially if one is interested in teaching strategies of gathering information, such as interviewing, direct observation and note taking, Internet search strategies, and so forth. Going deeply into process in that way ends up adding substantially to the amount of time in writers' notebooks, in advance of a draft. Then, teaching students how to discard much of that information and use selected bits to actually say something meaningful takes still more time. Other units, however, such as inquiry into sentences, can benefit from a week or so of intense observation and are in fact more powerful if they do not drag on. The appendix provides some ideas of the duration of various units of study in genres.

Types and Examples of Units of Study

- Beginnings—literate lives, notebooks, shared text, independent reading
- Genres—poetry, picture books, feature articles
- Practices—managing attention and activity, responding to others' writing, reading clubs
- Functions—writing for social action, persuasion, aesthetic response, satisfying curiosity
- Text features—sentences, transitions, multimodality, design and arrangement
- Process elements—revision, invention, use of notebooks across the process
- Language—dialects, multilingual resources, changing English

---

I discussed genre studies fairly extensively in Chapter 13, and in Chapter 4 I talked about how a year's journey through varied social structures of reading tends to progress. Here, let me describe a few other kinds of units of study. Some units can be about a particular kind of literate purpose. I have mentioned that writing for social action might be one such purpose and that another might be writing in online social networking environments. Writing in response to literature (or in service of learning anything) is another possible purpose of writing that could be a unit of study; it's really not a genre so much as a specific function writing can serve (see Chapters 7 and 9 on writing in response to literature and other tools for thinking).

Units of study can also be about particular actions that writers carry out in the process of making a text. Some people have done units of study on how to be a good partner, or a helpful responder to other writers. A couple of weeks of attention to that form of talk can help the structure of writing partnerships become more useful to both partners. Another stage of the process that can prove beneficial as a unit of study is revision. Usually, in a revision unit, students return to pieces they have completed earlier in the year, or even the year before, and they explore ways that piece could still be revised and made substantially different, even if the previously published version was fine with them. The purpose is to build the conception that writing can always be reworked, that it's always possible for things to be otherwise. These explorations of particular aspects of writing as a process are designed to deepen and refine students' habits so that their work in the following cycles will be more powerful and independent.

Themes or concepts can be another organizing principle for a unit of study. Texts whose content can be related within a big idea may be of widely varying genres. Selecting a variety of forms just reinforces the focus on the deeper themes the texts are addressing. Of course, caution is in order here, because choosing a text because it addresses a theme is a way of imposing an interpretation on other readers, and one that's bound to be partially inappropriate for some students and will undoubtedly short circuit readers' own initial moves in the process of interpreting. But on occasion, a limited amount of thematic work can be helpful when the concept being explored is one that supports students' learning to think more socially and critically. In Chapter 6 I discussed the critical concepts of groups, power, and fairness, and a thematic study of one of these abstractions or of the relationships among the three could provide lenses for students' subsequent reading experiences. In our book *For a Better World* (2001), Katherine and I provide an extensive list of critical concepts, and spending time studying any of these, such as race, gender, money, or representation can help to build a conceptual framework for reading that would prepare students for democratic participation.

Beginnings

It is the start of the school year, and the kids start rolling in. There is no end to them, it seems, as 150 or so shuffle in and out of the classroom on the first day. It's a kind of crisis, this crowded chaos of unknowing—their teacher not knowing them, them not knowing the path that this class will run. So much needs to be built. I, the teacher, need to get to know the kids. They need to know me, how I think and what I value—and unfortunately, I can't just put that in a handout or into a lecture for the first day. They need to know one another, respect their differences, and appreciate their individual and collective strengths and resources. We need to become a community. They need to start building reading and writing lives upon their existing literacies—which means we need to get to some real reading and writing ASAP. But a class period is a small window—more like a keyhole—and it is just not at all possible to squeeze all that through this small opening of time and attention at once. Where to begin? Our options are these:

1. *Our existing literacies.* A week or two, fading as a reading or writing agenda ramps up. This begins the year on the basis of the wide range of competencies and resources students bring to the class. See Chapter 2.
2. *Building a writing life and writers' notebooks.* Three to four weeks, plus another week for a very quick written project. This is a way to begin

building habits of academic literacy upon existing literate lives. Notebooks, furthermore, allow students to bring in their interests, life histories, and language. The agenda of writing-to-think provides a strong foundation of literacy-as-thinking. See Chapter 3 for literate life material and Chapter 11 for writing-to-think.

3. *Building a reading life and independent reading.* Around four weeks. Beginning by asking students to choose books they want to read provides a fairly easy (in a good way) and motivated beginning to the year. As you confer with them individually, asking about their responses and pushing them to try new kinds of thinking, you can get to know them (though in a different, somewhat less personal way than is afforded by writing).

4. *A brief, whole-class reading experience.* One week. Begin with a couple of short stories—or a set of thematically related texts that might include a poem or two, an essay, a feature article—can be a way of initiating the work of building a community. I would suggest finding texts that are appealing to young people (probably written for them) and are emotionally powerful, leaving them laughing, crying, or freaked out. The purpose here is to allow students to respond with their own thinking— to allow them to be provoked—to get them into dialogue with one another. This experience can provide a reference point for future conversations. In order to foster a sense of togetherness and to avoid failure and frustration right off the bat, these texts need to be within an appropriate level of difficulty and need to be read in class (teacher reading aloud and/or students reading silently). It's also useful if the selected texts ask for some thoughtfulness (contain enough ambiguity to invite interpretation and active meaning making). Even though the focus is on student thinking, this is also an important moment for the teacher to make initial steps toward mentoring students into valued ways of reading and talking (see Chapters 5 through 9).

From these possibilities, teachers choose one or the other for varied reasons, including personal preference or interest. It might also be the case that students' schedules don't settle for some stretch of time, that class rosters are up in the air for a while, and that state of affairs might lead one to begin with option 4. In most cases, it seems to me that option 1 followed by either 2 or 3 (but not both at once, except in cases of double periods) would make the most sense. Then, if 1 were followed by notebooks, I would very possibly move them to independent reading after that. (It is also possible that I would follow an initial writing cycle with another one—a genre study of memoir or poetry, for example.) If I did independent

Some Possible Units for the Start of the Year

Studying our existing literacies

Notebooks and building writing lives

Independent reading and building reading lives

A few short, shared texts—introducing a few types of thinking

Possible Units for Early in the Year: Objectives and Sources of Evidence	
Objectives	**Forms of Evidence**
1. Existing literacies (Chapter 2)	• Detail and range in observation and description of literacy practices • Evidence of understanding the connection of everyday literacies to academic ones • Evidence of engagement in inquiry processes—writing, talking, and outside-class research notes
2. Writing lives and notebooks (Chapters 3, 7, and 10)	• Evidence of attention to exploring and finding times, places, tools, habits, and materials for writing in and out of class • Sufficient numbers of entry (some long) in notebook • Variety of different kinds of thinking and writing in the notebook • Development of thoughtfulness, reflection, connections, and interpretation in the notebook
3. Reading lives and independent reading (Chapters 3, 4, and 5)	• Evidence of attention to developing times, places, habits, and texts for reading in and out of class • Evidence of substantial progress in developing reading agendas that carry across books • Evidence of an increased and still increasing amount of completed reading (in pages or books) • Records of thoughtful preparation for and reflection from conversations with other readers about reading processes and habits
4. Whole class with short texts	• Evidence (teacher and student records) of engagement in conversations with partners, small groups, and whole class • Evidence of engaged participation in response activities—written, drawn, enacted, and spoken • Evidence of development of responsiveness—the habit of answering the texts one reads • Evidence of envisioning and listening (see Chapter 6)

FIGURE 17–1 Possible Units for Early in the Year: Objectives and Sources of Evidence

reading before notebooks, I would most assuredly get notebooks started right after. Sometimes, however, with independent reading and writing front-loaded in the school year as I'm suggesting—even with extensive shared inquiry into habits of thought and literate lives—everyone just feels too isolated. In that case, a dose of option 4, a shared text or two, can be a corrective to the centrifugal force of everyone spinning off after their own independent interests. Each of these units—as will be the case in each study I describe—has its own objectives—the reasons for deciding it in the first place. These objectives really have to make sense to you, the teacher—or else they are not really the motives that drive your teaching and your students' learning. So if the reasons I present do not work for you, it's important to adjust them to the goals you are really pursuing in making the decision you do. Figure 17–1 lists three or four objectives for each unit beginning the year.

Figure 17–2 shows a rubric for a unit investigating literate lives, as a way of making institutional peace with a unit that might seem at first impossible to grade. (I very often do not use rubrics, and if I do, I introduce them very late in a unit of study, in order to prevent every conversation being about grading rather than about the content we are studying. However, I offer it here as a compromise for people who may be having a difficult time imagining how the curriculum I am describing can fit within the institutional structures of some schools and systems.) I am also using this initial unit to establish a principle—that the few governing objectives of any unit also provide the criteria for assessing student progress.

Criteria	Evidence of Excellence	Evidence of Adequacy
Detail and range in observation and description of literacy practices	Detailed, extensive, and varied descriptions of everyday literacy practices in notebook and extensive reports to the teacher, as assigned, but beyond the assigned topics	Everyday practices named and sometimes described, but not especially detailed or varied and may stick to things already discussed in class
Evidence of understanding the connection of everyday literacies to academic ones	Thoughtful comments in notebook about how everyday practices are connected to the practices valued in an educated life; well beyond the connections discussed beforehand in class	Connections drawn between everyday and academic literacies, but mostly, they stick closely to those we have discussed, or else are less than fully thought through
Evidence of engagement in inquiry processes—writing, talking, and production of research notes	Observed by teacher fully engaged in class, plus written notes and reflections as homework at least four times per week	Participated in class activity satisfactorily but produced written notes or reflections outside class only a couple of times per week

FIGURE 17-2 Rubric for Study of Existing Literacies

Planning for Real People

Planning units of study is not only about setting goals or plotting a sequence of lessons or activities. High-quality planning also requires thinking in advance about the actual human beings involved, imagining how they will engage with the invitations that make up this journey. In this book, I've advanced the perspective that teachers should remain focused on the assets that adolescents bring to a teaching-learning interaction. So we should make all our plans with these questions in mind:

1. What experiences have students already had, and which kinds of experience can therefore add to their repertoire?

2. How do I picture them carrying the knowledge, skill, attitudes they will develop in this unit into the real lives they will live beyond school?

3. What strengths and resources do I already know students will bring to this inquiry?

4. How can the work tap into what they already know?

5. What capacities are we going to be adding to what they can already do, and what support will be needed for those students to whom this material is newest and creating the steepest learning curve?

The first two questions ask us to situate this unit into students' life stories, past and future. First, in deciding on the value of a unit and the themes that we should emphasize, it's worth considering what previous years have been like. If students have often been reading whole-class novels and writing essays about them (and it's a good bet they have), then that increases the urgency of expecting them to learn to choose books and read independently and to tune into their own thinking as writers. If I know they did lots of independent reading in class at the end of last year, perhaps I could begin with that and then move more quickly toward reading partnerships. Too often, we English teachers keep giving students the same narrow set of experiences, even though the possibilities for the range of literacy practices we should support are so wide. It's not rigorous to keep perseverating on the same practices year after year, especially in an environment in which literacy practices are so dynamic and changing.

The second question, about how I see my unit as supporting practices in a literate life beyond school, is also essential. I need to make sure that the things I'm asking students to do—not just the outcomes but the practices themselves—have something to do with the things people choose to do in a real reading and composing life. I have tried to emphasize, throughout this book, the continuity between literacy as it's practiced by the uncoerced and a high-quality curriculum in class.

For any unit, a teacher is well served by planning for the resources students will bring to the work. For independent reading, when students are going to be asked to develop intentions as readers and to pursue those intentions across texts, we can plan to help them draw on engagements with other stories—like movies, television, and the stories their friends and families tell. From those, they can develop an initial agenda: "Let's see if I like scary books, too." For a unit of study on writing argument, we should take stock of the many oral argument strategies they already have developed, and inquire with them into the social conditions that make those strategies, which are really social moves, work. In order to have a curriculum that is built on assets, rather than one that attempts to correct perceived deficits, this move of planning to receive strengths is absolutely essential.

One special kind of planning for strength will direct our attention to the multilingual students we teach. I need to think about the special resources they bring, in order to open the curriculum to them and to help bridge the distance that they will likely feel between where they are now and where I'm asking them to go. Furthermore, I know that the resources they bring—the difference that often gives them trouble if it's not acknowledged as a strength—can substantially enrich the possible conversations this class can have. What are the key terms in this unit—say, revision, memoir, or interpretation—in their first language? What different shades of meanings might they have, and how might those shades of meaning help us think more three dimensionally about the concept they represent? I may not have access to this information, especially if their first language is from a language family with which I am not familiar—but the kids have access to it. I need to learn from them and their families. How is the literacy practice we're developing in this unit different in the culture from which they come? How do they argue over there? What brings them together with other readers? The point isn't that we leave them as they are and exempt them from developing the practice we're targeting, but it is certainly important to enable them to switch between cultural practices, rather than subtracting what they know in order to teach them something new. And we will all understand better what we are doing when we see how it is different from other possibilities.

As I have said earlier, it's important to plan for multilingual students to write-to-think in their first language as part of developing writing experiences. They will have access to ideas and ways of thinking in that language that may feel distant from their English-speaking world. There may be books in their language that do similar kinds of things to the text we are studying—that treat similar themes, that are formed in similar genres, or that are used for similar

> ### TECHNOLOGY NOTE
>
> Many, perhaps all, teachers of multilingual students live in the tension between a policy pushing learners to transition into English and a belief that continuing literacy development in their first language is also important. They struggle to maintain high expectations for both things, though the system supports the first, usually more than the second. It takes political work and courage to make an education for multilingual students additive rather than subtractive.

purposes in people's lives. While it's easy to make mistakes in doing this, since we are clearly out of our realm, we're safer if we use the student's expertise and that of her family and wider community. If schools can just learn to tap into their knowledge, the presence of immigrant and multilingual students can bring new richness and rigor to all we do, making the curriculum more accessible to them and more diverse and global for monolingual students whose cultural and linguistic repertoires are, by comparison, more local and narrow.

The final question in my list above asks something different. We've been taking stock of the resources students bring to the work, and for every individual, it's important that we find those. Also, it's important to anticipate the experience of those kids for whom this unit is going to be an uphill climb. For them, it's most important that the teacher become clear about the most essential goals of this unit, so that we can keep working on those goals with the kid rather than becoming distracted into a hundred other difficulties. If we have chosen those goals well, these will be things that are important to reading or composing, and that can help make people substantially better thinkers with text. We want to be able to devote full attention—ours and the students'—to those things, keeping our eyes on the prize, rather than being distracted by a million perceived imperfections. So we have to plan ways for all students to access the curriculum we are actually teaching, making sure we're planning other units that can address other important goals. In a genre study, then, we have to figure out how the readers will all be able to access the text, especially if some of the touchstone texts are adult level. When reading a text with the whole class, we have to take a serious look at its difficulty and ask whether everyone's eyes really need to be on the print in order to get the experience we mean to provide. (As I have said, many of the texts that teachers demand that students read are too difficult for a large number of students. It's just a fact, and it always has been so. Insisting more intensely will not solve that problem.) If the reading is difficult, then we have to ask if writing is really useful. Are we just assigning writing to have something to grade? Is it possible to remove the added burden from the reading experience so that we can concentrate our energies on the real purpose? It's a matter of fairness and justice to devote a disproportionate amount of our planning and thinking to those students who are more likely to be disadvantaged by the curriculum we are creating.

Plotting Out Units

How should the year progress? How can a teacher decide what comes next and what after that? While there is no right answer, no necessary sequence, there are a couple of narratives that have guided what I have presented in this book. One is that the class ought to *receive students as already literate and build forms of literacy that are valued in the academy upon existing literacies.* Though that is initiated in the beginning of the year, as I've said, it continues through the year, a home base that the class returns to again and again, since literate lives are what the class is designed to produce.

I've also argued that students *use writing as a tool for thinking about the world they know and then they go through multiple cycles of making something out of that thinking,* that dialogue with the world. The structure there is more like a musical one of theme and variations. Students explore themes in their notebooks that then become the material for variations in different genre studies.

In reading, students move through different social seasons, *from more individual toward the more complex and social work involved in small reading groups.* This story sees students beginning in independent reading, moving through partners, and perhaps coming into reading clubs in spring. Whole-class experiences are designed not so much to deposit a book as content inside students but as opportunities to mentor students into literate practices that many people find valuable.

Teaching is built as much by deciding what not to do as by deciding what to do, and no teacher will do all these things. Still, these narrative structures do, I think, make sense for organizing whatever units a teacher does select. It won't work to start the year putting students who don't even know themselves as readers into reading clubs, and it won't work to start the year with a genre study that is furthest from students' experience and without an exploration of students' writing territories. Though English teachers have certainly attempted to build literacy classrooms without attending to students' existing literacies, that hasn't always worked in students' interests. This approach to curriculum has especially disadvantaged the vast majority of students who won't be English majors, and there is ample reason to believe that that kind of dissociated planning will be ever less effective in the literate world into which we are all emerging.

It is also important to attend to the weight one gives to reading versus writing. Though for me, reading is one of the most pleasing and satisfying things in life, I often worry that in school, we might end up succumbing to a traditional habit of privileging reading over writing. The most typical thing in English education in the U.S.A. is still for students only to write essays (actually

One draft for a sequence of units–for you to slaughter, redesign, or adapt

I have left room here for you to insert four weeks of explicit test prep before the test day.

- Investigating literate lives (2 weeks)
- Notebooks and writing lives (4 weeks)
- Making an initial project from notebooks, no assigned genre (2 weeks)
- Independent reading and reading lives (4 weeks)
- Genre study of poetry (3 weeks)
- Shared (short) novel with emphasis on interpretation and social critique (3 weeks)
- Reading partnerships extending work on interpretation and critique (3 weeks)
- Writing in response to literature, using notebooks from the past six weeks (3 weeks)
- Genre study of argument (4 weeks)
- Language study using sentences from last two cycles (one week)
- Writing cycle with no assigned genre and big finish celebration (3 weeks)

arguments) about books, with attention to the books themselves being the only writing instruction they receive. This is an inadequate preparation for a participatory culture in which making things is of increasing value. It's also an education in sitting quietly and taking it, rather than speaking out. Education for democracy has to be about voices, and students need the experience of taking the first turn in a conversation, asking a public to attend to something the writer wants to bring forth. At the same time, there are a certain number of English teachers who have figured out, after the past forty years or so of the field's development, how to teach writing in a high-quality way, even though they may not feel confident enough about reading to provide teaching of a similarly thoughtful and rigorous character.

Another Sacrificial Draft of a Reasonable Compromise in a Sequence of Units

- Investigating literate lives (2 weeks)
- Independent reading (4 weeks)
- Critical concepts: groups, power, fairness— with short texts (one week)
- Whole-class novel with emphasis on interpretation and critique (4 weeks)
- Writer's notebooks narrowing toward things that need addressing in the world (3 weeks)
- Writing for social action (4 weeks)
- Unit of study in memoir (4 weeks)
- Unit of study in short fiction (4 weeks)
- Reading clubs (4 weeks)
- Writing cycle in choice of genres (4 weeks)
- Independent reading/literate lives (2 weeks)

They are reciprocal and mutually reinforcing processes, to be sure, but a good curriculum in writing is not one that is always and only subservient to literature. And a good curriculum in reading is not one that always drags writing along like a heavy stone. We don't write at the same moment as we read, and given half a chance, most writers will too cheerfully leave their word processing program for their Web browser. (It's the scourge of a contemporary writer's life.) We need to plan carefully the purposes and process that need teaching in each mode and plan which one is in the driver's seat for a particular part of the year.

In planning a year, therefore, it takes some concentration to decide how to move back and forth between reading and writing (and I include viewing and creating images in video as instances of reading and writing). It may be that they alternate, with a unit on reading followed by a unit on writing. It may also be that the year is divided between them. The most important question in deciding is what arrangement creates the least inefficiency and disorientation in switching between them. Which permits the greatest momentum, the greatest use of the recent past within the present? What creates the most logical order? Every context and set of purposes will require a different answer, and from one year to another, I know it's never seemed exactly the same to me. The teacher has to be constructing a story that makes sense to the people living it. Figure 17–3 provides a procedure for making a draft of a yearlong plan. If you're feeling at sea as you begin looking at a year, trying to figure out how to plan the teaching discussed in this book, that table can help you at least become aware of the decisions that have to be made. Another helpful resource might be Jim Burke's tenth chapter in *The English Teacher's Companion* (2008).

FIGURE 17–3

A Procedure for Designing a Year in English Language Arts Class

---

Steps Toward a Plan: Designing a Year

1. Mark the dates of any tests you have to give. If there is an important one in your grade level, mark out four weeks before that date for a unit that will acclimate students to that test's environment (see Chapter 16).

2. Analyze the underlying strengths that the test calls upon, as discussed in Chapter 16. Make note of them so that they can be included in the curriculum across the year, remembering that strength as readers and writers is going to do much more for students than test practice.

3. Plan how the beginning of the year will see students (and their teacher) taking stock of their existing literacies.

4. Plan how and when writing-to-think will get underway.

5. Plan when students will begin developing momentum and understandings of themselves and one another as readers through independent reading.

6. Plan an end to the year that connects students to reading and writing lives outside school.

7. Fit in perhaps two or three genre studies, planning backward from a publication date for each study (see Chapter 13).

8. Plan the journey through varied social arrangements for reading: independent, partners, small groups, and whole class (see Chapters 1 and 4). (You won't have time for everything.)

9. Arrange other units that are interesting and important to you and that you think will capture your students' energies, such as language study, a thematic study, a whole-class novel, or a unit of writing for social action.

10. Plan conversations with colleagues and administrators that will protect your planning of this curriculum.

Ending a Year

The purpose of the school year was to help students grow their literate lives, the uses to which they can put literacy academically, socially, spiritually, politically, personally, economically—across all the dimensions of life in which it might be useful. Such a purpose suggests certain endings to the year. After all, we encountered each student in the midst of their ongoing living and learning, then took them on a journey that we told them would be helpful. Maybe we should set them back down again in a place that invites them to take up their literacy practices. This is the moment to stick the landing, to try and make sure that all our contortions up until now have a chance to leave a lasting impression.

To that end, it can be useful to return to independent reading at the end of the year, supporting each student in developing a reading agenda, a stack of books she wants to read soon. Each kid is reminded of her favorite topics and types of books. She continues the project of developing favorite authors and maps out intellectual pathways through multiple texts. Most importantly, she develops intentions and momentum that can carry her into the break between school years.

I have also seen people productively take on writing for social action at the end of the year, though it's a longish unit, so it should not be underplanned as an afterthought. Students connect so intently to what is real, to purposes outside school, in such a unit that they often make plans to keep working on it through the summer. Sometimes they don't follow through on those plans, but treating themselves as if they are someone who *would* follow through is still a meaningful identity to adopt.

Because the Internet is likely to be an increasingly large part of young people's lives outside school, a unit of study on developing an online presence— integrating a blog and various social networking sites—can also meaningfully catapult students into a productive set of summer literacies. If school Web security will allow the establishment of blogs for students, then the unit might include developing the blog, titling it, and learning some habit of using a notebook for developing initial topics for blogging (which many bloggers do). Students can then explore attracting readers to their blogs by offering generous comments on other people's blogs, by announcing new posts through social networking, and by other strategies for raising the number of hits they receive. Again, the point is to engage students in some form of literacy that can carry on through the summer months.

Some people do projects that make the year add up. Deb Kelt, for instance, a teacher whose work I have discussed previously in this book, asks students to design a project—a set of slides on presentation software, a Web page, a poster, or a paper—in which they represent themselves as readers and writers, including how their work in this class contributed to that identity. Several teachers I've known use the requirement that they give a final exam to ask students to revisit their writing from the school year and show places where they can see that they grew as readers and/or writers from what they produced. This assignment can be the culmination of a portfolio process like the Learning Record, which asks students to analyze their growth along five dimensions of learning: confidence and independence; knowledge and understanding; skills and strategies; relationships between previous knowledge and new learnings; and critical reflection.

For more on the Learning Record, which I believe is the world's highest quality assessment tool, see Peg Syverson's website (Syverson 2006), which is the first thing that comes up if you enter "learning record" in an Internet search engine. These last strategies aren't designed to reach into students' out-of-school lives and sponsor projects that might continue; rather, they ask students to name and claim their learning and identity development from this school year.

Holding to Purpose

Jerry Harste has long said that curriculum is "a metaphor for the lives we want to live and the people we want to be" (Harste and Carey 2003, 491). A curriculum is more than just a sequence of units, a set of things to keep us and the kids busy. A curriculum, a course to run, is designed to transform all of us into new people, individuals in relation to one another, having participated in shared conversations with an eye toward becoming independent enough to move into new conversations and communities. As important as the design of our units may be, we can't get so wrapped up in putting together the pieces or composing surface structures that we lose sight of the larger, human life goals. Everything we do needs to serve a governing set of ideas, just as a writer has to make sure the parts of a composition contribute to her main purpose and principle in this particular text.

The most fundamental principle to which a literacy educator must adhere is a vision of each student's real, lived literate life, now as well as in the future. The interactions and activities we plan have to be contributive to each student composing such a life, not exclusively for the sake of more schooling, but for civic, personal, social, spiritual, professional, and aesthetic purposes, most of which are, in the long run, of more value to almost everyone than academic purposes. It is hard to support those extracurricular purposes within school-work without just turning them into schoolwork, but some school curricula get closer than others to doing exactly that with integrity.

And there is an important psychological dimension to work on literate lives. If we hope to have an impact on a life outside school, we must begin in dialogue with that life, asking students to bring it into school. We need to help them become appreciative of the things they are already doing that can connect to this curriculum, so that they will have in mind the practices that might be grown or transformed by this curriculum. And we need to show them that we respect them, their communities, and the things their people value, in order to have them feel safe negotiating the differences in values between what they already know and what we are asking them to learn. In addition to these relational and strategic purposes for regarding students as if they're capable and intelligent, such a perspective is also more accurate than the deficit perspective that so commonly prevails in school systems.

In addition to that deficit perspective, another trend in our collective life is constant distraction, as we try to attend to too many things, each of which seems to have high stakes. It is an environment hungry for our attention and in which there is seemingly no limit to people's and institutions' ability to reach us and distract us. At the same time, we are asked to accomplish things that require sustained attention and deliberate thought. That means, in order to do well, we have to learn to block many of the potential distractions and shape our own attention toward longer stretches of concentration on one thing. A curriculum that supports that habit, that attempts to addict students to a habit of focusing in, will go against the grain of the culture and of course the school system. But if, even as we focus our own attention in planning, we also *teach* them about attention and give them opportunities to make good and bad decisions about attention with our help, then we'll be preparing them for the clambering world outside school, too. There is no reason to think that an overcrowded curriculum will help them learn good attention habits or work habits.

Being recognized with respect as the person you are, and then being given the space to take seriously the complex work in front of you: that is an approach to curriculum in which each individual can create an identity, where they can affiliate with the groups that matter to them and cooperate with other groups. Part of what a curriculum does is make identity positions available to the people who participate in it. Students walk into English class wondering who they can be here, and the curriculum answers that. I began Chapter 2 with a quote from John Trudell in which he rejected school because they wanted him to make something of himself and "I knew that I already was something." He needed to be recognized for who he was.

Also, however, a curriculum is about becoming, about a process toward something new. Maxine Greene, at the age of eighty, famously said, "Who am I? I am who I am not yet" (Pinar 1999). How do we resolve the teenage Trudell and the older Greene's perspectives? Because her worth is not under threat, Greene can face her own unfinishment. Because she has been recognized, she can change, can keep becoming. If we can convince our students that they are something, but that they aren't finished yet, and that the world isn't finished either, then maybe they can commit to the project of helping us create a world that is more worthy and more ready to receive their future selves.

Likely Genres and Possible Goals Within Them

Short Story–At Least 6 Weeks

- development of character
- creation of a full world around the main character
- consideration of varied plot possibilities
- control of time

(See *Time for Meaning*, Chapter 8 [Bomer 1995].)

Memoir–At Least 4 Weeks

- selection of telling incidents with special significance
- reflection on the meaning of memories
- generous reconstruction of scenes
- control of time

(See *Time for Meaning*, Chapter 9 [Bomer 1995] and *Writing a Life* [K. Bomer 2005].)

Poetry–4 Weeks (Multiple Poems from Each Student)

- control of image
- design of lines and stanzas as reader experience

- attention to sound of language
- intensity of meaning and purposeful exploration of truth

(See *Time for Meaning*, Chapter 7 [Bomer 1995]; *For the Good of the Earth and Sun* [Heard 1989]; and *Crafting a Life* [Murray 1996].)

Essay–At Least 4 Weeks

- control of governing idea or concept drawn through text
- transitions in the journey of thought
- relationship of big ideas to concrete information and observation
- reflective thinking and interpretation

(See *Time for Meaning*, Chapter 10 [Bomer 1995]; *The Essay* [Heilker 1996]; and *Crafting a Life* [Murray 1996].)

Picture Books–At Least 6 Weeks

- images that extend meaning beyond words
- pages and page turns as interactive design
- overall design of the book
- vivid, concrete, compressed language

(See *In Pictures and In Words* [Ray 2010].)

Drama (Single Scenes)

- dialogue that matches style, character, and purpose
- expression of meaning through characters' actions toward one another
- exposition embedded in dialogue
- setting and action amenable to visually interesting staging and movement

Comic Strips and/or Cartoons (or Graphic Stories)–At Least 4 Weeks

- identifiable characters across frames
- visual representations of time passing and movement
- dialogue appropriate to style
- abbreviated drawing style

(See *Understanding Comics* [McCloud 1999].)

Public Argument (to Change Minds and Behavior of the General Public)–At Least 4 Weeks

- a written personality that is credible and engaging
- anticipation of readers' questions and objections

- evidence that is explicitly relevant to claims
- design for delivery and circulation of the text

(See *Writing to Persuade* [Caine 2008]; *For a Better World*, Chapters 7 and 8 [Bomer and Bomer 2001]; and *Compose Design Advocate* [Wysocki and Lynch 2007].)

Policy Argument (to Change Rules or Laws Governing Communities)– At Least 5 Weeks

- explicitness about the policy problem that needs change
- address to appropriate audience to affect policy
- explicit answering of opposition claims
- specificity about how the policy affects particular people

(See *For a Better World*, Chapter 8 [Bomer and Bomer 2001].)

Textual Argument–(to Affect How Others Think About Texts and the Issues They Talk About in Response to Texts)–At Least 6 Weeks

- clear framing of an interpretive purpose
- evidence from text that is relevant to claims
- analytic, interpretive explanations about the text
- clear subsections to the argument, arranged logically, with clear relationships among sections

(See *Rewriting* [Harris 2006], *They Say/I Say* [Graff and Birkenstein 2006], and *Writing About Reading* [Angelillo 2003].)

Posters–At Least 3 Weeks

- visual design that makes an argument
- clarity of message
- purposeful selection and compression of limited visual and textual evidence
- reasoned plan for delivery and circulation

(See *Compose Design Advocate* [Wysocki and Lynch 2007].)

Feature Articles–At Least 6 Weeks

- information from direct observation, reading, and interviews
- engaging style that makes topic interesting to readers
- moves between everyday, familiar life and special knowledge
- clear design along with reasons for multiple sections of article

(See *Time for Meaning*, Chapter 10 [Bomer 1995].)

Websites–At Least 4 Weeks

- visual design that is appropriate for purpose
- ease of navigation and logical link structures
- depth of content to keep reader at site
- design of activity to get hits at site

(See *Don't Make Me Think* [Krug 2000].)

Also consider these genres: radio documentaries, video documentaries, short films (fictional).

REFERENCES

Adger, Carolyn Temple, Walt Wolfram, and Donna Christian. 2007. *Dialects in Schools and Communities.* 2d ed. Mahwah, NJ: Erlbaum.

Agar, Michael. 1994. *Language Shock: Understanding the Culture of Conversation.* New York: William Morrow.

Albers, Peggy. 2010. *Literacy, the Arts, and Multimodality.* Urbana, IL: National Council of Teachers of English.

Allen, David. 2002. *Getting Things Done: The Art of Stress-Free Productivity.* New York: Penguin.

Allington, Richard. 2005. *What Really Matters for Struggling Readers.* New York: Allyn & Bacon.

Alvermann, Donna E., and Margaret C. Hagood. 2000a. "Critical Media Literacy: Research, Theory, and Practice in 'New Times.'" *Journal of Educational Research* 93 (3): 193–205.

———. 2000b. "Fandom and Critical Media Literacy." *Journal of Adolescent and Adult Literacy* 43 (5): 36–46.

Alvermann, Donna E., Kathleen A. Hinchman, David W. Moore, Stephen F. Phelps, and Diane R. Waff, eds. 2006. *Reconceptualizing the Literacies in Adolescents' Lives.* 2d ed. Mahwah, NJ: Erlbaum.

American Library Association. 2010. "Censorship in the Schools." Accessed November 27, 2010. Available at www.ala.org/ala/aboutala/offices/oif/ifissues/censorship schools.cfm.

Anderson, Carl. 2000. *How's It Going? A Practical Guide to Conferring with Student Writers.* Portsmouth, NH: Heinemann.

Andrews, Larry. 2006. *Language Exploration and Awareness: A Resource Book for Teachers.* 3d ed. Mahwah, NJ: Erlbaum.

Angelillo, Janet. 2003. *Writing About Reading: From Book Talk to Literary Essays, Grades 3–8.* Portsmouth, NH: Heinemann.

Apple, Michael. 2004. *Ideology and Curriculum.* 3d ed. New York: RoutledgeFalmer.

Atwell, Nancie. 1986. *In the Middle.* Portsmouth, NH: Heinemann.

Avi. 1991. *Nothing But The Truth.* New York: Scholastic.

Bakhtin, M. M. 1981. *The Dialogic Imagination*. Translated by M. Holquist and C. Emerson. Austin: University of Texas Press.

Barber, Benjamin R. 1992. *An Aristocracy of Everyone: The Politics of Education and the Future of America*. New York: Oxford University Press.

Barnes, Douglas, and Frankie Todd. 1995. *Communication and Learning Revisited: Making Meaning Through Talk*. Portsmouth, NH: Boynton/Cook.

Beers, Kylene. 2003. *When Kids Can't Read—What Teachers Can Do*. Portsmouth, NH: Heinemann.

Beers, Kylene, Robert E. Probst, and Linda Rief, eds. 2007. *Adolescent Literacy: Turning Promise into Practice*. Portsmouth, NH: Heinemann.

Black, Rebecca W. 2007. "Digital Design: English Language Learners and Reader Reviews in Online Fiction." In *A New Literacies Sampler*, edited by M. Knobel and C. Lankshear. New York: Peter Lang.

Bomer, Katherine. 2005. *Writing a Life: Teaching Memoir to Sharpen Insight, Shape Meaning—and Triumph over Tests*. Portsmouth, NH: Heinemann.

———. 2010. *Hidden Gems: Naming and Teaching from the Brilliance in Every Student's Writing*. Portsmouth, NH: Heinemann.

Bomer, Randy. 1995. *Time for Meaning: Crafting Literate Lives in Middle and High School*. Portsmouth, NH: Heinemann.

———. 1996. *Reading Discourses: An Ethnography of Cohesion and Difference in an Urban Sixth-Grade Classroom's Community of Readers*. New York: Columbia University.

———. 2006. "Reading with the Mind's Ear: Listening to Text as a Mental Action." *Journal of Adolescent and Adult Literacy* 49 (6): 2–13.

———. 2007. "The Role of Handover in Teaching for Democratic Participation." In *Adolescent Literacy: Turning Promise into Practice*, edited by K. Beers, R. E. Probst, and L. Rief. Portsmouth, NH: Heinemann.

Bomer, Randy, and Katherine Bomer. 2001. *For a Better World: Reading and Writing for Social Action*. Portsmouth, NH: Heinemann.

Bomer, Randy, Joel E. Dworin, Laura May, and Peggy Semingson. 2008. "Miseducating Teachers About the Poor: A Critical Analysis of Ruby Payne's Claims About Poverty." *Teachers College Record* 110 (12): 2497–531.

———. 2009. "What's Wrong with a Deficit Perspective?" *Teachers College Record*. Accessed November 27, 2010. Available at: www.tcrecord.org. ID Number: 15648.

Bomer, Randy, Melody P. Zoch, and Ann David. 2010. "Redesigning Memoir: A Design-Based Investigation of Materiality and New Literacy Practices in an Elementary Classroom's Writing Workshop." In *59th Yearbook of the National Reading Conference*, edited by R. T. Jimenez, V. J. Risko, M. K. Hundley and D. W. Rowe. Nashville, TN: National Reading Conference.

Bomer, Randy, Melody P. Zoch, Ann David, and Hyounjin Ok. 2010. "New Literacies in a Material World." *Language Arts* 88 (1): 9–20.

Braddock, Richard, Richard Lloyd-Jones, and Lowell Schoer. 1963. *Research in Written Composition*. Champaign, IL: National Council of Teachers of English.

Britton, James. 1982. "Shaping at the Point of Utterance." In *Prospect and Retrospect: Selected Essays of James Britton*, edited by G. Pradl. Portsmouth, NH: Heinemann.

Brown, David West. 2009. "Coming to Terms with What It Means to Teach and Learn Grammar." *American Speech* 84 (2): 216–27.

Burke, Jim. 2008. *The English Teacher's Companion*. 3d ed. Portsmouth, NH: Heinemann.

Buzan, Tony. 2000. *The Mind Map Book*. New York: Penguin.

Caine, Karen. 2008. *Writing to Persuade*. Portsmouth, NH: Heinemann.

Calkins, Lucy McCormick. 1994. *The Art of Teaching Writing*. 2d ed. Portsmouth, NH: Heinemann.

———. 2001. *The Art of Teaching Reading*. 1st ed. New York: Longman.

Calkins, Lucy McCormick, Kate Montgomery, Donna Santman, and Beverly Falk. 1998. *A Teacher's Guide to Standardized Reading Tests: Knowledge Is Power*. Portsmouth, NH: Heinemann.

Cazden, Courtney B. 1988. *Classroom Discourse: The Language of Teaching and Learning*. Portsmouth, NH: Heinemann.

Christenbury, Leila. 2006. *Making the Journey: Being and Becoming a Teacher of English Language Arts*. 3d ed. Portsmouth, NH: Heinemann.

Christenbury, Leila, Randy Bomer, and Peter Smagorinsky, eds. 2008. *The Handbook of Research on Adolescent Literacy*. New York: Guilford.

Christenson, Peter G., and Donald F. Roberts. 1998. *It's Not Only Rock & Roll: Popular Music in the Lives of Adolescents*. Cresskill, NJ: Hampton.

Cintron, Ralph. 1997. *Angel's Town: Chero Ways, Gang Life, and Rhetorics of the Everyday*. Boston: Beacon.

Cizek, Gregory, and Samantha Burg. 2006. *Addressing Test Anxiety in a High-Stakes Environment: Strategies for Classrooms and Schools*. Thousand Oaks, CA: Corwin.

Cole, Michael. 1996. *Cultural Psychology: A Once and Future Discipline*. Cambridge, MA: Harvard University Press.

Collins, James. 1996. "Socialization to Text: Structure and Contradiction in Schooled Literacy." In *Natural Histories of Discourse*, edited by M. Silverstein and G. Urban. Chicago: University of Chicago Press.

Collins, Suzanne. 2008. *The Hunger Games*. New York: Scholastic.

———. 2009. *Catching Fire*. New York: Scholastic.

Cowan, Peter. 2004. "Devils or Angels: Literacy Discourse in Lowrider Culture." In *What They Don't Learn in School: Literacy in the Lives of Urban Youth*, edited by J. Mahiri. New York: Peter Lang.

Crenshaw, David. 2008. *The Myth of Multitasking: How "Doing It All" Gets Nothing Done*. San Francisco: Jossey-Bass.

Crystal, David. 2006. *The Fight for English: How Language Pundits Ate, Shot, and Left*. Oxford, UK: Oxford University Press.

Czikszentmihali, Mihaly. 1990. *Flow: The Psychology of Optimal Experience*. New York: Harper.

Dewey, John. 1938. *Experience and Education*. New York: Macmillan.

Dudley-Marling, Curt. 2007. "Return of the Deficit." *Journal of Educational Controversy* 2 (1). Accessed November 27, 2010. Available at www.wce.wwu.edu/resources/cep/ejournal/v002n001/a004.shtml.

Duffy, Gerald G., and James V. Hoffman. 1999. "In Pursuit of an Illusion: The Flawed Search for a Perfect Method." *The Reading Teacher* 53 (1): 10–16.

Dworin, Joel E., and Randy Bomer. 2008. "What We All (Supposedly) Know About the Poor: A Critical Discourse Analysis of Ruby Payne's 'Framework.'" *English Education* 40 (2): 101–21.

Edwards, Derek, and Neil Mercer. 1987. *Common Knowledge: The Development of Understanding in the Classroom*. London: Methuen.

Eggers, David. 2006. *What Is the What: The Autobiography of Valentino Achak Deng*. New York: Vintage.

Elbow, Peter. 1981. *Writing with Power*. New York: Oxford University Press.

———. 1998. *Writing Without Teachers*. New York: Oxford University Press.

Electronic Literature Organization. 2010. "To Facilitate and Promote the Writing, Publishing, and Reading of Literature in Electronic Media." Accessed November 27, 2010. Available at www.eliterature.org/.

Eliot, T. S. [1922] 1971. "The Waste Land." In *The Complete Poems and Plays 1900–1950*. New York: Harcourt Brace & World.

Elley, Warwick B. 1991. "Acquiring Literacy in a Second Language: The Effect of Book-Based Programs." *Language Learning* 41 (3): 375–411.

Fader, Daniel N., and Elton B. McNeil. 1979. *Hooked on Books: Program and Proof*. New York: Berkeley.

Fiore, Neil. 1989. *The Now Habit: A Strategic Program for Overcoming Procrastination and Enjoying Guilt-Free Play*. Los Angeles: Jeremy P. Tarcher.

Fish, Stanley. 1980. *Is There a Text in This Class?* Cambridge, MA: Harvard University Press.

Fleischer, Cathy, and Sarah Andrew-Vaughan. 2009. *Writing Outside Your Comfort Zone: Helping Students Navigate Unfamiliar Genres*. Portsmouth, NH: Heinemann.

Flynn, Elizabeth A. 1986. "Gender and Reading." In *Gender and Reading: Essays on Readers, Texts, and Contexts*, edited by E. A. Flynn and P. P. Schweickart. Baltimore: Johns Hopkins University Press.

Ford, Richard. 2006. *The Lay of the Land*. New York: Knopf.

Fulwiler, Toby, ed. 1987. *The Journal Book*. Portsmouth, NH: Boynton/Cook.

Gilles, Carol. 1993. "'We Make an Idea': Cycles of Meaning in Literature Discussion Groups." In *Cycles of Meaning: Exploring the Potential of Talk in Learning Communities*, edited by K. M. Pierce and C. Gilles. Portsmouth, NH: Heinemann.

Gilligan, Carol. 1982. *In a Different Voice: Psychological Theory and Women's Development*. Cambridge, MA: Harvard University Press.

Goldhaber, Michael H. 1997. "The Attention Economy and the Net." *First Monday* 2 (4). Accessed November 27, 2010. Available at http://firstmonday.org/htbin/cgiwrap/bin/ojs/index.php/fm/article/view/519/440.

Goodman, Kenneth S. 1967. "Reading: A Psycholinguistic Guessing Game." *The Journal of the Reading Specialist* 6 (4): 126–35.

———. 2003. "Reading: A Psycholinguistic Guessing Game." In *On the Revolution of Reading: The Selected Writings of Kenneth S. Goodman*, edited by A. D. Flurkey and J. Xu. Portsmouth, NH: Heinemann.

Goodman, Yetta M., and Ann M. Marek. 1996. *Retrospective Miscue Analysis: Revaluing Readers and Reading*. Katonah, NY: Richard C. Owen.

Graff, Gerald. 1993. *Beyond the Culture Wars: How Teaching the Conflicts Can Revitalize American Education*. New York: Norton.

Graff, Gerald, and Cathy Birkenstein. 2006. *They Say/I Say: The Moves That Matter in Academic Writing*. New York: Norton.

Greene, Maxine. 1988. "What Are the Language Arts *For?*" *Language Arts* 65 (5): 474–81.

———. 1995. *Releasing the Imagination: Essays on Education, the Arts, and Social Change*. San Francisco: Jossey-Bass.

Gustavson, Leif. 2007. *Youth Learning on Their Own Terms: Creative Practices and Classroom Teaching*. New York: Routledge.

Guthrie, John T., and Donna E. Alvermann. 1999. *Engaged Reading: Processes, Practices, and Policy Implications*. New York: Teachers College Press.

Guzzetti, B. J., and M. Gamboa. 2004. "Zines for Social Justice: Adolescent Girls Writing on Their Own." *Reading Research Quarterly* 39 (4): 408–37.

Hanks, William F. 1996. *Language & Communicative Practices*. Boulder, CO: Westview Press.

Harris, Joseph. 2006. *Rewriting: How to Do Things with Texts*. Logan: Utah State University Press.

Harste, Jerome C., and Robert F. Carey. 2003. "Pursuing Diversity." In *Handbook of Research on Teaching the English Language Arts*, edited by J. Flood, D. Lapp, J. R. Squire, and J. M. Jensen. Mahwah, NJ: Erlbaum.

Harste, Jerome C., Virginia Woodward, and Carolyn Burke. 1984. *Language Stories and Literacy Lessons*. Portsmouth, NH: Heinemann.

Heard, Georgia. 1989. *For the Good of the Earth and Sun*. Portsmouth, NH: Heinemann.

Heckman, James J., and Paul LaFontaine. 2008. "The Declining American High School Graduation Rate: Evidence, Sources, and Consequences." *VoxEU* 13 February. Centre for Economic Policy Research. Accessed November 27, 2010. Available at www.voxeu.org/index.php?q=node/930.

Heilker, Paul. 1996. *The Essay: Theory and Pedagogy for an Active Form*. Urbana, IL: National Council of Teachers of English.

Hillocks, George Jr. 1975. *Observing and Writing*. Urbana, IL: National Council of Teachers of English.

———. 1986. *Research on Written Composition: New Directions for Teaching*. Urbana, IL: National Conference on Research in English.

Hillocks, George Jr., and Michael W. Smith. 2003. "Grammars and Literacy Learning." In *Handbook of Research on Teaching the English Language Arts*, 2d ed., edited by J. Flood, D. Lapp, J. R. Squire, and J. M. Jensen, 721–37. Mahwah, NJ: Erlbaum.

Hobbs, Renee. 2010. *Copyright Clarity: How Fair Use Supports Digital Learning.* Thousand Oaks, CA: Corwin.

Huey, Edmund Burke. [1908] 1968. *The Psychology and Pedagogy of Reading.* Cambridge, MA: Massachusetts Institute of Technology Press.

Hynds, Susan. 1989. "Bringing Life to Literature and Literature to Life: Social Constructs and Contexts of Four Adolescent Readers." *Research in the Teaching of English* 23 (3): 30–61.

———. 1997. *On the Brink: Negotiating Literature and Life with Adolescents, Language and Literacy Series.* New York: Teachers College Press.

Hynds, Susan, and Donald L. Rubin. 1990. *Perspectives on Talk and Learning, NCTE Forum Series.* Urbana, IL: National Council of Teachers of English.

Intrator, Sam M. 2005. *Tuned In and Fired Up: How Teaching Can Inspire Real Learning in the Classroom.* New Haven: Yale University Press.

James, William. 1890. *The Principles of Psychology.* Accessed November 28, 2010. Available at http://psychclassics.yorku.ca/James/Principles/.

Jennings, Carol. 1999. "Girls Make Music: Polyphony and Identity in Teenage Rock Bands." In *Growing Up Girls: Popular Culture and the Construction of Identity,* edited by S. R. Mazzarella and N. O. Pecora. New York: Peter Lang.

Jordan, June. 2003. "Nobody Mean More to Me Than You and the Future Life of Willie Jordan." In *Some of Us Did Not Die: New and Selected Essays.* New York: Basic Books.

Keene, Ellin Oliver. 2008. *To Understand: New Horizons in Reading Comprehension.* Portsmouth, NH: Heinemann.

Keene, Ellin Oliver, and Susan Zimmermann. 2007. *Mosaic of Thought: The Power of Comprehension Strategy Instruction.* 2d ed. Portsmouth, NH: Heinemann.

Killgallon, Don. 1998. "Sentence Composing: Notes on a New Rhetoric." In *Lessons to Share on Teaching Grammar in Context,* edited by C. Weaver. Portsmouth, NH: Boynton/Cook.

Kist, William. 2005. *New Literacies in Action.* New York: Teachers College Press.

Knobel, Michele, and Colin Lankshear. 2008. "Remix: The Art and Craft of Endless Hybridization." *Journal of Adolescent and Adult Literacy* 56 (1): 22–33.

Krashen, Stephen. 2004. *The Power of Reading.* 2d ed. Portsmouth, NH: Heinemann.

Kretzmann, John P., and John L. McKnight. 1993. *Building Communities from the Inside Out: A Path Toward Finding and Mobilizing a Community's Assets.* Skokie, IL: ACTA.

Krug, Steve. 2000. *Don't Make Me Think: A Common Sense Approach to Web Usability.* Indianapolis, IN: New Riders.

Kuh, George D. 2009. "The National Survey of Student Engagement: Conceptual and Empirical Foundations." *New Directions for Institutional Research* 2009 (141): 5–20.

Lam, Wan Shun Eva. 2007. "Re-Envisioning Language, Literacy and the Immigrant Subject in New Mediascapes." *Pedagogies: An International Journal* 1: 171–95.

Lambert, Wallace E. 1975. "Culture and Language as Factors in Learning and Education." In *Education of Immigrant Students,* edited by A. Wolfgang. Toronto: Ontario Institute for Studies in Education.

Langer, Judith A., Arthur N. Applebee, and National Institute of Education (U.S.). 1987. *How Writing Shapes Thinking: A Study of Teaching and Learning.* NCTE Research Report; No. 22. Urbana, IL: National Council of Teachers of English.

Lankshear, Colin, and Michele Knobel. 2003. *New Literacies: Changing Knowledge and Classroom Learning.* Buckingham, UK: Open University Press.

Lattimer, Heather. 2003. *Thinking Through Genre: Units of Study in Reading and Writing.* Portland, ME: Stenhouse.

Lenhart, Amanda, Mary Madden, Aaron Smith, and Alexandra Macgill. 2007. *Teens and Social Media.* Washington, DC: Pew Research Center.

Leu, Donald J., Charles K. Kinzer, Julie L. Coiro, and Dana W. Cammack. 2004. "Toward a Theory of New Literacies Emerging from the Internet and Other Information and Communication Technologies." In *Theoretical Models and Processes of Reading*, edited by R. B. Ruddell and N. Unrau. Newark, DE: International Reading Association.

Lipsitz, George. 1997. "Cruising Around the Historical Bloc: Postmodernism and Popular Music in East Los Angeles." In *The Subcultures Reader*, edited by K. Gelder and S. Thornton. London: Routledge.

Marx, Sherry. 2006. *Revealing the Invisible: Confronting Passive Racism in Teacher Education.* New York: Routledge.

Mathieu, Paula, and Diana George. 2009. "*Not* Going it Alone: Public Writing, Independent Media, and the Circulation of Homeless Advocacy." *College Composition and Communication* 61 (1): 130–49.

McCloud, Scott. 1999. *Understanding Comics: The Invisible Art.* New York: Paradox.

McDermott, Terry. 2003. "Parental Warning: Explicit Lyrics." In *Da Capo Best Music Writing 2003*, edited by M. Groening. Cambridge, MA: Da Capo Press.

McIntosh, Peggy. 1988. "White Privilege and Male Privilege: A Personal Account of Coming to See Correspondences Through Work in Women's Studies." Wellesley, MA: Wellesley College Center for Research on Women.

McQuillan, Jeff. 1998. *The Literacy Crisis: False Claims, Real Solutions.* Portsmouth, NH: Heinemann.

Mehan, Hugh. 1979. *Learning Lessons: Social Organization in the Classroom.* Cambridge, MA: Harvard University Press.

Mercer, Neil. 2000. *Words & Minds: How We Use Language to Think Together.* London: Routledge.

Moje, Elizabeth B. 2000. "'To Be Part of the Story': The Literacy Practices of Gangsta Adolescents." *Teachers College Record* 102 (3): 651–90.

Moline, Steve. 1995. *I See What You Mean: Children at Work with Visual Information.* York, ME: Stenhouse.

Murray, Donald Morison. 1996. *Crafting a Life in Essay, Story, Poem.* Portsmouth, NH: Boynton/Cook.

National Council of Teachers of English. 1994. *Resolution on Language Study.* Urbana, IL: National Council of Teachers of English.

————. 2004. "NCTE Beliefs About the Teaching of Writing." Accessed January 5, 2011. Available at www.ncte.org/positions/statements/writingbeliefs.

————. 2005. "Position Statement on Multimodal Literacies." Accessed January 5, 2011. Available at www.ncte.org/positions/statements/multimodallitearcies.

————. 2009. *A Report of the NCTE Review Team on the July 2009 Draft of the Common Core English Language Arts Standards (College and Career Readiness)*. Urbana, IL: National Council of Teachers of English.

————. 2010a. "Anti-Censorship Center." Accessed November 27, 2010. Available at www.ncte.org/action/anti-censorship.

————. 2010b. "NCTE Position Statement: The NCTE Definition of 21st Century Literacies." Accessed November 27, 2010. Available at www.ncte.org/positions/statements/21stcentdefinition.

The New London Group. 2000. "A Pegagogy of Multiliteracies: Designing Social Futures." In *Multiliteracies: Literacy Learning and the Design of Social Futures*, edited by B. Cope and M. Kalantzis. London: Routledge.

Nystrand, Martin, Adam Gamoran, Robert Kachur, and Catherine Prendergast. 1997. *Opening Dialogue: Understanding the Dynamics of Language and Learning in the English Classroom*. New York: Teachers College Press.

Olson, Carol Booth, and Robert Land. 2007. "A Cognitive Strategies Approach to Reading and Writing: Instruction for English Language Learners in Secondary School." *Research in the Teaching of English* 41 (3): 269–303.

O'Neill, Cecily. 1994. *Drama Structures: A Practical Handbook for Teachers*. Portsmouth, NH: Heinemann.

————. 1995. *Drama Worlds: A Framework for Process Drama*. Portsmouth, NH: Heinemann.

Passel, Jeffrey S., and D'Vera Cohn. 2008. *U.S. Population Projections: 2005–2050*. Washington, DC: Pew Research Center.

Pateman, Carole. 1970. *Participation and Democratic Theory*. Cambridge, UK: Cambridge University Press.

Pearson, P. David, and M. C. Gallagher. 1983. "The Instruction of Reading Comprehension." *Contemporary Educational Psychology* 8: 317–44.

Pearson, P. David, L. R. Roehler, J. A. Dole, and G. G. Duffy. 1992. "Developing Expertise in Reading Comprehension." In *What Research Has to Say About Reading Instruction*, edited by S. J. Samuels and A. E. Farstrup. Newark, DE: International Reading Association.

Perl, Sondra. 1979. "The Composing Processes of Unskilled College Writers." *Research in the Teaching of English* 13 (4): 317–36.

————. 1980. "Understanding Composing." In *To Compose: Teaching Writing in High School and College*, edited by T. Newkirk. Portsmouth, NH: Heinemann.

Pettitt, Tom. 2007. "Before the Gutenberg Parenthesis: Elizabethan–American Compatibilities." Accessed January 6, 2011. Available at http://web.mit.edu/comm-forum/mit5/papers/pettitt_plenary_gutenberg.pdf.

Pilgreen, Janice L. 2000. *The SSR Handbook: How to Organize and Manage a Sustained Silent Reading Program*. Portsmouth, NH: Boynton/Cook.

Pinar, William F. 1999. *The Passionate Mind of Maxine Greene: "I Am . . . Not Yet."* New York: Routledge.

Prensky, Marc. 2001. "Digital Natives, Digital Immigrants." Accessed November 11, 2010. Available at http://www.marcprensky.com/writing/Prensky%20-%20Digital %20Natives,%20Digital%20Immigrants%20-%20Part1.pdf.

Pressley, Michael, and Peter Afflerbach. 1995. *Verbal Protocols of Reading: The Nature of Constructively Responsive Reading*. Hillsdale, NJ: Erlbaum.

Pressley, Michael, S. VanEtten, L. Yokoi, G. Freebern, and P. VanMeter. 1998. "The Metacognition of College Studentship: A Grounded Theory Approach." In *Metacognition in Theory and Practice*, edited by D. J. Hacker, J. Dunlosky, and A. C. Graesser. Mahwah, NJ: Erlbaum.

Probst, Robert E. 2004. *Response and Analysis: Teaching Literature in Junior and Senior High School*. 2d ed. Portsmouth, NH: Boynton/Cook.

Putnam, Robert D. 2001. "What Makes Democracy Work?" In *The Last Best Hope: A Democracy Reader*, edited by S. J. Goodlad. San Francisco: Jossey-Bass.

Rabinowitz, Peter J., and Michael W. Smith. 1998. *Authorizing Readers: Resistance and Respect in the Teaching of Literature*. New York: Teachers College Press.

Ray, Katie Wood. 2006. *Study Driven: A Framework for Planning Units of Study in the Writing Workshop*. Portsmouth, NH: Heinemann.

———. 2010. *In Pictures and in Words: Teaching the Qualities of Good Writing Through Illustration Study*. Portsmouth, NH: Heinemann.

Resau, Laura. 2007. *Red Glass*. New York: Random House.

Rex, Leslie, David West Brown, Linda Denstaedt, Laura Haniford, and Laura Schiller. 2005. "Understanding and Exercising One's Own Grammar: Four Applications of Linguistic and Discourse Knowledge." *English Teaching: Practice and Critique* 4 (3): 111–40.

Rief, Linda. 1992. *Seeking Diversity*. Portsmouth, NH: Heinemann.

Rist, Ray. 1970. "Student Social Class and Teacher Expectations: The Self-Fulfilling Prophecy in Ghetto Education." *Harvard Educational Review* 70: 257–301.

Romano, Tom. 2000. *Blending Genre, Altering Style*. Portsmouth, NH: Heinemann.

Rosenblatt, Louise M. 1978. *The Reader, The Text, The Poem: The Transactional Theory of the Literary Work*. Carbondale, IL: Southern Illinois University Press.

Rosenthal, Robert, and Lenore Jacobson. 1968. *Pygmalion in the Classroom: Teacher Expectation and Pupils' Intellectual Development*. New York: Holt, Rinehart & Winston.

Santman, Donna. 2005. *Shades of Meaning: Comprehension and Interpretation in Middle School*. Portsmouth, NH: Heinemann.

Schoenbach, Ruth, Cynthia Greenleaf, Christine Cziko, and Lori Hurwitz. 1999. *Reading for Understanding: A Guide to Improving Reading in Middle and High School Classrooms*. San Francisco: Jossey-Bass.

Scholes, Robert. 1986. *Textual Power: Literary Theory and the Teaching of English*. New Haven: Yale University Press.

Schreiber, Peter A. 1991. "Understanding Prosody's Role in Reading Acquisition." *Theory Into Practice* 30 (3): 158–64.

Schwartz, Adam. 1994. "Where Is It Written?" In *Coming of Age in America*, edited by M. Frosch. New York: New Press.

Short, Kathy Gnagey, Jerome C. Harste, and Carolyn L. Burke. 1996. *Creating Classrooms for Authors and Inquirers*. 2d ed. Portsmouth, NH: Heinemann.

Smagorinsky, Peter. 2007. *Teaching English by Design*. Portsmouth, NH: Heinemann.

Smith, Debra, and Kathryn F. Whitmore. 2005. *Literacy and Advocacy in Adolescent Family, Gang, School, and Juvenile Court Communities*. Mahwah, NJ: Erlbaum.

Smitherman, Geneva. 2000. *Talkin That Talk: Language, Culture, and Education in African America*. London: Routledge.

Sommers, Nancy. 1980. "Revision Strategies of Student Writers and Experienced Adult Writers." *College Composition and Communication* 31 (4): 378–88.

Stafford, William. 1978. *Writing the Australian Crawl: Views on the Writer's Vocation*. Ann Arbor: University of Michigan Press.

Steele, Claude M. 1997. "A Threat in the Air: How Stereotypes Shape the Intellectual Identities and Performances of Women and African-Americans." *American Psychologist* 52: 613–29.

Straw, Will. 1997. "Communities and Scenes in Popular Music." In *The Subcultures Reader*, edited by K. Gelder and S. Thornton. London: Routledge.

Suarez-Orozco, Carola, and Marcelo M. Suarez-Orozco. 2001. *Children of Immigration*. Cambridge, MA: Harvard University Press.

Sullivan, Andrew. 2010. "The Daily Dish." Accessed November 27, 2010. Available at http://andrewsullivan.theatlantic.com/the_daily_dish/.

Syberson, M.A. 2006. "The Learning Record." Accessed November 27, 2010. Available at www.learningrecord.org/.

Todorov, Tzvetan. 1981. *Introduction to Poetics*. Minneapolis: University of Minnesota Press.

Trimbur, John. 2000. "Composition and the Circulation of Writing." *College Composition and Communication* 52 (2): 188–219.

U.S. Census Bureau. 2010. "American Factfinder." Accessed November 27, 2010. Available at http://factfinder.census.gov/home/saff/main.html?_lang=en.

U.S. Department of Education National Center for Education Statistics.

Valencia, Richard. 2010. *Dismantling Contemporary Deficit Thinking: Educational Thought and Practice*. New York: Routledge.

———, ed. 1997. *The Evolution of Deficit Thinking: Educational Thought and Practice*. London: Falmer.

Valenzuela, Angela. 1999. *Subtractive Schooling: U.S.–Mexican Youth and the Politics of Caring*. Albany: State University of New York Press.

Varenne, Hervé, and Ray McDermott. 1999. *Successful Failure: The School America Builds*. Boulder, CO: Westview Press.

Vipond, Douglas, and Russell A. Hunt. 1984. "Point-Driven Understanding: Pragmatic and Cognitive Dimensions of Literary Reading." *Poetics* 13: 261–77.

Vygotsky, Lev S. 1978. *Mind in Society: The Development of Higher Psychological Processes.* Cambridge, MA: Harvard University Press.

———. 1987. *Thinking and Speech.* In *The Collected Work of L. S. Vygotsky, Vol. 1: Problems in General Psychology*, edited by R. W. Rieber and A. S. Carlson. New York: Plenum Press.

Welch, James. 1986. *Fool's Crow.* New York: Penguin.

Wells, Gordon. 1999. *Dialogic Inquiry: Toward a Sociocultural Practice and Theory of Education.* Cambridge, UK: Cambridge University Press.

Wertsch, James V. 1991. *Voices of the Mind: A Sociocultural Approach to Mediated Action.* Cambridge, MA: Harvard University Press.

———. 1998. *Mind as Action.* New York: Oxford University Press.

Wheeler, Rebecca, and Rachel Swords. 2006. *Code-Switching: Teaching Standard English in Urban Classrooms.* Urbana, IL: National Council of Teachers of English.

Whitin, Phyllis. 1996. *Sketching Stories, Stretching Minds: Responding Visually to Literature.* Portsmouth, NH: Heinemann.

———. 2005. "The Interplay of Text, Talk, and Visual Representation in Expanding Literary Interpretation." *Research in the Teaching of English* 39 (4): 365–97.

Whitney, Diana, and Amanda Trosten-Bloom. 2010. *The Power of Appreciative Inquiry: A Practical Guide to Positive Change.* San Francisco, CA: Berrett-Koehler.

Wiggins, Grant, and Jay McTighe. 2005. *Understanding by Design.* 2d ed. Alexandria, VA: Association for Supervision and Curriculum Development.

Wikipedia. 2010. "Xylem." Available at http://en.wikipedia.org/wiki/Xylem.

Wilhelm, Jeffrey D. 2008. *You Gotta BE the Book: Teaching Engaged and Reflective Reading with Adolescents.* 2d ed. New York: Teachers College Press.

Wittgenstein, L. 1969. *On Certainty.* Translated by D. Paul and G. E. M. Anscombe, edited by G. E. M. Anscombe and G. H. von Wright. New York: Harper.

Wolfram, Walt. 1998. "Dialect Awareness and the Study of Language." In *Students as Researchers of Culture and Language in Their Own Communities*, edited by A. Egan-Robertson and D. Bloome. Cresskill, NJ: Hampton.

Worthy, Jo. 2000. " 'On Every Page Someone Gets Killed!' Book Conversations You Don't Hear in School." In *Struggling Adolescent Readers: A Collection of Teaching Strategies*, edited by D. W. Moore, D. E. Alvermann, and K. A. Hinchman. Newark, DE: International Reading Association.

Worthy, Jo, and Karen Broaddus. 2002. "Fluency Beyond the Primary Grades: From Group Performance to Silent, Independent Reading." *The Reading Teacher* 55: 334–43.

Worthy, Jo, Megan Moorman, and Margo Turner. 1999. "What Johnny Likes to Read Is Hard to Find in School." *Reading Research Quarterly* 34 (1): 12–27.

Wysocki, Anne Frances. 2004. "Opening New Media to Writing: Openings and Justifications." In *Writing New Media: Theory and Applications for Expanding the*

Teaching of Composition, edited by A. F. Wysocki, J. Johnson-Eilola, C. L. Selfe, and G. Sirc. Logan: Utah State University Press.

Wysocki, Anne Frances, and Dennis A. Lynch. 2007. *Compose Design Advocate: A Rhetoric for Integrating Written, Visual, and Oral Communication.* New York: Pearson Longman.

Zinsser, William. 1976. *On Writing Well.* 3d ed. New York: Harper & Row.